Technology,
innovation and
enterprise.

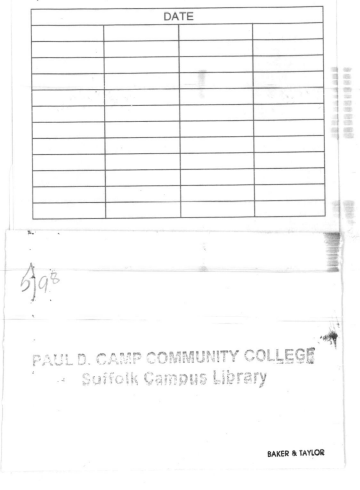

DATE			

TECHNOLOGY, INNOVATION AND ENTERPRISE

Technology, Innovation and Enterprise

The European Experience

Edited by

Dylan Jones-Evans

and

Magnus Klofsten

First published in Great Britain 1997 by
MACMILLAN PRESS LTD
Houndmills, Basingstoke, Hampshire RG21 6XS and London
Companies and representatives throughout the world

A catalogue record for this book is available from the British Library.

ISBN 0–333–67396–4

First published in the United States of America 1997 by
ST. MARTIN'S PRESS, INC.,
Scholarly and Reference Division,
175 Fifth Avenue, New York, N.Y. 10010

ISBN 0–312–17546–9

Library of Congress Cataloging-in-Publication Data
Jones-Evans, Dylan.
Technology innovation and enterprise : the European experience /
[with contributions and compiled by] Dylan Jones-Evans, Magnus
Klofsten.
p.   cm.
A collection of "mini-dissertations" by 11 authors who summarize
their doctoral research and additionally clarify and develop issues
"not prominent" in their original works.
Includes bibliographical references and index.
ISBN 0–312–17546–9
1. High technology industries—Europe—Management.   2. Small
business—Europe—Management.   3. Technological innovations—Europe–
–Management.   I. Klofsten, Magnus.   II. Title.
HD62.37.J66 1997
658.5'14'094—dc21   97–7760
                                                                          CIP

This book is printed on paper suitable for recycling and made from fully managed and
sustained forest sources.

10   9   8   7   6   5   4   3   2   1
06   05   04   03   02   01   00   99   98   97

Printed and bound by Antony Rowe Ltd, Chippenham, Wiltshire

Contents

List of Figures and Tables

Figures

Tables

List of Abbreviations

AE	Academic Entrepreneurs
BCG	Boston Consultancy Group
CEO	Chief Executive Officer
DTI	Department of Trade and Industry
IE	Industrial Entrepreneurs
MINT	Managing the Integration of New Technologies
MR	Mean Establishment Rank
NIH	Not invented here
NTBF	New Technology-Based Firm
OEM	Original Equipment Manufacturer
PIMS	Profit Impact of Market Strategy
R&D	Research and Development
RTO	Research and Technology Organisations
SEK	Swedish Krona
SMART	Small Firms Merit Award for Research and Technology
SME	Small and Medium-Sized Enterprises
TENS	Transcutaneous Electrical Nerve Stimulation
VIT	Technical Research Centre of Finland

Notes on the Contributors

Erkko Autio is Associate Professor at the Institute of Industrial Management, Helsinki University of Technology, Finland.

Steve Conway is Research Fellow at the Technology Management and Policy Unit, Aston University, UK.

Margarida Fontes is a researcher at the Instituto Nacional de Engenharia e Technologia Industrial in Lisbon.

Peter Heydebreck is managing director of INNO, an innovation management consultancy group in Karlsruhr, Germany.

Dylan Jones-Evans is Professor of Small Business Management at the University of Glamorgan Business School in the UK.

Magnus Klofsten is Director of the Centre for Innovation and Entrepreneurship and Senior Lecturer in Marketing and Entrepreneurship at Linköping University, Sweden.

Asa Lindholm Dahlstrand is Research Associate at the School of Technology Management and Economics at the Chalmers University of Technology, Gothenburg.

Maria Lindqvist is Senior Lecturer at the Institute of International Business, Stockholm School of Economics, Sweden.

Colm O'Gorman is Lecturer in Business Administration at the Michael Smurfit Graduate School of Business, University College Dublin, Republic of Ireland.

Besrat Tesfaye is Senior Lecturer in the Department of Business Administration at Stockholm University, Sweden.

1 Introduction

'You get a little bit of satisfaction from employing people, providing jobs for people and designing new products and finding people want to buy it . . . it would be nice to think that you could make a lot of money out of it as well, but that's not so important – that would be the icing on the cake . . . your own business ultimately gives the freedom, but you work a damn sight harder – I've never worked so hard in my life than for the last three years. It's very hard but it gives you the illusion that you have some control over what you are doing, and the long term objective is that I've got things that I would like to do, and working for myself gives me the right to choose when I do it.' – technology-based owner manager (Jones-Evans, 1992)

Through the efforts of scientists and engineers who, like the example above, have chosen the path of self-employment, the development of small technology-based firms has been one of the industrial success stories of Europe, making a significant contribution to employment in high-technology industries, wealth creation at a regional and national level, and the development of significant technological innovations, particularly within growth industries. Whilst we have yet to see the development of large corporations such as Apple and Microsoft, the creativity, flexibility and innovativeness of the technological entrepreneurs who have made the decision to develop and grow their own firms have ensured that, in many sectors, Europe is keeping up, if not overtaking, developments in other parts of the world.

This is quite different from the accepted thinking of the role of small firms 30 years ago, when pioneering researchers such as Ed Roberts of MIT and Arnie Cooper of Purdue University started their investigations into the phenomenon of 'spin-offs' in regions which have now become world-famous as incubators of entrepreneurially-oriented innovative firms, such as Route 128, Boston, and Silicon Valley, California. At that time, there was very little appreciation of the contribution of the small firm sector to the development of technology and innovation within developed economies. Indeed, economists such as Galbraith (1967) argued that the smaller organisation's contribution to technological innovation was relatively insignificant and that economic progress through technological change could only be carried forward by larger companies:

mention has been made of machines and sophisticated technology. These require, in turn, heavy investment of capital. They are designed and guided by technically sophisticated men. They involve, also, a greatly increased elapse of time between any decision to produce and the emergence of a saleable product. From these changes come the need and opportunity for the large business organisation. It alone can deploy the requisite capital; it alone can mobilise the requisite skills (Galbraith, 1967:4).

However, the re-examination of the contribution of small firms in western economies (Bolton, 1971; Birch, 1979), coupled with the diversity and complexity of technology, has led to an explosion in the number of small technology-based firms in both Europe and the USA. As Jones-Evans and Westhead (1996) indicate, there are a number of different factors to explain why there has been a growth in the number of small technology-based firms in Europe.

THE DEVELOPMENT OF SMALL TECHNOLOGY-BASED FIRMS IN EUROPE

A number of small technology-based firms may have been established by individuals who were 'pushed' into entrepreneurship because of unemployment or the threat of redundancy (Storey, 1982). For example, recent research by Keeble (1994), in his analysis of survey evidence from founders of new technology-based firms (NTBFs) in the UK, noted that over 40 per cent of founders whose business was located in an old industrial peripheral region (associated with high levels of unemployment) indicated they had been 'pushed' into forming their new venture. In addition, the fragmentation methods chosen within technology-based industries include the decentralisation of production to smaller plants (Howells and Green, 1986) which remain in the ownership of the large firm; a shift in production to small firms from large ones through franchising and licensing (Dodgson and Rothwell, 1991); and the disintegration of production to independently-owned small firms through outsourcing, subcontracting and employee buyouts and corporate venturing (Howells, 1987).

The development of new scaled-down production equipment suited to small-batch production has encouraged business start-ups, with the increasing trend towards flexible specialisation and customisation within high-technology industrial sectors (Perry, 1990; Garnsey, Galloway and

Mathison, 1994) encouraging the creation of specialist new firms in sectors where economies of scale are no longer relevant or important for competitive advantage (Aydalot and Keeble, 1988). For example, lower barriers-to-entry and the absence of significant economies of scale have led to a dramatic increase in the number of new computer service firms in these new market niches (McQueen and Wallmark, 1982; Olofsson and Wahlbin, 1993; Jones-Evans and Kirby, 1995). The emergence of generic technologies, most notably information technology, that are knowledge-intensive rather than capital- and labour-intensive have opened up new market niches which small firms are in a position to exploit (Rothwell, 1994b; Autio, 1997). This has therefore encouraged a growth in the number of firms engaged in micro-electronics, computing, telecommunications and information technology. The decreasing costs of micro-processor technologies have offered NTBFs a competitive advantage which enables them to compete with larger organisations. Some small technology-based firms have been established to maximise the competitive advantages offered by the decreasing costs of micro-processor technologies, enabling them to compete directly with larger organisations. This has occurred both in manufacturing industries, with the introduction of computer-aided design and manufacture (Rothwell, 1994b) and in service sector industries (Kirby and Jones-Evans, 1997). Indeed, the study by Brynjolfsson *et al.* (1993) showed that the average size of industrial firms in manufacturing and in technical services industries is decreasing, and that this development can be attributed to the diffusion of information and communication technologies (ICT) in industrial structures. The uncertainty engendered by technology-based competition has also created opportunities for small innovative firms dependent upon fast imitation and improvement rather than traditional research-based strategies (Charles, 1987).

Changes in cultural values such as the growth of the 'enterprise culture' (Ritchie, 1991), combined with more favourable attitudes towards industrial production and wealth creation (Rothwell, 1994b), have encouraged scientists and technicians within universities and industrial companies to consider self-employment as an alternative to their current employment (Olofsson, Wahlbin and Tovman, 1987; Olofsson and Wahlbin, 1993; Utterback and Reitberger, 1982). In addition, government policy at European and national level has actively encouraged individuals to become self-employed or to start their own business (ENSR, 1994). Indeed, one of the main policy initiatives in the European Commission's Research and Technological Development programmes aims at positive discrimination to encourage SMEs to become actively involved in different research and development (R&D) activities. In addition, government, universities, local authorities and various financial institutions have actively attempted to encourage the formation and growth of new knowledge-based firms (Massey, Quintas and Wield, 1992; Westhead and Storey, 1994).

THE ROLE OF SMALL TECHNOLOGY-BASED FIRMS WITHIN EUROPEAN ECONOMIES

Therefore small technology-based firms, contrary to the prophecies of writers such as Galbraith, have become important for technological innovation within developed economies, as well as employment and wealth creation. Various researchers have demonstrated the valuable contribution of small technology-based firms to technological innovation within a number of high-technology industrial sectors (Freeman, 1971; Acs and Audretsch, 1988). Such industrial sectors are usually characterised by fast-changing markets, low capital intensity and small dependence on economies of scale, and are thus better suited to smaller firms, due to the entrepreneurial nature and lack of bureaucracy in decision-making within such organisations (Rothwell, 1994b). In the UK, comprehensive research into the relationship between firm size and the level of innovation (Robson and Townsend, 1984) has revealed that small firms' share of innovations, during the period 1945–83, had increased by over 50 per cent and now accounts for over a quarter of the total number of innovations in the UK. Moreover, in certain sectors, such as computing services and scientific instruments, their contribution is highly significant, with small companies developing the majority of innovative products and processes. An examination of this study by Monck *et al.* (1988), comparing the proportion of total manufacturing employment in small firms and the proportion of innovations undertaken in this sector, showed that over the period 1958–83 there had been a considerable improvement in the 'innovative productivity' of small companies, which rose from 0.6 to 0.99 over the 25-year period. A similar comparison was carried out on US data (Acs and Audretsch, 1988:201) which showed that, whilst large manufacturing firms introduced 2608 innovations in 1982, and small firms contributed slightly fewer (i.e., 1923), small firm employment was about half as great as large firm employment. Therefore in US manufacturing, the average small-firm innovation rate in manufacturing was 0.322, compared to a large firm innovation rate of 0.225.

Technology-based small firms have become increasingly important to future national industrial employment in both Europe (Oakey, 1991a;

Lumme, Kauranen and Autio, 1994; Klofsten, Jones-Evans and Lindell, 1996) and the USA (Phillips, Kirchhoff and Brown, 1991). For example, a recent analysis of employment within the UK high-technology industrial sector in the period 1987–91 found that while total employment in firms with 100 or more employees was reduced by 83 419 jobs, total employment in firms with 1 to 99 employees increased by 26 766 jobs (Jones-Evans and Westhead, 1996). In addition, a number of studies show that technologically innovative small and medium-sized enterprises (SMEs) in the UK have a higher-than-average growth in assets, retained profits and exports (Wynarczyk and Thwaites, 1994). Moreover, such firms tend to have lower closure rates than businesses in other sectors (Westhead and Cowling, 1994; Westhead and Storey, 1994) and have demonstrated high degrees of resilience, especially within times of recession (Wynarczyk, 1996). In ageing Western economies such as the UK, small companies are considered to be important as 'knowledge-intensive' industries, aiding the transformation from a skill-based to a knowledge-based economy (Doutriaux and Simyar, 1987). During periods of technological change, large establishments and large companies cease to grow and expand, and SMEs, owing to their greater flexibility, are in a better position to face uncertainty (Maillat and Vasserot, 1988). Moreover, the quality of jobs provided in such firms tend to be significantly better than those in traditional manufacturing industries (Monck *et al.*, 1988; Storey, 1994).

THE IDEA BEHIND THIS BOOK

This book sets out to examine small technologically innovative enterprises in Europe from the viewpoint of ten new researchers' doctoral theses which examine different aspects of the creation and development of this sector. For researchers and academics, it provides a rich source of information on small technology-based firms in Europe, drawing on nearly 600 references. In addition it describes, in some detail, the various methodologies utilised to undertake the ten different studies, including qualitative techniques (Jones-Evans, Tesfaye, Fontes and Conway), quantitative data analysis (Heydebreck, Autio, O'Gorman Lindholm and Lindqvist), and a detailed case study approach (Klofsten and O'Gorman). For owner-managers and policy-makers, each chapter attempts to develop practical recommendations for future action based on the findings of the research studies.

This book, in itself, is an innovative enterprise in that it is the first time that a collection of PhD dissertations in the field of management have been brought together to examine one theme. There were a number of reasons for this.

First of all, the editors felt that many journal articles which are based on results from an individual's dissertation will, because of space limitations, present only a small part of the overall study. As a result, the reader tends to get only a 'flavour' of the main findings of the doctoral thesis. One of the principal aims of this book was to offer researchers the opportunity to present a holistic view of their work, including a detailed description of the previous studies which had influenced their research enquiry, a detailed methodology, the main findings and results, and policy and research implications for the future. Therefore, in effect, this book is a collection of 'mini-dissertations', each of which would capture, in one chapter, the core of the doctoral research which would not normally be published within a journal article. In addition, with the exceptions of the Scandinavian countries, most PhD dissertations are not published, and thus gaining access to the main results of the research is often very difficult.

Second, the development of such a book will give researchers the opportunity to reflect on the findings of their doctoral work and to clarify and develop issues which were not prominent in the original version, especially with regard to implications for researchers today, and for developing specific policy issues which have evolved since the dissertation was submitted. All the authors in this collection are experienced researchers who may have changed their outlook and perception of their particular disciplines since they formulated their initial research questions during the process of writing the dissertation. A whole chapter dedicated to their work gives each author the opportunity to reflect on their research and to articulate any new insights which may arise from the results. Finally, it is also hoped that the book presents a barometer of recent European doctoral research in the field of study of small technology-based firms.

STRUCTURE OF THE BOOK

One of the main concepts behind the development of the book is that it would describe the different aspects of business development and innovation process, including creation and development, the evolution of the firm into growth, different types of networking activities as the firm expands, and various development strategies when the firm is established in the market-place. Therefore academics and practitioners can examine some of the main factors affecting the growth and management of small technology-based firms at different stages in their development.

THE CREATION AND EARLY DEVELOPMENT OF SMALL TECHNOLOGY-BASED FIRMS

In Chapter 2, Dylan Jones-Evans examines the previous occupational background of the owner-managers of UK small technology-based firms, and its influence on the management of the business. The study arises from recent research which has indicated that an examination of the previous experience and expertise of the entrepreneur, gained in previous occupations, may be highly relevant in determining the possible success of a new venture. This is particularly true where the specific expertise of the entrepreneur forms the main strategic advantage of the business, as in the case of small technology-based firms. Utilising a typology based on previous organisational background, the research examines the results of an exploratory qualitative study of 38 technical entrepreneurs in the UK, concentrating on an examination of the effect of previous management experience on the functions undertaken by the technical entrepreneur within a small technology-based firm. The study concluded that, in general, entrepreneurs assume responsibility for functions in which they had previous experience although, unlike other studies of entrepreneurship, there is very little reluctance by these individuals to delegate responsibilities for management roles of which they have very little prior knowledge or experience.

In the third chapter, Besrat Tesfaye examines the patterns in the formation of the small technology-based firm originating from the university sector in Sweden. The study describes and analyses the formation of small technology-based firms originating from academic institutions, and identifies the factors conditioning this process. The study recognises that whilst each entrepreneurial process is unique and that a common pattern of firm formation and development may not always be presumed, it is nevertheless important to understand that the nature, interaction and impact of the multitude of variables which mould perceptions of opportunity, desirability and feasibility of an entrepreneurial action can provide a basis for distinguishing the patterns of formation and development of emerging organisations.

Margarida Fontes, in Chapter 4, examines the development of NTBFs in Portugal, with the aim of developing a better understanding of the way these firms are created, and subsequently develop, within less advanced economies. In particular, she addresses the role that NTBFs play in the development of new innovations, and also as disseminators of new technologies. The empirical study described in the chapter shows that NTBF formation and survival in a peripheral economy is indeed a complex undertaking, due to the lower technological opportunities and to the more limited demand for technology-based products. However, it also uncovers a variety of methods and sources used by entrepreneurs to identify and access the relevant technological knowledge and the proactive responses of the young firms to environmental constraints. In addition, the study indicates that NTBFs perform two major roles, namely a challenging role (whereby they break with the inertia of existing organisations by acquiring, developing and introducing 'absent' technologies into the market) and a more long-standing technology transfer role (in which they act as synthesisers of knowledge and technology, which they subsequently pass to the market). In performing these roles, these firms act as a vehicle for the acquisition, absorption and development of new technology at country level, contributing to an improvement in the nation's technological capability. Therefore, each of the next three chapters examines a different but complementary aspect of small firm development from the viewpoint of three different European cultures.

GROWTH OF THE SMALL FIRM

The second set of research, presented in Chapters 5 and 6, examines the process of small firm growth. In Chapter 5, Magnus Klofsten concentrates on examining the early development process of technology-based enterprises in Sweden, attempting to address the issues as to why the vulnerability of newly established firms leads to many not surviving their first years. Defining the attainment of survival of the early stages of development as the establishment of a business platform, this study identifies the necessary criteria for managing a young technology-based firm in order for it to achieve a business platform. The research indicates that it is indeed possible to identify the existence of a business platform, and that failure to establish such a platform will eventually cause the firm to fail and disappear from the market. The existence of a business platform, or lack of one, can be determined by ranking the firm according to eight aspects of achievement integral to its development process, and thus the minimum requirements for achieving a business platform can be determined.

In contrast, the work of Colm O'Gorman in Chapter 6 concentrates on examining the strategy literature to explain the growth of those few SMEs characterised by sustainable high growth. The research itself attempts to identify the business strategies of high growth businesses through a survey that compared high growth and low growth indigenous Irish companies. Case evidence from two businesses in the wholesale sector is also presented to illustrate these results which, by focusing on the strategies pursued by high growth businesses, should be of direct benefit to researchers, policy-makers and individual owner-managers of SMEs seeking high growth.

NETWORKING AND THE SMALL TECHNOLOGY-BASED FIRM

In the third set of chapters, the authors examine the different networking abilities of small technology-based firms. In Chapter 7, Erkko Autio addresses the development of small firms from three different countries from the point of view of the systemic model of innovation, where there is a complex interaction between the small technology-based firm and the environment in which it operates; this view of the technological innovation process has, by and large, yet to be implemented in research on NTBFs. The empirical part of the study develops and empirically tests a model that classifies NTBFs into science-based firms and engineering based firms. The two categories are defined in terms of the functional relationship between the NTBF and the articulation process of basic technologies. In the model, NTBFs are analysed in terms of the systemic knowledge conversion process to which they are attached. The main factors investigated in the study include technology contributions from various internal and external sources of technology, the use of various technology transfer mechanisms, and the functional contributions provided by NTBFs.

In the next chapter, Steve Conway examines the external sources of inputs in the development of successful technological innovation within small firms, especially the use of different networks. Particular emphasis is placed on the role and importance of informally derived inputs into the innovation process that have been sourced from outside the innovating firm. The role of a variety of external actors, such as users and suppliers, is then discussed in relation to these small-firm innovations.

Chapter 9, by Peter Heydebreck, builds on the premise that it is useful to study networks of technology-based firms and organisations, because they are linked together in patterns of co-operation and affiliation (which is defined as technological interweavement). The focus of the study is on the different forms of technological interweavement, and whether the impact of technological interweavement is dependent on different context factors. In addition, the study attempts to recognise whether firms can intensify their networking and manage their relationships more efficiently. In the study, both surveys and case studies are used for firms in Germany, Sweden and Switzerland. The results show that whilst firms' needs for external technological resources are often met on a regional level, the main problem for firms not taking advantage of external technological resources and know-how is a lack of awareness of what is available. In particular, NTBFs' needs for market-related services are not given the necessary attention, and there is a distinct lack of entry services (low cost, low risk) aimed at finding solutions for smaller problems which have been more precisely defined by firms. The study suggests the methods that may be implemented in helping small technology-based firms intensify their networking and manage their relationships more efficiently.

FURTHER DEVELOPMENT OF SMALL TECHNOLOGY-BASED FIRMS

The final two chapters examine the different processes which established small technology-based firms may undertake later in their development. In Chapter 10, Maria Lindqvist examines the process of internationalisation within small technology-based firms in Sweden, concentrating on the speed of internationalisation, the pattern of foreign market selection and the types of entry form used to access foreign markets. Some of the factors that were found to influence the process of internationalisation were managers' previous experience of foreign operations, ownership structure and certain technology characteristics, such as levels of innovation and technology, although the size of the firm and its R&D intensity had lower impacts than expected.

Åsa Lindholm, in Chapter 11, seeks to improve knowledge about technology-related ownership changes through examining the different forms of spin-offs and acquisition of small technology-based firms, concentrating on contrasting divestments and entrepreneurial spin-offs. Several analyses are made (case and survey studies), based on data from empirical studies of Swedish industry. The results indicate that technology-related acquisitions are increasingly important for the sourcing of technology among Swedish manufacturing companies. Growth and innovation are found to be higher among acquired firms than among the non-acquired firms, both before and after the acquisitions. The study also suggests that spin-off parents often fail to take advantage of growth and innovation in spin-off firms, especially in cases of entrepreneurial spin-offs, even though informal co-operation is common after the spin-off.

2 Technical Entrepreneurship, Experience and the Management of Small Technology-Based Firms

Dylan Jones-Evans

INTRODUCTION

The last decade has witnessed a growing enthusiasm for entrepreneurs as catalysts for economic development and change, with increasing attention being paid to the role of small technology-based companies as contributors to both technological innovation and employment in high-technology industries. Such small technology-based firms display a distinct form of entrepreneurship, mainly because of the dependence of the venture on the owner-manager's high degree of technical expertise, translated into new technologies, products or processes. As Cooper and Bruno (1977:20) have stated, 'for a new technology-based firm, the primary assets are the knowledge and skills of the founders. Any competitive advantage the new firm achieves is likely to be based upon what the founders can do better than others.' Using a typology based on the influence of the previous occupational experience of technical entrepreneurs, this chapter will explore the effect of previous management skills and knowledge on the current management position assumed by the individual owner-manager within the small technology-based firm, as well as any perceived future role in the business.

PREVIOUS RESEARCH ON TECHNICAL ENTREPRENEURSHIP

A number of early studies recognised the general importance of the previous occupational background of the technical entrepreneur on the management processes of small technology-based firms. For example, Cooper (1971a) demonstrated that technical entrepreneurs were often involved in businesses which were closely related to what they did before, and that the characteristics of the organisation the entrepreneur leaves to start a new

11

business may be directly related to the nature of the new business established. In fact, the influence of previous experience gained with other employers prior to starting a small business has become generally recognised as a relevant indicator of success within small companies (Chandler and Jansen, 1988; Stuart and Abetti, 1988; Mayer, Heinzel and Muller, 1990; Willard, Kruger and Feeser 1992; Klofsten, Jones-Evans and Lindell, 1996). Many of these studies have noted that such skills and knowledge are usually of a technical nature, forming the foundation of the products and services to be developed by the company and, ultimately, the markets targeted. However, whilst research has recognised the importance of previous technical experience on influencing the technology-based small firm, there has been considerable discussion regarding the often highly academic nature of the technological skill and creativity within this type of entrepreneur, leading to some scepticism regarding their ability to manage a commercial enterprise. Many of the early studies found that technical entrepreneurs rarely possessed management expertise comparable to their technical skills (Schrage, 1965; Cooper, 1971b; Litvak and Maule, 1972) which was generally attributed to a lack of a formal business education, coupled with work experience which tended to be in the technical area.

This orthodox view of technical entrepreneurs – having low management experience and high technological expertise – was originally associated with those emerging from a research-based academic environment (Schrage, 1965; Roberts and Wainer, 1966; Wainer and Rubin, 1969). However, investigations conducted by Cooper (1970a) recognised that a different type of technical entrepreneur might exist, whose previous experience had been gained within large industrial organisations. Subsequent research independently examining these two types of technical entrepreneur has shown that significant differences exist in the technical and management experience gained by each type. Studies of academic-based technical entrepreneurs frequently demonstrated that they had very little exposure to management skills such as marketing or finance, and had very little concept of business (Klofsten *et al.*, 1988; Samsom and Gurdon, 1990). On the other hand, technical entrepreneurs who had emerged from industrial organisations tended to have considerable managerial experience in interpersonal skills, decision-making and analytical skills, as well as marketing expertise (Braden, 1977; Knight, 1988).

Therefore, the type of organisation from which technical entrepreneurs emerge might affect the management and technical experience gained by the individual entrepreneur, and consequently the management of the small technology-based firm established by such an individual. Indeed, it has been suggested that the degree of management experience of technical entrepreneurs may affect the way the new venture grows, and that, at a certain stage of growth, entrepreneurs may no longer have sufficient management skills to run the business. The lack of management experience may lead to problems if the company grows to the stage where the management responsibilities increase to the point where strong leadership and delegation is needed (Greiner, 1972). As Firnstahl (1986) has shown, technical entrepreneurs can face a number of problems as the business grows, including the delegation of technical tasks to other employees (despite having the capability to do them quicker and better than the employee), shifting from the role of specialist to generalist, watching others achieving a technical competence within the organisation superior to one's own, and learning the new job of general manager (including the tasks of strategic planning and human resource management). This may prove very difficult to those entrepreneurs possessing high technological expertise, and subsequently, if an entrepreneur with little management experience continues to lead the venture beyond the start-up phase, then the organisational performance of the company will suffer (Flamholtz, 1986). For example, research carried out by Rubenson and Gupta (1990) indicated that founders with scientific or engineering backgrounds remain in control of the companies they founded for shorter periods than do founders whose previous experience was in business.

In the case of 'academic' entrepreneurs, their greater technological expertise can lead to significant problems as the small technology-based firm grows, especially if the business is highly dependent on the individual entrepreneur to provide the necessary technical expertise on which the competitive advantage of the business is based. Whilst Maidique (1980) has argued that technological entrepreneurs can continue to be involved in product development whilst retaining control as managing director, considerable difficulties may arise in maintaining technological advantage, as often the technical entrepreneur is the only person within the organisation with the necessary skills and experience to make the relevant technical decisions. In many cases, delegation may be difficult for individuals possessing a high degree of technical expertise, not only because they fear reduced technical quality, but because they have a genuine desire to continue to be involved on the technology side of the business. For example, in a study of the transition from scientists to managers, Peck (1986) suggested that, for the business to succeed, the entrepreneur's relationship with the product must change from direct to indirect involvement, with a sharp departure from the 'hands-on' orientation of the typical scientist. Such a change in roles may be difficult for entrepreneurs whose backgrounds are predominantly technological, despite indications that the future success of the small technology-based firm may rely on the ability of the entrepreneur to tie together the two strands of technical and management experience and expertise (Litvak and Maule, 1982; Stoner, 1987; Utterback *et al.*, 1988).

METHODOLOGY

Research Questions

As explained above, technology-based entrepreneurs may emerge from an academic or an industrial background. Indeed, while there have been numerous studies examining technical entrepreneurs from both academia and commercial organisations, no one study has attempted to differentiate between these quite different occupational backgrounds. This is despite evidence, as discussed earlier, that different organisational experiences may result in the entrepreneur developing different degrees of management and technical experience, which may subsequently affect the management and strategy of the new venture.

Therefore the central research question in this study is whether the previous occupational background of the technical entrepreneur directly affects the management of the small technology-based firm. In particular, the study will examine:

(a) the previous technical and management experience of the entrepreneur, including specific experiences of management functions such as finance, marketing, sales, R&D, manufacturing and project administration;

(b) the technical entrepreneur's previous experience as it relates to his current managerial and technical position within the company, and how responsibilities are delegated either internally within the company or to other external sources;

(c) the future role of the entrepreneur within the venture and the technical and management needs of the firm.

The study will therefore attempt to differentiate between occupational backgrounds, according to data gathered during the interview. Although the methods used to differentiate between the types of technical entrepreneur have been catalogued in detail elsewhere (Jones-Evans, 1995), a summary of the four different types identified in the study will be given later in this chapter.

Research Strategy

Whilst there have been studies in the USA which have examined the previous occupational background of the technical entrepreneur, the lack of European research in this area, especially in the UK, suggests that the study to be undertaken should be largely exploratory, and consequently any results should be generated inductively from the data collected. Such an inductive approach, developed from systematic empirical research, would be more likely to fit the data, and would therefore be more plausible and accessible than the speculative nature of deductive theory. The adoption of a qualitative methodology would also be the most relevant method of describing the 'technical entrepreneur', and such an approach can result in an intensive and extensive study of the individual or situation as it is in the present and the past, thus providing 'a wealth of information' for the development of hypotheses for later testing through quantitative studies (Smith, 1967). In fact, several important exploratory studies in entrepreneurship and business development (Collins, Moore and Unwalla, 1964; Scase and Goffee, 1980) have adopted an inductive, qualitative methodological approach to the examination of the small business owner-manager, predominantly because, as Bygrave (1988) states, the heart of the entrepreneurship process will be found in the descriptive background.

The methodology to be adopted should also best reflect the main objectives of the research, and as Romano (1989) observed, consideration should be given to the relevance or usefulness of research and the most appropriate methodology must be selected to fulfil this goal. To date, much of the research in entrepreneurship has tended towards the use of quantitative research instruments (Churchill and Lewis, 1986). This has also been the case in recent examinations of the technical entrepreneur's previous experience. For example, in a study of the impact of entrepreneurial and management experience on the early performance of technical ventures, Stuart and Abetti (1988) used quantitative methodology to examine the characteristics of the technical entrepreneur, and measured the amount (in years) of the experience of the entrepreneur and her new venture team. Not surprisingly, they concluded that it was not the amount, but the type of experience that was important in determining new venture success.

Therefore, taking into account the above considerations, it was decided to adopt a qualitative multiple-site process, as it was felt that this was the best approach for conducting an exploratory study of the relationship between the previous occupational background of the technical entrepreneur and the strategy of the new technology-based venture. The main conclusions of the study, although tentative, could then be tested quantitatively, using a larger sample of technical entrepreneurs.

Research Design

As Paulin *et al.* (1982) pointed out, the research design dimension, whilst complementing the research strategy, focuses more on the degree and formality of research methods and structure. Although the adoption of a qualitative research strategy approach offers the researcher the choice of a number of different research designs (Bryman, 1989), it should be emphasised that the design to be adopted should also directly complement the research purpose. In the UK study, a multiple-site qualitative process was adopted, as it was considered that this was the best approach for conducting exploratory research: furthermore, data had been gathered in other countries such as, the USA. Whilst the degree of 'richness' of data gathered through the use of the multiple-site approach may be questioned, it can be argued that whilst detail is sacrificed, the multiple-site approach offers a greater opportunity for studying a number of organisations, and hence potentially greater generalisability (Bryman, 1989). Consequently, events and processes in one well-described setting are not wholly idiosyncratic, and by comparing sites or cases one can establish the range of generality of a finding or explanation and, at the same time, pin down the conditions under which that finding will occur (Miles and Huberman, 1994).

Identifying the Sample

For the purposes of this research, a technical entrepreneur is defined as the founder and current owner-manager of a technology-based business: that is, as primarily responsible for its planning and establishment, and currently having some management control within the organisation (Jones-Evans, 1995). This differs from notable studies such as Smith (1967), who suggested that an entrepreneur could be an individual who, whilst being responsible for the setting up of a new venture, would not necessarily have to be involved in its subsequent management.

In identifying a suitable sample of 'technical entrepreneurs', the study adopted the methodology of an earlier study into industrial innovation (Langrish *et al.*, 1972), and utilised a government innovation award scheme, SMART (Small firms Merit Award for Research and Technology), which is directed towards the promotion of innovation within small ventures with less than 50 employees. As the award emphasised technological innovation and novelty within small independently owned ventures as its main criteria (Department of Trade and Industry (DTI), 1991), the owner-managers sampled from these businesses would provide a representative sample of technical entrepreneurs, as defined above, in the UK.

Data Collection

Taking into consideration both practical and geographical considerations, a sample of 102 SMART award winners (from a total of 290 winners) were identified for the study. A letter was sent to the managing directors of all 102 businesses, as identified in the SMART directories. As expected, a number of technical entrepreneurs refused to take part in the project, mainly because of past participation in other similar projects. This may be an increasing problem in management research in the UK, especially in the study of award-winning firms.

Overall, the reaction to the letter and the follow-up telephone call was favourable, with 76 companies indicating a willingness to participate in the study. However, eight companies could not be accommodated within the time-frame of the interview schedule, as they had indicated that an interview would only be possible at a time that was not suitable for the study. Moreover, a further seven companies had to cancel the meetings on the day of the interviews, and the financial constraints of the study made another visit to the region impracticable. This left 61 companies as a sample for the main study.

As this stage of the research was predominantly exploratory it was considered prudent to pilot the questionnaire thoroughly. In order to facilitate access, eight SMART winners from the UK regions of the West Midlands, East Midlands and Wales were chosen at random. Although many of the questions remained the same, the focus of the final questionnaire used in the main study was altered considerably as a result of the pilot. Therefore, the pilot respondents were not included in the main study, as the questionnaire was constantly being changed and developed throughout the piloting procedure. Visits were made to the remaining sample of 53 SMART winners, employing the same data collection techniques as in the pilot. All visits were carried out on a regional basis, which served to reduce both financial and time constraints. In two of the interviews, the tape recorder failed to work, thus losing valuable data (this is one of the main drawbacks of such a method, although in all the other interviews there were no recording problems).

The interview instrument took the form of a series of questions designed to elicit full information, which would enable a more detailed examination of the issues arising from the preliminary research. These would cover the entrepreneur's previous occupational background, especially previous technical and management experience and expertise; specific details on the small technology-based firm, including information on such issues as strategy and management, as well as standardised data such as turnover, employees and ownership structure; the novelty and origin of the technologies developed by the small technology-based firm; and the entrepreneur's personal history. Most of the questions asked were largely open-ended, in order to explore fully the participants' experiences, and how they affected the new entrepreneurial venture. Although the questionnaire was mainly standardised to enable a comparison between types of entrepreneur, this was confined to the themes under study, and considerable latitude was employed in the probing of the respondent for the relevant information.

After obtaining access to the companies, there were no problems with the interview process itself. All the respondents were willing to answer the relevant questions, with only one of the entrepreneurs questioned refusing to give specific information on his company's turnover figures (information which, incidentally, can be obtained from official sources at Companies House). In fact, some of the interviews continued for nearly three hours. The main problem encountered with the respondents was the unsuitability of some of the companies visited for the purposes of the research which, despite 53 companies being visited, resulted in a total of only 38 viable interviews. (Six of the winners were in fact 'garden-shed' operations run by inventors with no commercial or management function within the business; these individuals were all retired technologists who operated independently, and regarded the SMART competition as a way of financing their 'hobby'. In the cases of five of the winners interviewed, the researcher had to conduct the interview with a member of staff who was not the technical entrepreneur, and in one company, a take-over bid had been successful since the interview had been arranged, and the original technical entrepreneur was no longer the managing director of the company.) Although the sample could have been screened more thoroughly, the limitations of using a database with such a small potential population meant that securing access was one of the primary objectives of the data collection. However, the size dimensions of the sample of 38 firms were similar to that of the original database of 290 winners in 1988 and 1989.

Data Analysis

As with Bhave (1994), all 38 interviews were fully transcribed to generate case studies, adopting the approaches suggested by Miles and Huberman (1994) to methodically reduce the vast amounts of data for analysis, supporting this through using a combination of traditional coding and data reduction methods such as cutting and pasting (Riley, 1990). One of the methods to be utilised in displaying the data was to be the use of narrative text, which not only presents an accurate description of what is being studied (Strauss and Corbin, 1990), but also enables the full richness of the entrepreneur's experiences to be exhibited, as in previous studies of entrepreneurial behaviour (Collins, Moore and Unwalla, 1964; Smith, 1967; Scase and Goffee, 1980). In addition, an array of matrices and displays was used to condense the qualitative information, and make it accessible in compact forms (Miles and Huberman, 1994). These tables are not intended for quantitative analyses, but rather as a means of tracking the different characteristics of technical entrepreneurs and their firms across different qualitative variables. From these tables (2.2–2.7), a summary of the salient issues arising from the data was made, enabling direct analysis and comparisons between different categories. Analysis of each case-study was carried out individually, and then collectively analysed as a representative sample of technology-based small firms.

TYPOLOGY OF TECHNICAL ENTREPRENEURS

Taking into consideration some of the findings of previous research in the USA, as indicated in the literature review, the development of a typology – based on the previous occupational or organisational background – may be a possible instrument in differentiating technical entrepreneurs, and examining the management of small technology-based ventures. Much of the considerable growth in the field of entrepreneurship studies has tended to concentrate on identifying certain traits or characteristics associated with entrepreneurs that make them different from other individuals in society (Churchill and Lewis, 1986). These include the need for achievement (McClelland, 1961); locus of control (Rotter, 1966); a propensity towards risk; and personality deviancy (Collins, Moore and Unwalla, 1964; Kets De Vries, 1977). However, such empirical investigations, whilst being both rigorous and methodologically sound in their approach, have yet to find any trait that is strongly and consistently associated with entrepreneurship, with a number of studies (Brockhaus, 1980, 1982; Hull, Bosley and Udell, 1980; Carland, 1982; Stoner and Fry, 1982; Begley and Boyd, 1986; Lorrain and Dussault, 1988) highlighting many discrepancies in the ability of these models to predict entrepreneurial characteristics. In particular, this research has demonstrated considerable inconsistency in identifying a set of characteristics by which those individuals can be termed entrepreneurs or entrepreneurial (Stevenson, 1988). A number of writers have also presented the view that such studies have little relevance to a current examination of entrepreneurs and their firms, and feel that such personality analysis tools have only resulted in providing researchers with the consummate entrepreneur (Duffy and Stevenson, 1984; Aldrich and Zimmer, 1986). In fact, as Woo, Dunkelberg and Cooper (1988:165) recognised, 'Entrepreneurs are not homogeneous. They come from diverse backgrounds, exhibit different management styles, and are motivated by different factors. Yet to describe each possible combination of these characteristics would be cumbersome and impractical.' This has led to researchers departing from differentiating entrepreneurs from the rest of the population and instead adopting an approach which attempts to distinguish between different types of entrepreneur.

Therefore, with increasing evidence of the relative failure of behavioural-based models as indicators of entrepreneurial behaviour, the use of typologies as a means of examining different types of entrepreneur has gained increasing favour in entrepreneurship research (Smith, 1967; Stanworth and Curran, 1976; Gibb and Ritchie, 1981; Routamaa and Vesalainen, 1987). As Davidsson (1988:89) stated:

> a useful typology of entrepreneurs has a potential of high theoretical – and therefore also practical – value. If stringent sub-groups can be successfully established, even such abstracted theory as used within economics may benefit from empirical studies of entrepreneurship. Even larger is the potential progress that the field of entrepreneurship and small business research itself can make if uniform concepts are developed and greater care is taken as regards what kind of entrepreneurs results apply to.

Whilst some studies have attempted to build typologies based on a number of matching characteristics (Ettinger, 1983; Chell, Haworth and Brearley, 1991), researchers have, more recently, begun to differentiate between entrepreneurs on the basis of one dominant characteristic. For example, Robinson, McDougall and Herron (1988) developed a model whereby entrepreneurs were distinguished by their new ventures' strategies, while others such as Dubini (1988) have categorised entrepreneurs according to their motivations to start up a new enterprise.

Whilst technical entrepreneurs have been recognised as representing a distinct form of entrepreneurship, displaying characteristics which are quite different from other types of entrepreneur (Cooper, 1971a; Cooper and Bruno, 1977; Roberts, 1991b), there has been very little research which has attempted to distinguish between different types of technical entrepreneur, the exception being the study by Braden (1977) which differentiated technical entrepreneurs according to the entrepreneur's primary purpose for forming the business. This is despite evidence from the literature that technology-based entrepreneurs can be increasingly grouped according to their different occupational background.

Early studies into technical entrepreneurship identified the research-based academic environment – including non-profit organisations, namely non-profit research institutes, government research centres and universities – as the predominant background from which technical entrepreneurs emerged (Schrage, 1965; Roberts and Wainer, 1966; Wainer and Rubin, 1969; Cooper, 1971a). More recent research by Samsom and Gurdon (1990:441) specifically identified these individuals as 'scientist-entrepreneurs', namely:

> the scientist whose primary occupation, prior to playing a role in the venture start-up, and possibly concurrent with that process, was that of clinician, researcher or teacher, affiliated with a university, research institution and/or hospital . . . the industrial scientist who, during his industrial affiliation, had usually been exposed to corporate and managerial cultures, was thus not included.

They showed that this type of technical entrepreneur was an individual with no exposure to either the business world or entrepreneurship: not one of the scientist-entrepreneurs examined had any formal business training whatsoever, with team management and interpersonal skills the most frequently mentioned lack of skill, followed by marketing and finance. Two other studies, from Canada (Knight, 1986) and Sweden (Klofsten *et al.*, 1988) found similar results.

Research carried out by Cooper (1970a; 1970b) recognised a different type of technical entrepreneur: the individual who had 'spun out' from a large industrial organisation. Subsequent studies have indicated that these entrepreneurs have quite different characteristics from those originating from an academic environment. For example, a study by Knight (1988) of 133 spin-off ventures from large corporations showed that the entrepreneur had gained considerable experience of interpersonal skills, decision-making and analytical skills and marketing management.

As well as differences in management experiences between the two types, research by Roberts and Hauptmann (1986) has suggested that the organisational background may determine the degree of technological sophistication of the firm's products. In an examination of technological entrepreneurs in the biomedical field, a classification was devised according to the technological attributes of the founders' professional background and experience:

> Entrepreneurs who held predominantly R&D or research positions were encoded as 'high' on technological sophistication of their professional background, and all the others were encoded as low . . . Entrepreneurs whose previous employment was predominantly in universities or hospitals were encoded as 'high' on relevance and technological sophistication of their industrial background, those with medical or pharmaceutical industrial experience were encoded as 'moderate', and the rest as low. (Roberts and Hauptmann, 1986:111–12)

Therefore, in terms of organisational background, the research suggested that technical entrepreneurs may be differentiated according to their previous occupational background, and that both the management and technological sophistication of a new technology-based venture may vary according to this background. To date, whilst there have been numerous studies examining technical entrepreneurs from both academia and industrial organisations, no one study has attempted to differentiate between these quite different occupational backgrounds, and the effect that the competencies developed within these previous 'incubator' organisations may have on the possible success of the new venture.

In order to examine the effect of the technical entrepreneur's different experiences and expertise on the strategy of the small technology-based firm, this research study has adopted a similar approach to Smith (1967) and attempted to build a typology of technical entrepreneurs which is based on their previous occupational background, and the associated management and technical experience (Jones-Evans and Steward, 1991; Jones-Evans, 1995). Through a qualitative examination of the general occupational experience of the technical entrepreneur in the innovation process at previous companies worked for, it was possible to classify the individual technical entrepreneurs into four broad categories, namely 'research', 'producer', 'user' and 'opportunist'.

1. *The 'research' technical entrepreneur, with an academic knowledge-oriented institutional background.* The 'research' technical entrepreneur has been involved in scientific or technical development, either at an academic level at a higher educational establishment, or within a non-commercial research laboratory (such as working for a government body). This classification is very close to Samsom and Gurdon's (1990) definition of the academic-entrepreneur.

2. *The 'producer' technical entrepreneur, with an industrial organisational background, involved with the production and development of technology.* The 'producer' organisational background is one in which the entrepreneur has been involved in the direct commercial production or development of a product or process, usually within a large organisation.

3. *The 'user' technical entrepreneur, with an industrial organisational background and peripheral technological experience, either in technical sales or support services.* The third classification is the 'user' technical entrepreneur. This individual's background will have been in support or in a peripheral role in the development of the technology (e.g., technical sales or marketing). Alternatively, the 'user' technical entrepreneur may have been involved as an end-user in the application of the specific product or technology (perhaps in support services such as technical support), but without direct involvement in the actual development of the technology.

4. *The 'opportunist' technical entrepreneur, with no industrial technical background whatsoever.* The fourth type of technical entrepreneur identified is the non-technical 'opportunist' entrepreneur, an individual who has identified a technology-based opportunity, but who has no technical experience, or whose previous occupational experience is within non-technical organisations.

The coding of these occupational backgrounds into the four specific categories is discussed in more detail elsewhere (Jones-Evans, 1995). However, it should be noted that these typologies were arrived at from a careful qualitative analysis of the data in the interviews pertaining to the previous occupational background of the technical entrepreneur, using the various techniques of data reduction as recommended by Miles and Huberman (1994), where data reduction refers to the process of selecting, focusing, simplifying, abstracting and transforming the 'raw' data of the field notes. As such, the assessment of qualitative data gathered would, to a significant degree, be greatly dependent on the value judgement and observations of the researcher. Therefore, the grouping of the sample of technical entrepreneurs into four different types was based on the qualitative judgement of the researcher, rather than any series of quantitative variables.

As Table 2.1 shows, the firms in the study have been grouped into the four different types. These typologies will be used to examine whether the previous occupational background of the entrepreneur has any influence on the managerial roles undertaken by such individuals within the small technology-based firms they initiate. Whilst it may be argued that the 'user' and 'opportunist' technical entrepreneurs could be grouped together (as a group with little or no technical expertise), there are quite distinct differences between these two types, and as this is an exploratory study, it was felt prudent to differentiate between them.

Table 2.1   The occupational background of the sample of technical entrepreneurs

Research technical entrepreneur	*Producer technical entrepreneur*	*User technical entrepreneur*	*Opportunist technical entrepreneur*
($n = 11$)	($n = 15$)	($n = 6$)	($n = 6$)
Abbey Biosystems	Beran	Aber Instruments	CSE
Biocell	Bucon	Eng. Systems	Hereford Herbs
BPS	Boverton	IDS	NKR
Cell Adhesions	Cirrus	RK Drury	Optimised Control
EST	DC Clarke	Seaward	PC Marine
HE Associates	Ensigma	Talbot Helifix	Somerset Fruits
HMI	Fiox		
Mupor	Hunt		
Newcastle Photo	Hydramotion		
Novocastra	Interprise		
S&C Thermofluids	Isle Optics		
	NET		
	Rice		
	RJ Pond		
	Warwick Design		

RESULTS AND ANALYSIS

Previous Technical Experience of the Entrepreneur

'Research' Technical Entrepreneurs

In terms of academic qualifications, ten out of the eleven 'research' technical entrepreneurs had achieved qualifications to doctoral level in their particular technological discipline (Table 2.2). In those cases where the entrepreneurs had a pure academic research background – Novocastra, Newcastle Photometrics and EST – the technical expertise and experience was high, with all of them having worked for a number of years in research positions in their particular technological discipline, often at the leading edge of their science.

The same applies to those 'research' entrepreneurs with some minor experience of a 'producer' occupational background. All demonstrated high technical experience, having worked in research positions within academic or

Table 2.2 Highest educational qualification achieved by type of technical entrepreneur

Qualification	Research technical entrepreneur	Producer technical entrepreneur	User technical entrepreneur	Opportunist technical entrepreneur
PhD	Abbey Biosystems Biocell Cell Adhesions EST HE Associates HMI Mupor Newcastle Photo Novocastra S&C Thermofluids	Cirrus Interprise		
Postgraduate		Bucon		Optimised Control
Graduate	BPS	Boverton Ensigma Fiox Hydramotion Isle Optics NET Warwick Design	Aber Instruments Engineering Systems IDS Seaward	Hereford Herbs PC Marine
Technical qualification		Beran DC Clarke Hunt Rice RJ Pond		NKR Somerset Fruits
No qualifications			RK Drury Talbot Helifix	CSE

governmental posts, and in commercial organisations. For example, the technical entrepreneur in Biocell, despite working in two 'producer' occupations, had been a research scientist throughout his career, whilst in the case of Abbey Biosystems the technical entrepreneur, although moving from an academic department to technical consultancy and finally technical entrepreneurship, was still predominantly involved in technological innovation within the medical instrumentation sector. Only one technical entrepreneur – from Mupor – did not hold a technical position in the 'incubator' organisation prior to start-up. However, the duration of this position as a general manager was only a couple of years, and was preceded by 19 years of technology-based occupations in the field of synthetic organic chemistry.

'Producer' Technical Entrepreneurs

In terms of educational qualifications, the majority of the 'producer' entrepreneurs had qualified to degree level or better, whilst a third of the entrepreneurs – RJ Pond, DC Clarke, Hunt Power Drives, Beran Instruments and Rice Associates – had gained technical qualifications through apprenticeships within larger companies. The technical experience of the 'producer' technical entrepreneurs from previous employment was fairly high, although as their careers progressed there seemed to be an underlying pattern of movement from a relatively technologically-intensive occupation to a more management-based occupation. Over half of the 'producer' technical entrepreneurs had occupations with a direct technological element prior to initiating their own business, with the remainder of this type of entrepreneur becoming involved in management-intensive occupations such as divisional manager (Cirrus Research), marketing manager (Fiox), general manager (Bucon), works manager (DC Clarke), technical sales (Hydramotion), technical development manager (Interprise), and technical manager (Beran). It would be expected that the technical expertise of such individuals would be high when entering such a post from a technical background, but may diminish if the individual retains this management position for a considerable period of time.

'User' Technical Entrepreneurs

The technical qualifications of the 'user' entrepreneur are divided between those who gained a general technology-based first degree (Seaward, Aber Instruments, Engineering Systems, and IDS) and those who had none (RK Drury and Talbot Helifix). Apart from Aber Instruments, the other three qualified 'user' technical entrepreneurs had businesses based on the technological areas in which they qualified, although they had also gained some general experience of the use of technology. For example, the entrepreneur in Seaward had previous experience as an electronic test engineer, whilst the owner-manager of Engineering Systems had a support role as a research technician within an academic department, although neither had been involved in the actual development of technology, only its use (thus differentiating them from the research and producer technical entrepreneurs). In the case of the entrepreneurs from RK Drury and Talbot Helifix, both had previous 'hands-on' experience in using technology, although they had no formal qualifications.

'Opportunist' Technical Entrepreneurs

Although the educational background of 'opportunist' technical entrepreneurs, similar to their previous occupational background, was varied, two of this type had developed their technological expertise in an educational institution prior to the immediate establishment of their own business. In the case of the entrepreneur from Optimised Control, this was a Master's course in 'special automation', whilst the entrepreneur from PC Marine undertook a degree course in 'nautical studies'. In both businesses, the initial technical expertise was based on the skills gained by the entrepreneur during his educational course, and prototype work developed during this time. Neither had any previous occupational technical experience: the entrepreneurs from PC Marine and Optimised Control had been a yacht captain and a management consultant respectively, prior to undertaking a technical education course. The technical entrepreneurs from CSE and NKR had developed their technical expertise in their spare time, as a private 'hobby', whilst the entrepreneur from Somerset Fruits had gained some experience of working with technology within previous non-industrial occupations, mainly as a schoolteacher. In the case of Hereford Herbs, the entrepreneur appeared to have minimal technical knowledge, as he had no previous technical qualifications or experience, having previously worked as a civil servant prior to buying an agricultural business.

Previous Management Experience of the Entrepreneur

'Research' Technical Entrepreneurs

Other than the management of R&D projects, the 'research' technical entrepreneur had very little previous experience of specific management functions such as marketing or finance (Table 2.3). This was especially the situation with the entrepreneurs from EST, Newcastle Photometrics and Novocastra, who had conducted their entire careers, prior to establishing the new venture, within an academic institution. As an academic lecturer, the

Table 2.3 Previous management experience of the technical entrepreneur, by occupational background

Management function	Research technical entrepreneur (n = 11)	Producer technical entrepreneur (n = 15)	User technical entrepreneur (n = 6)	Opportunist technical entrepreneur (n = 6)
Finance		Bucon Cirrus Hydramotion Warwick Design	Aber Instruments IDS RK Drury Seaward	CSE Optimised Control PC Marine
Manufacturing	Biocell BPS Mupor	Beran Boverton Bucon Cirrus DC Clarke Fiox Hunt Hydramotion Interprise Isle Optics NET Rice		Hereford Herbs Somerset Fruits
Marketing	Abbey Biosystems BPS Mupor	Bucon Interprise Cirrus Fiox Hunt Rice	Aber Instruments IDS Seaward Talbot Helifix	CSE
Project leadership	Abbey Biosystems Biocell BPS Cell Adhesions EST	Beran Bucon Cirrus DC Clarke Hunt	Talbot Helifix	PC Marine CSE

	HMI Mupor Newcastle Photo Novocastra S&C Thermofluids	Interprise Isle Optics NET RJ Pond Rice Warwick Design		Somerset Fruits
R&D	Abbey Biosystems Biocell BPS Cell Adhesions EST HE Associates HMI Mupor Newcastle Photo Novocastra S&C Thermofluids	Beran Boverton Cirrus DC Clarke Ensigma Fiox Hunt Hydramotion Interprise Isle Optics NET Rice RJ Pond Warwick Design	Aber Instruments Eng. Systems	
Sales	Abbey Biosystems	Beran Boverton Bucon Cirrus Fiox Hunt Hydramotion Isle Optics NET Rice Warwick Design	Aber Instruments IDS Seaward	CSE

entrepreneur from EST had not developed any specific functional management skills. Instead, his previous experience was predominantly technical, with management experience limited mainly to project management, either working as part of a team, or individually on a particular experiment. No direct knowledge of management functions such as sales, marketing or finance was gained, with very little practice in managing resources or people. As shown earlier, such a case-study is frequently proposed as indicative of the typical background of an academic technical entrepreneur: predominantly technology-oriented with no functional management experience.

This was certainly not the case with the entrepreneurs from Novocastra and Newcastle Photometrics. For example, the entrepreneur from Newcastle Photometrics had gained increasing experience of management with each academic position, with a gradual movement away from 'hands-on' technical tasks towards the overall management of research projects. For example, within his current academic position at the time of the study, the entrepreneur's role had gradually evolved from a purely scientific function to that of a facilitator and manager:

> Purely I would say that I have moved from an experimental scientist role to a managerial overseeing role. I get less and less into the laboratory and I spend my time looking to the actual projects and overseeing the science of it. Management was an evolving situation – as the research group grew, then one had to develop the managerial skills to cope. Administration is a big part of it, then one realises that motivation is equally as important as just providing an environment . . . so I would say that man-management has been the main effort in the last three years to make sure that one can see what people are like.

The management experience of the other 'research' technical entrepreneurs was varied, with a number of these 'research' technical entrepreneurs having had some commercial experience within manufacturing organisations prior to initiating a small business, although the large majority of their careers had been spent within academic institutions. Despite taking this factor into account, there is very little evidence of a functional expertise of management, although the research suggests that this may depend on whether the entrepreneur had gained industrial experience prior to or after entering an academic career. For example, those technical entrepreneurs whose industrial experience preceded their research-based occupations seemed to have gained insufficient personal and functional management skills. Similar to the technical entrepreneur in EST, their management skills were limited to project management only, with negligible experience of functions such as finance or marketing. The technical entrepreneur from HE Associates is a typical example: 'Management responsibilities were only in the project management sense. Marketing to a certain extent, but very limited – it wasn't really my responsibility in the project. Science-based management was just project management, and again there was no formal training.' The same situation was found in Cell Adhesions, where the technical entrepreneur's industrial and academic experience was very much limited to technical tasks. Similarly, in the cases of the entrepreneurs from both S&C Thermofluids and Biocell, there was only limited exposure to management skills within the organisation for which each individual previously worked.

According to the survey, the 'research' entrepreneurs with direct management experience were those who had left a research-based position to take up a developmental 'producer' occupation within a manufacturing organisation, namely BPS, Mupor, HMI and Abbey Biosystems. However, the degree of management experience tended to vary considerably. For example, the technical entrepreneurs in Mupor and HMI had gained little management experience within positions at research organisations, with management skills being acquired during a brief experience of industry prior to start-up. In both these cases, the functional management skills gained were of a broad general nature, with no expertise acquired in specific management functions. Whilst the entrepreneurs in BPS and Abbey Biosystems had both worked in 'research' occupations prior to joining a manufacturing organisation, they gained considerable experience of management whilst working in a research environment. For example, in the case of Abbey Biosystems the entrepreneur, whilst working in an academic department, was involved in the development of applied research which had commercial, rather than academic, priorities:

I was developing medical instrumentation for use in hospitals . . . if you are working in that sort of environment, you can't just do research. You actually have to do product development – you may want to call it that, but at the end of the day you can't use laboratory lash-ups on patients. You have to go through all the procedures you go through in a company in making the device socially acceptable and relatively inexpensive if you are having to use it on patients. I quickly came to the conclusion that what I was involved in, even though it was in an academic environment, was commercial product development.

Subsequently, the technical entrepreneur transferred his entire research team from the academic institution, and established a small technology-based organisation. In this particular case, commercial considerations outweighed the scientific considerations. As a result, manufacturing knowledge was gained through the academic position but, more importantly, marketing skills were also acquired, albeit in an indirect manner

> [With] my contact with marketing people in companies, one became familiar with their thinking, you became familiar with their market survey figures, how those were gathered. I spoke to a lot of customers, competitors and so on. The other marketing experience was direct contact with clinicians, i.e., the end users. When you place a product, what do they say about it, what things do you take notice of and what things do you ignore? Whereas as an academic, you're not able to sift one sort of information from the rest.

Therefore, in this case, the entrepreneur's experience of marketing was developed through relationships with both the external customer, and through contact with the commercial world. Moreover, the entrepreneur was seconded to a large manufacturing company as technical consultant for one year prior to the establishment of his first new venture, which greatly influenced his decision to start up. This experience resulted in exposure to more specific managerial skills, along with managerial solutions to commercial problems, including commercial project management, increased awareness of the importance of the function of sales in product development, and more specific manufacturing skills. As stated, this commercial experience led directly to the formation of a company by the technical entrepreneur, which was similar in size and composition to the research group previously managed by the entrepreneur in his academic department. In fact, it can be suggested that the commercial experience enabled the technical entrepreneur to move the research group from an academic base to a more commercial one.

'Producer' technical entrepreneurs

It is expected that those entrepreneurs who have worked within technical positions in a commercial organisation will, unlike 'research' technical entrepreneurs, gain considerable experience of management functions such as sales or marketing, predominantly through a relationship with other departments in the commercial company. This is indeed the case with the sample of entrepreneurs identified as originating from a 'producer' background, with only two individuals demonstrating limited experience of management: RJ Pond and Ensigma (Table 2.3). In the case of RJ Pond, the technical entrepreneur's previous management experience was limited to the management of design projects, whilst in Ensigma, the entrepreneur's management experience was restricted to an R&D role, albeit within a large manufacturing organisation:

> I have no direct experience of manufacturing or sales or marketing. In that position when I was project managing this product development, I had cause to liaise with engineering, and through them the operations manufacturing group and also marketing, but I was never directly involved. For example, I didn't spend any time on the shop floor actually working on any product built. Never spent time in the marketing department . . . I simply relied on their experience and took instructions on what they required of me.

However, such an experience seems atypical of the occupational background of the 'producer' technical entrepreneurs, with the other 13 case studies in this typology having had a considerable breadth of management experience (with experience of at least two management functions). The technical entrepreneur from Cirrus Research had previous experience of all the functions required in a technology-based commercial organisation, including R&D, manufacturing, marketing, sales, finance and project leadership. This had been achieved through a succession of positions within manufacturing organisations, originating with technical management positions, but then progressing to divisional responsibilities within large companies. This eventually resulted in a senior management position, with no technical obligations, prior to the establishment of his own venture: '[In this job] I didn't have any responsibility for production whatsoever – it was a very formal system. I was in charge of marketing, sales and development. I did a course for accounting – it was good training, but there wasn't much technical responsibility.'

With regard to the entrepreneurs from Rice Associates and Hunt Power Drives, both had considerable experience of R&D, manufacturing, marketing and sales, but not finance. In the case of Hunt Power Drives, the financial function within the incubator firm was carried out by a central accountant for the whole company, whilst in Rice Associates the entrepreneur was running his own small engineering company, and preferred to use an external book-keeping service. In fact, there seems to be evidence of very little previous knowledge of finance and accounting by the 'producer' technical entrepreneurs, despite their experiences within commercial organisations. Apart from Cirrus Research, only three other entrepreneurs had gained any experience of finance. In Bucon, the technical entrepreneur had gained experience as a general manager of a large manufacturing subsidiary, whilst in the examples of the individuals from Hydramotion and Warwick

Design, the experience was gained within smaller organisations. For example, in establishing a completely new division within the 'incubator' organisation, the entrepreneur from Warwick Design gained financial 'know-how', in conjunction with other management skills such as sales and marketing:

> I did some finance and accounts. At one point, I opened a new division in Australia, so I set that up and had to run it, running the accounts and keeping the books; developing the business, meeting the clients, doing the design. With regard to sales, I was 'mailshooting' people, following up with phone calls, going to see them, making a presentation, and going back with their design proposal.

In over half of the 'producer'-based companies examined – Hydra-motion, DC Clarke, Boverton, Interprise, Fiox, Beran, Isle Optics and NET – the entrepreneurs had previous experience of technical positions within small manufacturing companies. As a result, their involvement with functions such as manufacturing and sales was far closer to the customer than those entrepreneurs within larger organisations. For example, in the case of Boverton, the entrepreneur's occupation within the incubator organisation was predominantly R&D. However, as he explains, he was directly concerned with the marketing side of the business:

> With the sales side, we were sort of hand in glove. There were sales engineers on the road who got the initial enquiries, but either we would go out with the sales engineers to a customer or work independently, so I was very much involved with the sales and marketing side, down to even in fact taking decisions on what areas of marketing we should follow.

'User' Technical Entrepreneurs

As Table 2.3 shows, the management skills of the 'user' technical entrepreneur varied considerably. In some cases, such as RK Drury and Talbot Helifix, the management skills developed were peripheral to the technological needs of the company. In both cases, the entrepreneurs had been users of technology within their own businesses, gaining management skills relevant to the 'running' of those firms. In the case of Talbot Helifix, the entrepreneur was not only responsible for the marketing and sales function of four subsidiary companies, but was also responsible for the strategic role of the main business:

My actual managerial responsibilities at the time was as chairman, which really meant I ran the management group meetings where all the directors met and discussed the administration and management of the company on a monthly basis. I was still largely responsible for sales and marketing and was also running a small subsidiary company.

On the other hand, the technical entrepreneurs in both Seaward and IDS gained specific management skills within a technological support function of a large manufacturing organisation. The entrepreneur from Seaward, in his role as marketing manager for a large manufacturing company, learnt skills in specific management functions:

There was a lot of experience and training in finance and obviously marketing. I had exposure to finance and accounts during this time, because I had to make sure that to work with the European divisions, I had to take in, not necessarily financial information, but certainly projected forecasts and that sort of thing, and tie it back into the overall European picture... I was eventually responsible for all the market planning within the company.

With regard to the 'user' entrepreneurs who had some previous 'producer' occupational experience, the complexity and degree of management skills developed within these large manufacturing organisations was comparatively low. In the case of Engineering Systems, the entrepreneur gained minimal experience of management, both as an apprentice in a manufacturing company and as a specific user of engineering technology: 'There was nothing that would relate to running a small business either at the university or when I was serving my apprenticeship. So there was no background of any managerial experience in small business.'

The technical entrepreneur from Aber Instruments gained no management skills within his first employment position as a development engineer in a large manufacturing organisation. However, after leaving this firm, he established a small business, which resulted in the acquisition of a number of relevant business skills.

'Opportunist' Technical Entrepreneurs

As stated earlier, the 'opportunist' entrepreneur is characterised as having no previous direct technical background, and as a result, the types of occupations from which such individuals will emerge to establish technology-based small firms can vary greatly. Consequently, the degree of management experience gained in previous occupations can be considerably different, as this sample demonstrates (Table 2.3). For example, the entrepreneur from NKR, following a period of military service, had developed no experience of management functions whatsoever, whilst in the case of PC Marine, the entrepreneur spent the majority of his career as an insurance manager, which was followed by a period as a yacht captain. On the other hand, some individuals had gained experience of running their own businesses prior to the current start-up, as in the cases of Hereford Herbs and CSE. In CSE, the entrepreneur gained considerable management experience in establishing a successful retail business:

> I was managing director of the company and had complete responsibility for decision-making, with about 35–40 people in the company at the end and a budget of £500 000. The only thing involved was man-management and marketing, and I was responsible mainly for the latter. It was my job to tell the public what we had, and get them in through the door.

Whilst the entrepreneur from Optimised Control had only limited experience of financial management after one year within a management consultancy, the entrepreneur heading Somerset Fruits had some previous experience within industry, especially in the development of manufacturing systems. However, in this case, the majority of the entrepreneur's career was as a teacher and college lecturer prior to start-up.

The Current Management Role of the Technical Entrepreneur in the Small Technology-Based Firm

'Research' Technical Entrepreneurs

Table 2.4 presents the technical entrepreneur's current involvement in different management functions within the small technology-based firm. With regard to the 'research' technical entrepreneur, individuals categorised under this type had previous experience of R&D activities, and therefore it is not surprising that all except one of these 'research' technical entrepreneurs had assumed responsibility for R&D within their businesses. One example is the technical entrepreneur from Biocell, who had utilised his previous technical and management experience gained in a research organisation directly within his new venture, this time in the market-place. As he explained:

> Biocell manufactures and markets gold-labelled immune reagents for the specific purpose of visualising proteins and micro-molecules at the sub-cellular level . . . these are used in exactly the kinds of research areas that

I was involved with for the last 15 years, so it has come directly from my research experience ... I am doing commercially what I only did in research before – that is what has happened.

Table 2.4 Delegation of management functions within the small technology-based firm: 'research' technical entrepreneur

Management function	Technical entrepreneur	Other director/s	Venture staff	External	Not required
Finance	Biocell HE Associates HMI S&C Thermofluids	Abbey Biosystems	EST	BPS Cell Adhesions Mupor Newcastle Photo Novocastra	
Manufacturing	Biocell Mupor	Newcastle Photo	BPS Novocastra	Abbey Biosystems EST HE Associates HMI	Cell Adhesions S&C Thermofluids
Marketing	Biocell EST HMI Mupor Newcastle Photo	Abbey Biosystems	BPS	Novocastra	Cell Adhesions HE Associates S&C Thermofluids
Project Leadership	Biocell BPS Cell Adhesions EST HMI Mupor Newcastle Photo Novocastra	HMI	Abbey Biosystems		HE Associates S&C Thermofluids
R&D	Abbey Biosystems Biocell Cell Adhesions EST HE Associates Mupor Newcastle Photo Novocastra S&C Thermofluids		BPS		
Sales	EST HMI Newcastle Photo	Abbey Biosystems	BPS Mupor	Biocell Novocastra	Cell Adhesions HE Associates S&C Thermofluids

The exception among 'research' technical entrepreneurs was BPS, where the entrepreneur had assumed the position of managing director of the company, preferring to leave the responsibility for the technology with his venture team. This was despite previous experience of the technological process developed within the new venture.

The majority of the technical entrepreneurs, including those from Biocell and BPS, had also assumed their previous position of project leadership within the organisation. Two of the cases of technical entrepreneurs who did not take up leadership positions, S&C Thermofluids and HE Associates, were in partnerships, and considered most of the tasks equally shared between the directors of the firm. In the case of Abbey Biosystems, the technical entrepreneur, although the initiator of the venture, had assumed more of a technology consultant role. The company was managed by experienced professionals: the managing director was an ex-BOC (British Oxygen Company) employee with expertise in marketing and sales who, for the previous four years, had headed a spin-off BOC division in Florida very successfully; the responsibilities for both engineering management and sensor technology development were held by two other experienced individuals.

In the areas of finance, marketing and sales, there emerged a tendency by the technical entrepreneurs to take on responsibilities for functions in which they had no previous experience. In some of the cases, such as EST and HMI, this was due to a lack of finance in attracting suitably qualified staff to the company. In the case of HMI, this resulted in the technical entrepreneur taking on personal responsibility for marketing, sales and finance:

So at the moment as MD, I'm supposed to be responsible for the whole thing – responsible for finance, marketing and sales because there is nobody else to be responsible for it. However, we need sales and marketing. The problem is at the moment that sales and marketing skills are expensive. A good quality marketing department would cost a fortune and a salesman on the road is highly expensive. In planning the substantial expansion, we have incorporated into that a certain amount of consultancy costings. We can't afford, certainly for another year, people of that skill.

Other technical entrepreneurs, such as those from Biocell and Newcastle Photometrics, had assumed responsibility for the functions of sales and marketing because, although they had no previous experience of either management function, they had extensive knowledge of the market. In the case of Newcastle Photometrics, the technical entrepreneur himself was a potential user and intimately appreciated the needs of his customers. In fact, his university research group was being used to actively test the feasibility of the product as part of its research. Moreover, the company produced relatively low numbers of units, and sold them with a high profit margin. As a result of this strategy, marketing and sales could be targeted personally at specific individuals within the technical entrepreneur's scientific field, without a great need for marketing/sales expenditure and effort. The company was also the first innovator of this product, which gave it a very strong competitive advantage.

The responsibility for finance, although undertaken by a number of the entrepreneurs, was largely entrusted to other experienced members of staff, with only two of the sample entrepreneurs utilising external accountants. In fact, there was very little use of external individuals for the management of functions within these organisations, despite a general lack of experience in the areas of management. One of the exceptions was Novocastra, where the technical entrepreneur had appreciated his company's deficiencies in the areas of sales and finance, and had concentrated on those management competencies in which he has sufficient experience, namely the technical leadership of his venture, and input into R&D, using external distributors for both the marketing and sales of the venture's products. This took sufficient pressure away from the new enterprise, enabling it to concentrate its resources on its particular strengths of innovation and technology, rather than attempting to market products where there may be sufficient technical sales knowledge, but no commercial experience.

Three organisations – S&C Thermofluids, Cell Adhesions and HE Associates – perceived no need for marketing and sales functions for their ventures. In the case of S&C Thermofluids and HE Associates, both were small development organisations whose main function was not product manufacture, but the provision of specific technical expertise to larger companies. In both cases, no marketing or sales was required by the company because of the high technical expertise of the entrepreneurs and the demand by larger firms for this expertise. Manufacturing responsibilities were not undertaken by the vast majority of the 'research' entrepreneurs. Although Newcastle Photometrics, Novocastra and BPS carried out manufacturing in-house, they produced custom products in small batches. Subcontracting was the most popular method of manufacturing, mainly because companies wished to retain their position as R&D organisations only.

'Producer' Technical Entrepreneurs

With the 'producer' technical entrepreneur, there were again a high number of entrepreneurs with responsibilities for both project leadership and R&D

within the small company (Table 2.5). Exceptions to this were found in the cases of Ensigma and RJ Pond, where the technical entrepreneurs were responsible for the R&D function alone. In Ensigma, the other areas of management were delegated to venture staff within the company, whereas in the case of RJ Pond, a conscious decision had been made to keep the company as free of administration as possible, with marketing, sales and even manufacturing subcontracted out:

> I mean I do have my own firm anyway, but from a manufacturing point of view, there's no way I can see I want to do that at the moment. First of all you get into large organisation operation; you tend to lose touch with the design aspects. For that reason, I have sold the licence to a company in Stroud who market and manufacture these valves, but I'm intimately involved with it. I supply the technical side of the thing, and also the oilfield contacts, as I meet quite a few people in the course of my work.

However, a number of entrepreneurs were undertaking both technical and management tasks within the company. This is understandable, considering the previous management backgrounds of some of these entrepreneurs. For example, the entrepreneur from Warwick Design had developed expertise in both development and design, as well as sales and finance. In common with some of the 'research' entrepreneurs, there was an underlying impression that these specific managerial roles had been assumed through necessity, rather than desire:

> Both myself and my fellow director are involved as much as possible in day to day project work, because basically we are product designers who have to do the other things to keep the company going. I now do less design and more writing letters . . . my role has definitely changed. It's a necessary evil really . . . I'm ideally best skilled at being a designer, but being a designer in isolation or being a designer in a bigger company or another company which isn't my own is not fulfilling enough from a career point of view. So in order to get out of that, you have to grow and expect to take on these other jobs. It's very hard to keep a global view of what the company is doing and focus down on working on individual design problems.

Although three of the entrepreneurs – from Cirrus, DC Clarke and RJ Pond – subcontracted marketing and sales to distributors, these two functions were undertaken by the majority of the entrepreneurs, often in conjunction with responsibility for R&D. Most of the 'producer' entrepreneurs had previous management experience of either sales or marketing.

Table 2.5 Delegation of management functions within the small technology-based firm: 'producer' technical entrepreneur

Management function	Technical entrepreneur	Other director/s	Venture staff	External	Not required
Finance	Bucon DC Clarke Hydramotion	Boverton Fiox Interprise Isle Optics NET	Cirrus Ensigma	Beran Hunt Rice RJ Pond Warwick Design	
Manufacturing	Boverton	Beran Bucon Fiox Hunt Hydramotion Interprise Isle Optics		Cirrus DC Clarke Ensigma NET Rice Warwick Design	RJ Pond
Marketing	Beran Boverton Bucon Fiox Hydramotion Interprise Isle Optics NET Warwick Design	Rice	Ensigma Hunt	Cirrus DC Clarke RJ Pond	
Project leadership	Beran Boverton Bucon Cirrus Hunt Hydramotion Interprise NET Rice Warwick Design	Ensigma Fiox			DC Clarke Isle Optics RJ Pond
R&D	Boverton DC Clarke Ensigma Hydramotion Isle Optics NET Rice RJ Pond Warwick Design	Beran Bucon Hunt Interprise	Cirrus Fiox		

Table 2.5 Contd.

Management function	Technical entrepreneur	Other director/s	Venture staff	External	Not required
Sales	Beran Boverton Fiox Hunt Isle Optics Interprise NET	Bucon Rice	Ensigma Hydramotion Warwick Design	Cirrus DC Clarke RJ Pond	

In the case of Hydramotion, the technical entrepreneur had no formal management experience of marketing, but was assuming responsibility within his organisation for this function, predominantly because of a lack of personnel with adequate expertise. Despite the majority of the 'producer' technical entrepreneurs having gained experience of manufacturing within their previous occupations, only one of these individuals – from Boverton Electronics – had assumed responsibility for this function within his organisation. In general, the manufacturing function within ventures headed by such entrepreneurs had been either subcontracted to other organisations, or delegated to another director within the company. In most of these cases, the manufacturing function had been delegated to other individuals or organisations, because the entrepreneur's role had changed to that of assuming overall responsibility for the business as managing director, as in the cases of Bucon, Beran, Interprise and Hunt. In Hunt Power Drives, responsibilities for different functions had been slowly devolved to other individuals within the organisation, despite the technical entrepreneur's substantial previous experience of management, especially manufacturing.

The majority of the 'producer' technical entrepreneurs did not take responsibility for financial matters within their companies, choosing instead to delegate this function either to other directors, or preferably to external accountants. In the case of Boverton Electronics, the entrepreneur decided to concentrate on managing the technical and sales functions within the company, whilst leaving financial matters to his fellow director:

> Basically I am more technical, I don't particularly want to get involved with the financial side, and my partner is the opposite way round. She was the financial accounts director of the other company, so between us we think we have got a well balanced managerial team. Although we know a little about what the other does, we don't really get involved in that. If there is anything financial, it goes to my partner, who could probably do it in a quarter of the time and with more expertise.

In two of the sample companies – Fiox and Ensigma – the leadership of the organisation had been assumed by another individual. This enabled the entrepreneur to concentrate on his particular expertise. In the cases of both RJ Pond and DC Clarke, neither entrepreneur required project management skills as they were both 'one-man' development companies.

'User' Technical Entrepreneurs

As the 'user' technical entrepreneurs had been predominantly involved in a technical support role such as marketing, usually within manufacturing organisations, it is expected that such individuals would undertake responsibility for the marketing function within their entrepreneurial venture. The findings of this study support this premise: the entrepreneurs from Aber Instruments, IDS, Talbot Helifix and Seaward Electronics all had previous experience of marketing, and were currently responsible for this function within their organisations (Table 2.6). As the entrepreneur from Seaward explained:

> The marketing experience gained was very important to me. We rely on that because our products are relatively low technology and rely very heavily on my experience in the marketing side to develop the business . . . it was crucial and gave me the ability to want to start the business in a more professional fashion having had that experience.

Of the six 'user' technical entrepreneurs, only the owner-manager of IDS was directly involved with the sales function, although this was a result of strategic customer liaison in his other position as managing director.

No 'user' technical entrepreneur had taken responsibility for the manufacturing function. Instead, in the majority of businesses headed by this type of entrepreneur, manufacturing had been devolved to other staff within the venture, with the exceptions of RK Drury and Talbot Helifix. Whilst both of these ventures were one-man development organisations, RK Drury, as a development company, did not require manufacturing facilities. On the other hand, the entrepreneur in Talbot Helifix had subcontracted the manufacturing tasks, which was also the situation with the other management functions in the company apart from marketing:

> The manufacturers are all sub-contractors. The R&D are all contracted out. The financial and accounting services are all sub-contracted – they are done by our accountants. The marketing has been the subject of a DTI study, and we are implementing their recommendations. Sales will be

done through commissioned representatives whom we are busy recruiting at the moment. I have adopted this management structure in order to allow the maximum expansion with the minimum of staff which will enable me to keep a tight control on the costs.

Table 2.6 Delegation of management functions within the small technology-based firm: 'user' technical entrepreneur

Management function	Technical entrepreneur	Other director/s	Venture staff	External	Not required
Finance	Aber Instruments RK Drury	Eng. Systems	IDS Seaward	Talbot Helifix	
Manufacturing		Aber Instruments	Eng. Systems IDS Seaward	Talbot Helifix	RK Drury
Marketing	Aber Instruments IDS Seaward Talbot Helifix			Eng. Systems	RK Drury
Project leadership	Aber Instruments Eng. Systems IDS Seaward Talbot Helifix				RK Drury
R&D	Eng. Systems RK Drury	IDS Aber Instruments		Seaward Talbot Helifix	
Sales	IDS		Aber Instruments Seaward	Eng. Systems Talbot Helifix	RK Drury

Only two 'user' technical entrepreneurs were directly involved with the development of the technology: those from RK Drury and Engineering Systems, who were both former users of their venture's technology. Again, the majority of this type of entrepreneur assumed the role of managing director within their organisations, with the exception of RK Drury who, as a one-man operation, felt that he did not require that particular function.

'Opportunist' Technical Entrepreneurs

As Table 2.7 shows, the entrepreneur from CSE was the only individual from the 'opportunist' background to have had previous experience of running an organisation. Nevertheless, all the 'opportunist' technical entrepreneurs had assumed responsibility for the overall leadership of the company. Within this role, a number of the entrepreneurs had undertaken the functions of finance and marketing. In the case of CSE, the entrepreneur was involved in a partnership with a technologist, and supplied the management functions of the company, whilst the other partner was responsible for the

Table 2.7   Delegation of management functions within the small technology-based firm: 'opportunist' technical entrepreneur

Management function	Technical entrepreneur	Other director/s	Venture staff	External
Finance	CSE NKR Optimised Control PC Marine Somerset Fruits	Hereford Herbs		
Manufacturing	Hereford Herbs Somerset Fruits	PC Marine		CSE NKR Optimised Control
Marketing	CSE NKR Optimised Control Somerset Fruits	Hereford Herbs PC Marine		
Project leadership	CSE Hereford Herbs NKR Optimised Control PC Marine Somerset Fruits			
R&D	Somerset Fruits	CSE NKR Optimised Control PC Marine		Hereford Herbs
Sales	CSE Somerset	NKR	Optimised Control	Hereford Herbs PC Marine

development of the product: 'The roles will be clearly defined in the company as it grows. My brother will be in charge of the technical side and I will be in charge of the management side . . . my strong point is marketing and my brother's is design – it's all about marketing, money and the product and that's the mix we need.'

The entrepreneur from Somerset Fruits was the only one directly involved with the development function within his organisation. In the other cases, the majority of the 'user' entrepreneurs had formed partnerships with technical individuals to provide the necessary skills on which the business was based, although in the case of Hereford Herbs, the technology was bought in. With regard to the manufacturing function, again there seemed to be a trend towards subcontracting, with only one of the entrepreneurs – from Somerset Fruits – assuming responsibility for this function, mainly because of substantial previous manufacturing experience.

The Perceived Future Role of the Entrepreneur within the Small Technology-Based Firm

'Research' Technical Entrepreneurs

With regard to the perception of the future role of the entrepreneur within the new venture, approximately half of the 'research' technical entrepreneurs saw themselves remaining in the same position within the company in the near future, whilst the others intended to change their functions within the company (Table 2.8). The entrepreneurs from Biocell, Newcastle Photometrics and Novocastra perceived their role as changing from a distinct functional managerial role to a more strategic position within the company, mainly in order to enable themselves to plan the future of the small firm more effectively. As the owner-manager of Newcastle Photometrics stated:

> Both directors have to move away from working at a desk or a bench on a day to day basis, and put in a middle management structure that deals with it as I would now. Then I am going to have to stand back and oversee it in a more global planning way, and make general policy decisions for the company and leave the day to day running to a manager with presumably some substructure to that.

On the other hand, three of the entrepreneurs perceived that they would relinquish management responsibilities to other individuals within the organisation as it grew, mainly in order to devote more time and effort to the development of the innovative technological capabilities of their businesses.

As the entrepreneur from Mupor indicated:

> I don't see my role as MD changing, in that I will still retain overall interest in what is going on, but I shall have somebody else doing the day to day. It is not an easy thing to delegate responsibility in a small firm because one always feels that no-one can do the job as well as you can. I guess the only practical thing that comes out of that is that there is an element of truth in so far as all the methods that we use here were invented by me and there isn't a job here that I can't do. So you think – whatever this guy has done, is it right, could it be any better? But we are doing so many things that I can't keep track of everything.

Table 2.8   The proposed future management role of the technical entrepreneur within the small technology-based firm, by occupational background

	Research technical entrepreneur ($n = 11$)	*Producer technical entrepreneur* ($n = 15$)	*User technical entrepreneur* ($n = 6$)	*Opportunist technical entrepreneur* ($n = 6$)
Remain responsible for technical function	Cell Adhesions S&C Thermofluids	DC Clarke RJ Pond Rice	RK Drury	
Move from management to technical function	EST HE Associates Mupor	Ensigma Interprise Isle Optics Warwick Design		
Remain responsible for management function	Abbey Biosystems BPS HMI	Fiox Cirrus	Eng. Systems Talbot Helifix	CSE Hereford Herbs NKR Optimised Control PC Marine
Move from technical to management function	Biocell	Hydramotion NET		
Move from functional management to strategic role	Newcastle Photo Novocastra	Beran Boverton Bucon Hunt	Aber Instruments IDS Seaward	Somerset Fruits

Therefore, although in the case of the 'research' technical entrepreneurs there is evidence of a gradual movement away from functional management roles in the company towards either a strategic or technical position, there seems to be no conclusive proof of a definite trend.

'Producer' Technical Entrepreneurs

In the sample of 'producer' technical entrepreneurs, all the individuals had previous experience of either team/project leadership, or the management of R&D. As Table 2.8 shows, there also seemed to be a movement away from management functions (as in the case of 'research' technical entrepreneurs), towards either a more strategic role within the company or a technically-based position. In the case of Hunt Power Drives, the entrepreneur intended to change his role to become more compatible with his previous leadership experience, rather than having responsibility for a particular management function. Similarly, in Bucon, the entrepreneur envisaged less personal involvement in the day-to-day running of the business, switching from having to be involved with assembly problems, to attending exhibitions to determine future opportunities in the market-place. He perceived his role as changing to become more of an ambassador for the business, especially in the pursuit of new customers:

I would like to see less day to day involvement for me on the technical side because it is possible to buy people who can do that . . . what I want to do is to get more involved in the high level sales and less involved in the technicalities of it, because in order for us to grow, we need to be able to obtain the right sort of business. We don't want to be scrabbling and just competing on price – I want to compete on what we can offer the customer.

On the other hand, the technical entrepreneur from Isle Optics was sharing the responsibility for many of the management functions of the company with his partner, and envisaged their respective roles becoming less diffuse in the future:

The ultimate plan is to build the company up to such a size, maybe 10–20 people, and we would then move into the areas of responsibility within the company that best suited us. I would then become much more responsible for R&D and a bit less responsible for things like marketing and those sorts of aspects. My partner would become much more responsible for manufacturing and less responsible in other areas. So we would move to positions where we were much more comfortable.

Despite previous evidence of the 'producer' technical entrepreneurs' greater experience of management, only two entrepreneurs – from Hydramotion and NET – intended to relinquish responsibility for technology in favour of greater control of a management function of the venture. In the case of Hydramotion, the technical entrepreneur saw himself eventually becoming totally removed from the development of the product, and becoming more responsible for the marketing of the company: 'As it grows, I would find myself getting more removed from the nitty gritty of development. I would be involved purely on the administration of development, and more involved in the actual overall marketing of the company.'

Overall, the shift in management responsibilities by the 'producer' technical entrepreneur was very similar to that experienced by the 'research' type: from responsibility of particular management functions towards either a strategic role in the company, or a technology management position. There was also very little evidence of a desire by technical entrepreneurs to take up management functions in the company, despite earlier evidence of the previous development of management competences by these individuals.

'User' Technical Entrepreneurs

Again, there was a similar desire by 'user' technical entrepreneurs to adopt a more strategic position within the venture, although half of the entrepreneurs – namely RK Drury, Talbot Helifix, and Engineering Systems – intended to remain responsible for the same management position (Table 2.8). If their companies completed the growth from entrepreneurial ventures to professionally managed organisations, then the entrepreneurs from both IDS and Seaward envisaged their roles developing to those of full-time managing directors of the company, with a more formalised professional structure of functional directors. The entrepreneur would have overall responsibility for those directors. As the entrepreneur from IDS suggested:

> I've got to come back out of straight sales and back into managing my directors – where you have got a board of directors with specific responsibilities. I have to make sure that those people are managed – each of the directors will have a senior management team who will be doing the work for the directors. So that's where I see my role in the next two to three years.

'Opportunist' Technical Entrepreneurs

As Table 2.8 shows, none of the 'opportunist' entrepreneurs had a desire to change their responsibilities from a management function within their organisation to a technically-based position. This is not surprising, as most of this type of entrepreneur had no formal technical qualifications or experience. Furthermore, their previous competence was strong in different management functions, with most of the sample having clearly defined their role within the venture at start-up, unlike the other types of entrepreneur. Only one entrepreneur, from Somerset Fruits, endeavoured to change his current role within his organisation, away from the management of various functions and towards a more strategic role in the organisation: 'I would like to pull away from doing everything in the company, and that's why I want it to grow. When it grows you can afford people that actually specialise in the various areas and then you do that task more efficiently.' However, this may be due to the entrepreneur's initial assumption of responsibilities for a number of management functions in which he had no previous competence, coupled with a lack of ability to delegate the other functions of the business.

IMPLICATIONS OF THE RESULTS FOR POLICY, PRACTITIONERS AND FURTHER RESEARCH

To date, previous research has only examined the entrepreneurs originating from either an academic (research) or industrial (producer) background, although Gupta, Raj and Wilemon (1986) did indicate that an individual with a 'user' background within a large organisation could possess both technical and marketing skills. However, their paper did not suggest that such individuals would subsequently establish small technology-based firms. In addition, there is almost no evidence in published research findings of 'opportunist' technical entrepreneurs initiating and managing a small technology-based firm and, as a result, the characteristics of both the 'user' and 'opportunist' entrepreneur cannot be specifically compared to the findings of previous studies into technical entrepreneurship. Therefore, one of the major findings of this research is the non-technical experience of a number of owner-managers of small technology-based firms.

With regard to the technical qualifications of the technical entrepreneurs studied, nearly three-quarters of the sample had qualified to degree level or better, with over a quarter obtaining a doctoral qualification. Only two of the sample had no formal qualifications. In terms of occupational background, all of the 'research' technical entrepreneurs, apart from the entrepreneur from BPS, had qualified to doctoral level in their particular technical discipline. This is not surprising considering the academic positions that many of this group held before establishing their own firms. With regard to 'producer' entrepreneurs, all were technically qualified within their disciplines, although only two of the 'producer' enterpreneurs had doctoral qualifications. This may suggest that many of the previous studies that have shown technical entrepreneurs qualified to PhD level may have concentrated on organisations headed by 'research' entrepreneurs. Whilst two of the 'user' entrepreneurs had no technical qualifications, all of the others had qualified to degree level within a technical subject, whilst the 'opportunist' entrepreneurs had various types of qualifications, ranging from postgraduate to no qualifications.

Therefore, with regard to comparisons to other general studies of technical entrepreneurship (Cooper, 1971b; Roberts, 1991b), the findings are broadly similar: technical entrepreneurs are relatively well qualified, with a high number technically qualified above degree level. This finding is not itself surprising, because as Cooper (1973) pointed out, small technology-based businesses are often based upon the founder's knowledge. However, the findings do call into question Storey's (1994) assertion that a PhD in a scientific subject is increasingly becoming a necessary passport for business formation in this area, since a number of the larger firms represented in this sample have owner-managers from a 'user' background qualified to degree level only (Jones-Evans, 1992). Indeed, a recent study of the development of small technology-based firms in Sweden showed a similar result: of the five fastest growing firms, only one had been initiated by an owner-manager with a PhD (Klofsten, 1996). Further quantitative research is needed, especially within a European context, which will test the relationship between educational qualifications and business performance, especially within technology-based firms.

There is little evidence of experience in management functions such as marketing or finance, even in the case of those 'research' entrepreneurs with previous commercial experience (Table 2.3). This broadly agrees with the findings of studies discussed in the literature review, such as that of Samsom and Gurdon (1993) who discovered that marketing and finance were two areas in which 'scientist-entrepreneurs' had very little previous experience. However, the findings of this research do not correspond to the other conclusions of that particular study (i.e., that team management and interpersonal skills were the most frequently mentioned lack of skills in 'research' or 'scientist' entrepreneurs). All of the 'research' technical entrepreneurs in this study had considerable experience of managing R&D projects, in many cases evolving from a purely technical role within academic research projects to responsibility for other individuals working together as a team. The inter-personal skills developed during the supervision of small research teams may, in many cases, be directly transferable into the management of a small research-based new venture. Not surprisingly, the study also found that those 'research' technical entrepreneurs who had gained industrial experience after previous employment in academia, unlike those who had moved from industry into academic research, were, in general, more likely to have gained functional management skills that were transferable into the small firm. Therefore, whilst the study suggests that the 'research' technical entrepreneur has low experience in functional management skills, it casts doubts over the findings of other studies which have examined 'academic' entrepreneurs, finding that management skills (such as team-building) may be high in a number of 'scientist' or 'research' entrepreneurs, mainly because of the team-building nature of much of academically-based scientific research.

In terms of management experience, the 'producer' entrepreneurs are similar to the 'research' technical entrepreneurs in having considerable competence in both project management and R&D functions. However, there is evidence of a greater experience of other management functions, with the majority of the entrepreneurs having familiarity with either manufacturing, marketing or sales. A third of 'producer' entrepreneurs even had previous experience in finance and accounting. This agrees broadly with the findings of the literature review concerning this type of entrepreneur (with the 'industrial' background).

Therefore, in terms of technical experience, both 'research' and 'producer' technical entrepreneurs had substantial technical experience, having worked in R&D positions within their previous organisations prior to start-up. However, as has been suggested, while most 'research' entrepreneurs were still involved in the development of new technologies within the 'incubator' organisation when they left to initiate their new venture, 'producer' entrepreneurs had progressed into the management hierarchy within their organisations. Consequently, their technical knowledge on start-up, although substantial, would not be as current as that of the 'research' technical entrepreneurs.

'User' technical entrepreneurs had relatively little experience of manufacturing and R&D, showing a higher relative experience in the functional areas of marketing, sales and finance than do other types. However, most of the 'user' technical entrepreneurs started their careers in technical positions before shifting into responsibilities for management functions within their organisations. The 'opportunist' technical entrepreneurs, as would be expected from individuals with a diversity of occupational backgrounds, had no one particular management strength although, like the 'user' technical entrepreneur, there was very little evidence of technical experience with regard to management functions such as R&D or manufacturing. As with the management experiences gained by such individuals, there was a diversity in the technical qualifications gained, although in terms of actual formal technical experience, only the entrepreneur from Somerset Fruits gained some initial engineering experience at the beginning of his career. In the other cases, the technical expertise had been gained through educational qualifications or part-time interests.

Therefore, whilst the majority of the technical entrepreneurs interviewed had considerable management experience in the areas of R&D management and project leadership, there is very little evidence of previous experience in the functional areas of management such as finance, manufacturing, marketing and sales (Table 2.3). This supports much of the previous research examining technical entrepreneurship, which showed that in general, technical entrepreneurs tended to have a low experience in management functions (Klofsten *et al.*, 1988; Samsom and Gurdon, 1993). On initial analysis, this suggests that small technology-based firms in the UK have a major need for management training. If these businesses, as Storey (1994) suggests, are to play a key role in the development of a high quality small firm sector in the UK, then there may be a need by support organisations such as Training and Enterprise Councils (TECs) to target initiatives towards the development of management skills in such firms. However, Storey (1994) also asserts that it has still to be demonstrated that the training of owners, managers and workers within a small firm exerts a significant influence on the performance of the firm. Whilst there have been criticisms of this suggestion by Storey, researchers should take up the challenge of determining whether such a relationship between training and small firm success exists, especially in sectors where the owner-managers demonstrate a high degree of skill competence, but low management competence.

The predominant current role of the technical entrepreneur within the small technology-based firm is in the overall management of the small technology-based firm, although there were exceptions, such as the cases of the entrepreneurs from Abbey Biosystems, Ensigma and Fiox. This in itself is not surprising, as the majority of the technical entrepreneurs examined had considerable previous experience of project and team management within both academic and commercial organisations. Given that there is very little evidence of technical entrepreneurs having previous competence in the functional areas of management, such as finance, manufacturing, marketing and sales, it is not surprising that the entrepreneurs in this study had tended not to assume responsibility for these functions. However, the majority of the technical entrepreneurs had assumed responsibility for marketing within their businesses, with less than half of these actually having had any formal marketing experience in their previous occupations. Two general reasons were given by these entrepreneurs for assuming an important management responsibility in which they had no previous competence. First, it was suggested that 'buying in' specific marketing expertise would be expensive for a small technology-based firm. This was also the case in those firms where the entrepreneur was responsible for the finance function within the business, but without any formal financial experience. In fact, the evidence suggests that, as the business grows, the entrepreneur may relinquish responsibility for finance, although this may take a number of years. This is not the case with any of the other functions, such as manufacturing or sales. Second, many of the entrepreneurs questioned felt that they were the 'best people' to market their 'personally-developed' technologies. In some cases, such as Newcastle Photometrics, the business sold a unique product in very small batches at a very high profit, and consequently the marketing effort required at this stage of the firm's development was minimal, and managed personally by the entrepreneur. These findings are similar to Roberts's (1991b) examination of sales and marketing within a sample of high technology firms in the USA.

In examining the ventures in which the technical entrepreneur did not have responsibility for different management functions, a number of conclusions may be drawn. With regard to finance, although a number of technical entrepreneurs had, as suggested earlier, assumed responsibility for this function within their businesses, the majority either brought in specific financial skills at director level, or were utilising external accountants. In terms of manufacturing, over a third of the sample subcontracted to other sources, which was to be expected in the cases of small R&D organisations with no in-house manufacturing facilities. Consequently, they would either subcontract the manufacturing to other sources or, in some cases, not require manufacturing at all. A similar situation exists with the sales function. Although over a third of the technical entrepreneurs surveyed were responsible for sales within their organisations, a number either used external distributors to sell their firm's products, or had no need, as development firms, for this function within their businesses. Although there does not seem to be any emerging trend in the process of externalisation of functions within the smaller firms surveyed, it is not surprising to find that in most of the larger businesses, as a formalised management structure and system emerged, the technical entrepreneur delegated the functions of finance, manufacturing and sales to other staff within the venture.

As stated earlier, the majority of the entrepreneurs examined were responsible, within their respective firms, for the functions of marketing, R&D and the venture's overall management, which suggests that many technical entrepreneurs may wish to retain control of the management of the firm, as well as its technical direction.

In examining the relationship between the previous occupational background of the technical entrepreneurs, and their current role within the new venture, some significant differences emerge, according to the four types identified. As the results demonstrate, the 'research' technical entrepreneurs were predominantly involved in the technical management and leadership of their companies, with R&D responsibilities kept in-house. Despite having had little experience of management functions, a number of these entrepreneurs assumed responsibility for marketing and sales, either through necessity – because of a lack of finance to employ suitable staff – or because of a close understanding of the needs of the market. The function of finance within the venture was also only assumed when the business was fairly small, and could not afford suitably qualified staff. The 'research' technical entrepreneur undertook almost no manufacturing responsibilities, except in cases – Biocell and Mupor – where the entrepreneur had gained previous experience in this area. Instead, the manufacturing function was either delegated to other staff within the venture or, preferably, to subcontractors.

In the ventures headed by 'producer' technical entrepreneurs, the individual entrepreneur was again mainly involved with the overall management of his business, and had responsibility for R&D. However, despite the strong involvement by the entrepreneur in the function of R&D, it is proportionally less than for the 'research' technical entrepreneurs, with six of the entrepreneurs delegating this responsibility to other individuals within the organisation; again, the responsibility for R&D was not externalised. Despite the 'producer' entrepreneurs' previous experience of manufacturing, there was comparatively little current involvement in this function within the small technology-based firms. Instead, the function tended to be delegated either internally (to other directors) or externally (to subcontractors). With regard to the functions of marketing and sales, a number of the entrepreneurs had previous experience of this function, and this was reflected in their personal involvement in the management of these functions. In the area of finance, there was generally little personal experience, and thus a reluctance to undertake responsibility for it. As with the 'research' entrepreneurs, a number of the 'producer'-led ventures externalised their financial function to accountancy practices. However, there seems to be a trend with this type of entrepreneur towards having a partner (or another director within the firm) who has specific skills in finance and accounts.

In this case of 'user' technical entrepreneurs, as with the 'research' and 'producer' technical entrepreneurs, overall management responsibilities were assumed for their businesses. With this type, there was a tendency to concentrate specific management skills on that function in which the entrepreneur had a specific expertise, namely marketing. Again, the majority of the ventures had their finances managed by individuals other than the entrepreneur, despite evidence of a greater competence gained in previous occupations within this function.

The 'user' technical entrepreneurs, who had no previous experience of manufacturing, did not assume responsibility for this function within their firms, preferring instead to delegate the responsibility to other venture staff and, in the case of one of the businesses, to another company. In the management of R&D within ventures led by the 'user' technical entrepreneur, there was comparatively less personal involvement by the technical entrepreneur than there was by the other two types of 'research' and 'producer', with two entrepreneurs accessing technology from outside the venture. This is probably due to the low amount of previous experience of R&D gained by the entrepreneur.

As with the other three types of technical entrepreneur, the 'opportunist' entrepreneur had undertaken full responsibility for the overall management of the venture. However, unlike the other three types, the 'opportunist' entrepreneur tended to have considerable competence in the area of finance, thus being able to undertake responsibility for that function within the venture. As expected of this 'non-technical' entrepreneurial type, the 'opportunist' entrepreneur had almost no responsibility for R&D, with the venture being predominantly dependent on a partnership with other technologists to provide the technical competence for the company. With regard to manufacturing, the 'opportunist' entrepreneur had only assumed responsibility in those cases where there was previous experience, with the preference being to subcontract this function externally. In sales and marketing, despite only one 'opportunist' technical entrepreneur having previous experience, half of this type had assumed responsibility for this function.

Therefore, although there are exceptions, it would seem that the majority of technical entrepreneurs tend to undertake management functions within their ventures of which they have previous management competence. For example, nearly all of the 'research' technical entrepreneurs were responsible for the R&D function within their organisations, while the 'user' technical entrepreneurs undertook the marketing function within their ventures. However, there was a tendency on the part of a number of entrepreneurs to undertake functions in which they had no previous competence. There has been very little detailed research which has examined the different responsibilities of the entrepreneur and their subsequent effect on the management of the firm, and there is a need for studies to be undertaken to examine this important area of interest.

As has been described earlier, previous research has suggested that the role of the technical entrepreneur within the small firm should change as the venture grows. This would seem to be the case with this study, with a tendency for the technical entrepreneur to move away from management functions towards a more strategic role within the venture as the firm grows. A few of these entrepreneurs had very little management experience, but nevertheless considered growth to be within their own personal capabilities; this is quite different from some of findings of the literature review, although recent research by Smallbone, Leigh and North (1995) has suggested that for any firm to grow successfully over an extended period, it needs to develop an organisational structure in ways that enable the entrepreneur to delegate responsibility for operational tasks and focus more on planning and higher level strategic functions. Also of interest is the fact that a small number of the sample, after assuming a management position within their ventures, intended to move back to a technical role within the business. This suggests that some technical entrepreneurs may wish to avoid some of the major problems highlighted by Firnstahl (1986) regarding the delegation of technical responsibilities within small technology-based ventures.

With reference to the previous occupational background of the technical entrepreneur, there seems to be a general trend by the 'producer' and 'user' entrepreneurs away from functional management roles and towards a more strategic position within the venture. In the case of 'opportunist' entrepreneurs, the management positions seemed already well-defined within the small technology-based firms. There is also a definite trend among the more technically-oriented entrepreneurs – the 'research' and 'producer' entrepreneurs – to move away from management roles within the venture and towards more responsibility for technology.

CONCLUSION

This study has explored the different occupational backgrounds of a sample of technical entrepreneurs in the UK, and their effect on the management of the small technology-based firm. Although there has been no specific research which has examined in detail the previous occupational background of the technical entrepreneur, other research studies indicated that a positive relationship may exist between the previous experience and expertise of the individual technical entrepreneur, and the management and strategy of the new venture. In general, the results of this study strengthen these findings, and show that the previous technical and management competences of individual entrepreneurs have a strong influence on a number of aspects of management within the small venture, not least the delegation of management functions. Consequently, the research strongly implies that an examination of the different competences such individuals bring to their new ventures may be as valid and useful a method of assessing the success of new technology-based ventures as previous approaches such as psychological or traits models. Further research should be carried out on a larger, and more varied sample (i.e., including non-technical ventures) to determine the exact relationships between personal experience and the management of a new venture. This may enable the formalisation of competency research as a tool for use by policy-makers and support agencies alike in assessing the needs of smaller firms.

The research supports the findings of the different studies into technical entrepreneurship, which have identified two main types of technical entrepreneur: those with an 'academic' and those with an 'industrial' background. However, whilst previous research has attempted only to examine one type, without comparison to the other type, this research has compared different types of technical entrepreneur. In addition, the study has identified the 'user' and 'opportunist' technical entrepreneurs as two distinct types of owner-managers of technology-based small firms; they possess quite different experience and expertise from the two types recognised in the literature.

A number of specific findings have emerged from this qualitative exploratory study which suggests that the previous experience of the technical entrepreneur (especially the degree of management and technical experience gained) may influence the nature of the management of their organisations. First, the results are broadly similar to other surveys of technical entrepreneurs: in general, the management experiences of such individuals is minimal and the degree of technical expertise is high. However, an examination of both management and technical experience by type of entrepreneur (according to the previous occupational background) does reveal differences. Indeed, as Stuart and Abetti (1990) have suggested, it is not the amount of experience but the type of experience which is important, and its relevance to the needs of the firm and the market. Consequently, technical entrepreneurs may need to analyse which particular competences they bring to the business, and which other competences are needed to fit in with the small firm's strategy. Financial institutions and policy-makers may also take this result into account when developing financial or support packages for such individuals. This result also suggests that, unlike many other past examinations of technical entrepreneurs, future research should consider analysing, in detail, the previous occupational experience of the individual when evaluating personal entrepreneurial factors, and the way in which they may affect the small technology-based firm. In particular, as Reuber and Fischer (1994) indicate, there is a need to develop an instrument to examine not only the relevance of the depth and breadth of experience, but also to measure the expertise of individual owner-managers and its relevance to the needs of the small firm.

A study of the management role of the technical entrepreneurs within their businesses has revealed that, within this exploratory study at least, technical entrepreneurs have begun to overcome some of the problems highlighted by Firnstahl (1986) in the management of small technology-based firms. In this respect, therefore, technical entrepreneurs in the USA and the UK are similar, although a more detailed comparative study is needed to directly support this finding. This chapter has also attempted, among other matters, to answer the question posed by Schrage (1965) over 30 years ago, in a study of academic entrepreneurs; namely, 'Who should run an R&D organisation? Should our three physicists seek a business manager to head their organisation while they devote their time to scientific pursuits, or should one of them run the company?' Indeed, this finding, if confirmed by a larger quantitative study, may be relevant to the future support needs of small technology-based ventures. As individual technical entrepreneurs, in this study at least, seem to prefer to concentrate on their own particular area of functional expertise, it may be pertinent for different agencies to target support towards the development of a network of accountants, subcontractors, marketing consultants and distributors around small technology-based firms, which would complement the expertise and experience of each individual entrepreneur. This supports some of the more general findings of a recent report by the OECD (1994), which suggested that one of the main reasons for enterprise survival was the availability of management advice from both private and public sources, and those of Storey (1994), who suggested that the package of assistance (which would include elements of information, advice, financial assistance, provision of managerial resources and assistance with obtaining new premises) should vary markedly from one firm to another.

This research has therefore provided a qualitative study of technical entrepreneurship in the UK, building on previous research in this area of study undertaken within the USA in regions such as Silicon Valley and Route 128, Boston. Subsequent research, especially within the UK, may take into consideration some of the findings indicated within this chapter, especially if, as Roberts (1991b) suggests, high-technology entrepreneurship is to grow and develop in other areas of the world. In order to study technical entrepreneurs in detail, more work needs to be carried out, which not only considers different personal characteristics of the individual entrepreneur (as previous studies have done) but which also examines the effect of the technical entrepreneur's previous occupational background in influencing the success of high-technology enterprises.

3 Patterns of Formation and Development of High-Technology Entrepreneurs

Besrat Tesfaye

INTRODUCTION

New technology-based small companies with roots in the research milieu, especially universities, have attracted much attention in Sweden in recent years. Traditionally, research results from universities have been transferred to industrial organisations and some of the most prominent companies in Sweden have their origins in these technologies. From the early 1980s, however, an increasing number of researchers have been founding companies in an attempt to commercialise their research results (McQueen and Wallmark, 1982; Olofsson, Wahlbin and Tovman, 1987; Olofsson and Wahlbin, 1993; Tesfaye, 1991). In the peak years, 1982–3, the number of new companies with roots in universities was more than twice the number noted in 1980 (Reitberger, 1987). This development is believed to have an important social significance, in terms of technological advancement, industrial rejuvenation and job creation, and society has responded by establishing support mechanisms for these companies. A rich flora of innovation/technical centres – or research parks, as these are sometimes called – have evolved around the host universities. By 1993, sixteen such centres had been established. A major part of these companies are still located in close proximity to the universities of origin.

The companies have some similarities to earlier developments including the Palo Alto (Silicon Valley) in San Francisco (Cooper, 1971a) and the 'Cambridge phenomena' in England (Segal Quince, 1985), but are reported to be younger and smaller (Olofsson, Wahlbin and Tovman, 1987). Some researchers, however, are of the opinion that the association made with the development of other high-technology companies that are commonly regarded as high growth industry does not follow (Steen, 1991). Philips, Sundberg and Uhlin (1991), for example, point out that the 'idea' of university-related companies should be distinguished from university related companies themselves.

THE RESEARCH AREA

The development of spin-off companies from Swedish universities has been catalogued in a number of studies (McQueen and Wallmark, 1982; Olofsson and Wahlbin, 1984, 1993; Olofsson, Wahlbin and Tovman, 1987; Klofsten *et al.*, 1988). A major part of this research focused on the quantitative aspects of these companies, including the population, employment and turnover, acquisition of resources, and links.

The research area is multidimensional and can be approached from various angles: for example, the founders, the companies, the nature and role of the support mechanisms, the implication for the host university and policy aspects. As a research problem each dimension is complex and multifaceted. The focus in this study is on the factors that may condition the pattern of the start-up and initial development of new, small technology based companies from academic research institutions. The questions addressed include: what characterises the start-up process? What factors condition the pattern of start-up and initial development of an academic spin-off? Can a common company formation pattern for academic spin-offs be distinguished? Are there similarities to spin-offs originating in other research milieux, such as industrial organisations?

Researchers contend that the foundations of the pattern of development of an organisation are laid down in the formation phase and emphasise the need for studying the emergence of new companies. Fundamental decisions about the future direction of a company, including location, size, market, and administrative style, are presumed to be made during the formation period (Stinchcombe, 1965; Kimberly and Miles, 1980; Katz and Gartner, 1988; Tucker, Singh and Meinhard, 1990), criticised entrepreneurship literature for neglecting the process of company formation, contending that descriptions and analysis of company formations relate to established organisations and not companies in creation. A similar criticism is forwarded by Scott (1987:141), who stated that 'the question of organisational creation, or founding, is of fundamental importance to the study of organisations. Understanding the process that culminates in an organisational founding would have significant policy and practical implications.' Similarly, Katz and Gartner (1988:437) indicated that 'emerging organisations are likely to be small, fragile, and volatile. The process of organisational emergence may be analogous to the types of interactions that take place at the atomic and subatomic levels of physics.' Gartner (1985) further contends that research tends to capture momentous glimpses of a long and complex process and calls for a longitudinal orientation.

THE OBJECTIVE OF THE STUDY

The objective of this study is to gain some understanding of the forces that condition the emergence and initial development of new companies from research conducted in a university. The methodological approach has two objectives:

(a) studying the process of formation of university spin-offs during a long period may give insight into the conditions for commercialising research results through entrepreneurship;
(b) by relating to spin-offs from non-academic environments and prior research indications, some understanding of the emergence of technology-based small companies may be gained.

From a societal point of view, such knowledge may be important in designing policies and tailoring supportive programmes where these are considered to be desirable. From a theoretical perspective, existing frameworks may be strengthened and new questions formulated.

THEORETICAL BACKGROUND

The subject of entrepreneurship has been approached from various perspectives by scholars of different disciplines, including economics, sociology, psychology, anthropology, history and political science. Whilst the volume of literature is impressive, this chapter will only consider those theories and models that closely relate to the basic hypotheses of the study.

Conceptual Models of Company Formation

McClelland (1961) perceived company formation as a coincidental interaction of motivation (need for achievement) and opportunity. Watkins (1976) proposed the same hypothesis but added a third interactive variable, namely skills. The basic assumption underlying this model is that individuals with a higher need for achievement would take an entrepreneurial initiative upon perceiving an opportunity irrespective of other barriers. Watkins suggested an exception with regard to the need for skills on the grounds that these are fundamental in a complex world.

Shapero and Sokol (1982) perceived entrepreneurship as a societal function and proposed a coincidental interactive model. The underlying assumption is that entrepreneurship is preconditioned by negative displacements and positive pulls given that prospective founders perceive the action to be desirable and feasible.

Company Formation Process Models

The perception of company formation as a process is common to the major part of entrepreneurship literature. As regards the nature of the process there are many variations. Some researchers propose the view that company formation processes vary and may not follow a common pattern (Ruhnka and Young, 1987; Katz and Gartner, 1988). Others argue that there is an inner logic that is common and can be conceived (Crone and Crone, 1971). A cursory look at the proposals reveals wide variations in terms of the number of the phases, descriptive variables and characteristics of company formation processes. For example, Galbraith (1982) proposes five phases distinguished along functional variables, Gartner (1985) four phases based on various company formation activities, Watkins (1975) five phases based on activities, Hult and Odéen (1986) five activity-based phases, and Susbauer (1975) 12 stages based on unspecified variables. Kazanjian (1988) takes a middle line and proposes that a distinctive company formation pattern can be distinguished in cases where, for example, investors actively control the development of the company. In internally financed, independent company formations, this would be unlikely.

Influences on Company Formation

Allowing for the fragmentation of the research, the review of research identifies the following influences:

(a) economic and socio-political factors that can be regarded as those constituting the 'macro-environment' (Schell and Davig, 1981);

(b) the 'entrepreneurial environment' defined as a subset of the macro-environment; it consists of variables that are presumed to be of special significance for entrepreneurship (Cooper, 1971b; Draheim, 1972; Johannisson, 1978; Pennings, 1982).

In addition, there are factors that can be attributed to the entrepreneur, including:

(a) family background (McClelland, 1961; Collins, Moore and Unwalla, 1964; Roberts and Wainer, 1968; Boswell, 1972);
(b) religious affinities (Weber, 1930);
(c) social class (Dahmén, 1953);
(d) education and career (Boswell, 1972; Cooper, 1973; Watkins, 1975; Cooper and Dunkelberg, 1981; Brockhaus, 1982; Utterback and Reitberger, 1982; Hult and Odéen, 1986);
(e) personality traits (McClelland, 1961, 1965, 1969; Collins, Moore and Unwalla, 1964; Kets de Vries, 1970; Stanworth and Curran, 1973; Brockhaus, 1982; Klandt, 1987; Davidsson, 1989);
(f) incubation factors that are directly/indirectly related to the place of employment of the prospective entrepreneur (Cooper, 1971b; Little, 1977);
(g) situational factors such as unemployment, conflict, displacement (Liles, 1974).

As indicated, much of the research on entrepreneurship focuses on the individual (entrepreneur) and environmental factors, whilst company formation process studies are commonly linked to organisational life-cycles and growth problems.

DEFINITION OF SOME CONCEPTS

Some concepts in this study may have been previously used in a different context or the reader might misunderstand the meanings attached to the term here. The central concepts relate to the founders, their activities, the companies they create, and the environment in which the companies emerge.

Entrepreneur, Entrepreneurship

The entrepreneur in this study is defined as the person(s) who initiates and manages, in a personal way, a new, independent company. The term 'company founder' has been used as synonymous with the entrepreneur. 'Entrepreneurship' denotes the activities of an entrepreneur.

Company Formation Process, Entrepreneurial Process

Company formation process refers to the series of activities and decisions undertaken in founding a company. The entrepreneurial process defines the notion that company formation is an interactive process with each preceding phase shaping the pattern of the following phase.

Technolog]y-Based, High Technology

The terms have been used alternatively and denote companies founded by individuals with an academic education and which are research-intensive. Intensity of R&D refers to the proportion of resources diverted to research activities during the company formation process.

Spin-Off, Incubator Organisation (Environment), Entrepreneurial Environment

Spin-off refers to a company founded on an idea/product that has been developed in a context other than the company itself. The concept of incubator is closely linked to spin off and denotes the places where the initial development of the idea/product and the skills underlying a new company takes place, commonly the former employer. The entrepreneurial environment is defined as a pool of material and immaterial resources and is presumed to be what the prospective founder perceives it to be, (i.e., given the general environment, the key variables constituting the entrepreneurial environment may be individual).

METHODOLOGY

Critics of methods in entrepreneurship research contend that researchers presume existing companies' development as static and historical (Kimberly, 1980; Katz and Gartner, 1988). Katz and Gartner point out that company formation process studies are based on retrospective data and fail to capture the dynamics of an emerging organisation. Kimberly emphasises the need for a dynamic approach that encompasses organisational development over a longer period of time. A review of the literature indicates that the creation of a new organisation and the impact of this process on the development of a company has not been well researched. It was further suggested that such an understanding may call for a 'within-the-company' perspective: that is, studying how they 'tick', and what makes them 'tick'. In view of the form of the research questions, and the nature of the phenomenon studied, the case study approach has been considered to be an appropriate strategy for this study. The study is based on multiple cases and varying sources of data have been used. The research has been conducted in a series of steps, with each step shaping the following one. The first step in the research process was to review the literature on entrepreneurship, followed by a pilot case study which included two companies. Prior research indications and the findings of the pilot study were incorporated into a preliminary frame of reference for defining the parameters of the research problem.

On the occasion of the first interviews, there were a total of 21 companies that were spin-offs located at the innovation centre, High Tech Hill in Stockholm. All the companies were contacted and interviewed. For purposes of more profound interviewing and follow-up study, the number of cases was narrowed down to eight, four spin-offs from the Royal Institute of Technology and four case formations originating in various industrial organisations. During the follow-up interview in 1991, one of the industrial cases was excluded. The criteria used in selecting the cases included; spin-off status, start-up date, entrepreneurial status, and the type of company. In collecting data, several sources have been used: personal interviews comprising approximately 75 interview-hours with 23 respondents at two intervals, telephone and personal interviews with personnel from the university affiliated innovation centres, and secondary sources including data from catalogues on university spin-offs and research reports. This has been continuously upgraded as to serve as a 'data bank' on university spin-offs in Sweden. The first interviews were conducted in the months of May–July 1987. Between 1987 and 1991, only sporadic contact was maintained.

The second round of interviews was conducted in the months of March–June 1991. By this time, one company had been bankrupted, one case was under discontinuance, one case had been acquired, three had moved to another location and two were still at High Tech Hill. However, apart from the acquired spin-off, all the founders could be located. In the case of the acquisition, the first acquirer of the company was interviewed. One entrepreneur requested he be left out on the grounds that he was involved in crucial negotiations; he was thus excluded from the study. In analysing the data, the respective case groups were first compared internally and then as case groups, (i.e., university spin-offs versus industry spin-offs). Finally, the indications were compared to prior research.

Patterns of Formation and Development of the Case Companies

This section of the chapter describes and analyses the characteristics of the cases as these progress from initiation to start-up and infancy. Excerpts from the case study illustrating differing company formation patterns are presented as an introduction to the section. The case formations with roots in the Royal Institute of Technology (KTH) are referred to as 'academic entrepreneurs' (AE) and those cases with roots in industrial organisations as 'industrial entrepreneurs' (IE). This is followed by a discussion of the selection of the key descriptive variables and the sequencing of the process. The progress of the case formations is then sequentially described and the main characteristics of the respective phase analysed. In concluding this section, the case groups are compared for similarities and differences and the indications are summarised and commented upon.

An Illustration of Company Formation Patterns

This section shows a pattern to the route that company founders may follow in initiating and starting up a new company. The three case excerpts presented are intended to illustrate variations in company formation and how the process is perceived and related by the case founders:

> well, this can be regarded as an attempt to apply a basic research concept. It has to do with the technical side, market need, developing a cost-effective method, extend one's network of contacts and gather information. (AE – first interview)
> This has been a difficult and slow process. One has no time for the company. Everything becomes chaotic. This is also a mental process, a qualitative change. First of all one learns to communicate, acquires new skills, let us say, in administration. There is a change of attitude, for example towards the dependency on research grants. (AE – second interview)

> I continued with the R&D work, while my partner concentrated on the organisational start-up. We had previously succeeded in acquiring a long-term business contract, a side-line activity which we hoped would finance the company. We contacted a bank, a prospective customer, and the Swedish Trade Council (Exportrådet) helped with advice. We have a consultant working for us almost full-time. We have a bank credit, and we have access to some financing from the Development Fund, which we have not utilised. (IE – first interview)

We have continued to develop more or less according to plan. We had hoped to launch the product somewhat earlier, but the R&D phase took much longer than expected. We altered our plans in some areas, especially on the market side. But a major part of our plans have been accomplished. (IE – second interview)

It began as a side-line activity which gradually began to demand more and more attention. I leased a room from High Tech Hill, bought some second-hand machines, some shelves and set up a laboratory. I succeeded in securing some external financing and began producing and selling small amounts to a small number of clients mainly distributed by post. (AE – first interview)

The process is one big tumult, an experiment with different ideas. When the first idea proved to be intangible on a longer perspective, I diverged into another. I will probably continue in the same way until I hit on something big. But it is not just experimenting, a qualitative change also takes place: one begins to think big, views customer-product relations differently. (AE – second interview)

The case illustrations may not give a phase-related description of a company formation process. However, they touch upon some important aspects of company formation including:

- the circumstances underlying each case formation
- the resource base
- the contact establishment
- the activities that the cases tended to emphasise
- the founders' interpretation of the business concept and of the process
- the factors affecting the process of business formation

The company founders themselves do not appear to perceive the process as either chronological and/or logical. Their descriptions include terminology such as 'chaotic' and 'tumultuous', and their narratives appeared to be rather diffuse and jumpy. They emphasise qualitative factors, such as 'personal development', rather than quantitative accomplishments, such as profit or turnover.

Characteristics of the Company Formation Process

Researchers commonly describe company formation in terms of sequential stages (Crone and Crone, 1971; Greiner, 1972; Hofer and Schendel,

1988; Kimberly and Miles, 1980; Churchill and Lewis, 1983). A cursory look into the literature, however, reveals a wide variety of approaches in describing the process:

(a) the process can be related to critical factors including financial and human resources, and managerial abilities (Churchill and Lewis, 1983);
(b) organisational development can be described in terms of variables such as management style, and strategic goals (Cooper, 1981), or shifts in functional focus (Galbraith, 1982);
(c) one can consider the type of financing required;
(d) there may be a combination of different variables including the characteristics of the companies as they develop, the resource base, major benchmarks (strategic goal), and primary risks (Ruhnka and Young, 1987).

Subsequently, the terminology employed to distinguish between the respective stages (phases) of the formation and development process exhibit a rich variation. Thus the initial phase of the company formation process may be referred to as: the project phase, seed stage, concept, pre-start-up, R&D financing, idea phase, initiation phase, and so on (Webster, 1976; Hult and Odeén, 1986; Ruhnka and Young, 1987).

Sequential models commonly reflect an implicit assumption that all companies develop through similar stages with an equal opportunity for establishment and growth (Crone and Crone, 1971; Greiner, 1972; Kimberly and Miles, 1980; Churchill and Lewis, 1983). Some researchers, however, are of the opinion that there is no 'typical' company formation (Vesper, 1990; Burgelman, 1983). Gartner (1984) contends that researchers describe a specific dimension(s) of a multidimensional process and thus fail to capture the diversity of emerging organisations. At the same time, Burgelman (1983) emphasises the role of stage models in systematising narratives.

This study also suggests that company formation cases are likely to be conditioned by a unique interaction of various factors and may not follow a similar pattern. Further, the degree of variation among individual cases seems to depend on the specific descriptive variable being considered. For example, in relating the company formation process to the concept development, differences between the product/non-product based cases became evident. Further variations were indicated with regard to resource requirements, and the establishment of appropriate networks. In terms of functional focus, too, company founders do not seem to emphasise similar activities at specific stages, and similar variations were observed in organisational structure.

One interesting observation made in attempting to describe the company formation process was the tendency among different case formations to 'merge and/or disperse' as these progressed from lower to higher stages. Thus, at the initial phase, the respective case groups (academic and industrial) appeared to be internally relatively homogeneous (disregarding differences in underlying business concepts). Gradually, however, internal variations between the case groups became more evident.

The Descriptive Variables

The selection of the variables is based on prior research and the indications from the case descriptions and include:

(a) concept development, which is assumed to be cyclical and consists of idea generation, engineering (prototype/model development), market test, commercialising (Baumback and Mancuso, 1987);

(b) characteristics of the companies (organisational development) which have been defined in terms of core concept (underlying product), and organisational complexity (structure, functional specialisation, leadership, network, turnover, and employees);

(c) resource base, which refers to key requirements and actual sources at the various phases of the process;

(d) functional focus, which describes the specific aspects of company formation activities that are emphasised at a particular phase of the process;

(e) network refers to the establishment of appropriate contacts with individuals and institutions;

(f) major benchmarks are goals that need to be accomplished in order for the company to progress from a lower into a higher phase.

The Phases

Despite the diversity in company formation patterns illustrated, there are attributes that may distinguish different levels of development. Companies in formation, for example, tend to emphasise core concept initially. This internal focus gradually tends to give way to market outlook, after which an organisational consolidation takes place. In the final stages of start-up, a concentration of resources on production and marketing efforts can be observed. Based on this observation, the case formation processes have been distinguished into four sequential phases:

- initiation
- acclimatisation

- consolidation
- start-up and infancy

However, it must be emphasised that company founders may not do the same things at the same time, or in the same manner.

The Initiation Phase

The point of initiation of a new company may not coincide with formal registration (legal accountability) in that this phase is often preceded by pre-initiation company formation activities. Therefore, considered from the point of formal registration, the level of development of the case companies varies. Allowing for the individual variations, the likely scenario for the two case groups (academic and industrial) can be laid down.

At the earlier stages of the initiation phase, the academic commonly maintains his or her position, still retains access to research facilities including funds previously granted, leases a room from the incubator (at a close proximity), and attends to the legalities of company formation, such as the acquisition of basic resources for registration (SEK50 000 minimum capital for a joint-stock company) and registration fees, other legal formalities, and so on. In other respects, the academic continues to work as previously. Company formation is likely to be regarded in the same way as any other promising research project, and might not even enjoy the status of a side-line activity. Formally, however, the spin-off process has been initiated and the academic's attention is divided between the company and ordinary work. During this phase, the academics estimated the percentage of working hours committed to the company at between 10 and 50 per cent. In one case only, one of the founding team had taken leave of absence and committed all his time to the company.

The situation for the industrial entrepreneur at the early stage of this phase is different. The industrial entrepreneur has either resigned or lost her job. A working prototype has to be developed and the entrepreneur has no access to research funds and/or facilities and little possibility of acquiring external financing at this stage. She will therefore undertake an income-generating activity in order to finance the development of the business idea. In one case, the company founder took on a consulting job, and in another case, the two founders began by establishing a side-line activity; in a third case, the founders had previous assignments that generated some financing.

Table 3.1 summarises the main characteristic of the initiation phase. Here, characteristics refer to the attributes that distinguish the respective phase of the company formation process, including organisational aspects, resources, nature of the network, organisational (company founders') goals and the activities that tend to be emphasised.

Table 3.1 Some characteristics of the initiation phase by variable and entrepreneur

Variable	Academic entrepreneur	Industrial entrepreneur
Core concept	Product	Product/software
Characteristics:		
Organisation format	Informal	Informal
Functional specialisation	Low	Low
Decision making:		
Normalisation	Low	Low
Centralisation	High	High
Leadership	Founder/s	Founder/s
Employees	None	None
Turnover	None	None
Production	None	None
Functional focus	Product/development	Product/development
	Boundary establishment	Boundary establishment/ financing
Required key resources:		
Financial	Seed capital	Seed capital
Skills	General*	Technical skills
Sources:		
Financing	R&D funds	Personal savings
Skills	TH/interim† service bureaux	Interim consultants
Network	Local	Local/external
Major benchmarks	Working model/prototype	Concept development

* general skills encompasses the need for information in company formation including guidance in establishing institutional network, legal advice, and product evaluation.
† interim – provisional sources, such as temporary staff or a consultant.

As illustrated in Table 3.1, the companies are no more than 'research projects' and/or a business concept. Their organisation is basic, (i.e., simple routines without functional structure) with little or no functional specialisation, and there is no lead entrepreneur in the case of partnerships. The degree of normalisation is low, implying verbal agreements in the case of partners. The primary focus during this phase is on product development, but the cases tend to vary in intensity in pursuing the goals. The cases with earlier commitments, for example, tended to focus primarily on these. The academics continue to emphasise R&D (and engineering) but also make efforts towards defining a business concept, commonly in consultation with personnel at the Innovation Centre. The industrial cases with less developed products, on the other hand, tended to focus primarily on the technical aspects of the company formation, primarily engineering (modelling, testing, screening). At this phase, functional focus and organisational goals tend to be indistinct.

The founders themselves do not appear to make such a distinction. With regard to networking, the academics tend to depend highly on the support services, while the industrial cases seek out personal contacts, including friends, colleagues and acquaintances. In both cases, family support (passive or active) appears to have been important. The first formal contacts with various public institutions also takes place at this stage. Therefore, the establishment of networks at this point thus appears to be based on the individual and is likely to be related to the earlier career and life patterns of the founder(s).

The Acclimatisation Phase

Acclimatisation is a concept that is often associated with the process of adapting to new environments and conditions. In this study too, the term has been used with the same implication and denotes a phase under which the primary emphasis lies in identifying an 'environmental fit' for preconceived ideas. For the company founders, this phase implies an establishment of a new pattern of life whereby they begin to perceive themselves as entrepreneurs and define their role accordingly. Indications of shifts in the life patterns appear to be more evident among the academics. They tend to increase their commitments in terms of time and other resources, make efforts to extend market contacts and develop an independent organisational structure (i.e., extricate themselves from the academic world both physically and mentally). Upon entry to this phase, two of the academic cases resigned their posts and one committed about 70 per cent of his working hours to the company.

The course of behaviour upon entry to this phase, however, is conditional on the preceding phase. One example is whether and how well the founders have accomplished their benchmarks. A second is whether they have secured resources including financing and information. Third, and perhaps the most important, is whether they have abandoned their previous commitments (i.e., unfinished research projects, commissioned assignments and side-line activities).

The academics had access to varying amounts of research funds during the initiation phase. Consequently, this case group had shown little concern for financing previously. They could stretch research resources. At this stage, however, research grants have commonly been used up and other sources of financing have yet to be considered. Thus, they begin a frenetic search for financing, mostly without success. A common alternative under these circumstances was 'freelancing' as consultants or taking on commissioned research contracts: 'it was not easy. At one point I worked as a consultant' said one AE. Despite continued emphasis on R&D, and need to acquire finance, the primary area of concern among the academics during this phase appears to be the market. They made increased efforts to compile and convey market information, participated in the appropriate technical fairs and began establishing market contacts. Subsequent activities suggest that this was decisive in defining the business concept. In one case, the product was reviewed and a new test model designed, whilst in another case the underlying core concept was abandoned. Only one case proceeded to testing the product model.

Two of the industrial cases began this phase by acquiring a 'permanent' location. One case proceeded to develop a test model while the software company began market testing of the product. In this case, further product development was related to specific customer needs. The industrial cases had basic financing secured during the initiation phase. One case had established a profitable side-line activity whilst the second case was financed internally (by the founders' own resources) and had modest needs for financing due to reasonable requirements for product development. The focus at this point appears to have been on establishing customer relations, a time-consuming process as illustrated by one case, where more than two years of intensive efforts were required to establish a business relation with a single customer. Table 3.2 presents a summary of the main characteristics distinguishing the acclimatisation phase.

One distinguishing characteristic of this phase is the multi-functional focus. Another is the outward direction of the focus, particularly in the case of the academics. The cases were still R&D-intensive but had some characteristics of engineering companies (i.e., more design, development, screening and testing), had little in-house production (commonly model/ test prototypes), had no employees, very little turnover, and an informal organisation with some routines. The key resources were primarily generated internally but also through the local network, including former colleagues, friends and acquaintances, and contacts mediated through the incubator, particularly in the case of the academics. The academics further established working relations with professional bureaux such as accounting and legal offices. Although the companies remained small, further changes can be observed in terms of concept clarity, organising, resource base and normalisation of appropriate networks, and so on.

Table 3.2   Some characteristics of the acclimatisation phase by variable and type of entrepreneur

Variable	Academic entrepreneur	Industrial entrepreneur
Core concept	Product	Product/software
Characteristics:		
Organisation format	Informal	Informal
Functional specialisation	None	Low
Decision making:		
Normalisation	Low	Low
Centralisation	High	High
Leadership	Founder/s	Lead entrepreneur
Employees*	None	None
Turnover	Some	Some[†]
Production	In-house	In-house
Functional focus	Test product financing market	test product market relations
Required key resources:		
Financial	Seed capital	Seed capital
Skills	General	Technical skills
Sources:		
Financing	Seed capital	Seed/start-up capital
Skills	Marketing skills, administration	Location, technical skills, marketing
Network	Local/external	External/local
Major benchmarks	Business concept	Test model

* Employees refers to permanent staff excluding founders.
[†] Turnover shown on the books probably originated from side-line activities or research grants.

The Consolidation Phase

The main difference between the consolidation phase and the preceding phases is the increased focus on internal aspects, primarily organisational development. With regard to the extent and nature of the measures undertaken, however, the case groups vary.

To the academics, this stage appears to have been important in that this implied interpreting and implementing new experiences and information. Two of the academic cases produced and sold the first test products upon entry to this phase. This appears to have been decisive in that the remaining part of this phase was conditioned by the outcome (response) of this test. One case company recruited a professional manager who immediately began reorganising the company and, as a result, new employees (a research team) were recruited and an export promotion office opened in one of the prospective export markets. At the same time, there began a period of intensive experimenting and testing in order to finalise a product model.

The remaining two cases abandoned their respective core concepts (in one case totally, in the second case partially) at this point and began 'dusting off' previous research and 'juggling' with new ideas. Gradually, one case diverged into R&D and technical consulting. In essence, the company underwent a bankruptcy reorganisation implying a change of ownership and a new organisational structure, with increased emphasis on functional specialisation. New partners were brought in and the company moved into a new office complex. The second case settled for an 'R&D and engineering' concept and continued more or less as previously. The two industrial cases with early market contacts emphasised the development of product models and/or a finished product. The primary concern appears to have been securing production facilities. One case decided on external manufacturing, while the second case settled for a small in-house partial production. In both cases, additional resources including skills were acquired through informal sources such as family members, former colleagues and friends, but also some consultancy services.

If we look at different types of cases, then some differences can be observed. For example, the academics depended on support services and professional skills, whilst the industrial cases tended to maintain a multi-focus strategy with a primary emphasis on the organisation of production and/or sales combined with consolidation of internal and external resources. A product-based case had hired a consultant, began recruiting new employees, and looking for a suitable location, as well as reaching an agreement with an external manufacturer and entering into a contract. The software case had extended its customer base and was generating some income. In this case, too, the company was reorganised, implying a change of leadership, new formalities for decision-making, functional specialisation, and temporary employees. Within the industrial case group, skills were primarily acquired through formal sources including consultants, temporary employees, and professional bureaux. In Table 3.3, the primary characteristics of this phase are depicted. Under this phase too, the case companies remain small. In absolute terms, the companies have no (or very few) employees, and limited turnover which commonly is generated through side-line activities and sale of test products.

Table 3.3   The main characteristics of the consolidation phase variable and type of entrepreneur

Variable	Academic entrepreneur	Industrial entrepreneur
Core concept	Product/consulting	Product/software
Characteristics:		
Organisation format	Informal	Single
Functional specialisation	Low	High
Decision making:		
Normalisation	Low	Low
Centralisation	High	High
Leadership	Founder	Lead entrepreneur
Employees	None	Few
Turnover	Low	Low
Production	In-house	In-house
Functional focus	Market test/organising	Management/expanding capacity
Required key resources:		
Financial	Start-up/seed capital	Start-up capital
Skills	Marketing	Production resources
Sources:		
Financing	Internally generated	Internally generated
Skills	Interim consultants	Employees
Network	Extended	Extended
Major benchmarks	Extended market identification	Verified concept Customer relations

In considering the levels of the development in terms of product development and the clarity of the business concepts, some differences can further be observed. The organisational structure is primarily informal and decision-making highly centralised. Qualitatively, however, some important changes have taken place. In all cases, the contact networks have been extended, the resource base (capacity, skills) has increased, and the case founders have acquired new skills and manage some administrative functions that had been considered difficult in earlier phases. In terms of complexity, two industrial cases appear to have advanced more quickly in that their companies have the contours of formal structures, a management profile and are functionally specialised.

Start-Up and Infancy

The point of start-up in this study coincides with the first sale or pending order, implying the formal launch of the company on to the market. Infancy refers to the later stages of the start-up phase and is intended to imply an increase in sales volume and not progress to a higher level of growth. In terms of functional focus, the start-up phase may be said to be characterised by an increased emphasis on production, marketing and sales organisation.

The type of organisation and resources required may be unique, but will partly depend on the nature of the core concept, the market, and organisational strategy. Thus, product-based cases with large market prospects are organised differently compared to a consulting business. Likewise, the cases with in-house production require solutions that may differ from cases with external manufacturing. Further, in relation to the initiation phase, the start-up phase differs in that some cases companies had shifted to alternative concepts and/or initiated a complementary activity. The shifts have not always been successful: 'we communicated through contacts, by telephone and sometimes spontaneous ads. We also attempted ... larger presentations but were losing money because customers backed out and we were not compensated for our expenses. In addition, it was difficult to reach the small and medium companies' (IE).

For these cases, the start-up phase implies continued efforts for survival with few benchmarks. Thus start-up is more or less reduced to juggling and experimenting with alternative ideas and freelancing in order to generate income. For example, two cases had generated and tested two and three core concepts respectively. However, following start-up one of the cases decided to give up and was wound up. The second case consists of three separate core concepts, all with few commercial 'prospects', and the founder hoped for a new idea that could be developed into a commercially viable product. Allowing for such variations, the academic cases commonly continue to emphasise technology. During this phase, one case developed and succeeded in licensing a product, but also had some in-house production and limited sales; the second case secured a number of contracts, and the third case was engaged in the market testing of newer product models.

Marketing in the conventional sense appears to be seldom considered among the academic cases. The primary channels are personal contacts, recommendations from customers, and technical fairs where test models are exposed. The founders may engage in marketing (telephone calls, letters) for a short period, then production, installations, and so on, finally ending up in the laboratory/workshop. By the time they return to the telephone, the prospective customer has probably forgotten all about the previous call.

This is partly a question of a poor resource base, but may also indicate a lack of strategy. At this stage, there is a widening gap in progress within and among the case groups. The academic cases are smaller with no employees and an average turnover of under SEK1 million. They emphasise R&D activities, irrespective of their actual business concepts, which is perhaps a reflection of inherent aspirations for establishing R&D companies. Only one of the industrial cases appears to have maintained the original course of development and has made progress, while a second survived on freelancing and the third case was discontinued and acquired upon start-up: 'we have participated in a number of International Fairs and established valuable contacts including prospective Agents. But our original plans of export have been changed depending on the contacts that we have been able to establish during these Fairs' (IE).

In infancy, the first industrial case company had developed the contours of a small growth-oriented company with volume sales and new employees, and had intensified its efforts to get established in export markets. Except for one company, start-up capital was internally generated in all cases and informal sources in the acquisition of skills continued to be important, particularly for the academic cases. As illustrated in the summary presented in Table 3.4, expansion and growth in terms of turnover and employees has remained very modest and the companies continue to be small and informal.

Similarities and Differences

The academics appear to have progressed faster in terms of product development, which may be explained by the fact that they had prototypes upon initiation, and continued focus on the technological aspects of company formation activities. An additional aspect is that they had access to initial seed financing.

The company formation process initially appeared to be systematic in that they focused primarily on product development and, following initiation, the academic cases tended to emphasise several activities at the same time so that clear functional shifts were difficult to observe. In some cases, the companies were abandoned for a long time. They made no distinction between the various types of financing and more than likely focused on daily survival. The academics' requirement of skills varies over the phases and they maintained an informal organisational structure and continued to be the sole actors in their companies.

Table 3.4   Characteristics of the start-up and infancy phase by variable and type of entrepreneur

Variable	Academic entrepreneur	Industrial entrepreneur
Core concept	Product/consulting	Product/service
Characteristics:		
Organisation format	Informal	Single
Functional specialisation	Low	High
Decision making:		
Normalisation	Low	Low
Centralisation	High	High
Leadership	Founder(s)	Lead entrepreneur
Employees	None	Some
Turnover	Under SEK1 million	Over SEK3 million
Production	In-house	In-house/external
Functional focus	Marketing, Production	Production, Sales
Required key resources:		
Financial	Start-up/seed capital	Start-up/ working capital
Skills	Management, marketing	Management
Sources:		
Financing	Internally generated	Internally generated
Skills	Interim consultants	Employees
Network	Extended	Extended
Major benchmarks	Customer relations	Volume sales

The industrial cases differ in several respects. Concept development cycles (in product-based cases) appear to have been shorter and predominant. The founders tended to maintain a 'balanced' focus on the various aspects of company formation, and appear to have been relatively systematic in their approach. They seem to have introduced functional specialisation or at least some type of 'division of labour', probably due to the fact that they were partnerships. Contrary to the academics who initially had access to R&D funds, the industrial cases depended entirely on private and internally generated resources. The dominance of the need for technical skills probably reflects their backgrounds. In terms of establishing networks, the academics initially depended on informal and institutional contacts and professionals mediated by High Tech Hill, but gradually extended the appropriate network. The industrial cases primarily formalised previous contacts including personal, and institutional ones, together with those established while with the incubator organisation.

Another aspect is the survival/revival strategy of the respective case groups upon establishing the commercial intangibility of the underlying concepts. The academics initiated a period of 'juggling' with new ideas and/or dusting off previous research project. In one case, a prototype that had been lying in a cellar was dusted off and launched successfully. In another case, the founder noticed and promoted a product idea that later proved to be highly interesting. In a third case, the company founder diverged from product to services within the same technical area. It is interesting to note that the academics perceive this to be a normal course of company formation behaviour: 'some experimenting with different things is a kind of development. Besides, we can afford to fail. We are too small' (AE). Under similar circumstances, the industrial cases tended to 'naturalise' side-line activities that had been maintained for generating income and thus appear to have made little effort to develop alternative ideas/concepts.

They rather tended to appropriate a day-to-day survival strategy and seldom occupied themselves with the development of entirely new concepts. They maintained that they were aware that the company had already been discontinued and that they had not succeeded in developing an alternative idea/concept.

Can a Common Company Formation Pattern be Distinguished?

It is likely that companies develop through phases and that a company formation process can be described as such. However, this is related more to the common attributes of the companies than the descriptive variables that have been considered here. Thus, in the initial phase, the companies had established legal boundaries, but had very few resources (the founder(s) is the primary resource), vague goals and no commercial activities. During this phase, the companies and their founders are almost indistinguishable. The contours of the companies as independent organisational entities begin to appear in the acclimatisation phase. The founders probably begin to differentiate their 'role' from that of their companies. The symbiotic existence is still maintained but the companies begin to be visible. In the consolidation phase, the main focus is on structural aspects, including organisational form and management. The start-up phase implies that the companies have established a legal boundary, an organisational identity and goals. Therefore, in this phase, the companies can be said to have a span of control over their environment. However, the boundaries between the phases are overlapping and indistinct.

Considered in terms of the descriptive variables, a common company formation pattern could not be distinguished. Organisationally, some become relatively complex, while others maintain their initial form. In terms of absolute variables, phase distinctions are also not clear: some company formations are capital- or-technology intensive, requiring little human capital, whilst in others, the labour-intensive activities may lie outside the organisation itself (external manufacturer). In terms of functional focus too, there are many variations, with a clear example being those company formations based on earlier commitments. Company founders do not appear to emphasise the same things in the same phase. Their actions rather appear to be conditioned by daily needs, the commitment and skills of their founders, and accessibility of resources. Benchmarks also vary and therefore cannot be the basis on which a company formation pattern can be distinguished.

In conclusion, company formations are characterised by diversity and are unlikely to follow an established pattern. However, depicting company formation in terms of sequential stages is useful in organising data, in describing the creation of a new company, distinguishing needs and requirements, and identifying problems/implementing measures where this is required. In the following section, the main reasons underlying the diversity in the company formation patterns of the studied cases are discussed.

INFLUENCES ON THE PATTERNS OF COMPANY FORMATION AND DEVELOPMENT

The pattern of formation and initial development of a company is shaped by four groups of variables:

- the nature of the underlying concept (nature of the business)
- the level of gestation (pre-initial development)
- entrepreneurial factors
- the environment

The Underlying Concepts

Differences in the nature of the underlying concepts may affect the company formation process in that this precondition can produce variations in resource requirements, technical solutions and market strategy. For example, the software-based company had a short product development phase, needed few production facilities, had low marketing expenses, but was highly dependent on the personal contact network for establishing customer relations. The opposite is true for a product-based case involving a complex technical idea aiming at a highly structured market, dominated by a few well established suppliers. The illustrated variations may have an impact on the functional focus, organisational structure, financial structure, marketing strategy, sequential benchmarks, and so on.

Another aspect of this topic is the inherent risk of non-viability, which may lead to diversion or discontinuance. Divergence during the ongoing process affects the pattern of company formation in that new ideas need to be generated and developed. Consequently, functional focus, benchmarks, resource requirements and so on cannot be compared to uninterrupted case formations. However, the diverging cases may not be regarded as re-initiations as the existing resource base and level of development in terms of skills, experiences, network of contacts and so on may not be comparable to the initial conditions. One observation made was that the 're-initiations' tended to be accomplished relatively quickly and smoothly, even where product development was involved. Allowing for core-concept related variations, the two case groups tended to differ in several aspects considered over the spectrum of company formation.

Pre-Initiation Development

Company formation decisions seldom coincide with the level of concept development of the actual point of initiation of a new company. A large body of prior research presumes that a company exists only as an idea prior to start-up, and references made to 'gestation' (Reynolds and Miller, 1989), 'pre-venture' (Webster, 1977), 'pre-start-up', (Kazanjian, 1988) and similar concepts commonly denote the company formation process.

However, some researchers point out that company formation is preceded by idea generation and development activities, and the location of sources of financing (Kazanjian, 1988). Others make general references denoting the pre-initiation phase without elaborating on the specific activities (Susbauer, 1972; Watkins, 1976). Thus, very little is known regarding the effect of pre-initiation behaviour on the pattern of formation and development of a company.

As indicated in the preceding section, the initiation of the case companies was preceded by a gestation period of varying length and intensity in terms of the level of concept development, the scope and relevance of information obtained, planning activities, and network. Case formations based on vaguely defined business concepts tended to be long and sketchy, and in some cases this proved to have been an additional cause for divergence or failure. The company founders lacked insight into inherent incompatibilities, including the market, technology and resources. For example, in one case, the underlying technology proved to have become 'obsolete' in the market. The company founder maintained that earlier adjustments (improvements) would have been possible had he been aware of the actual conditions in the market prior to company formation.

The surviving industrial (and most progressive) case illustrates company formations based on relatively concise business concepts. Despite a poorly developed core concept, this case had access to market information, sources of resources including financing, and action plans defining benchmarks. Perhaps as a consequence, the company formation process appears to have been relatively straightforward.

Ultimately, pre-initiation gestation has to do with identifying, obtaining and processing requisite information. Thus, the information base underlying company formation decisions may be a good indicator of the level of pre-initiation development. The nature and amount of information required, the relevance of sources perceived and approached, and the speed and accuracy of the final interpretation of information obtained is decisive. This is evident from the cases.

The founders of academic spin-offs tended to seek general information on business practices but did so on a piecemeal basis (i.e., whenever a specific task needed to be done), and as a result their approach tended to be sketchy. In addition, it must be noted that academics tended to seek information within the framework of academic research, mainly because of their previous links with an academic network.

Among the cases originating in industry, the specific type of information required depended on the particular industry, product/idea, career and personal network of contacts. Cases with ideas and markets closely related to the incubation organisation had good knowledge of their prospective markets, and information appears to have been readily available in industries dominated by a few large companies. Furthermore, founders with previous administrative careers in smaller companies seem to have been well aware of the type of information required and the sources that could be approached.

Entrepreneurial Aspects

At the initial stages, the concept 'company' is inextricable from the founder and it is therefore probable that all aspects concerning the entrepreneur are of importance. Given this, the key entrepreneurial factors affecting company formation included: personal attributes, background variables, motives, risk-taking, career, family and attitudes. These touch upon the various spheres of life of the company founders, including the personal, family and social spheres.

The personal attributes observed appear to suggest that the company founders in these case studies have a strong belief in their abilities to accomplish whatever task they choose to undertake, as well as being inclined towards acting on their own initiative. They are keen on realising an idea and like to see the results of their efforts, and pursue their goals (tasks) energetically. They appear to be versatile and are often engaged in many 'projects' at the same time.

The background variables investigated included family background (entrepreneurial history in the family), education, skills, career and experience, and age. Not surprisingly for high-technology firms, the company founders were found to be highly qualified academically. The founders' educational backgrounds, skills and experiences may precondition company formation in that these are instrumental in developing a viable product (business concept) underlying a new technology-based company. It is likely that the prospective founder's decision to found a company is primarily based on the positive self-image (self-assessment) in this respect. Entrepreneurial fathers (or other family members) on the other hand do not appear to have been of significance, however. Indeed, the influence of parents rather appears to be limited to educational choice. Another observation made is that the academics appear to be more age-conscious than the industrial entrepreneurs.

A comparison of the motives of the respective groups of cases revealed academics to be primarily driven by offensive motives such as self-realisation, independence and money. The company founders with an industrial background, on the other hand, seemed to be primarily affected by a combination of defensive motives (such as dissatisfaction with their parent organisations) and offensive motives, including independence and self-realisation. Thus the motives underlying the company formation decision are closely inter-related and may include both offensive and defensive motives. Given the underlying motives, the entrepreneurial decision appears to be triggered by a single motive (an event or a new situation): this has been defined as a precipitating event. The motives triggering a company formation decision were of two kinds. For the academic, a new product (or rather the need to commercialise a new product on invention) was a primary reason for founding the company, whilst the industrial entrepreneurs were often involved in serious conflicts with their employers or were contemplating on other options at the time of the decision.

The company founders in this study appear to be risk-conscious and inclined towards risk reduction. The type and the perceived degree of risks involved in founding the companies differ. Internally compared, the industrial entrepreneurs differ with regard to their propensity to take financial risks depending on the size of the investment and share of liability in case of failure. The academic entrepreneur is a soft-starter (seldom committing large sums of money) and thus reduces the financial risk. On the other hand, industrial entrepreneurs are hard-starters and invest their own savings. Partnership (shared responsibility) is a way of reducing this risk. As to the significance of the risks, the academic entrepreneur is primarily concerned about the family and missing a viable business idea. Ethical considerations also appear to be specific to the academic types. Industrial entrepreneurs are also concerned about their family life but not about missing a viable idea, and the primary concern of this group is financial loss.

Career success/failure is relative and personal, and probably relates to goals and ambitions. The academics probably have a clear concept of future prospects and can easily retain their positions as they had numerous academic publications to their credit, and at least one patent. A similar assessment cannot be made for the industrial cases, but none appears to have conceived their career paths to have been unsatisfactory. They, too, felt they had a number of career options and that the risk of unemployment was minimal. The study suggests that career dissatisfaction had often to do with individual expectations and goals more than the objective rewards and prospects of the job. On the other hand, success and failure do not appear to be an issue in decision-making. Career aspects that appear to be important relate to the various attributes of the places of employment including:

- acquisition of special skills and experiences
- degree of exposure provided
- organisational climate
- R&D structure
- attitudes and norms
- career and wage prospects

The specific career-related preconditions for spin-off thus appear to consist of variables that in perspective may have negative (push) and positive (pull) effects on the prospective founders.

The founders tended to emphasise the role of the family. In many cases, family members were actively involved as owners, members of the board, and as personnel resources. Perhaps more important is the moral support the family provides, without which, the respondents often contended, the companies would never have succeeded. The academics tended to consider the ethical and social aspects of their actions, partly because they felt that they could be failing in their mission as researchers, but also because they felt that their actions may be conceived as opportunistic in that their researches were financed by public resources.

These entrepreneurial variables had an impact on the decision to found a company and shape its pattern of formation and development, and the unique interaction of these factors affects role perception, acquisition resources including skills, attitudes and motives, and ambitions for continued entrepreneurship.

Role Conception

One indicator of role clarity may be how the founders perceive themselves and their role. A second indicator can be the degree of involvement in the company formation process. A third indicator can be the degree of ease with which the founders acclimatise themselves to their role, (e.g, in terms of acquisition of skills, communication, etc). Role conception and development is probably related to various aspects of the founders themselves, including motivations, background, risk-taking propensity, earlier life-patterns and their family situation. Company founders previously exposed to business practices are likely to have less difficulty in associating themselves with an entrepreneurial role, and the fact that lack of role clarity appears to be pronounced among the academic cases probably supports this view. Considered in terms of the three indicators of role clarity, the industrial cases do not appear to have faced difficulties.

The academics continued to perceive themselves as 'researchers' but appeared to be less defensive on the occasion of the second interview than the first. Another observation made at this point was the continued lack of focus on the business, despite the fact that none of the founders entertained ideas of retaining their positions at the university. They maintained that they were still researchers and company formation was to be regarded as a continuation (completion) of a research project. Distinctions between the research and entrepreneurial role are marginal.

Role clarity and commitment appear to be important influences on the level of involvement in company formation activities and, consequently, the academics had few options for company formation, particularly in the first years. This type of multiple role-commitment appears to have affected the case formations in several ways, including slow start-up, sketchy functional focus, and poor and slow acquisition of complementary skills. Further, the founders themselves tended to conceive the process as tedious which can affect the desire to continue entrepreneurship.

The difficulty experienced by academics in role acclimatisation can be further observed in their emphasis on familiar activities (R&D), their language, and their hesitations concerning changes in their life path. After start-up, the academics tended simply to continue to work (and probably think) as previously. They often referred to the 'application' of a research project when discussing the company formation process. They could describe the technical merits of their 'projects' without making a single reference to the potential customer and market. Thus role development still appears to be slow, despite references to 'personal development, qualitative change' made by the case founders at the last interview. In the longer perspective, poor role development may imply role conflict and a diminishing desire to continue on the path.

Acquisition of Skills

As Schumpeter (1934) proposed, entrepreneurial skills probably have to do with the ability to perceive unique ways of combining existing resources. However, the requisite skills in perceiving the unique combinations are difficult to specify. In this study, for example, company founders encompass various roles, including researcher/inventor, innovator, entrepreneur and manager; the skills required for each one are likely to be different. Despite this complexity, three types of skills appear to be essential, namely technical, entrepreneurial and managerial. Whilst the significance of each skill is phase-related, elements of all the three types are a precondition for company formation. Differences in skills reflect upon many aspects of company formation behaviour including functional focus, decision-making procedure, networking, organising and leadership development. The fact that the academics continue to develop, however, indicates that skills can be acquired (learned). The implication is that skills and experiences in entrepreneurship are important in the initial stages but may not have a decisive impact on a longer perspective.

Attitudes

An attitude is commonly reflected in disposition towards something. Here, it is intended to describe the company founders' disposition towards various commitments in entrepreneurship. Attitudes are probably related to various individual aspects including motives, preconceptions of the entrepreneurial role, earlier patterns of life, family situation, and risk-taking propensity. The components of attitude-related influences including risk-taking propensity appear to have a direct impact on resource acquisition and level of investment. Apart from some initial R&D funding, the case formations were internally financed through personal savings, private loans and internally generated resources, or side-line activities. Equity financing was an exception; in these cases the shares of the companies were owned by the founders and their families (commonly the wives). This appears to have been a basic strategy and not a consequence of poor access to external financing.

One reason is the low risk-taking propensity (risk of failure), and another is the risk of losing control. For example, the academics were specific about maintaining personal autonomy irrespective of the prospects for their companies. Perhaps as a consequence, the case formations were characterised by chronic under-capitalisation and poor involvement as the founders were often undertaking temporary assignments in order to generate resources. Therefore the financial structure of a company is moulded by many factors, including the availability/accessibility of resources, and the perceived desirability.

Attitude-related financing strategies (internal financing) appear to have affected the case formations in that these fail to establish formal relations with external sources of financing. In the longer perspective, this may imply that the prospects of acquiring financing may decrease. Another aspect is that limited exposure to external financing may imply limited acquisition of financing management skills. The surviving industrial case company is an exception in that the founders had identified potential sources of financing and established formal relations in case this would be needed: they expressed their hope of locating an external partner willing to buy shares in the company. A similar attitude can be observed with regard to the acquisition of skills. The academics hesitated to acquire permanent employees and continued to depend on professional services. The primary reason was not the cost of permanent employees but the responsibility.

Ambitions

Ambitions in this study refer to the entrepreneurial goals of the company founders (i.e., what they want to achieve by establishing a company).

Ambitions probably relate to role conceptions, motives and risk-taking propensity, particularly fear of changing an established pattern of life. The academics' tendency to create companies resembling the academic environment may be an indication of this: they were intent on completing their research projects, and offensive motives such as financial gain were of low priority. Their ambitions inferred from the type of companies they tried to establish appears to support this suggestion:

> a research team with 4–5 members, group feeling, you know. Then if we succeeded in developing something viable, we would think of patenting. (AE).

> we want an R&D company with 7–8 members at the core. Then we can place new bits in different baskets and let each basket stand independently. (AE)

The ideal for the academics was a small, high-technology R&D company with a good research team. The emphasis on 'research team' is interesting in that it suggests that the academics will probably be the ones to relay new 'cultural' elements to industry, and not only become assimilated themselves. The higher level of involvement of the industrial cases with offensive motives, and the growth ambitions in the case of the surviving industrial company, is in contrast to the academics group:

> our ambition is to continue to expand, establish contacts in 20–25 countries. Prospectively, we would like to establish a partnership with a larger company that could inject additional resources in terms of capital, skills and perhaps a sales organisation. (IE)

The level of involvement, resource acquisition strategies and growth ambitions appear to be determined by the skills, role conception, ambitions and attitudes of the company founders. Thus success in terms of quantitative growth may not necessarily be related to the market potential of companies.

ENVIRONMENTAL ASPECTS

The environmental conditions in which the companies are started shape the process in various ways. In this study, the factors relating to the environment have been distinguished into those relating to the incubation and those relating to the entrepreneurial environment: the incubation environment includes factors that can be directly attributed to the former places of employment (incubator organisation) and indirect influences inherent in the association with a specific sector (spin-off conditions).

Incubation and Entrepreneurial Environment

The Incubator Organisation

A comparison of the two types of incubator organisations – academic and industrial – revealed these to be different in several respects. The academic institution was found to be conducive to spin-off company formation in that it provides specialisation in R&D (skills), access to R&D facilities, access to research funds, a permissive organisation, frustrations arising from poor career and wage prospects. The conditions for spin-off for university employees (former employees) contemplating company formation were found to be favourable in that:

(a) there are no patenting restrictions on academic researchers (an invention or patent is the private property of the researcher);
(b) seed-capital may be acquired through R&D grants (funds);
(c) formal/informal supportive services are easily accessible.

With regard to the defined aspects, industrial organisations were found to be conducive to spin-off in that they provided:

- skills and experiences in entrepreneurship
- a high degree of exposure (e.g., industrial contacts)
- frustrations that motivate spin-off
- permissive attitudes and norms towards entrepreneurship

Spin-Off Conditions

The conditions for spin-off that were of importance to company formation included patent practices (regulations), access to seed-capital, and the existence of (and access to support for) spin-off activities of former employees. In contrast, industrial organisations were found to be less favourable to the prospective founder in that they had relatively little access to R&D seed-capital through research grants, inventions developed within the industrial organisation (an eventual patent is the property of the employer) and support services due to informal obstacles (lack of information)

The incubation environment, including support services and links, appear to have been important, particularly to the academic cases. Access to support services and links to the university probably explain the survival of the academic cases, despite failure to commercialise the initial products. The local network, for example, has been an important gateway to external contacts including government offices, professionals, investors and customers. Local networks probably explain some of the regional variations in the rate of spin-offs from universities in Sweden, with universities with well established networks tending to have a higher rate of spin-offs (Wallmark and McQueen, 1986; Olofsson *et al.*, 1987; Tesfaye, 1993). The importance of university-affiliated supportive networks may not only depend on access to various resources, but also the moral support that these provide, with the respondents emphasising the sense of credibility and affiliation provided by the local environment. The existence of other small companies, particularly those with backgrounds in universities, was found to be an important condition for a company formation decision. These continue to be important to the academics in that they can easily affiliate themselves, even as business partners. In addition, such academic-based companies tend towards not only buying services from each other, but also providing informal advice and consulting.

The Entrepreneurial Environment

A second group of environmental factors found to have been of significance to the founders relates to the environment in which the companies are founded. Prior to deciding on an entrepreneurial career, the prospective founder is likely to consider the environment in which the company is to be founded and developed. The analysis of the environmental factors conditioning company formation indicated the following to be of importance:

- the availability of start-up capital
- access to necessary skills
- viability of suitable locations
- access to a market (customers)
- existence of positive references (credible examples)
- positive attitudes towards entrepreneurship

Initially, the case founders had very little interaction with the external environment. Compared to the industrial entrepreneurs, the academics appear to have perceived the entrepreneurial environment to be more favourable in that they expressed less concern for the material resources (including availability of start-up capital, skills, locations and markets). Their preconceptions were probably similar to an 'average researcher' and they made little effort to obtain information on specific areas such as capital sources and prospective markets. On the other hand, the academics expressed more concern for the immaterial incentives in the form of credible examples and societal attitude. The reverse is true for the industrial entrepreneurs, who expressed great concern for the availability of material resources but not the immaterial incentives.

With increasing need to interact, the environmental variables become important. The particular aspects of importance and the ease with which the interaction takes place appears to be related to internal strength of the company (especially in terms of internal resources, personal network, family involvement, etc.) and the nature of the companies.

Access to Resources and the Domestic Market

The case companies were founded in the mid-1980s when access to capital was readily available, and anything involving 'high technology' was considered to be an attractive investment. The low priority the founders seemed to attach to capital requirements may be related to this condition. In reality, this does not appear to have been the case: for example, in Klofsten *et al.*'s (1988) study of high-technology spin-offs, very few of the respondents had been able to acquire external financing. As mentioned previously, acquisition of resources is related to attitudes. However, availability of resources is likely to be perceived as an indication of the climate for entrepreneurship and thus an important condition for company formation.

Access to markets appears to be related to skills and to the structure of the industry. Young expanding markets in both manufacturing and technical services appear to be easier to penetrate than traditional or lagging markets. In the first type, market information appeared to be readily available, competition was low, and access was perceived to have been easy. In markets dominated by a few large companies with huge resources, acquisitions are more likely than new establishments, as was the case with one company in this study. Establishment in a highly concentrated market thus appears to require a solid resource base which new companies commonly lack. Another strategy would be to target a small niche and thus avoid 'rubbing the giants'. However, niche markets may not be easily penetrated due to horizontal integration/links. Further, niching appears to be short-lived in that companies which are solely dependent on niches have difficulty in maintaining their competitive edge and become easy prey for larger companies.

The industrial structure also appears to be unfavourable to companies producing R&D products, including patents. The cases that had produced patents were unable to attract domestic interest, with all three patents being exported after a fruitless search for domestic buyers. This may be attributable to the size of the market, but may also indicate structural problems and management philosophies that are unfavourable to unplanned innovations and new ideas. Therefore, market prospects for innovations (patents, licensing) in the domestic arena appear to be small.

Policies and Trends

Environmental variables that have impact on company formation behaviour may also include policy aspects such as taxation and the emphasis placed by the local environment on university spin-offs and innovations. Taxation is probably one of the main reasons for university staff to establish new companies: for example, two founders in the study had been forced to take personal loans to pay taxes.

The case descriptions also show taxation of income from royalties and additional activities to have been perceived as highly unfavourable, because the acquiring companies commonly apply different practices: for example, in some companies, royalties are linked to all the patents that the company has, and not to a specific patent. Thus the royalty received has very little to do with the specific patent. In addition, academic researchers commonly take loans to develop the patent but this does not affect the taxation of income from royalties. Another aspect of patents is that it they are difficult to protect. Whilst a patent is legally protected, it is at the same time a public document open to all and therefore, in the long term, is impossible to protect. As mentioned previously, this condition is favourable to company formation.

Taxation policies and economic trends are important influences for two main reasons. First, the private finances of the founders tended to be closely intertwined with those of the companies. Negative economic trends, affecting interest rates on housing, bank credit, and so on are thus likely to have an impact. Second, the company founders have developed to a stage where they have perceived the necessity for some external financing, and therefore limitations at this point of their development may thus have serious consequences. With a view to company formation behaviour, each of these variables probably impedes on role conceptions/development, attitudes, company formation strategy, and ambitions for growth and expansion.

Therefore, the company formation behaviour of the cases is characterised by diversity more than similarity, and a common pattern cannot be distinguished. The aspect that appears to be common to the case formations is the tendency to depend on internal financing and other resources such as skills. Here, too, there may be differences in the reasons underlying this tendency. Relative to the industrial cases, the academics' behaviour appears to suggest:

- unprocedural approach
- poor involvement

- sketchy functional focus
- introspective growth perspective

This is likely to be a 'typical' condition for soft-starters resembling the academic cases in this study. Soft-start (implying continued linkage to the research institutions) is not necessarily a poor precondition, as this was the primary strength of the academics relative to the discontinued industrial cases. However, this has an impact on the progress of the companies and implications for the exploitation of perceived opportunities. Presuming growth in terms of turnover and number of employees to be the measures of success, the surviving industrial case may be used as an illustrative example of the favourable impact of pre-founding conditions. Factors which distinguish this company from the preceding company formation patterns include: pre-initiation gestation, a successful partnership (person–concept compatibility), a sound resource base and strategic company formation behaviour. This mix of variables appears to be absent in the remaining cases.

In conclusion, the pattern of formation and initial development of an emerging organisation is closely linked to the specific preconditions underlying the creation of a new company. This study has identified some of the key variables. The significance of each combination of factors shaping each company formation is phase-related. A similar variation with regard to the required inputs has been observed. Each stage of development is thus predicated on the preceding one, and so the pattern of development during the initial stages is fundamental to organisational development. Conceptual models of emerging organisations need to depict this relationship, and not only the knots on the chain. The following section attempts to organise the indications of the study into a coherent structure that capture the intertwined and dynamic nature of entrepreneurial processes.

DEPICTING THE INFLUENCES ON COMPANY FORMATION AND DEVELOPMENT: A CONCEPTUAL MODEL

The key variables distinguished in the study affect three dimensions of company formation and initial development:

(a) how company founders perceive entrepreneurship;
(b) how the founders perceive the chances of succeeding;
(c) whether they perceive an opportunity.

The entrepreneurial decision is based on the perception that entrepreneurship is desirable, feasible and that there exists an opportunity. These perceptions are likely to be subjective and may not reflect the objective conditions: upon the initiation of the process, founders may find the conditions to be entirely different. Perception of desirability of an entrepreneurial action is fundamental to the company formation decision in that it affects perceptions of feasibility and opportunity.

An individual who does not feel strongly towards an entrepreneurial action is unlikely to contemplate problems of feasibility or be alert to business opportunities. Some of the founders in this study, for example, had chosen other means of commercialising research results on previous occasions. Their responses suggest that they had not perceived entrepreneurship to be desirable.

Perception of Desirability of Entrepreneurship

Perceptions of desirability are probably affected by individual values and norms moulded by social value systems. Given this, in contemplating an entrepreneurial action, prospective founders are likely to consider what they want to achieve and the options for such an undertaking and social rewards inherent in this role. Thus, perception of desirability of an entrepreneurial action appear to be affected by three groups of factors:

- the motivational mix
- readiness to undertake an entrepreneurial action
- a positive self-image

The Motivational Mix

The 'right' motivational mix underlying the company formation decision may be related to the psychological, sociological and cultural aspects of the prospective founder. Individuals who are keen on initiative and results may perceive entrepreneurship as a desirable option.

The variation in the hierarchy of the founders' motives further suggest that motives may be shaped by perceived prospects (expectations) and negative experiences. The emphasis on the independence motive can therefore reflect a search for an ideal situation and/or an escape from negative experiences (including an ongoing conflict or displacement). Similarly, self-realisation appears to be partly related to failure and/or fear of failure to commercialise a research result through alternative mechanisms (i.e., realise an idea).

Readiness

Readiness to undertake an entrepreneurial action may also be affected by the above factors. Prospective founders who are energetic, self-confident and keen on initiative and achievement are likely to perceive themselves ready for the challenge. Given this, prospective founders are likely to weigh the perceived risks against their private, family and career spheres. Prospective founders who perceive that they have the right skills for the undertaking, numerous career options, favourable private finances and a supportive family, are likely to perceive the entrepreneurship risk differently from others. Access to support services also probably strengthens the perception of readiness.

Self-Image

Self-image probably has to do with how prospective founders perceive their present role, social status, and so on. This could mean setting the 'social image' of their profession against the attitude towards entrepreneurship in the immediate environment and society at large. The perception of role is likely to be influenced by the existence of credible examples, primarily colleagues and acquaintances, but also a favourable entrepreneurial climate and infrastructure. Role perception is likely to further influence the conceived feasibility of an entrepreneurial action.

Perception of Feasibility

Feasibility is probably related to how the prospective founders perceive their own capabilities such as skills, knowledge and creativity, and how they view the objective conditions in the environment. Therefore, feasibility is likely to be related to perceived needs and requirements and the ease with which they think these can be acquired. Strong local networks probably play an important role in this respect, with the main point of reference likely to be other entrepreneurs, particularly those with whom the prospective founder can identify. These preconceptions, however, do not appear to be based on objective conditions but values inferred from environmental conditions, entrepreneurship culture and success stories. The founders in this study, for example, perceived availability/accessibility of startup to be favourable. However, none had made any efforts to contact potential sources of financing, as they 'presumed' the situation to be favourable due to many new companies in their immediate surroundings and society at large having been successful in this respect. Perceptions of desirability and feasibility are fundamental to entrepreneurship but may not condition an initiation of an entrepreneurial process. No matter how appealing the action may be perceived to be, entrepreneurship will not be realised without an opportunity.

Perception of Opportunity

Opportunity may be actual or perceived, and actual opportunity may be related to the motives and ambitions of the founders. A concept with evident poor market prospects may be considered to be an opportunity for some but not for others. Perception of opportunity also appears to be related to the self-conception of the founder: 'I am so creative that I know that I will come up with something' (AE). Perception of opportunity may further be affected by perceived feasibility and relate to the conception of the preconditions for the company and the pervading environmental conditions. Furthermore, the continued dynamic societal signals probably are important in influencing the individual perceptions of opportunity, in that a society that makes no investments towards creating opportunities in the form of education, the development of skills, and the social and industrial infrastructure cannot, in general, hope for creativity in the form of entrepreneurship.

Opportunity may be related to an invention or a new business concept and/or an incentive that facilitates the exploitation of vaguely defined business ideas. However, perceived opportunities need not imply products, concepts or a business opportunity. In some cases, it may represent an alternative to unfavourable outcomes such as, for example, a tax-reduction opportunity. Some companies, started for taxation purposes, can remain dormant for a period and be reactivated upon perceiving a business opportunity. One interesting aspect is that founders of such companies tend to be entrepreneurial: that is, alert, creative and often successful in perceiving opportunities. One example is a company that had been started up for the express purpose of accruing income from royalties from an earlier patent, but ended up by buying back the patent and establishing a joint multi-million business with a foreign company. The company was later reorganised into an R&D company, and a commercial organisation.

Therefore, allowing for the illustrated type of diversity, company formation is likely to occur when an individual perceives the notion of becoming an entrepreneur to be desirable, feasible and perceives an opportunity. The point of initiation of the entrepreneurial process, however, is likely to be precipitated by a single positive/negative event.

Perceptions of desirability, feasibility and opportunity may be fundamental to entrepreneurship, in that company formation is likely to be predicated on the interaction of these factors. However, this is not a static condition and may not predict an entrepreneurial process. Perceptions are subjective and may not reflect objective conditions, the perceived options for company formation may not exist, resources may prove to be inaccessible, and opportunities may not prove to be as tangible as perceived. The study showed many examples to this effect. Therefore, a gap exists between preconceptions and objective conditions, and consequently company formation behaviour is likely to reflect the gap between the preconceptions and the objective conditions. The nature and impact of the discrepancy between preconceptions and objective reality probably determines the actual desirability, feasibility and opportunity of entrepreneurship.

Actual Desirability, Feasibility and Opportunity

The stage-wise analysis of the case formations indicated variations in behaviour and suggested that a common company formation pattern may not be distinguishable. However, the approach proved useful in that some of the variables affecting the particular phase of the process could be observed. Thus, access to support services (information, access to appropriate network, requisite skills) appears to have been important to the academic cases at the initial stages. As the companies progressed to higher phases of the process, the significance of these variables tended to decrease. The company formation process in the case of the academics tended to be slow and sketchy, with primary emphasis on the technological aspects. Characteristic of these cases was:

- inadequate pre-initiation gestation
- low levels of involvement by the founders
- under-capitalisation
- sketchy functional focus
- informal organisational structure

Whilst the industrial cases differed internally, they appeared to be more procedural in their activities. This behaviour appears to have been conditioned by the interaction of the different aspects of the pre-founding factors and the environment. The primary entrepreneurial aspects that conditioned company formation behaviour included the following.

1. Self-image, skills and experiences, reflected in the definition of business concepts, role conception, and company formation strategy. Relative to the industrial cases, the academic case formations tended to be vague about their business concepts and the requirements of their role.

2. The nature of the motives, perhaps reflected in the goals and ambitions directing the course of development. The defensive nature of academics' motives, with emphasis on the completion of research projects, further appear to reflect on their ambitions for growth.
3. Risk-taking propensity prevalent in the risk-reduction (cautious) behaviour reflected in attitudes towards external financing including equity and acquisition of skills. The low risk-taking propensity among the respective groups of cases perhaps explains the high tolerance of under-capitalisation and low levels of capital investment.

The impact of lack of skills and experiences seems to decrease as the cases progress to higher stages, suggesting that these can be learned during the ongoing process. The aspects of the underlying concepts (opportunity), technological complexity and utility (tangibility) seem to be reflected in technology – resource incompatibilities, although the impact of encountered intangibility may depend on the existing conditions, particularly the entrepreneurial resource. However, the primary factors underlying divergence and discontinuity relate to the tangibility of perceived opportunity, thus implying this to be decisive. Likewise, the impact of environmental influences is probably at variance with entrepreneurial resources, including career backgrounds, links, skills, motivations and attitudes. The vulnerability of the process thus appears to be closely related to the attributes of the founders. In this respect, the preconditions for the academics (with backgrounds in, and links to, research institutions) appear to have been favourable, perhaps due to the supportiveness of this environment. The preconditions underlying the conception of desirability, feasibility and opportunity probably constitute the frame of reference for the desire to pursue entrepreneurship, and the commitment to succeed.

Thus the particular pattern of company formation behaviour probably reflects the gap between perceived and actual desirability and feasibility opportunity. Even though all the three aspects are fundamental to entrepreneurship, desirability is likely to be decisive. In cases where a lack of feasibility was encountered or where perceived opportunities proved to be intangible, the founders tended to generate new means and ideas for continuing the entrepreneurial process. In cases where entrepreneurship was no longer perceived to be desirable, the founders tended to discontinue: 'it is not only that we are short of ideas. We have somehow lost the initial zeal' (IE).

Actual desire to accomplish an entrepreneurial process is probably determined by the factors underlying the perception of desirability, the impact of the environment and situation factors manifest in the degree of commitment to the process, role development, the attitudes and ambitions of the founders. Actual feasibility may be affected by factors underlying the perception of feasibility, desirability and environmental variables, including accessibility of resources and societal trends. Indicators of actual feasibility may include the span of environmental control (i.e., resources, network, market). Actual opportunity too is likely to be affected by variables underlying perception of opportunity, desirability and feasibility factors and the objective conditions reflected in:

- opportunity–resource compatibility
- opportunity–market compatibility
- opportunity–person compatibility

The inter-relatedness of perceived and actual desirability, feasibility and opportunity can be conceptualised as in Figure 3.1. An entrepreneurial process is dynamic and it is probable that research efforts only capture momentary glimpses of multidimensional phenomena in constant change. Therefore, attempts to depict an entrepreneurial process may imply a simplification of a complexity that is difficult to envision. However, research efforts attempting to analyse the entrepreneurial process as a dynamic phenomenon may be useful in understanding the conditions for entrepreneurship and designing strategies that meet the requirements of entrepreneurs at the different phases of development, if this is what is wanted.

Applicability of the Model

With regard to the proposition that the entrepreneurial process may be conditioned by perceived and actual desirability, feasibility and opportu-

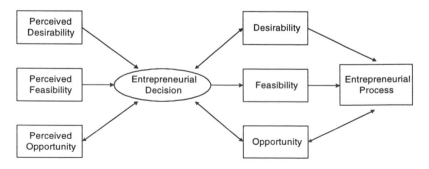

Figure 3.1   The entrepreneurial process

nity, there do not appear to be variations between the case formations. Comparing this with some of the conceptual models of company formation, the proposals in this study differ in some fundamental aspects:

(a) key variables may not distinguish prospective entrepreneurs (McClelland, 1961; Watkins, 1976);
(b) entrepreneurship cannot be predicated on situational factors such as shifts in the patterns of life of individuals or negative/push effects;
(c) an entrepreneurial event in itself may not predicate an entrepreneurial process (Shapero and Sokol, 1982). Thus the entrepreneurial event only describes a knot in a chain and not an entrepreneurial process.

These results give a very good illustration of the inherent fragmentation in entrepreneurship research, and the model incorporates these hypotheses and integrates the main knots on the chain of the company formation process. This can be a useful frame of reference in organising the multitude of factors affecting company formation behaviour.

CONCLUSIONS AND IMPLICATIONS FOR ACADEMIC-BASED ENTREPRENEURSHIP

The research results and the interpretations made have been discussed in the preceding sections of this chapter. In this section, only those conclusions that relate specifically to academic-based entrepreneurship will be presented. In concluding the chapter, the implications of the research are briefly discussed.

A major part of the key variables conditioning the formation of small technology-based companies with roots in academic institutions have been identified in prior research on entrepreneurship. With regard to the specific nature and significance of the influences, the results in this study differ in several respects.

Key influences on the supply of entrepreneurship that recur in prior research including entrepreneurial background, displacement job-related dissatisfaction and economic motives, are poor indicators of academic entrepreneurship. An academic's decision to found a company is unlikely to be predicated on these variables. The academic entrepreneurs had very limited knowledge of experiences in enterprise and innovation, emphasised non-economic motives, and entry into entrepreneurship was usually precipitated by a positive pull (i.e., a new product or a new business concept). Therefore academic cases, with backgrounds in an environment that nurture non-economic values and norms and alternative measures of results and accomplishment, are likely to mould similar values in their members. In the emergence of academic entrepreneurship, two interrelated groups of factors appear to have been of particular importance to the founders.

First, general changes in the academic climate have resulted in efforts to create a supportive R&D framework, stronger links to industry, financial support, and the establishment of appropriate mechanisms for commercialising research results. This development is likely to have influenced the preconceptions and attitudes of the academics themselves, who contended that entrepreneurship would have been inconceivable for them personally, and in the academic world in general, some years back.

Second, changes in societal attitudes towards entrepreneurship, especially the university spin-off phenomena, have led to an increasing focus on entrepreneurial initiative and efforts to improve entrepreneurial climate. This has an impact on the self-image of the academic and consequently the desirability for an entrepreneurial career: 'academics who found companies have nothing to be ashamed of. They use public funds for the benefit of all' (AE). Relative to the industrial cases, the academic case formation processes tended to be long and sketchy and characterised by:

- an emphasis on R&D
- a low level of involevement
- an unprocedural approach
- a low level of resource commitment and capital investment

In other words, the academics organise and conduct company formation activities much as they would a research project. The academics tend to 'think' and express themselves in a specific way, perhaps as researchers. They are therefore likely to be more receptive to individuals who have a thorough knowledge and understanding of how they 'tick' than to business 'experts'. In this regard, the role of individuals with academic backgrounds and long experience in the commercialisation of research results is not to be under estimated. The academics in this study made frequent references to the role of the initiator at High Tech Hill in their decisions and company formation: not only the expertise he provided, but the way he approached them and communicated with them. It is also therefore not surprising that the academics expressed preference for environments that are familiar (i.e., which 'feel' and function like an academic institution).

Further, the academics tend to imitate academic institutional organisation models. Thus, loosely designed, informal organisational solutions are likely to be conceived as attractive. Perhaps the primary role of the innovation centres is to mobilise individual resources, and create stimulating environments that facilitate this process. However tentative the indications of this research may appear, the implications can be important in policy and strategic decisions for stimulating academic spin-offs.

Implications for Policy and Research

The knowledge gained from this study can be useful for policy makers and practitioners, including financial institutions, universities, innovation centres and researchers with ambitions for an entrepreneurial career in several ways.

The conceptual model of company formation proposed in this chapter depicts entrepreneurship as a social process, and can be useful in designing aggregate and selective policies for stimulating entrepreneurship. For designing aggregate policies, the dimensions of entrepreneurship supply distinguished in the model can be used as decision and evaluation parameters. For academic entrepreneurship, societal attitudes are shown to be very important, and therefore measures for stimulating academic entrepreneurship need to be anchored in aggregate social policies that compound the various spheres of the lives of the individuals and the society.

For financial institutions, knowledge about the company's formation and the impact of this phase on the potential of a company can be useful in evaluating their investment, understanding the requirements and needs of company founders, and identifying problems and remedies at a very early stage. In the cases where risk-capital investment was involved, the investors tended to keep their involvement to the minimum and thus failed to perceive the problems of the companies in time. Thus investors may need to back academic spin-offs with complementary resources including skills in innovation management. One important result from this study is the impact that the incubation environment appears to have on academic spin-off. In order to stimulate entrepreneurial initiative, academic institutions need to nurture a permissive climate: for example, by integrating entrepreneurship education in undergraduate programmes irrespective of discipline.

For innovation centres, the knowledge gained may be valuable in designing services for the companies and stimulating an environment that suits the needs of the company founders. The study shows the needs and requirements of each entrepreneurial process to be phase-related: that is, company founders need different types of resources and incentives as their companies progress from the lower to higher phases of development. This calls for individually tailored services. Research on company formation presumes existing companies and provides no guidance on how to identify emerging organisations. Distinguishing the specific properties of emerging companies can be a basis for understanding the patterns of formation and development. In addition, the interaction between entrepreneurship and the theory of organisation are not clear. Research on the interaction of organisation theory and entrepreneurial processes can generate an understanding of the phenomenon and should be a challenge.

4 Creation and Development of New Technology-Based Firms in Peripheral Economies

Margarida Fontes

INTRODUCTION

New technology-based firms have been the object of extensive research in the more advanced Western countries, but little attention has been paid to this type of organisation in less advanced countries. This can be regarded as an indication of the lower relevance of the phenomenon in the latter, derived from the absence of favourable conditions for small technology-based firms' formation and survival. Despite this, NTBFs have nevertheless been created in these environments, thus emerging as an important, and relatively neglected, object of research.

This research attempts to fill this gap by studying the case of new technology-intensive firms created in Portugal in the last 15 years. These firms have been established with the objective of introducing completely new products or services, or of bringing to the Portuguese market products already available elsewhere but new (or particularly difficult to obtain) locally. These products embodied technologies that were new or only starting to diffuse in Portugal, with particular relevance to micro-electronics and information technologies. Some of these firms were created close to a research centre, often through the initiative of scientists/technologists willing to commercialise the results of their research work. Others were created by entrepreneurs leaving existing firms to exploit an idea or an opportunity they had identified.

In studying these firms, the researcher tried to evaluate whether they differed from NTBFs created in more advanced environments and to perceive the reasons behind the eventual differences. In other words, it was our objective to understand the impact of the conditions found in a less advanced country upon the creation and evolution of such firms. On the other hand, because NTBFs are characterised by their capacity to develop and introduce innovative applications embodying new technologies, it was also our objective to identify the roles this they could play in the technological development of laggard countries. Although this study concentrated in the case of Portugal, the conclusions can be possibly applied to similar environments, particularly other less advanced European countries.

Therefore, the objective of this research was to study NTBFs in Portugal, in order to gain a better comprehension of the conditions in which these firms are created and operate, and of the roles they are likely to play in a less advanced economy. The absence of previous research about this subject in Portugal made it necessary to rely exclusively on literature produced in other contexts as the basis for the research. On the other hand, the multidisciplinary nature of the problem required the analysis of different bodies of literature concerning firm creation, innovation and technological change, and less advanced economies and development.

THE ROLE OF NEW TECHNOLOGY-BASED FIRMS

Technological Dynamism and its Limitations

NTBFs have often been described as an important element in the process of technological change. Their association with a number of new technologies and with the emergence of new industries conveyed the idea of their potential contribution to technological development, economic growth and employment creation, as well as the revitalisation of 'peripheral' regions (Cooper and Bruno, 1977; Rothwell and Zegveld, 1982; Bollinger, Hope and Utterback, 1983; Oakey, Rothwell and Cooper, 1988).

An analysis of the arguments put forward regarding the potential role of NTBFs suggests that it is based on two orders of factors:

(a) firms' technological dynamism – that is, the ability to identify and develop new technologies with great potentialities and the entrepreneurial drive necessary to take them to the market;
(b) their capacity for fast growth, on the basis of the successful introduction of these new technologies.

Recently some doubts have been cast upon their ability to meet the expectations raised around them (Oakey, 1991b; Stankiewicz, 1994). However, these doubts are largely based on the fact that, in spite of a few individual cases of outstanding success, NTBFs have not, as a group, matched the expectations of fast growth, although they have fulfilled their role as technologically dynamic firms, challenging existing ways of doing things.

The point is that maybe such expectations were 'inflated' (Stankiewicz, 1994) and most firms did not necessarily have the willingness to grow (Bruno, McQuarrie and Torgrimson, 1992; Jones-Evans, 1996b), or the opportunity to achieve such growth. Whereas in some fields where technological opportunities are high, conditions may have existed for new firms to grow on the basis of the appropriation of their technological knowledge (Pavitt, 1984) – which may explain why a few experienced fast growth – this was not a general phenomenon. The explanation may lie both in the nature of the pioneering process – early entrants often experience difficulties in getting established and grow on the basis of the major innovation they introduced (Olleros, 1986; Teece, 1986) – and in the resilience shown by some large established companies. A number of these have revealed the ability to survive potentially damaging 'discontinuities', to incorporate the radical changes introduced by young technology-based firms, and even to recover leadership when they seemed to have skipped a major opportunity (Pavitt, 1991).

Recent research on the activities of small technology-intensive firms have contributed to their dissociation from the fast-growth perspective, directing attention instead to their role in the process of diffusion of new technology (Rizzoni, 1991; Autio, 1994; Stankiewicz, 1994). In doing that, these approaches shift the focus to aspects of NTBFs behaviour that emphasise their potential as technologically dynamic firms.

Therefore, it is possible to argue that the role of NTBFs can be primarily expressed in terms of their technological dynamism – which is an intrinsic factor associated with the very existence of the firm – and only secondarily in terms of their growth capacity, which can be regarded as a 'bonus' occurrence. Moreover, an analysis of the activities carried out by NTBFs suggests that their potential relevance as technologically dynamic firms goes beyond the initial ability to identify, develop and introduce a new technology/application.

The concept of 'technological dynamism', as it will be used in this research, encompasses two major roles performed by these firms, as described below.

1. The initial 'challenging role', implicit in the act of their creation. This role is often described in the literature. For instance Bollinger, Hope and Utterback (1983:5) summarise this view, pointing out that NTBFs are valuable, both because they sometimes carry out major product in-

novations, making 'contributions which extend the boundaries and constraints of technical know-how', and because of their impact upon existing firms, which view them as a threat and have to respond, improving the existing technology or acquiring the new one.

2. The more long-standing function as source and disseminator of new technologies: that is, their 'technology transfer role'. This role is well described by Autio (1994:260), who believed NTBFs 'develop technology internally and/or acquire it from external sources', act upon it in order 'to achieve the best possible fit with customer needs' and then 'transfer technology to customers through various interactions'.

Although these two roles have been separately approached in the literature, they are clearly complementary and together constitute the major contribution of this type of firm. NTBFs are created to develop and introduce a new technology/application, which improves or replaces the existing ones (often challenging the existing organisations). By that act, a firm is established which embodies a 'new combination' of technological competences, and whose basic role is to proceed as an agent of technology transfer, acquiring and delivering new technology.

However, as young, small and technology-oriented organisations, NTBFs have a number of limitations (particularly with regard to level of resources and breadth of skills) that can hinder the performance of these roles. They may act as a constraint upon their ability to commercialise the technologies their founders identified, developed and/or refined, or to go beyond the early stages and proceed in the technology transfer role. So their technological dynamism will only be fully expressed if other actors are involved. These actors include both established organisations and similar firms, who may be involved in the process of creation, or participate in the introduction of the new technology/ application, or act over time in a more or less symbiotic way with the young firm. There is ample evidence in the literature about the linkages that NTBFs establish with the environment, to compensate for their shortcomings (see, for example, Lawton-Smith, Dickson and Lloyd Smith, 1991; Roberts, 1991b; Rothwell and Dodgson, 1991; Saxenian, 1991; Van de Ven, 1993; McGee and Dowling, 1994; Mustar, 1994). Theorisation about the 'dynamic complementarity' between large and small firms (Rothwell, 1983, 1991), the emergence of the 'network organisation' (Miles and Snow, 1986), 'external growth' (Jarillo, 1989) and the social dimension of the emergence of new industries (Van de Ven and Garud, 1989), provides a more general framework that permits us to understand why their role can only be clearly expressed in a relational context. NTBFs are only one element of the process of technical and industrial change. Their ability to perform a role in such process depends on the presence of other elements, and on the relationship they are able to establish with them.

Technological Dynamism and Less Advanced Countries

A review of the literature found few studies (both Western and Asian) examining NTBFs in less advanced countries (see, for example, Senker, 1985; Kim, 1988; Ramos, 1989; Ayal and Raban, 1990; O'Doherty, 1990; Brunner, 1991; Sanchez, 1992; Valls, 1993) and even fewer references to the role of small technology-based firms in the development process. However, a careful analysis of these studies permits us to conclude that, in spite of the limited attention they receive, NTBFs in less advanced economies appear to have some potentialities, once a basic Science and Technology (S&T) infrastructure is present and some industrial development has occurred, thus permitting access to technological knowledge and the occurrence of market opportunities (Kim and Dahlman, 1992; Bell and Pavitt, 1993).

In fact, NTBFs emerged from most of these studies as firms showing great dynamism in technological terms, and with an innovative behaviour considerably above that of the 'average' local firm. Two particularly important components of their behaviour were their close interaction with the local S&T infrastructure, and their ability to access and absorb externally generated technology, adapting it to local needs. These features appeared to make them well suited to being one element in the process of gaining early competences in emerging technologies, in the 'catching-up' mode suggested by Perez and Soete (1988). However, the technological sophistication of the firms seemed to be largely a function of the sophistication of the markets: that is, more advanced firms will be more likely to emerge only when the market is receptive to them (Kim, 1988). This gives particular relevance to the role of government policies. Because the industrial structure is often weak and deficient in technological terms, and technological and market opportunities are not ample – or at least are not perceived as such by potential entrepreneurs – some support or even incentive for NTBFs creation and early establishment will be required (Kim, 1988; Ramos, 1989).

These results suggest that NTBFs 'technological dynamism' can be equally relevant in less advanced economies and that they can play an important role both as technology challengers and as technology disseminators. However, while the firms themselves are likely to be relatively similar to their counterparts in more developed countries, the conditions prevalent in the context where they operate imply that the way their roles are performed, and their impact on the country development, are likely to be different.

In performing these roles, NTBFs can have an important function acquiring, absorbing and diffusing (at country level) technologies from diverse sources, both local and foreign. Given the background and linkages of their founders, they can be a mechanism to exploit some of the new technological knowledge being developed by, or accessed through, the local scientific and technical infrastructure, which would not be directly used by established firms. They can thus contribute to a greater industrial orientation and usefulness of public research (which frequently accounts for most R&D undertaken at country level). On the other hand, NTBFs can also function as channels to technology generated in more advanced environments. They may convey new knowledge and technology into the country, eventually combining it with existing skills, and apply it in the development of new products (which can be similar to others existing elsewhere, or truly innovative applications). In doing that, they are contributing to the country's effective appropriation of the technology (Jevons and Saupin, 1991). When these activities impact upon sectors where the country has already gained some competence, they may bring about the formation of integrated clusters of development and even contribute to the creation of a pool of distinct competences in particular fields (Andersen and Lundvall, 1988; Carlsson and Stankiewicz, 1991).

THE CREATION OF NEW TECHNOLOGY-BASED FIRMS

The Process of Firm Creation

Firm creation can be regarded as a process of resource acquisition where capabilities, technology and funds are drawn, involving several sources and interveners (Smilor and Feeser, 1991; Van de Ven, 1993). This process is 'orchestrated' by the founders, who are often the major driving force behind creation (Oakey, Rothwell and Cooper, 1988). The founders are by no means the sole participants in this process, and the network of relationships they establish is crucial for firm launch and early operation (Larson and Starr, 1993; Lipparini and Sobrero, 1994). In the case of NTBF creation, a plurality of roles and of actors performing them has been identified (Kenney, 1986; Fairtlough, 1992; Autio, 1994). Some of these actors share the entrepreneurial role with the founder(s), having a determinant impact on firms' early life.

The view of NTBF creation that results from these approaches – a process involving several actors from different origins, establishing both a diversity of relationships between them and with the environment – denotes it as a strongly context-related process (Van de Ven, 1993; Gnyawali and Fogel, 1994). Therefore, their emergence in a given context depends on its ability to generate the 'inputs' – environmental conditions, actors and linkages – necessary for the creation of a technology-based firm. It can be further argued that the characteristics of the actors and of their relationships shape the organisation being formed and have a decisive influence on its evolution.

The 'Inputs' to New Technology Based Firm Creation

Technology-related 'inputs' – at the level of supply and demand – are likely to be predominant in the creation of NTBFs. In fact, looking at the process through which most of them emerge, it is possible to argue that their founders (and other actors in the creation process) identify and exploit technological opportunities that are being ignored or neglected by existing organisations. In doing that they are, to some extent, 'internalising' into a new organisation the externalities generated in the process of creation and diffusion of knowledge and technology. These externalities may assume the form of public knowledge – a 'public good' more or less widely available – or of more localised knowledge, only accessible to the interveners in a particular context (Dosi, 1988). While in the first case it may be procured by 'outsiders', in the latter, immersion in the environment where it is generated is indispensable. Therefore,

(a) the more extensive the externalities generated in a particular context, the greater the potential for technological opportunities to emerge;
(b) the wider the number of people exposed to the sources from which these opportunities emanate, the higher the probability that they will be identified and that an innovative idea will emerge.

Finally, the chances of turning that idea into a successful business will depend on the presence of a technology-oriented demand.

Countries vary with regard to their ability to provide the technological inputs that are critical to NTBF creation (Freeman, 1988; Bell and Pavitt, 1993). The presence of activities that produce advanced knowledge (Perez and Soete, 1988) – generating 'externalities' and people endowed with the skills necessary to profit from them – the multiplicity of channels through which information circulates (Oakey and White, 1993) and the level of demand for technology-intensive products (Dahlman and Westphal, 1982), are likely to differentiate between more and less advanced countries, making the environment less favourable to NTBF creation in the latter. In other words, a less complete and integrated 'national system of innovation' (Lundvall, 1988) can limit the emergence of technological opportunities as well as the circumstances where these opportunities are identified and exploited. On the other hand it may create 'gaps', and hence provide opportunities for new firms to fill these gaps, that will not exist in more advanced contexts.

NEW TECHNOLOGY-BASED FIRMS AND TECHNOLOGY ACQUISITION

The Nature of Firms' Technology Acquisition

To be able to perform their 'technology transfer role' over time, NTBFs need to go on developing and upgrading their initial technology base, and building up firm-specific competences (Pavitt, 1991). To achieve it, the firms need to ensure that they access advanced knowledge and technology, both generating it internally and establishing links with relevant external sources. However, NTBFs are small firms with scarce resources, both human and financial, and this dichotomy – scarcity of resources and the need to invest strongly in the acquisition of knowledge and technology – is a major problem.

The analysis of the literature on knowledge and technology acquisition by NTBFs permits a generic picture of their acquisition activities to be devised. With respect to internal acquisition activities, they are systematically described as:

(a) firms with limited resources, which will sometimes mean small teams, part-time activities and informality of organisation, as well as tight budgets (Oakey, Rothwell and Cooper, 1988; Littler and Sweeting, 1990);
(b) relatively specialised firms, although they are likely to exhibit a strong technology base in some fields where their competence is based (Meyer and Roberts, 1988; Pavia, 1990).

A potential problem is that scarce resources associated with a narrow specialisation may affect firms' ability to expand their technology base and absorb externally acquired technology. Finally, NTBFs are frequently less strong in non-technological areas, revealing some deficiencies at the level of business skills (Oakey, Rothwell and Cooper, 1988; Roberts, 1991b).

Given firms' internal constraints, external acquisition is likely to be indispensable to complement their in-house competences. Therefore the ability to access and use externally generated knowledge and to achieve complementarities with other organisations are critical (Rothwell and Dodgson, 1991; McGee and Dowling, 1994). Firms will have different requirements, which call for different inputs and different sources. However, a number of characteristics seem to be common to most NTBFs, namely that:

(a) they favour collaboration;
(b) they use informal know-how trading extensively;
(c) they give great importance to sophisticated suppliers (in some areas);
(d) they use technological linkages also as a means to access other skills and assets they do not possess (e.g., in areas such as production or marketing);
(e) they fear links with large firms, but may need them, in which case they often trade technological knowledge for access to complementary assets.

Finally, NTBFs – as compared with other small innovative firms – have a number of particularities that facilitate external acquisition. The origin and background of founders may facilitate insertion in knowledge/technology networks (Mustar, 1994), and the firms' strong and sometimes unique competences may raise the interest of other organisations in collaboration and be a passport to admission into international networks (Lawton-Smith, Dickson and Lloyd Smith 1991).

Conditions of Technology Access in Less Advanced Countries

Given the relevance assumed by external sourcing, location in more munificent environments – where firms can profit from the easier access to sources of knowledge and technology and from the synergies provided by the 'agglomeration effect' – is an advantage for NTBFs (Saxenian, 1991). Therefore, firms in less advanced countries have 'locational disadvantages', due to the deficiencies of the national system of innovation and their peripheral position in relation to the places where useful 'externalities' are generated (Perez and Soete, 1988). This makes the access to knowledge, embodied technology and human resources more difficult, limits the pulling effect of advanced consumer requirements, and impedes synergies with similar firms. Firms can try to obtain some of these inputs elsewhere, but may incur high costs in doing so. This problem is especially serious for small firms, whose scarce resources make it difficult to undertake extensive searches and expensive dislocations (O'Doherty, 1993; Feldman, 1994).

Despite the absence of research into technology access by NTBFs in these environments, it is possible to assume that such access is constrained by the conditions in which knowledge and technology are generated locally. First of all, less advanced countries inevitably develop proficiency in a limited number of fields, with a consequent impact on the range of expertise available (Walsh, 1987). This will have consequences both in terms of firms' internal acquisition – since it will restrict the level and type of skills and knowledge brought by the founders and possessed by the staff recruited – and in terms of external acquisition. Furthermore, given the conditions in which researchers in these contexts define their priorities – research conducted by academic organisations often follows international patterns and researchers are externally oriented (Walsh, 1987) – it is possible that a substantial part of the knowledge generated locally does not match the requirements of local firms, and that local researchers have little interest in collaborating with them (Balazs and Plonski, 1994).

The reduced presence of industrial participants in the process of technology generation, and the lack of technological awareness prevalent among a substantial number of firms (OECD, 1993), also hampers NTBFs, limiting the extent of technological linkages they can establish with other companies. Therefore, these firms will have few opportunities for industrial R&D collaboration, and will miss the interaction with suppliers (as sources of technology) and with customers (as providers of advanced requirements), being deprived of the learning opportunities provided by close user-supplier relationships (Andersen and Lundvall, 1988).

The limitations of the local context may lead firms to try to access knowledge and technology generated elsewhere. Assuming that, as with similar firms elsewhere, they rely strongly on sophisticated suppliers as sources of advanced embodied technology (Oakey, Rothwell and Cooper, 1988; Valls, 1993), the ability to access foreign suppliers of advanced inputs will be critical, given the deficiencies of the national markets (Kim, 1988; Lemola and Lovio, 1988). With respect to collaboration, firms in small economies will often seek partners abroad, due to the restricted and highly competitive nature of the national markets (O'Doherty, 1993). However, access to the international networks where collaborative R&D is carried out and information circulates is difficult for small firms (Dodgson, 1992). Participation in international collaborative projects (particularly in the European environment) has been suggested as a way into these networks; this route is available to firms which can offer unique knowledge and skills and thus are able to utilise the interest of large firms and research organisations in finding partners to comply with programme regulations (Dodgson, 1992; Valls, 1993). This alternative, however, should be approached with care, since it may lead to forms of 'exploitation' by large firms from more advanced countries, with little profit for the weaker firm/country (Walsh, 1987).

The above conclusions concerning the potential implications of the conditions prevailing in less advanced countries regarding technology acquisition obviously need to be tested on the basis of an analysis of the actual behaviour of NTBFs operating in these contexts. This will allow us to evaluate whether these limitations apply, and especially what are the firms' responses to the constraints they face at these levels.

THEORY-DERIVED HYPOTHESIS

The review and critical analysis of the relevant literature, and the subsequent conceptualisation of them, permitted us to reach the following conclusions.

1. NTBF creation is a context-related process. Since conditions differ according to the characteristics of the environment where this process occurs, it is argued that such creation depends on the ability of a context to generate a number of 'inputs' – environmental conditions, actors and linkages – that are defined as necessary to the emergence of this type of firm.
2. NTBF creation is based on the identification and exploitation of technological opportunities ignored or neglected by existing organisations. Therefore the likelihood that an innovative idea will emerge and be converted into a successful business will depend on the prevailing conditions with respect to the generation of technological opportunities, peoples exposure to the sources from which they emanate, and the presence of a technology-oriented demand. It is thus possible to argue that technology-related 'inputs'– at the level of supply and demand – are predominant in the creation of NTBFs.
3. Countries vary with regard to their ability to provide these technological inputs. A less complete and integrated 'national system of innovation' can limit the emergence of technological opportunities as well as the circumstances where these opportunities can be identified and exploited through the creation of an NTBF. But, on the other hand, it may create 'gaps', and

hence provide opportunities for new firms to fill these gaps, which might not exist in more advanced contexts. Deficiencies in the national system of innovation can also constrain the firms' subsequent evolution, making it particularly difficult for these firms to continue acquiring knowledge and technology, to find markets to absorb the results of their technological efforts and to establish complementarities with other organisations, in order to compensate for their insufficiencies.

4. The main feature of NTBFs is their 'technological dynamism', which invests them with two major roles: a 'challenging role', implicit in the act of their creation, whereby they break with the inertia of existing organisations; and a more long standing 'technology transfer role', acting as the source of the new technologies they acquire and deliver by several means. However, NTBFs have intrinsic limitations in terms of resources and capabilities, and thus their technological dynamism can only be fully exercised if other actors are involved.

5. Technological dynamism can be particularly relevant for less advanced countries, where NTBFs can be an important element in the 'catching-up' process. They may have a critical role in the access to new technological knowledge – both generated by the local scientific and technological infrastructure and obtained from more advanced countries – and in its transfer to the market, contributing to the development of indigenous capabilities in the new technologies and their application. A number of conditions are nevertheless necessary for this role to be played: the presence of some basic competences in the field; enough demand for sophisticated products;and supporting policies.

This conceptual framework allowed us to hypothesise that NTBFs created in less advanced economies resemble NTBFs created elsewhere, at the level of the characteristics that are intrinsic to the status of small firms founded by technologically-oriented people. However, their behaviour in these contexts is likely to be influenced by the weaknesses of the countries' systems of innovation, at the level of the factors with greatest impact upon their activities: the supply of and the demand for technology.

Therefore, the environment where NTBFs are created and operate may introduce some specificities concerning: rate of creation, type of firm created, innovative behaviour and roles played.

METHODOLOGY

The empirical search for evidence about the hypothesis presented above was carried out in the Portuguese context. Therefore one basic objective of the research was to evaluate whether and to what extent did the Portuguese firms differ from NTBFs elsewhere, and to understand the reasons behind the eventual differences. Two further objectives were:

(a) to evaluate the influence of the conditions found in an environment like the Portuguese one on NTBF creation, as well as the adaptations required for such firms to survive and evolve in this particular environment;
(b) to identify the roles that can be played by this type of firm in a less advanced economy.

In order to fulfil these objectives, and on the basis of the indications provided by the conceptual framework devised above, the focus of research was directed to two major issues:

(a) the process of firm creation;
(b) the analysis of the ways in which NTBFs acquire, develop and deliver the technology.

A definition of an NTBF was devised for the purpose of this research, namely: 'young independent firms involved in the development and/or diffusion of new technologies'. According to this, the firms studied satisfied the following criteria:

(a) newness: between one and fifteen years old (referring to 1991);
(b) independence: launched by individual entrepreneurs;
(c) technology base: created to exploit a new technology, including firms developing frontier technologies and their early applications and firms using them to create new or substantially improved products or services.

Most firms studied operated in fields which can be broadly included under the 'information technologies' umbrella. Biotechnology/speciality chemicals firms were excluded, given the very low incidence of firm creation in these areas in Portugal, and considering that firms in these fields are substantially different from ones based on information technology.

The characteristics of the problem being addressed suggested the adoption of an exploratory approach, drawing on the findings obtained for NTBFs in other contexts, but maintaining the flexibility necessary to identify the aspects peculiar to the context being studied. Such an exploratory approach called for the extensive use of qualitative research methods, which would permit an in-depth comprehension of the complex phenomenon being investigated (Van Maanen, 1979). It also recommended the division of the research into phases, where a less structured approach would be followed at the outset, an attempt being made to achieve a greater focus and to increase the level of formality in subsequent stages (Morton-Williams, 1977).

A combination of methods was therefore used to collect the empirical data. The identification of the population of Portuguese NTBFs required an intensive search, since information about this type of firm had not been systematically collected before. A first characterisation of the population was carried out, using a generic questionnaire survey, whose results also assisted in the selection of candidates for the subsequent research. Given the limited knowledge about these firms' behaviour in Portugal, a two-stage approach was adopted for the main body of research:

(a) a preliminary exploration was carried out on the basis of unstructured interviews with a small group of firms, which provided some orientations to the next stage;
(b) more detailed information was sought, using in-depth semi-structured interviews with a subsample of firms.

The choice of the semi-structured interview as the main data collection instrument was based on the opportunity it provides to explore the interviewee's views and attitudes, while keeping some structure in the way the data is collected and thus allowing for comparability among cases. Concerning the research, a balance was sought between depth and variety. The option of purposive sampling does not enable us to claim to represent the entire population of firms, but the inclusion of a variety of cases increased the generalisability of the findings.

The main body of research presented in this chapter is therefore based on detailed interviews with 28 NTBFs and five young technology-based subsidiaries of existing companies (used for comparative purposes), selected among the 123 firms that answered to the questionnaire (65 per cent response rate). The interviews were conducted between 1991 and 1993. About one-half of the firms were the object of more than one interview at different time periods, permitting us to follow their evolution over time.

The research was based on the following premises. In analysing the ways in which the firms' founders identified the opportunities, acquired the technology, converted it into marketable products or services and brought them to the market, an attempt was made to evaluate whether they were performing the 'challenging role' and which particular forms it assumed in that context. In analysing the ways in which operating NTBFs went on upgrading and expanding their initial technology base, building up firm specific competences and passing the results of their activities to the market, an attempt was made to evaluate whether they carried out the 'technology transfer role' and the difficulties they found in its performance.

THE CHALLENGING ROLE: THE PROCESS OF FIRM CREATION

According to the framework defined above, the challenging role is expressed in the process of creation of a new firm, which breaks with the inertia of existing organisations and introduces new ways of doing things. The creation of NTBFs is seen as a process through which technological opportunities are identified, and new technology is acquired, developed and turned into new applications that can then be taken to the market. This section addresses the conditions in which this process takes place in the Portuguese context.

The Identification of the Opportunity and the Acquisition of the Technology

Most Portuguese founders of technology-based firms followed a typical path of development. They identified a technological opportunity directly through their previous work and used the knowledge and skills acquired there to form the technology base of the new firm. In some cases, they even transferred a substantial part of the technology from the source organisation. This was the current situation among founders originating from research centres, and also in the case of a few founders originating from the electronics industry. However, in several cases, the technological opportunity was not identified directly through the founders' previous work, but through other, (more indirect) sources:

(a) on the basis of exposure to more technologically advanced sources (national or foreign), sometimes at least partly accessed through channels provided by the ex-employer;
(b) on the basis of the identification of a need – felt by the ex-employer or its clients – that was the basis for a search for new technological solutions, sometimes involving a substantial deviation from the fields where founders used to work.

Thus existing knowledge and skills, although important, could be of limited use, the founders often being required to acquire or develop considerably newer ones. These cases were more frequent among founders originating from industry.

The latter situation seems to be peculiar to the Portuguese context, being related to the local firms' relatively low technological level and dependence on external technology, and generally to the gaps in the Portuguese national system of innovation. It points to a limited role for Portuguese companies as technological 'incubators', and simultaneously reveals the important role assumed by technology obtained elsewhere: that is, from local research organisations (for industry-based founders) and/or from foreign sources. In fact, some founders were able to identify and gain access to technology being developed in a research environment and acted as agents of its transfer to the market. Others went beyond the local environment to identify opportunities, establishing their firms on the basis of knowledge or technologies obtained abroad through a diversity of means, including:

(a) knowledge and skills acquired through post-graduate research or work abroad;
(b) exposure to emerging knowledge through less tangible means (publications, international meetings, personal contacts);
(c) direct contact with foreign organisations.

Very often the outcome was a situation where technology and knowledge from different origins were combined, synthesised and exploited. This process was facilitated by the skills the founders had gained in their previous employment, but drew extensively on foreign sources.

The creation of firms strongly based on technological influences originating abroad can be seen as a way to overcome the country's limitations with respect to the generation of knowledge and technology. Some of these firms have indeed acted as pioneers, contributing to the introduction of new technologies in the Portuguese context, or at least guaranteeing their commercial exploitation (some of the technologies involved were not completely new at academic level but, given the approach of some academic organisations, it was very unlikely that transfer to the industry would have occurred through them (at least in the near future). Because of the structural gaps in the Portuguese national system of innovation, firms will possibly continue to be launched in fields scarcely exploited in Portugal, although it is possible to perceive, among more recent founders, a tendency to target fields where some expertise already exists locally. Some research-based firms, launched in the late 1980s, can be said to have performed a more 'relative' pioneering role: they carried out the first introduction of a new technology, which was not yet available at market level, but which was at least partly developed in a local research centre. The development of stronger local competences in a number of fields, which is currently under way (Marques and Laranja, 1994), can provide a seedbed for new firms and thus make more common this type of 'relative' pioneering, as compared to the 'absolute' one described above. Despite this, there still appears to be a role for the 'absolute' pioneer, despite the problems this posture may bring to the new firm.

Achieving Market Demand

Demand is a crucial element for the survival and growth of the new firm, and it was at this level that several of the firms interviewed confronted their greatest problems. Portuguese NTBFs not only faced the normal difficulties experienced by new firms attempting market entry, but were also hindered by the characteristics of the market they were addressing. The combination of limited demand for technology-based products and lack of trust in its local suppliers constituted a serious drawback for young firms trying to introduce advanced applications (Coombs and Fontes, 1993). It was particularly grievous in the late 1970s/early 1980s, when some older firms were created. One of the major problems confronted by these Portuguese firms is that the number of organisations prepared to quickly recognise the advantages of the products they commercialise – thus becoming early adopters – is relatively small. In general, the limited number of large and technologically advanced companies, with whom 'dynamic complementarities' (Rothwell, 1983) can be achieved – which are a powerful impulse to the activities of this type of firm in other contexts – is a real constraint to the development of the Portuguese ones.

In spite of the incontestable difficulties created by the conditions of the Portuguese market, if opportunities had not been identified at this level, most founders would not have decided to launch their firms. In fact, the Portuguese environment did generate some opportunities for small technology-oriented firms, although it also raised obstacles to their exploitation. These opportunities were often based on 'gaps' in the Portuguese national system of innovation, such as:

(a) problems in the supply of some sophisticated components, systems or services that existed elsewhere but which it was difficult for local firms to access, or which were represented by agents who lacked competence to solve complex customisation problems;

(b) the identification of particular needs of local firms willing to upgrade their technological level, whose requirements could be better met on the basis of customised development of products and systems, combined with some 'technological consultancy';

(c) the absolute absence of some product or service (i.e., the identification of a new need that led to the development of a product or service to satisfy it).

The type of opportunity identified had implications in terms of the receptivity of the potential market. Most firms were oriented to non-consumer markets (industrial or public) and ended up targeting one of two types of clients, namely more technologically-advanced companies whose needs were not being satisfied by the local market, or less advanced companies willing to upgrade (or presumed to be). The firms interviewed had different degrees of success with each group, which may help to explain the market difficulties faced by some of them.

Firms that were able to target niches composed of more sophisticated users experienced fewer problems, since their clients revealed some interest in novel solutions incorporating advanced technologies and were willing to buy them from local suppliers. A few of these clients could be described as 'lead-users' (von Hippel, 1986b), as they:

- absorbed a relevant part of firms' production
- acted as a test bed for the product
- contributed ideas, suggestions and (more rarely) technical inputs

These 'early adopters' were willing to try the products/services being introduced and their demand was crucial for the new firm, if this early adoption of products by a responsive customer eased the initial steps, it then guaranteed a continuing demand, as some firms later realised.

The objective of assisting the upgrading of less advanced companies met with less success. Firms addressing these clients were among those experiencing the most serious problems, with some being forced to move away from their initial markets, or to address others in parallel. Therefore, although the diffusion of advanced technology to less developed segments of the economy is crucial, and although a small technology-intensive firm may be better prepared than foreign suppliers to adjust the technology to the customer needs (given its flexibility and proximity to the user), it is also true that a small and relatively unknown firm may find it difficult to penetrate markets composed of companies with limited awareness of technology requisites, low internal capabilities, and often evidencing an absolute lack of trust in national producers. The realisation of such endeavour is clearly beyond the means of a few small firms, their efforts being mostly ineffective if not adequately backed.

Therefore, while some firms were able to find early clients with a steady demand for their products, others faced serious troubles with regard to market acceptance of the technologies they were introducing. Some of the latter were finally able to open a market after long 'desert-crossings', but others were forced to change more or less decisively the contents of their activities, in order to adjust them to the reality they were confronted with. These 'adjustments' – which indicate remarkable survival capabilities – included cases where:

(a) firms were forced to move to another activity;
(b) firms persisted in their chosen business, but were forced to alter the character of their products, 'downgrading' them to conform to the effective needs of their potential clients, or to undertake other (usually less sophisticated) activities in parallel.

On the other hand, some initially successful firms were later confronted with constraints derived from the limited market demand when required to replace the early lead-users, or when envisaging further growth.

The conditions at the level of demand made the creation and survival of NTBFs particularly difficult in the Portuguese context. However, the firms' intrinsic weaknesses may have contributed to an aggravation of the problems experienced by some of them. The conditions of the Portuguese environment might have called for even better marketing skills and for strategies targeted to the particular country circumstances. With a few exceptions, firms' founders had technical rather than business backgrounds, few marketing skills and little experience. On the other hand, strategies based on role models derived from more advanced countries were found to be relatively widespread, especially among the early founders, which pioneered the introduction of technologies emerging elsewhere in a still very closed and unaware market (Fontes, 1995a). It has to be recognised that without the drive and willingness to run risks revealed by these founders (which led us to label their approach 'missionary') the introduction of some technologies would have been slower and based on a greater dependence on imported technology, as opposed to indigenous development. However, their approach often failed to take into account the differences between the initial environments in which the technologies originated and the Portuguese one; in Portugal, supportive 'incubator' organisations, venture capital, large advanced clients and public procurement, as well as effective government policies, were generally missing. The fact that the type of organisation adopted – the NTBF – was itself an 'imported' organisational innovation, 'grafted' to a different environment, did not improve matters. In particular, the pioneers' approach to the market often neglected the profound technological and cultural gap between the local customers and those available to NTBFs in other economies. This prevented them from realising that, to reach their potential clients, they needed to conduct their activities in a different way. Such a perspective emerged with time and experience, and sometimes only after the firms were confronted with difficulties they had not anticipated.

The experience of the earlier pioneers was an important input for the subsequent founders, inducing less idealised views and more careful attitudes. As a result, most of the latter either were less prone to introduce very new technologies or, when they did introduce them, made sure that their move was adequately backed (e.g., by a good capital structure, the presence of other actors providing complementary assets or enhancing the firms' credibility, and the early identification of lead-users). Alternatively they followed a step by step approach, entering the market with less sophisticated products or a less demanding activity, with a view to upgrading them over time, evolving with their clients and benefiting from their growing trust; this approach had also been adopted by a few early pioneers, more aware of the conditions they were likely to face due to their better knowledge of the Portuguese market. Nevertheless, even when these more 'prudent' strategies were adopted, firms in some fields were still confronted with difficulties. More adequate strategies and several forms of external backing – which multiplied with time – were found to afford firms better conditions to persist in their efforts or to achieve eventual adjustments, but the demand conditions still make the creation of an NTBF a complex undertaking.

The Difficulties Associated with New Technology-Based Firm Creation in Portugal

The conclusion that can be derived from the analysis of the creation process is that Portuguese NTBFs have undoubtedly performed the challenging role hypothesised above.

1. Their founders identified technological opportunities not being profited from by existing organisations, and created innovative organisations to exploit them.

2. They acquired and developed new technologies not yet available in the country (or not used at industrial level) and took them to the market in the form of innovative products or services.
3. Their efforts were important from the country's standpoint, since the firms' active involvement in the development of the technologies (as opposed to simple purchase) permitted the endogenisation of competences, thus contributing to an increase in the country's technological capabilities.

However, several founders experienced great difficulties in the performance of such roles, which perhaps was inevitable. In fact, the Portuguese environment does not create particularly favourable conditions for NTBFs at the level of the factors that are critical to their emergence:

(a) technological opportunities are not extensively generated;
(b) the possibilities to gain advanced skills which permit the identification and exploitation of these opportunities are not abundant;
(c) the low demand for technology-based products does not lead to many market opportunities;
(d) important elements are still missing among the mechanisms to stimulate would-be entrepreneurs (e.g., there are several incubators, but venture capital is scarce);
(e) there are few large technology-based companies prepared to sponsor the creation of technologically-oriented firms, or to act in ways that complement their efforts.

Therefore, it is not unexpected that, in spite of the attempts registered over a period of time to create more favourable conditions at the level of support to creation, NTBFs are still relatively few. Whilst there was an effective increase in NTBF formation in the late 1980s/early 1990s – which can be explained by the development of support mechanisms combined with a period of economic boom – their numbers have not increased considerably. Besides, the ensuing recession appears to have held up this process, and has even forced a number of NTBFs (including some firms which were part of this research) to close down or to accept acquisition. The incidence of problematic situations and the absence of cases of resounding success may have acted as *negative* role models. In addition, except for some 'pockets' where firms were created on the basis of local competence development in a given field, they tend to be relatively isolated, which makes their efforts less effective.

Therefore, if the importance of NTBFs as 'challengers' is accepted and their promotion is envisaged, it may be necessary to act at levels that go beyond the simple mechanisms to support new firm launch. If the basic

elements in the creation of NTBFs are the emergence of technological opportunities, the presence of people with the capacity to identify them, and
market opportunities which will allow them to turn into successful businesses, any intervention, to be effective, should be oriented to the root of
the problem: the supply of (and especially the demand for) technology.

THE TECHNOLOGY TRANSFER ROLE: ACQUISITION, ABSORPTION AND DISSEMINATION OF TECHNOLOGY BY NEW TECHNOLOGY-BASED FIRMS

An examination of the ways in which the Portuguese NTBFs acquired and
absorbed knowledge and technology and passed the results of their efforts
to the market was carried out in order to evaluate whether and how they
performed a technology transfer role. This section addresses the process of
technology acquisition and dissemination, and analyses the difficulties
the firms faced in achieving it.

Acquisition versus Dissemination: The Strengths and Weaknesses of New Technology-Based Firms

It was found that the ability of NTBFs to perform the technology transfer
role varied. Being associated with continuity of innovative performance,
it required firms to be successful in the introduction of the new products, to
survive as technology-intensive firms and to go on acquiring and developing new technologies and transferring them to the market. Firms showed
different behaviours with respect to this issue, which can be explained by
their diverse proficiency regarding two domains: technology and the market.

As a rule, NTBFs were found to be more efficient as technology
acquirers than as technology disseminators. Most of the firms studied were
able to continue acting as agents of technology acquisition, absorption and
development over time. Despite the difficulties they sometimes experienced in identifying and obtaining the necessary knowledge and technology, as well as the constraints imposed by the scarce internal resources,
the firms interviewed developed a variety of acquisition strategies and
practices, which corresponded to adaptive responses to the conditions of
their environment (a more detailed discussion of firms' internal and external acquisition strategies and practices is presented in Fontes, 1995b). The
older firms, which frequently originated in technological fields where
expertise did not exist locally, experienced the greatest difficulties. They

often went through long and relatively solitary learning processes, concerning the development of in-house competences and the establishment of a network of relevant relationships, with foreign linkages usually being privileged. The younger firms frequently benefited from the development of national competences in some fields which, directly or indirectly, facilitated access to complementary knowledge.

With respect to the dissemination aspect, firms exhibited a greater variety of behaviours. While most firms were able to convert the technology into marketable applications and make them available to a small set of advanced users, only a few could be said to have achieved their diffusion beyond this relatively limited number of informed clients. The reasons behind different market performances have already been addressed in the previous section. As was the case with the early product introduction, firms were confronted with markets showing diverse levels of resistance to the new technologies/products being commercialised, and revealed different degrees of proficiency in addressing them. In time, some firms which had been relatively successful in finding early users for their products were also able to extend their activities to a growing number of clients, while some less successful ones were finally able to get established in the market, after long 'desert-crossings' or arduous adjustments. However, several firms continued to experience difficulties with respect to the market acceptance of their products. Others, which had an early success with a few 'lead-users', were later confronted with difficulties in expanding their initial market or in replacing the first clients, given the gap between them and the wider market.

Although the firms went through a learning process – which permitted them to gain some marketing skills and experience and to establish their strategies for the complex markets they were addressing – and although the environment conditions also registered some improvements (particularly in some fields), the market remained a problematic area for Portuguese NTBFs. Even relatively successful firms were sooner or later confronted with the limits of the Portuguese market: if growth was envisaged, internationalisation was a requirement. This situation frequently occurs to NTBFs, given the 'niche' character of their markets, and is inevitable in small economies (Freeman, 1988; O'Doherty, 1990). However, Portuguese NTBFs attempting foreign expansion were confronted with both the resource problems common to small firms everywhere *and* the 'low-tech' image of Portugal in international trade, which made it difficult to accept Portuguese firms as technology-intensive producers. The number of firms that developed sophisticated products eventually found some initial market for them – usually among a few more advanced clients

– but realised that they would not be able to survive only on the basis of that activity. In addition, they also realised that they could not grow on the basis of the local market, suggesting that demand problems are likely to be a 'fact of life' for most Portuguese NTBFs. Therefore, this is something that founders should envisage and be prepared to deal with.

The constraints faced at the level of the demand may also have repercussions on firms' efforts concerning knowledge and technology acquisition. The limited market success can restrict firms' capacity to continue upgrading and expanding their technological competences, thus reducing the impact of their efforts at this level. These continued market difficulties may threaten firms' survival or force them to reconvert their activities, which represents a loss of expertise in country terms. While some were able to retain the more advanced component of their activity in parallel to those activities 'downgraded' to adjust to the conditions of the market, a few completely reconverted their activities, thus losing part of their competences.

It is possible to conclude that the major strength of Portuguese NTBFs lies in their ability to acquire, absorb and transform new technology, making the results of their efforts available to a set of more aware users, who might have experienced greater difficulties in accessing it if these firms did not exist. A few firms also contributed to a wider dissemination of that technology, but even these had a set of advanced clients, which often formed the core of their client portfolio. Given the relevance of NTBFs as acquirers of technology and the role they play in the development of national capabilities in their area of activity, it seems pertinent to describe in more detail the most salient aspects of their contribution in this field.

New Technology-Based Firms as Acquirers, Synthesisers and Developers of New Technology

As was pointed out above, most firms continued to be involved in the acquisition and development of new technology, with more or less intensity, over time. However, the forms assumed by these activities were diverse, as was their impact. The research examining the process of technology acquisition by Portuguese NTBFs led us to conclude that the type of linkages the firms had established with their environment was one differentiating aspect, since it influenced both the ways firms accessed technological knowledge and their ability to share it with other organisations. The identification of different behaviours led to the definition of a typology of firms (Figure 4.1), based on their relationship with the external environment. The basic factors behind this classification were:

- the type of technological linkages firms had established at start-up and their evolution
- the role firms attributed to relationships with external sources of techno- logy

---

SYMBIOTIC

Firms with a 'symbiotic' relationship with a source of science and technology/since start-up, which they use extensively to leverage their capabilities in core areas (fre- quently spin-offs from research).

LINK+

Firms with a privileged link with a source of science and/or technology since start-up or early years, which supplements in-house capabilities in fields where these are weaker.

INDEPENDENT

Firms that rely largely on their in-house capabilities, and use a variety of formal and informal links with local sources in an 'opportunistic' basis, to acquire skills and/or knowledge, which complement their own.

AUTONOMOUS

Firms whose relationships with local sources are weak or virtually absent, either be- cause competences do not exist locally, or because firms are unable to access them and have therefore built an extensive in-house autonomy. Firms which considered it essential to complement in-house activities with external inputs have sought expertise elsewhere, either by using local contacts to gain access to foreign sources, or by integrating international networks, generating a major subgroup: the Autonomous- Integrating.

Figure 4.1 Typology of firms according to their technological relationships

This typology will be used to support the discussion about the functions per- formed by NTBFs regarding the technology acquisition dimension (for more details about the generation of this typology and the characteristics of each type, see Fontes and Coombs, 1995). The functions performed by Portuguese NTBFs as vehicles of technology acquisition (which will be subsequently used to encompass also the absorption and development elements) can be de- scribed along two major lines:

(a) transferring knowledge and technology from local academic research to the market;

(b) acquiring and absorbing technological knowledge developed outside the country and turning it into national competences.

A further function these firms perform concerns the increasing concentration of the techno-industrial network in their field of activity, encompassing technology acquisition and its dissemination through the establishment of different forms of collaboration with similar technology-intensive organisations, and the creation of close user-supplier relationships with advanced suppliers and progressive users.

Transfer of Technology Between Local Research and the Industry

Several firms were created on the basis of transfer of results from academic research, while others were able to establish linkages with research organisations, either at start-up or over time. The relationships thus established – whether of an 'organic' type like the 'Symbiotic' firms, or more occasional like the 'Independent' ones – represented a 'short-circuit' to the laborious and frequently ineffectual process of transfer between the two worlds, thus representing an important achievement of NTBFs. These links favoured the transfer of a variety of tangible and intangible inputs among organisations, with benefits for both groups. They contributed to a leverage of the individual efforts of every participant, with a positive impact on the overall capabilities at country level. Table 4.1 summarises the more relevant impacts identified, and the relative role played by every type of firm.

The *bridge* that was established between the two environments permitted more than the immediate movement of information or technological knowledge. It also allowed a certain *adjustment* as industrial companies became better able to define their requirements and therefore to gain access to inputs that met their needs more precisely, and research organisations had a window on market requirements (which was helpful in defining research directions more appropriate to the needs of local industry). Sometimes, firms' particular needs led research organisations to address fields neglected up to then, thus filling a 'gap' at country level. More generally, the development of a common language facilitated further relationships with similar organisations.

Finally, links with local research organisations were important as channels to foreign sources. Even some 'Autonomous' firms, which held that links with research organisations were not very useful, ended up recognising their relevance to access inputs originating from outside the target organisations, but accessible through them.

Table 4.1   Transfer between academic research and industry

	Symbiotic	Link+	Independent	Autonomous
Preferential relationships: keep a channel open between organisations permitting movement of information, knowledge and people (both ways)	H	H	–	–
Occasional contacts: greater use of research inputs by industry; increased awareness of research organisations about industry needs and market requirements	L	M	H	L
Creation of bridge between two different environments permitting development of common language, which facilitates further contacts	H	H	H	L
Presence of firms operating in a field stimulates research organisations to re-orient research to its development	–	–	M	M
Local research organisations act as channels to foreign sources, where other inputs can be obtained	H	H	M	M

H – High impact or very frequent.
M – Medium impact or less frequent.
L – Low impact or infrequent.

Accessing and Absorbing Foreign Technology

A second fundamental role performed by NTBFs entailed acquiring and absorbing technological knowledge developed outside the country and turning it into national competences. This process involved:

(a) accessing technological knowledge not available in the Portuguese context (or whose development was not carried out with an industrial orientation);
(b) achieving a synthesis between knowledge obtained elsewhere and knowledge and skills developed locally, with the firms (or their founders) functioning as the 'meeting point' and the 'integrator' for inputs coming from several origins (local research, local industry and from abroad).

In gaining competences in these 'absent' technologies, and in applying them in the development of products or services (often oriented to the needs of the local market), as opposed to simply purchasing and using them, NTBFs acted as agents of their endogenisation at country level, rather than their simple introduction. This process can thus be described as a 'higher level' transfer of technology from more advanced environments, contributing to improve the national technological capabilities.

Table 4.2   Forms of access to foreign technology

	Symbiotic	*Link+*	*Independent*	*Autonomous*
(Close) relationships with foreign suppliers	*M*	*M*	*H*	*H*
Partnerships or supplier relationships with foreign companies or with MNE subsidiaries acting locally	*L*	*L*	*L*	*L*
Integration in international networks in the field	*L*	–	–	*L*
Participation in international collaborative R&D projects	*H*	*L*	*M*	*M*
Use of local research organisations as intermediaries to foreign sources	*H*	*M*	*M*	*M*
Extensive use of a variety of scanning mechanisms to access research spill-overs	*M*	*M*	*H*	*H*

H – High impact or less frequent.
M – Medium impact or less frequent.
L – Low impact or infrequent.
MNE – Multinational Enterprise.

The search for foreign sources sooner or later became a necessity, whether or not the firm had been started up using knowledge or technology acquired abroad. The firm was either required to continue resorting to foreign sources or was forced to look for them when new knowledge not available locally became necessary. The extent of this acquisition process depended on firms' ability to build (or keep open) channels to the places where the expertise existed, which differed according to the methods favoured by each type of firm to access these inputs (Table 4.2). A more complete description of the methods used to identify and access the foreign technology and of the conditions in which it was combined with existing skills and knowledge can be found in Fontes and Coombs (1995).

The process of absorption and further local development of the acquired technological knowledge entailed the combination of the new skills and knowledge with the competences obtained through in-house acquisition practices. When available, links (close or opportunistic) with other local organisations were often used to support this task, and awareness of the requirements of local customers was a relevant element in this process. The end result was often a 'new combination', encompassing elements from a variety of origins (local and foreign), of which the NTBFs acted as the integration vehicle.

The importance of this process of acquisition and internalisation of technology generated outside the country does not negate efforts to create strong local competences in a number of fields. Indeed, a situation where a firm acquiring new technologies elsewhere achieves some sort of integration between the new technological knowledge and the competences developed locally in a particular field – thus contributing to the expansion and upgrading of the national capability in it – will have the greatest impact upon the country's development.

The Growing Concentration of the Industrial Network

It was precisely in fields where some critical mass was being developed – at both academic and industrial level – that the activities of these firms was most effective. In fact, isolated and desegregated attempts are intrinsically fragile, and although they may be important in raising awareness about the technologies, are likely to be much less effective than more integrated ones (Van de Ven, 1993). The activities performed by NTBFs – particularly by those more integrated in technological and market terms – contributed to an increasing density of the technological network at industrial level. Their principal contribution was expressed in two areas:

(a) the establishment of technological relationships between technology-intensive organisations;
(b) the establishment of close user-supplier relationships with progressive clients.

The opportunities to establish technological relationships with local industrial organisations – other than of the user-supplier type – were constrained by the relatively small number of technologically-advanced companies. Some firms were indeed very 'lonely' and complained about the lack of a technologically dynamic industrial community. This may explain why several of them were so eager to obtain contacts with foreign firms. However, informal know-how trading (von Hippel, 1987) among R&D people from different firms was frequent, especially when favoured by geographical proximity. A few firms inferred that contacts with people from the few local companies with R&D departments were more useful than those with university researchers.

The growing number of NTBFs, as well as the activities of a few large firms and/or their technology-based subsidiaries, was contributing to an increase in the opportunities for more extensive collaboration. Particularly relevant was the emergence of a network formed by a number of 'Symbiotic' firms spinning off from the same research centre, which had established among themselves (and with the centre) a web of formal and informal linkages, and whose activities were in some cases extended to a few 'outsiders', acting in adjacent fields. Equally promising were the attempts to build a 'cluster' of firms (with complementary competences and linkages in a given field) around a large company, which was achieved through the acquisition of existing small, technology-intensive firms and the creation of subsidiaries. The basic premise in both cases was to build a 'critical mass' which would fully utilise the efforts of the individual participants.

The establishment of close user-producer relationships with local companies – both with technology-intensive companies and with other technology-aware customers – was another step towards the growing density of the technological network. This type of relationship was more often associated with the one-way transfer of technology from NTBFs to their clients. Although in some cases NTBFs (and a few other technology-intensive firms) functioned as suppliers of advanced and often customised inputs to each other, generating a two-way movement of technological know-how, this was not the prevailing situation. NTBFs resorted extensively to foreign suppliers for sophisticated inputs, while technical co-operation with customers was seldom mentioned. In spite of their openness, a substantial proportion of the 'aware clients' was not technology-intensive. Therefore the technology-intensive supplier acted as a disseminator of advanced technology among firms that understood the advantages of the new solutions, but had no capacity to devise them.

Several of these advanced clients would have nevertheless been able to resort to foreign companies, and satisfy their needs on the basis of imported technology. The fact that they trusted local firms instead favoured the building-up of national competences in the development and use of the technologies involved. Both clients and suppliers mentioned a number of benefits derived from a close link with a local company, some of which are typical of the process of development of complex technologies (Lundvall, 1988):

(a) product customisation to the client's needs as opposed to the use of a standard product offered by the foreign supplier;
(b) the condition of principal client/supplier as against the situation of being only a marginal one (frequent in relationships between Portuguese companies and foreign ones);
(c) the advantages of proximity in terms of both development and after sales support;
(d) the guarantee of a continuity of supply/demand, with consequent impact upon firms' motivation to upgrade the competences and to continue innovating.

The establishment of this type of close relationship favoured a learning process. As a result, NTBFs could go on expanding their technological competences and adjusting them to the needs they identified on their markets. However, the adjustment to the clients' needs was beneficial for the small supplier only when it targeted niches composed of demanding clients, which allowed it to develop truly innovative products, or when the clients' technical requirements also evolved over time, enabling them to assimilate increasingly complex products and services. When these processes took place, a sort of 'virtuous circle' was induced. If not, such adjustments could reveal themselves to be dangerous for the supplier's future prospects, particularly if foreign expansion was envisaged. In fact, the 'specific needs' of Portuguese firms could be relatively unsophisticated, and thus not serve as basis for international expansion. For that reason, NTBFs selling in the European market frequently pointed out that, in devising a product, they had in mind the foreign market because the sole consideration of the Portuguese one did not allow them to be competitive enough. Therefore, new technology-based firms were frequently confronted with the contradictory requirements of fitting into the environment where their early survival was based, and those associated with the more long-term objectives of foreign expansion.

THE IMPACT OF NEW TECHNOLOGY-BASED FIRMS ON THE PORTUGUESE NATIONAL SYSTEM OF INNOVATION

It was hypothesised that NTBFs could play two major roles, which would be particularly important in less advanced countries (Figure 4.2).

1. *A challenging role*, expressed in the process of their creation, and associated with 'shaking' the status quo. Their founders would identify technological opportunities and, breaking with the inertia of established actors, would create innovative organisations to exploit them in the market
2. *A technology transfer role*, associated with continuity of innovative performance. Firms would go on consolidating their initial technology base, expanding it through the acquisition of new knowledge and technology and transferring the results of this activity to the market.

It was also suggested that, in performing these roles, NTBFs created in less-developed countries had an important function of acquiring, absorbing and diffusing (at country level) technologies from diverse sources. In the case of technologies new to the country, firms' activities would permit the development of endogenous competences in them, thus 'internalising' the technological knowledge at country level.

This analysis of Portuguese NTBFs has attempted to evaluate whether they were performing all or part of these roles, and their degree of success in achieving the 'acquisition/absorption/diffusion' functions. The results of the empirical research confirmed that the group of firms interviewed has undoubtedly performed the challenging role. Their founders have been able to acquire and develop new technologies and have created a new organisation, which introduced the respective applications into the market. The performance of the technology transfer role required that firms were successful in the introduction of the new products and went on acquiring and developing new technologies and transferring them to the market. Firms showed different behaviours with respect to this issue, which were largely related to their market performance. Some firms were

CHALLENGING ROLE	TECHNOLOGY TRANSFER ROLE
Associated with 'shaking up' the status quo	Associated with continuity of innovative performance
Identify technological opportunity	Achieve the wider introduction of the new products
Access/acquire new technology from diverse sources	
Use it to create new firm	Survive as a technology-based firm
Bring application(s) to the market	Consolidate technology base/build specific competences
	Continue acquiring/developing/diffusing new technology

Figure 4.2   The roles played by NTBFs

relatively successful in the market, finding early users for their products and extending their activities to a growing number of clients. However, several firms had difficulties in convincing the potential users of the advantages of their products, or were unable to go beyond a few advanced clients.

The Impact of New Technology Based Firms' Acquisition and Diffusion Efforts

The above conclusions about the unequal ability of Portuguese NTBFs to perform the roles hypothesised suggested that the impact of their technology acquisition and diffusion efforts would become more clear if it was expressed at a number of levels related to firms' evolution. Similarly, it also seemed sensible to address separately the impacts pertaining to two domains where these firms revealed different capacities:

(a) the process of acquisition of technological knowledge and development of competences in the new technologies at country level;
(b) the process of market diffusion of these technologies.

Three impact levels were identified. Level 1 corresponds to the launch process: that is, to the activities performed by the founders which led to the identification of an opportunity, the access and further development of technologies that were new or not widely used in Portugal, and their conversion into products or services which could be taken to the market. By developing capabilities in these technologies, NTBF founders have contributed to the creation of endogenous competences, which also permitted an increase in the country's absorptive capacity for subsequent developments in the field. In bringing these technologies to the market, they have first of all raised the awareness about them and their applications among potential users and have also made them available to at least a set of more advanced ones. Figure 4.3 presents the technology and market impacts corresponding to this level.

Level 2 corresponds to a situation where the firms were able to establish a good user-supplier relationship with one client or a small group of clients (usually informed users). The guarantee of a certain continuity of demand provides an incentive for firms to upgrade and expand their initial technology base and to pass the results to their clients. However, given their dependence on a few clients, firms are in a vulnerable position, which may threaten the continuity of their technology acquisition and diffusion efforts (Figure 4.4).

Activities	Impact
Acquire new technology. Develop marketable applications. Create firm to commercialise them. Introduce applications in the market: the sell them to at least one or a small set of initial clients.	<u>Technology</u>: Access technology not yet available in the country. Endogenous development permits 'internalisation' of the knowledge at country level. <u>Market</u>: Raise the awareness about the uses of the technology. Make its applications available to at least a set of more advanced clients, introducing completely new products, or increasing the accessibility to products similar to others existing elsewhere.

This is a transitory stage, although firms can remain in this stage for some time (e.g., in the case of part-time ventures or of firms experiencing early market difficulties). Firms will either evolve to another stage or go out of business.

Figure 4.3   Impact: Level 1: 'introduce technology'

Level 3 corresponds to a stage where the firms were able to extend their activities to a wider range of clients, either by expanding the client base for the same product or its extensions, or by developing new products, targeting other advanced clients in new niches. The greater stability achieved by these firms gives them better conditions to develop their in-house technological competences, namely permitting them to increase the level of resources devoted to it. It also makes them more effective as suppliers (Figure 4.5).

Firms in Level 2 and Level 3 will similarly contribute to improving the technological capabilities at country level, although the lower vulnerability of the latter gives greater consistency to their efforts. However, since the range of users that are reached by firms' activities is different, the impact of their technological efforts at market level will be diverse. Firms in Level 2, by taking the technology to a set of more aware users, will be particularly important in facilitating their access to new developments, and in devising applications more adequate to their needs. Depending on the forms assumed by their expansion, firms in Level 3 will either perform a similar function for a wider range of advanced clients, or have a greater diffusion role by also taking the technology to other types of clients: that is, they may reach users who might not have been aware of the technology's potential if the firm had not made it available to them, or

Activities	Impacts

Firms have the guarantee of a certain continuity of demand from a small set of advanced clients for
 	
   the first product/service
   other products/ services
 	
Continue acquiring/ developing new technology to upgrade existing products or to develop new ones
	Technology:
	Have motivation to upgrade and expand initial technology base. Build firm-specific competences contributing to consolidation of country's technological capabilities in the field
	
	Likely to establish links with other organisations to complement internal acquisition, contributing to densify a network in the field
	
	Market:
	Contribute to diffuse advanced technology among a set of more aware users by: providing access to technology that they might not know about otherwise; devising applications that satisfy more closely their needs; guaranteeing local supply of a technology they would otherwise import.

Firms are vulnerable, given the dependence on one or few clients, which may fail at any moment. This may threaten continuity of technology acquisition and retention of developed competences. May also make firms less reliable as suppliers, because there is no guarantee of continuity of supply.

Figure 4.4   Impact: Level 2: 'improve accessibility'

which might have resorted to standard imported technology instead of using a solution more appropriate to their level of requirements.

The expansion beyond the early stage associated with Level 1 was not always straightforward, with several firms being unable to impose their products. This situation would either force firms to close down, or else adopt one of the responses described above: either a 'downgrade' or a move to a new field where the skills and knowledge could be applied. In the case of firms closing down, a loss of expertise is inevitable, unless part of the competence is re-absorbed (e.g., acquisition or founders/employees either moving to other companies or creating new ones). Firms forced to 'downgrade' are a particular case, with the degree of loss in country terms depending on whether or not they keep some activity in the initial field. Those which do may be able to retain the technical competences acquired, although they may not be so motivated to consistently upgrade and expand them, thus reducing their contribution in purely technological terms.

In terms of the *use* of the technologies, firms that move closer to the technological needs of their clients and bring them the new advances in a 'simpler' form may be performing an important role in the process of diffusion. If they have success in this approach and expand the client base among this subset of less sophisticated users, they may approximate the Level 3 market impacts. If they are also able to raise the awareness of these clients, leading them to increase their technological requirements (or are able to maintain some more sophisticated clients in parallel) they may equally continue contributing to the expansion of technological competences in the field.

Activities	Impacts
Expand range of clients: on the *basis of the same product*(or extensions), either by reaching other clients locally, or entering foreign markets or, through diversification, *developing new products* for other niches (often still targeting advanced clients) In both cases, firms usually maintain a 'core' portfolio of more advanced clients, often including early lead-users. Continue acquiring/ developing new technology to upgrade existing products or develop new ones.	Technology: Same as Level 2, but with greater guarantee of continuity and possibly with more resources (human and financial). Market: Continue performing roles described in Level 2 for 'core' portfolio of more advanced clients, but simultaneously. Bring application to wider range of clients, some of whom might not be aware of it if the firm did not reach them or would resort to standard imported technology instead of using solution more adequate to their needs. Although having relatively advanced clients as main target, they have a wider impact because of the broader range of clients reached, in the different niches addressed.

Are less vulnerable as firms. From technological capabilities standpoint, are better prepared to retain the competences and to upgrade and expand them. They are also more reliable as suppliers, guaranteeing a continuity of supply, and passing technological evolution to the clients.

Figure 4.5   Impact: Level 3: 'contribute to diffusion'

Among the firms interviewed, several had moved to Level 2 – after more or less troubled start-up periods – but relatively few had attained Level 3. Failure to move beyond Level 2 could derive from operation in fields where there were few clients prepared to buy firms' products, but could also be caused by firms' lack of skills to search for other clients. Most of the firms that moved to Level 3 achieved this through diversification of products and hence of the niches addressed; only a few reached this level by substantially expanding the number of customers for a given product. For some firms, this route had difficulties because they had undertaken customised development, which made this alternative less feasible.

Despite this, some of these firms were also trying to develop more standard products in parallel, or to conceive 'modules' that could be applied in different products. A number of firms were also attempting expansion in the number of customers by addressing foreign markets. Figure 4.6 presents a schematic description of the alternatives of progression along these levels.

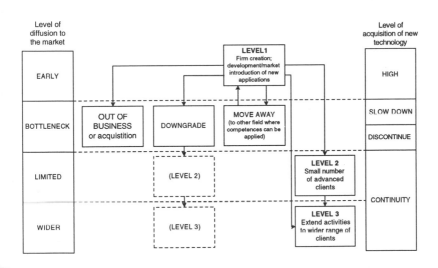

Figure 4.6   The evolution of NTBFs on the three impact levels

Therefore, one of the basic conclusions of this research is that most NTBFs interviewed were particularly effective in acquiring, absorbing and developing new technology and in bringing its applications to the market, making them available to a set of advanced users. However, they were generally less effective in diffusing these applications beyond a relatively limited number of more aware clients. This is not necessarily a failure of the Portuguese NTBFs, since it is exactly the first of these roles that is more often performed by similar firms elsewhere (Oakey, Rothwell and Cooper 1988; Littler and Sweeting, 1990; Autio, 1994). However, Portuguese firms act in a different context where advanced users are less frequent. Therefore, their inability to gain other customers, and their limited market proficiency more generally, can become problematic.

The Limitations of Firms and the Need for Complementarities

Portuguese NTBFs, as with similar firms elsewhere, were found to exhibit a number of limitations, intrinsic to their youth, their scarcity of resources, and their sometimes low competence in non-technological areas, which inhibited the full exploitation of their potential. The characteristics of the Portuguese national system of innovation not only brought additional difficulties, but also implied that firms' weaknesses could not be compensated for by the actions of other actors, who are present in other contexts, but are absent or show lower initiative in Portugal.

Considering the complexity of some markets and the weaknesses revealed by the firms, both at the level of resources for a wider promotion of their products and at the level of the skills to market them more extensively, it could be questioned whether NTBFs – at least, relatively unbacked ones – are the best vehicle to introduce some new technologies, particularly in more conservative sectors. In fact, despite their 'missionary approach' and their technological competences, most of the firms studied revealed clear limitations when it came to conveying their products beyond a restricted range of already aware users. Because market resistance to new technologies and lack of trust as regards national suppliers are relatively widespread behaviours (particularly in the manufacturing industry), Portuguese NTBFs are often confronted with difficulties whose solution requires a conjugation of efforts far beyond the capablities of a young, small firm. On the other hand, experience has shown that the founders' drive and willingness to run risks were important elements in the early introduction of some new technologies in Portugal, and that the approach followed by these firms enabled the creation of national competences in the acquired technologies. Therefore NTBFs have an important role to perform when the activities involved are adequate for small specialised firms. However, given the conditions where they operate, their ability to perform these activities will be greatly enhanced if they are helped in overcoming their insufficiencies and supported in their efforts.

This can be achieved through the involvement of existing organisations or through government initiatives. The first is important because it permits the building of several types of complementarities, as was demonstrated by the example of other countries and as was confirmed in the Portuguese case by some experiences of partnerships, risk capital initiatives and close user-supplier relationships. Government intervention may also be necessary, especially in areas where the complementary organisations are absent. It is particularly important at the level of demand, either directly (through public procurement) or indirectly in stimulating the demand for some technologies and their applications. The scarcity of advanced users has a negative impact upon the rate of industrial diffusion of the new technology (Carlsson and Jacobsson, 1994) and creates great difficulties for technology-intensive suppliers (Rothwell, 1994a). Therefore government policies which foster the technological awareness of the incumbent firms, encourage them to increase their technological level and persuade them to resort to local suppliers are necessary. They are especially relevant in the case of some less advanced segments in which Portugal specialises, where they may promote an effective integration between the country's traditional capabilities and the technologies being introduced by the NTBFs.

The results of this research suggest that assistance could be more fruitful when it:

(a) supports firms in overcoming their critical weaknesses at the level of the market, and sometimes at the level of production;
(b) backs their initial efforts, namely giving them enough margin to endure slow market entries, persisting in their efforts until the market becomes more responsive or it becomes evident that a strategic change is required;
(c) enhances the credibility and visibility of relatively unknown companies;
(d) provides resources for the expansion of their activities;
(e) assists their internationalisation efforts;
(f) contributes to the promotion of the technologies being developed and commercialised by them;
(g) facilitates the access to sources of technology and to support mechanisms which allow firms to upgrade and expand their technological competences (e.g., support to R&D and product development).

Acquisition by other firms may also be a solution to be carefully considered when it appears to be the best path to retain the acquired competences or to ensure that they are more efficiently transferred to the market. Indeed, several cases of acquisition were identified among the older NTBFs (six out of the 14 firms created before 1986), some of them having come very close to needing a 'rescue' operation. Most of these cases were still too recent to assess their outcome. However, in parallel with cases which appear to be positive so far, there were some negative experiences – firms which ended up closing down afterwards, or whose partners failed to meet the expectations – which led other NTBFs to approach this alternative with care.

CONCLUSIONS

This research attempted to evaluate the impact of the conditions prevailing in a less advanced country like Portugal upon the creation and evolution of NTBFs, and to devise the roles that these firms could play in such a context. It was found that NTBF creation and operation in Portugal can indeed be a complex undertaking. Technological opportunities are not extensively generated, the chances to gain early access to advanced knowledge and technology are not numerous, and the demand for technology-based products is limited. Mechanisms to support entrepreneurs and young firms are a recent development; and complementary organisations, which in other contexts compensate for the shortcomings of NTBFs, are often absent or show a lower initiative. However, the analysis also uncovered a variety of methods and sources used by the founders to identify and access the relevant technological knowledge, and the young firms' proactive responses to the environmental constraints.

With respect to the roles played, it was suggested that NTBFs can perform two major roles:

(a) a challenging role, expressed through their creation, which breaks up with the inertia of existing firms;
(b) a technology transfer role, synthesising internal and external knowledge and technology and passing it to the environment;

It was further suggested that, in performing these roles, NTBFs operating in less advanced countries would contribute to the acquisition and diffusion of new technologies at country level. It was found that the Portuguese firms studied did, in fact, have an important function as vehicles for the acquisition, absorption and development of technological knowledge. They accomplished it both at start-up and over time, by accessing the knowledge generated in the local S&T infrastructure and turning it into marketable applications, and by absorbing technological knowledge developed outside the country, eventually making a synthesis with local knowledge and skills. In developing competences in the new technologies and their application, as opposed to their simple purchase and use, these firms contributed to a strengthening of the country's technological capabilities. Their activity was particularly beneficial when they also achieved integration between the new technological knowledge and local competences.

Portuguese NTBFs also had a role in the market diffusion of these technologies, but the impact of their efforts at this level varied. As a rule, they emerged as particularly effective in turning the acquired technology into marketable applications and in taking them to a set of already aware users. However, they were much less effective in conveying their products or services beyond these more informed clients. Although a similar conclusion could be reached regarding most NTBFs located in advanced countries, this feature was found to cause serious problems to the Portuguese firm, because sophisticated clients are less frequent in Portugal. For this reason, the market impact of firms' efforts was often limited, despite a few cases where they were able to attain a wider range of customers (sometimes also including less advanced ones). The market performance of Portuguese NTBFs was hindered by the local market conditions – market resistance to novelty, a lack of trust in local suppliers, the limited number of clients prepared to act as 'lead-users' – and aggravated by firms' own limitations, such as resource constraints, absence of reputation and a lack of marketing skills, which left them poorly equipped to face the difficulties they were confronted with. They also lacked the presence of a more dynamic industrial community, where synergies could be achieved.

The supply of, and demand for, technology were initially defined as the factors with the greatest impact on NTBFs' performance. The research concluded that while most firms studied found ways to circumvent the problems at the level of technology supply, technology demand emerged as a more serious constraint, inhibiting the full exploitation of their potential, and sometimes even threatening their survival. A limited market success, or even the failure to pursue their initial activities, could also impact upon firms' ability to retain the technological competences developed and to continue upgrading them. This would reduce even more the impact of their efforts and, in the long run, represent a loss of expertise in country terms.

Therefore it was concluded that if the innovative drive and the acquired competences of NTBFs are to be fully profited from, they need to be supported in their efforts. This can be achieved through the involvement of existing organisations, thus permitting the development of beneficial two-way relationships. The intervention of the government will also be required when the necessary complementarities cannot be established. It will be particularly relevant at the level of demand, where measures to increase the technological awareness of existing organisations and to encourage them to upgrade, as well as to directly or indirectly increase the use of local firms as suppliers, appear to be fundamental.

5 Management of the Early Development Process in Technology-Based Firms

Magnus Klofsten

INTRODUCTION

Young technology-based firms have attracted considerable attention since the early 1980s. They are a vital source of innovation and are instrumental in disseminating new technology throughout the market. Many are spin-off firms created in areas close to universities or large, technology-intensive businesses, such as Cambridge (UK) and Silicon Valley (USA). In the Linköping region, where the author of this chapter is situated, about 400 technology-based firms in computer-related fields have been created during the past 15 years. The high founding rate and the growth of these firms have generated an interesting sample of small technological ventures to study.

Researchers often emphasise the importance of studying the development of young, small-scale firms. The creation of a firm and its early development process are critical events, and the results of early decision-making and action will considerably influence a firm's later development (Kimberly and Miles, 1980). Even so, contemporary research is mostly concerned with the problems of older, established firms (Aldrich, 1985), with comparatively little research examining the creation process of the firm (Tucker *et al.*, 1990), especially where technology-based firms are concerned (Kazanjian, 1988). This is despite the fact that both practical and theoretical benefits may be gained by studying the process of creating a firm (Scott, 1987). Therefore a closer investigation of these processes is highly relevant, and the purpose of this chapter is to describe and analyse the early stages in the development of the technology-based firm and how to manage that process successfully. Below are the three key definitions to be used in this study.

Business platform	A state of affairs whereby an enterprise has an input of business resources and is able

	to use these to promote corporate survival and growth in reasonably normal business circumstances
Early development process	Begins with the realisation of the idea whereby one or more founders take concrete action to set up a commercial enterprise. The process is said to be concluded when a business platform has been established
Technology-based firm	A firm whose strength and competitive edge derives from the engineering know-how of people who are integral to the subsequent transformation of this know-how into products or services for a market.

RESEARCH QUESTION

Earlier studies have shown that newly established firms are vulnerable and that many fail to survive their first few years of existence. For example, Olofsson, Petterson and Wahlbin (1986) discovered that nearly 50 per cent of all new firms in their sample failed during the first two years. Whilst this study did not focus on technology-based firms, other studies from the USA (Roberts, 1968; Bruno and Cooper, 1982; Bruno, McQuarrie and Torgrimson, 1992) have demonstrated that technology-based firms tend to have a higher survival rate than their non-technological counterparts. For example, a study of technology-based start-ups by Timmons and Bygrave (1986) showed a complete failure rate ranging from 14.7 per cent to 35 per cent over the first five years of the firm's existence (a mean of 20 per cent). This is dramatically different from the characteristically high and early failure rate of non-technology-based start-ups.

Despite this, it is not uncommon for even technological firms to fail, and it seems that young firms are, by their very nature, vulnerable. As time goes by, the firms that survive become more resilient. This chapter particularly addresses the vulnerability issue of the young firm on a micro-level, mainly because when a firm's vulnerability has declined sufficiently, it is said to have achieved a business platform. Therefore, the key question for discussion is: what are the necessary criteria for managing a young technology-based firm in order for it to achieve its business platform?

The following section discusses the characteristics of a business platform: that is, those aspects making up the platform and their several levels of maturity. The methodology adopted for the study is then reviewed and a comparative analysis of individual studies is then made. Finally, the more important findings are discussed, namely the conclusions that may be drawn from the study and their implications.

BACKGROUND

Characterising the Business Platform

What makes new firms vulnerable? Research examining this question is often carried out on a macro-level, where large samples of firms are grouped together and analysed. In many cases this research is related to the population ecology approach which takes up to main causes to explain the vulnerability of new firms, namely the liability of newness (Stinchcombe, 1965; Carroll and Delacroix, 1982; Singh, Tucker and House, 1986) and the liability of smallness (Aldrich and Auster, 1986; Wholey and Brittain, 1986; Singh and Lumsden, 1990).

The liability of newness is a consequence of inadequate internal co-ordination (of internal structures and processes) or inadequate links to the outer environment (establishment of effective mutual relationships). Singh, Tucker and House (1986) found that the liability of newness was mainly a consequence of the latter. Vulnerability can be due to a firm's failure to establish external relationships in sufficient number and quality (cf. Olofsson, 1969, 1979): the 'environmental anchoring, and anchoring processes'.

The liability of smallness can be due to the specific difficulties of small firms, such as the lack of supply of seed capital, and a taxation and business legislative system that does not take account of the small firm's special problems or its competitive disadvantage *vis-à-vis* large firms (Aldrich and Auster, 1986). It may be difficult to strictly separate the concepts of newness and smallness since the factors associated with both concepts are often similar. Nevertheless, it is important to establish a distinction between a firm being 'new' and a firm being 'small', as the problems associated with established small firms are often different from those of newly-founded ventures (Wholey and Brittain, 1986).

Studies have indicated that a firm which is growing and developing progressively can reach a point where it becomes more stable (cf. Kimberly, 1980, 'getting off the ground'; Gibb and Scott, 1986, 'base for potential development'). Meyer and Goldstein (1961) show that firms which survive their first two years are more likely to continue to be viable. For example, studies conducted by Freeman, Carrol and Hannan (1983) on American semiconductor firms indicate that the corporate mortality rate was greatest during the first two years and declined thereafter.

A distinct characteristic of many young firms is their instability, which can often lead to a greater risk of failure and early disappearance from the market. Firms that manage to get through the critical early development process become more viable, and therefore will have established a business platform. As a result, these firms will become less vulnerable with a greater chance of surviving and developing, but this is conditional on the business platform being maintained, with no dramatic changes in the corporate environment: a dramatic change means a change that the firm cannot prevent, such as the loss of a key person or a rapid decline in the market potential, and so on. To achieve a business platform, two criteria must be satisfied, namely:

- the securing of the input of resources into the firm
- the development of an ability by the firm to manage and utilise such resources

Achievement of a business platform allows a great deal of latitude for generating and managing its resources. This ability is not temporary but long term, as it is a question of becoming a more mature business firm.

A business platform is subject to external and internal factors. External factors include the establishment of strong relationships with customers, vendors and financial backers in order to acquire the resources it needs. Internally, the firm must establish a sufficiently effective structure, business administration system and core group expertise in order to maintain and develop important relations. More precisely, the firm's vulnerability is considered to be directly related to its ability to develop the eight aspects described in the following section. These aspects are intended to give a holistic view on a micro-level of the early development process, including the characteristics of the development of the firm, the entrepreneur, other people closely concerned with the development and the external flow of resources into the firm.

There are several situations which fit the description of a business platform. In some firms, business activities may require many relationships with the market, combined with a sophisticated level of administration and a well-defined organisational structure. In other cases, it may suffice to have only a few key relationships and a rudimentary, informal organisational structure. Therefore, a business platform is unique for each firm and related to the actual type of business conducted.

The business platform delimits a firm's early development process. Early development begins with a realisation of the business concept, where the founders initiate activities clearly intended to lead to the creation of a firm for selling a product or service. It ends when the business platform is established. The time needed for this can vary, with some firms having the ability to complete the early development process quickly, while others never get off the ground.

PREVIOUS RESEARCH

Generally, access to research and literature aimed at the level of the firm, which describe the early development process in technology-based firms, is poor. Often, only certain factors are discussed such as the characteristics of the entrepreneur or the environment. Much of the research into organisational founding is on the macro-level, particularly within the population ecology approach. The review of the literature in this chapter is intended to give a holistic view from the micro-level of the early development processes of technology-based firms. Three areas are addressed, namely:

- the firm's development process
- the people behind the setting up of a firm
- the environment, networks and resources

The Firm's Development Process

It is characteristic that developing firms must solve a number of important problems (Greiner, 1972; Kazanjian, 1988). This applies to firms who find themselves in both the early and later stages of development. What emerges from the literature are the following characteristics with regard to the firm's early development process.

1. The firm's early development phase is characterised by creativity and the development of ideas (Adizes, 1987; Kazanjian, 1988). Normann (1975) states that firms in an early stage of development have a seed idea from which the initial planning is done. It is from this that the product is created, the market defined and the business idea developed. The firms are at this time usually driven by vision, and ideas on the future are imprecise.

2. The business is strongly directed towards developing a finished product for the customers (Greiner, 1972; Kazanjian, 1988). The firm is therefore product-oriented (Adizes, 1987).
3. It is a question of quickly defining a market which is sufficiently large and profitable. (Miller and Friesen, 1984; Kazanjian, 1988). However, the firm usually has difficulty in giving priority to that market which it should aim for. It is occupied with making good use of incentives and possibilities which turn up without being directly conscious of whether they are to its advantage or disadvantage (Greiner, 1972; Adizes, 1987).
4. Usually the firm has an informal administration, governance and control. The organisation structure is informal and flexible (Mintzberg, 1973; Miller and Friesen, 1984). It follows that as the firm develops and more people become involved, co-ordination and communication problems arise (Greiner, 1972). To achieve effectiveness, the basic functions such as finance, sales, marketing and production should be established (Kazanjian, 1988). Adizes (1987) is of the opinion that the firm should strive to be systematic in its work if it does not want to run the risk of landing in the 'founder trap'. This is characterised by an unclear division of labour and a short planning horizon. It is important that a structure exists where flexibility and creativity are promoted (Normann, 1975).

The Founders of the Firm

The second part of the literature review emphasises the importance of individuals during the early development stages (Mintzberg, 1973; Miller and Friesen, 1984). Usually the founder(s) or entrepreneur(s) are the central actors who, through their ideas and activities, govern the firm (Adizes, 1987; Kazanjian, 1988). The firm's potential is intrinsically linked to their qualifications and abilities. After looking at studies aimed at entrepreneurs' experiences, abilities, knowledge and education, the following can be said.

1. Entrepreneurs often set up firms linked to the branch or business area where they have previously been working (Cooper and Bruno, 1977; Brockhaus, 1980), and usually the entrepreneurs are between 30 and 40 years old.
2. Previous experience of firm ownership is an advantage when setting up a firm (Meyer and Goldstein, 1961).
3. Entrepreneurs are often technically skilled but poor in the areas of marketing, finance and so on (Greiner, 1972; Kazanjian, 1988). Studies such as Utterback and Reitberger (1982) show that entrepreneurs have a long professional background in a wide range of areas over and above technology.

4. Educational levels vary but those who set up technology-based firms are usually well educated with perhaps an ordinary academic degree, a master's degree or a doctorate (Cooper, 1971b; Utterback and Reitberger, 1982). How the level of education influences development is difficult to judge since substantial research in this area is lacking.

An important factor in entrepreneurship research is the team of people who are involved in the early development. Susbauer (1967) and Utterback and Reitberger (1982) found that a firm was often set up by several people. In those cases where it is a question of several founders, the firms show greater growth as compared with firms with one founder. One explanation for this is that the founders complement each other, for example with regard to competence and networks (Cooper and Bruno, 1977). The SAPPHO project (Achillades *et al.*, 1971) showed that success in the commercialisation of innovations depends on the strength of the team which develops the innovation. However, the importance of the founder(s) usually diminishes as the firm develops. Adizes (1987) points out that as the firm develops, it may grow to a point where the needs of the business may exceed the personal capacity of the founder(s). In such instances, a leadership crisis arises which may result in the founder(s) transferring the leadership of the firm to a professional manager (Greiner, 1972; Kazanjian, 1988).

Several studies emphasise the importance of studying the motivation leading to the founding of small firms (McClelland, 1961; Stanworth and Curran, 1976, 1986). Entrepreneurs are often described as people with a driving force, deeply involved in the development of, and with the ability to create, something new (Schumpeter, 1934; Adizes, 1987). Birley and Norburn (1985) suggest that the driving force behind entrepreneurs and their personal motivation are closely related during the early period of development. The driving force behind the decision to establish a business can include the desire to be one's own boss, to earn more money, to make good use of possibilities, to avoid unemployment and a dissatisfaction with one's work situation. Even if the prospect of studying motivation is attractive, it must be emphasised that this is very difficult to measure and analyse (Meyer and Goldstein, 1961).

From research examining entrepreneurial qualities and characteristics, different types of entrepreneur have been defined. Each type has a particular influence on the early development of the firm. The most well known entrepreneur types are 'the Craftsman' and 'the Opportunist' (Smith, 1967), with the latter having a greater ability than the former to create growth and development in a firm, due predominantly to obvious social and extrovert qualities.

The Firm's Environment, Networks and Resources

The third area in the literature review is the firm's relationship with the external environment. Singh, Tucker and House (1986) state that a contributing factor to early failure rates among small firms is the lack of effective exchange relationships (i.e., small firms are not supplied with resources to a sufficient extent). It is therefore important that they are anchored, at an early stage, to the exchange environment (Olofsson, 1969, 1979). Yuchtman and Seashore (1967) are of the opinion that the firm's efficiency is related closely to its ability to acquire resources.

In a discussion on external relations, an important subject to consider is networking. Networks can be described at different levels. For example, so called agglomerations of firms promote the addition and development of new firms (Cooper, 1981; Oakey, 1984). Larsen and Rogers (1984) point out that the expansive formation of firms in Silicon Valley is a result of correct infrastructure. With regard to networks at firm level, Birley and Norburn (1985) found that the founder(s) first took advantage of informal networks (relatives, family and friends, etc.), before turning to more formal networks (financiers, lawyers and accountants, etc.). A well-established network is a prerequisite for development. Furthermore, relations with important actors in the network gives credibility (Birley and Norburn, 1985; McKenna, 1985).

The most important relations are naturally those with customers, not only for the sake of income but in developing personal contacts. Roberts and Wainer (1968) found that many independent firms were developed from a subcontracting relationship with larger organisations. Utterback and Reitberger (1982) suggested that customer relations built up during the previous job could benefit the entrepreneur's current company. Other important relations in young firms' development are financial (Bollinger, Hope and Utterback 1981; Cooper, 1981). It can, however, be difficult to gain access to capital since financiers judge investment in such firms as risky. As a result, entrepreneurs must initially finance the firm through their own funds (Dahmén, 1950; Dunkelberg and Cooper, 1983; Knight, 1986). Important sources of finance over and above their own funds include advance payment from customers (Utterback and Reitberger, 1982) and loans from governmental organisations such as the National Swedish Board for Technical Development (NUTEK) (Olofsson and Wahlbin, 1984). Firms who have access to capital early on often exhibit faster growth compared with those firms which fail to be financed in this way (Bruno and Tyebjee, 1984).

THE BUSINESS PLATFORM

Essential Aspects of a Business Platform

Therefore, based on the review of contemporary literature above, eight aspects of achievement are defined as being essential to the description and analysis of the early development process of a technology-based firm. Four of these eight aspects deal with the development process itself.

1. The formulation and clarification of the business idea. Development of a commercial firm requires a business idea that will allow it to pursue commercial activities.
2. The development to finished product. An important step in the process is the development from product concept to a finished product that is acceptable to customers in the market-place.
3. The definition of market. A firm cannot effectively offer its wares in all markets. It must define a market which is large enough to enable the firm to turn a profit.
4. The development of an operational organisation. The firm must have internal functions for managing and resolving problems.

Two other aspects particularly concern key actors such as the founders, Chief Executive Officer (CEO), board members, and so on, The capabilities of these will influence the development of the firm as the firm is not run by the entrepreneurial founders alone.

5. The core group expertise. The creation and the running of a firm require different types of expertise. If essential expertise is lacking in the firm, it must be provided from outside sources. This may be done through external recruitment or by creating a qualified board of directors.
6. The commitment of the core group and the prime motivation of each actor. During the early stages of the development process, there must be strong commitment and a strong driving force on the part of the key firm actors.

Two final aspects concern the flow of external resources. A basic assumption is that the firm must be supplied with vital resources for survival and development. This means several types of resources in several areas, with each resource complementing the others. The aspects defined below are a natural division of the firm's access to external and internal resources.

7. Customer relations are vital to all business firms since they are essential for creating a customer base, the source of operating revenue. Good customer relations are created through effective marketing and internal teamwork, (for instance, on the product development side).
8. Other firm relations include a wide diversity of business associations, but particularly important are those which provide the firm with financial resources.

Aspects: Three Levels of Maturity

To measure the development of the aspects along a time continuum, and to determine the demands placed on each en route to a business platform, three levels of maturity have been defined: low (*L*), intermediate (*I*) and high (*H*). The levels *L* and *H* are extreme points on a scale. The ranking *L* means that the level of maturity of an aspect is non-existent or very limited, whereas *H* indicates that a maximum development has been achieved. The *I*-level is defined as a point where the firm has taken a substantial step toward the *H*-level.

Table 5.1 illustrates how the level of maturity is assessed. Idea formulation and description can be thought of as a progression from no clear business concept whatsoever (*L*) to a tentative formulation (*I*) that is superseded by an operable concept (*H*). In the earliest stage (*L*) there may be no established relations with customers, but eventually a customer base may materialise and the product will be tested (*I*), and finally the new firm may be accepted as a reliable vendor (*H*). In other words, it may be assumed that further development of each aspect will lead to a higher position on the scale. Remember that it is not a scale with precisely defined intervals but rather a labelled progression. Caution must be exercised when comparing the *L*, *I* and *H*-levels of the various aspects since there is no time conformity.

METHODOLOGY

Since the research subject is the corporate development process, it is natural to select a case study approach. Study of a process implies a time horizon, and the case approach allows a review of both historic and contemporary stages in the development process. It also allows the object to be reviewed in detail and in depth, in order to create a comprehensive picture.

Table 5.1   Yardstick for measuring level of maturity

ASPECTS Commercial Development:	Low level (L)	Intermediate level (I)	High level (H)
Idea formulation and clarification	Idea is vague. Business concept not yet articulated.	Clear, articulate understanding of the uniqueness of own products and know-how. First step towards a business concept is taken.	Business concept in initial version. It defines users (customers), their needs and ways to satisfy these.
Development of finished product	No finished product exists. Working model or prototype may be available.	Beta product is tested on pilot customers.	Finished product available and with key customer acceptance.
Definition of market	Market not clearly defined. Perhaps tentative efforts to find customer categories.	Early mapping of customer categories but no priorities set.	Market basics are defined. One or more profitable niches.
Organisational development	No organisational structure. No key functions. Informal *ad hoc* contacts.	Reduced overlapping of functional roles. Co-ordination of internal/external activities.	Operable organisational structure that enables problem-solving, including integration/co-ordination of key internal/external functions.
Key actors:			
Core group expertise	Necessary business and technological expertise is lacking.	Necessary business and technological expertise available.	Corporate association to actors with high and well-matched business and technological expertise.
Prime mover and commitment	No driving force to develop a business enter-prise. Founder(s)	No strong driving force to create business enterprise. Small-scale com-	At least one highly committed actor striving to create a business

	treat idea as a hobby.	mitment with personal orientation.	enterprise. Strong commitment of corporate staff.

External Resources:

Customer relations	Underdeveloped customer relations. Sales procedure is non-existent.	Sufficient quantity and quality of customer relations. Pilot selling and sales evaluation.	Sufficient quantity and quality of customer relations. Market acceptance. Opportunity for continued sales.
Other firm relations	No relational network for complementary resources. Shortage of capital.	No variety in other relations. Financial relations established for capital supply.	Network to supply capital, management, credibility, etc.

Source: Klofsten (1992:142).

Three firms were selected from the following criteria. They were judged to be available and the access to data was very good. The cases were independent in that they were not a part of a concern or a larger firm and they had to be different in terms of background, markets and products. All of them were studied through personal interviews, both face-to-face and over the phone. The data collection began during the spring of 1985. From that date and until May 1987, thirty interviews were conducted, of which 18 were held face-to-face and the others by telephone. The total interview time was 50 hours, of which 45 were on site hours and the other five telephone time. Between June 1987 and the autumn of 1990, there was passive surveillance of the cases. During a follow-up phase in the autumn of 1990, three face-to-face interviews (totalling 11 hours) were held. The respondents had a good insight into the firm's development, and included one or more of the founders, the CEO and other key staff, as well as outsiders such as shareholders or board members. In addition, a review was made of pertinent corporate data such as minutes of board meetings, contracts, business plans, market plans, annual reports, sales promotion material and other documents. Access to such data was very good.

The investigation was given early support by the management teams in each firm. The project was presented to the respondents prior to the interviews. At the same time, a request was made for documentary matter on the development process. Respondents were allowed to read and comment on the written interview protocol and the relevant case study to ensure accuracy.

The analysis was conducted in several steps. First of all, each individual case was analysed in accordance with the two main aspects of the business platform (in other words, the input of business resources and the ability to manage these). This indicated whether or not the firm had been able to achieve a business platform. Thereafter, the firms were analysed according to the above eight aspects and their level of achievement was measured *(L, I* or *H)*. The levels which were decided for each aspect were discussed with the respondents in order to control the verifiability of the specific levels attained. These findings were later used to define more precisely the criteria necessary to achieve a business platform.

THREE CASE STUDIES

Case Study no. 1: Instrutec Inc.

Background

Instrutec was founded in the autumn of 1980 by three engineering students from the Institute of Technology at Linköping University. The firm was located in Linköping. The basic business activity was the continued development and marketing of a system of products for linking text-television and Videotex. Maximum turnover was about SEK9 million (about US$1.2 million). In 1986, the firm had 18 employees and a turnover of SEK8 million (about US$1.1 million). In the later part of 1989 (10 years after its founding), the firm went bankrupt.

Resource Input

Corporate development was characterised by a cautious start-up followed by a relatively strong expansion and then stagnation. The resources input, which was not particularly good at start-up, follows roughly the same pattern. The available resources included the know-how of the founders, savings, income from an occasional sale and premises which were let by the municipal authorities at a subsidised rate. The following year, resources were increased through bank loans and credits, equipment from Philips and revenue from the sale of the first information system.

Corporate expansion was especially strong between 1982 and 1984. Sales increased and the firm landed several large orders. Important relationships were established with small and major customers, suppliers, retailers and financial backers. Interest in the firm's products and other signals from the market indicated that Instrutec had achieved a certain degree of credibility. Then the upward trend turned. Sales declined throughout 1985 and never again reached the 1984 level. Few new customers were obtained. Stagnation led to a drying up of the resources generated internally by the firm. Viewed against the backdrop of the entire period, it could be seen that Instrutec found it difficult to acquire sales revenue that would allow it to carry its own weight. Several liquidity crises occurred, and continued survival required an outside supply of capital.

Ability to Manage Resources

From the time of founding and until 1984, there was a continued improvement in the firm's ability to manage resources. Thereafter, the situation neither improved nor directly deteriorated. During the first two years, the Instrutec staff consisted of two forceful founders and a few employees, but none had experience or in-depth knowledge of business operations. The basic organisational functions existed, but corporate authority and division of labour was indistinct. The liquidity crises of 1982 resulted in changes intended to improve and strengthen the organisational structure.

New owners came into the picture and contributed much-needed expertise by taking seats on the board. A new CEO was externally recruited and gained support both inside and outside the corporate borders. As a result, Instrutec became a more mature business firm. From 1985 onwards, the previous positive developments stagnated as the firm stopped recruiting personnel and no further expertise was added. This was due to at least two factors. The first was that yet another new CEO was appointed at the beginning of the year. He did not have the support of the personnel and especially not of the original founders. Another factor was a negative corporate climate caused by a bonding between the CEO and the external owners.

Did Instrutec Attain its Business Platform?

Instrutec was close to a business platform but never really achieved it. The input of resources increased considerably during an expansive period, only to stagnate later. The same applies to the management of resources. It is worth noting, however, that the firm had difficulty generating financial resources during the development process, and survival was dependent on outside funding. Corporate ability to manage resources was adequate.

Case Study no. 2: OptiSensor Inc.

Background

OptiSensor was founded in the autumn of 1983 by NordInvent (a Swedish development company) and was located in Gothenburg. The business was created to exploit an invention, the optical touch tangent. During 1986, the firm had three employees and the maximum turnover was SEK0.5 million (about US$70 000). In the autumn of 1990 (seven years after its founding), a decision was made to close down the operation of the firm.

Resource Input

Despite financial backing from two large industrial groups, four venture capital companies and a development firm, no large-scale business activities were ever initiated. Access to resources was fairly good. At the time of founding and during the continued development, the owner group contributed the necessary capital. In addition, OptiSensor had access to an administrative apparatus, premises, a contact network, manufacturing and development resources. Prior to the actual founding of the firm, considerable resources were put into an investigation of the technical possibilities and commercial applications from which OptiSensor could benefit.

It was hoped that the business relations with ASEA and Electrolux would eventually result in sales revenue. Despite several years of joint effort, commercial success was never forthcoming, neither with the original two partners nor others who came later. Accordingly, the financial input from sales was either very low or non-existent during the entire period. OptiSensor had a constant need for new capital to finance its business activities. Outside capital was contributed on four occasions, the largest sum being about SEK5 million (about US$700 000).

Ability to Manage Resources

OptiSensor's ability to manage its resources was adequate and relatively stable. The very simple organisational structure set up at the time of founding was retained throughout the development stage. The founders and the core group were motivated, committed and mutually complementary. The idea behind the corporate structure was to have a limited administration and buy the administrative support from outside firms. In retrospect, it could be questioned whether this was the best solution. No major problems in co-ordinating the business activities were apparent. The problem seems to have lain in another direction. OptiSensor was entrapped by its strong dependency on ASEA and Electrolux. The consequence of this became apparent when Electrolux encountered financial and internal problems and when OptiSensor's contact person at ASEA was relocated.

Did OptiSensor Attain its Business Platform?

OptiSensor never reached its business platform and, in fact, was never even close. The firm never made any sales to speak of and so never generated sufficient working capital. The ability to manage its resources was adequate.

Case Study no. 3: Sutec

Background

Sutec was founded in the spring of 1980 by four employees of the Aircraft Division at Saab-Scania. The firm was situated in Linköping. Sutec's basic business activity was to develop remote-control unmanned undersea craft. During 1986, the firm employed 28 people and had a turnover of SEK26.5 million (about US$3.5 million). In 1989, a larger governmental organisation became the main shareholder of the firm.

Resource Input

The firm's development is characterised by a cautious start-up followed by continuing expansion. As time passed, the input of resources increased. At the time of founding, the firm had a relatively good supply of resources. Saab-Scania was the most important business ally since it supplied the prototype of the undersea craft, documentation and a functioning market network. Saab-Scania continued to pay the salaries of Sutec's founders during the first year and supplied skilled personnel when the need arose. Early resources were secured through a loan from the Regional Development Fund and a few modest orders.

Following the first sale of the underwater craft near the end of its second year of operations, the firm began to expand. In the preceding year, Sutec had established business relations with two large customers who later became the source of more than half of the turnover. Other new customers appeared on the scene and Sutec was able to generate enough sales revenue to allow it to be self-financing. The capital contribution from owners, bank credits and loans were important complements, but seem not to have been especially significant for the achievement of a business platform.

Ability to Manage Resources

During the entire development process, the firm continued to improve its ability to manage resources. At the time of founding, the firm consisted of four forceful, experienced and mutually complementary founders The organisational structure was quite simple, with a functional structure being established when the business was founded and retained throughout the entire development process, except for the changes made at the end of 1985 when a new CEO was appointed and minor organisational changes were made.

As the second year of operations drew to a close, Sutec had become noticeably better at managing its resources. This included recruitment of the first external member of the board, alliances with other companies and the creation of the first sales firm in the USA. The personnel increased continually and, by the spring of 1987, Sutec had 28 employees. During 1984, the firm became a more mature business firm. New owners appeared on the scene and took a seat on the board. This improved the firm's business competence. A relatively distinct organisational structure defined the areas of authority and responsibility. At this point, Sutec had 16 employees.

Did Sutec Attain its Business Platform?

Sutec definitely achieved its business platform. It succeeded in generating internal funds that allowed it to be self-financing, and improved its ability to manage resources. Although outside capital was supplied during the development stage, the firm could have survived without it.

COMPARATIVE ANALYSIS

Three levels for each of the eight aspects of achievement used to measure the maturity of a business platform were defined earlier. Table 5.2 illustrates the achievement of the individual cases and the time required. It can be seen that the two firms that failed to achieve a business platform were not able to become self-financing. Their ability to manage their resources is judged to be adequate, but their ability to generate and manage resources gives no clear indication of exactly what is required to achieve a business platform. This is better done by examining the eight aspects of achievement and the level of maturity each requires. Evaluation of needs is mainly based on the two cases that failed to reach a business platform. In this way the relevant shortfalls can be determined.

The first step is to distinguish between the aspects related to external input of resources and aspects that have to do with resource management. The first category consists of aspects with an external orientation. This includes development from product idea to finished product, definition of a market, customer and other firm relations. Aspects which are tied to resources management are internally orientated. These include the formulation and clarification of the business idea, development of an operational organisation, core group expertise, and the commitment of the core group and the prime motivation of each actor. Which aspects related to the external input of resources are lacking? The following evaluations seem to apply.

1. Development to finished product. OptiSensor is the only case that did not achieve an *H*-level. A product was developed but was not accepted by major reference customers. The firm had nothing to offer the market. This aspect is not mature enough to generate the necessary resources. It seems that a business platform cannot be achieved unless the *H*-level of this aspect is fulfilled.
2. Definition of market. Both Instrutec and OptiSensor reached the *I*-level and succeeded in finding relevant categories of customers. Market priority was not clear, and neither was the question of where the most valuable customers were to be found. The customers chosen did not generate enough revenue. This indicates that an *I*-level is not enough; an *H*-level is required.
3. Customer relations. OptiSensor is the only one of our cases that failed to reach the *H*-level. Only small sporadic sales were made, and there is no sign of any agreement for continued purchases by old or new customers. There is no indication that the firm was accepted as a credible supplier. To reach a business platform, an *H*-level on this aspect is required.
4. Other firm relations. All the cases achieved the *H*-level. The question is whether an *H*-level really is necessary, and analysis indicates that it is not. In the OptiSensor case, there seems to be an overabundance of other firm relationships at the time of founding. In the other two cases, an *I*-level gives sufficient quality and quantity. An *I*-level seems to be adequate.

An evaluation of these four aspects allows two claims to be made. First, Instrutec failed to become self-financing, and failed to reach the *H*-level of market definition. This is true despite the fact that Instrutec reached the necessary levels in the other three aspects. The second claim is that all three cases show an overabundance of other relations. This is most apparent in the OptiSensor case. The firm had considerable problems in getting the necessary resources.

Table 5.2   Comparison of the achievements of each case

Aspect	Instrutec	OptiSensor	Sutec
Idea	*L*-level at TOF but *I*-level less than 1 year after TOF.	*L*-level at TOF but *I*-level at 6 months after TOF.	*I*-level at TOF but *H*-level 1 year after TOF.
Product	*L*-level at TOF, *I*-level 1 year later, *H*-level 1.5 years after TOF.	*L*-level at TOF, *I*-level 1.5 years later.	*L*-level at TOF, *I*-level 1.5 year later, *H*-level 2 years after TOF.
Market	*L*-level at TOF but *I*-level less than 1 year after TOF.	*L*-level at TOF but *I*-level more than 1 year after TOF.	*I*-level at TOF but *H*-level slightly more than 1 year after TOF.
Organisation	*L*-level at TOF but *I*-level 2 years after TOF.	*I*-level at TOF.	*L*-level at TOF, *I*-level 1 year later, *H*-level 4 years after TOF.
Expertise	*I*-level at TOF, *H*-level 2 years after TOF.	*H*-level at TOF.	*I*-level at TOF, *H*-level 1 year after TOF.
Prime mover and commitment	*H*-level at TOF.	*H*-level at TOF.	*H*-level at TOF.
Customer relations	*L*-level at TOF, *I*-level 1 year later, *H*-level 2.5 years after TOF.	*L*-level at TOF, *I*-level 2.5 years after TOF.	*L*-level at TOF, *I*-level 1.5 year later, *H*-level 2 years after TOF.
Other relations	*L*-level at TOF, *I*-level 1 year later, *H*-level 2.5 years after TOF.	*H*-level at TOF.	*I*-level at TOF, *H*-level 1 year after TOF.

TOF = Time of founding.
Source: Klofsten (1992:144).

Earlier it was pointed out that management of the resources did not cause serious problems in any of the cases. The following evaluations concern the minimum levels required for aspects with an internal orientation.

1. Formulation and clarification of the business idea. Instrutec and OptiSensor reached an *I*-level and thereby took the first step toward a business concept. It seems that both firms were aware of the uniqueness of their products and know-how. This aspect was sufficiently developed to allow a business platform to be achieved.
2. Development of an operational organisation. Here too, both Instrutec and OptiSensor reached the *I*-level. This indicates that each has an organisational structure that satisfies its needs. An *I*-level is necessary to reach a business platform.
3. Core group expertise. All the cases have access to *H*-level expertise. This indicates that when a firm reaches the *I*-level, it has a competence that is sufficient for that situation. An *I*-level will allow a business platform to be achieved.
4. Commitment of the core group and prime motivation of each actor. All three cases were at the *H*-level when the firm was founded. The business operations were characterised by active problem-solving: for instance, in the development of new products, working the market and establishing relationships. Even if the results seem different in each case, a strong driving force and a strong commitment on an *H*-level seems to be a prerequisite for a business platform.

Where the internally orientated aspects are concerned, all three cases reached the levels necessary for achieving a business platform. There is a slight surplus of expertise, but otherwise the aspects are precisely developed to the minimum levels.

DISCUSSION

Previously, it has been pointed out that firms which have achieved a business platform can have different internal structures and external relationships. This study indicates that it is possible to achieve a business platform in a firm with a basic and informal organisation, and only a few key customers if these are stable and generate the greater part of the revenue. This is of course a generalisation. A firm's ability to manage and generate resources is directly related to the eight aspects discussed above and to achieve a business platform, corporate maturity in all aspects must have progressed past the minimum level. It is expected that most of the externally orientated aspects must mature to the *H*-level, while an *I*-level will suffice for most of the internally orientated aspects.

1. Formulation and clarification of the business idea. Corporate growth and progress requires that the firm has a business idea that indicates a commercial direction. It is important that this idea is clarified so that the special know-how which makes up the commercial springboard is understandable and can be spread internally and externally. This is the first step towards establishing a business idea and is quite sufficient for achieving a business platform. It is not necessary to have a fully developed business idea when the firm is founded.

2. Development to finished product. A product is something that satisfies the needs and wants of customers. If there is no product, the firm naturally has nothing to offer. Once the product is available, it must gain acceptance by one or more reference customers. The firm has then proven that it is capable of satisfying the market's needs and wants.

3. Definition of market. A firm defines its market when it decides who it intends to do business with. It is not enough just to choose some customer category that vaguely seems to suit the purpose: the firm must define a market which is large enough and profitable enough to ensure survival. If this task is successful, the firm will have resources for future growth and development.

4. Development of an operational organisation. The running of business operations requires the existence of an organisational structure that facilitates functional co-ordination. This structure should take advantage of the firm's inherent flexibility and innovative ability, and be fairly effective at internal co-ordination and at maintaining and developing external relations. It is not necessary to have a formal structure: the main thing is that everyone is agreed upon how it will work.

5. Core group expertise. A business firm must have technological and commercial competence to develop its products and market, but access to expertise is not a goal in itself, and neither is it necessary for the achievement of a business platform. More important is having access to expertise for solving the firm's real problems.

6. Commitment of the core group and the prime motivation of each actor. A basic requirement for corporate development is that at least one person is highly motivated and that the other key actors are committed to the business idea. A firm without commitment and a driving force will not be able to implement change or carry out the activities required for achievement of a business platform.

7. Customer relations are necessary for internal financing and ultimate survival. It is not enough to sell now and then to different customers. A customer base must be qualitatively and quantitatively strong enough to generate operating revenue if it is to gain acceptance as a credible vendor.

8. Other firm relations. These relations complement the customer relationships. The firm may sometimes need additional capital, management know-how, or other 'oil' in its machinery. It is not necessary to have a high level of in-house expertise in all areas, but the firm must always have access to working capital.

Earlier studies of new firms show that the liability of newness is mainly due to the inability to secure an outside supply of capital. It is difficult for a new firm to define a large, profitable market that can serve as springboard to the resources necessary for growth and development. To sum up, it could be said that the internally oriented aspects do not cause any major problems and the ability to reach a business platform is not directly tied to their development.

Can a Mature Aspect Compensate for an Immature One?

It is pertinent to ask whether a low level of maturity in one aspect can be compensated for by a high level of maturity in another. First of all, concerning the externally oriented aspects, three of these – product, market and customer relations – must be on the *H*-level. In other words, an external input of resources cannot be satisfied if any of the aspects are on the *L* or *I*-level. If there is no finished product, the firm will not have anything to deliver. If the market is vague, there will be no long-term survival. If an adequate customer base is lacking, the firm will not be able to establish its commercial credibility.

As far as the other firm relations are concerned, it may be possible to operate when this aspect is at the *L*-level, if all the other externally oriented aspects are on the *H*-level. It is difficult, however, to imagine a scenario where the firm has so many outside resources that it does not need a network of vendors, financial backers and other business allies.

The internally oriented aspects cannot compensate for one another. Without a prime mover and commitment, the other aspects will not mature. Lack of an organisational structure cannot be compensated for by commercial expertise or a vague idea of how a strong organisation should operate. Rising above an *I*-level when minimum need is fulfilled will only lead to a over-abundance of expertise that cannot spill over into any other area. On the other hand, if the level falls, a vital ingredient in the development process will be taken away.

Therefore, if it is not possible to compensate within the categories, it would seem that it is not possible to compensate between the categories. The business platform rests on the fulfilment of two main criteria: a steady flow of resources into the firm, and an ability to manage these resources. These two criteria are mutually dependent but they cannot compensate for one another. In brief, it can be said that it is not possible for one aspect to compensate for another. It might be done in the firm relations aspect, but this scenario does not seem realistic.

Why are some of the Aspects so Difficult to Develop?

The case analyses show that there are differences associated with the various aspects: the levels of maturity to be achieved, the difficulties in reaching these levels and the time it takes to develop them. An aspect is said to be easy to achieve when it can be developed with few or no difficulties. Some of the aspects take time to develop but that does not necessarily imply that they are difficult. An aspect is said to be difficult when the firm cannot immediately develop it, even if both time and resources are available. There may exist some kind of barrier that cannot be overcome, or there may be forces inside or outside the firm that counteract the development process.

Two of the aspects existed on an intermediate level from the very beginning in the three cases studied. One, core group expertise, is easily assessed to determine how easy or difficult it will be to develop it to a high level. Aspects can be put in four categories.

1. Aspects for which it is easy to achieve an intermediate level, but difficult to achieve a high level (for instance, idea formulation and clarification, definition of market, and organisational development).
2. Aspects for which it is easy to achieve both intermediate and high levels, such as development of finished product, establishment of customer relations and other corporate relations.
3. Aspects which are on an intermediate level at the time of founding and which easily reach a high level (for instance, core group expertise).
4. Aspects which are on a high level at the time of founding, such as prime motivation and commitment.

Aspects which are Difficult to Develop

The study shows that when a firm is founded, there might be greater and lesser understanding about the direction the business activity should take. Some firms have a relatively clear business idea which was carefully thought out before the firm was formally established. Others have several options, and must decide how to set priorities. Generally speaking, it does not take very long to formulate and clarify the basic thoughts that lead to a business idea. However, it is not certain that the firm will ever get any further. In other words, it is not inevitable that a firm will follow the pattern presented by Normann (1975), which claims that at an early stage of development there normally is a seed idea from which a business idea can grow.

It is usually easy for a young firm to find relevant customer categories, but more difficult to set priorities and define a profitable market (cf. Miller and Friesen, 1984; Kazanjian, 1988). The firm will demonstrate a plan of action similar to that described in Adizes (1987). In other words, random investments in chances and opportunities as they turn up on the market.

Why are the two aspects, business idea and market definition, so difficult to develop? One explanation is that in order to achieve them according to the capabilities of the firm, there must be insight (an ability to recognise the market opportunities), as well as the needs and desires of the potential customers.

These two aspects are difficult to achieve because they are abstract and not easily grasped. A newly founded firm will find it easier to construct a problem and find a solution to it, than to start with problems that others have and try to solve them. For this reason it is easy to develop these aspects up to an intermediate level. In order to proceed further, there must be a more articulated acceptance by the actors outside the firm. It is not surprising that these aspects are difficult, but even if they have different make-ups, they are rather similar. The step from business idea to market is not very long. These two aspects partly overlap.

Studies reveal a characteristic organisational structure in young firms in that they are simple, flexible and informal (cf. Thain, 1969; Mintzberg, 1973; Miller and Friesen, 1984). There is no well-functioning organisation in the earliest stage, but as described by Kazanjian (1988), one will soon emerge and include the more important organisational functions such as accounting, marketing and production. This is sufficient for the business activity conducted at this point.

It is difficult to develop an organisational structure to a high level because there are sometimes forces within the firm that counteract the creation of formal structures. A well-functioning organisation implies an effective handling of internal and external problems and fairly well defined organisational roles and functions. This is not usually to the liking of the entrepreneur. What is wanted instead is a structure which allows flexibility and creativity.

A further explanation may be that it is difficult to create stability in a young firm, due in part to possible conflicts between the internal actors in the firm. It is not always easy to arrive at a company of actors that will benefit the young firm's growth and development.

Aspects which are Easy to Develop

Earlier studies show that a firm in an early stage of development tends to put a great deal of time and energy into product development (cf. Greiner, 1972; Kazanjian, 1988). This may be one of the main reasons why it is relatively easy to achieve a high level for this aspect. Product development has a high priority, because the key individuals in the firm usually have a 'technical bent' and are very interested in product development. In addition, if there is no product, there is nothing to sell. Product development is more tangible than market development. A finished product is an object that has been accepted by the end-user group and it is possible to exercise control over it.

As stated earlier, studies such as that of Roberts and Wainer (1968) indicate that many firms start their business activities as subcontractors to large companies. This is not confirmed in these cases. When the case firms were founded, there was no established customer base. However, from a very primitive level, customer relations were successively established until there was a base with sufficient quality and volume. In some cases the firm has been able to take advantage of previously established business networks (cf. Utterback and Reitberger, 1982).

The aspect of customer relations is easy to develop in that, like product development, it claims a high priority. Establishment of customer relations is generally regarded as being one of the basic stepping stones in business activity. Without customers, the firm will not be a long-term firm. A further reason is that customer relations is a rather tangible aspect. Establishment of a customer base is a perceptible event.

A vital component in business activities is the establishment of financial relationships (cf. Bollinger, Hope and Utterback, 1981; Cooper, 1981). The interspersion of such relations is considerable and includes venture capital companies, development companies and banks. Access to financial resources is generally good in the early stages of development and undercapitalisation is not a characteristic feature (cf. Goldstein, 1984).

Other studies of the entrepreneur's network indicate that this tends to be informal in the early stages but later shifts to a more formal type (cf. Birley, 1985). This is not confirmed in the study at hand. Instead, a formal network existed at the time of founding, one consisting directly of financial backers, subcontractors and product development partners (cf. Leonard-Barton, 1983).

Certain types of business relations are sometimes dubbed strategic, in the sense that they are more important than others because they increase the firm's market credibility (cf. McKenna, 1985). In this study, the firms established several strategic ties apart from customer relations (for instance, a link to a large corporation where joint engineering was conducted or ties to a number of owners who had a say in the activities of the new firm). Strategic relationships often exist when the firm is founded.

The very nature of other corporate relations gives us a clue as to why it is easy to develop. It is possible to establish financial relationships without having a finished product or a defined market. What is needed is credibility, so that financial backers feel fairly certain that they will recover their initial investment and receive a return on it. Vendor relationships serve to further illustrate why the aspect is easy to develop. Here it is the vendor who has a commercial interest. Why should a vendor turn down a relationship that falls within the framework of his business activities? Like product development and customer relations, this aspect is a straightforward event.

Aspects that are there from the Start

The first one, core group expertise, is on an intermediate level when the firm is founded, but later reaches a high level. The second, prime mover and commitment, is on a high level at the time of founding.

Earlier studies of entrepreneurial characteristics show that the new businessperson usually has experience of the relevant field (Cooper and Bruno, 1977; Brockhaus, 1980); a firm footing in technological matters but less experience of marketing (Kazanjian, 1988); a long-term background in business, but not necessarily with engineering experience (Utterback and Reitberger, 1982); and a high level of education that includes an academic degree of some kind (Cooper, 1971b; Utterback and Reitberger, 1982). Often the new firm is started by several individuals with well-matched qualifications (Susbauer, 1967; Utterback and Reitberger, 1982).

This study showed that the young firm has good access to core group expertise during its early stages of development. The initial value lies either on an intermediate level of maturity or, in some cases, a high level. The founders and other actors close to the firm are well educated, and in many cases have a long professional background in key areas. When there are several founders, they often have well-matched business and technological expertise. If some key area of competence is lacking, it is compensated for through the recruitment of a competent board of directors.

Core group expertise is an aspect that exists at the time of founding and there are several reasons for this, not least the fact that the firm is set up to exploit some special expertise. This makes up a kind of natural resource, available from the founders and key relations. Another reason, as can be seen from the above, is that other types of expertise are relatively easy to obtain, (for instance, by taking in new associates).

The early development process is identified by the presence of individuals who are prime movers and who have a strong commitment to the commercial activity. This is true for both founders and key associates (cf. Schumpeter, 1934; McClelland, 1961; Adizes, 1987). The fact that this aspect is available on a high level from the start is due to its being a requirement for both the actual founding of the firm and its continued development. This aspect is clearly the most fundamental and must be represented in all firms that intend to show commercial progress.

The Founding and the First Three Years

In the study, it was demonstrated that the situation at the founding of the firm is important because the levels of achievement on the aspects will affect the further development of the firm (Stinchcombe, 1965; Greiner, 1972; Kimberly and Miles, 1980). In general the following could be said about the founding:

(a) the majority of the aspects – formulation and clarification of the business idea, development of a finished product, definition of a market, development of an operational organisation and customer relations – are poorly developed; and
(b) few aspects – core group expertise, commitment of the core group and prime mover of each actor and other firm relations – are relatively well developed.

Some firms are founded without any pre-start-up activities. Others are founded after several years of planning and different activities and are therefore involved for a longer period in the development of the aspects prior to start-up. Such a pre-active period is similar to those which have been addressed as 'gestation' (Reynolds and Miller, 1989), 'courtship stage' (Adizes, 1987) or 'pre-start-up' (Kazanjian, 1988).

Those firms which are active before start-up show the highest total values on the aspects. A number of characteristics are common to such firms, including:

(a) most of the aspects will be poorly developed at the time of founding, which makes the firms very vulnerable;
(b) the aspects of core group expertise and other firm relations have been developed sufficiently and therefore little effort is required to attain high levels;
(c) some firms may be better equipped at start-up when it comes to the more difficult aspect of the development, such as aspect formulation and clarification of the business idea and definition of a market.

That is a difference which is later shown to be of great importance when trying to increase the odds to overcome the initial vulnerability and be a more stable firm. A possible explanation is that when a firm is strong on the difficult aspects at start-up, the easier aspects will be easier to develop as the firm grows.

During the development the firms experienced a shortage of capital, but in general this did not adversely affect their survival during the first two years of existence. This may suggest that, in some cases, the critical period of a firm's development may last longer than the two years suggested in other studies (Meyer and Goldstein, 1961; Freeman, Carrol and Hannan, 1983). However, what also emerges from the analysis is evidence that while a rapid development of these aspects takes place during the first two years of the firm's existence, it is also clear that further development of such aspects is highly improbable and that a stagnation in the level of achievement will begin after this early period.

The situation in the firms after the first three years of development is quite different. While some firms may still be very vulnerable, others will have passed this stage. Further development of the aspects in these particular cases will not take place. The firms which remain vulnerable will continue to develop, but they are unstable and may finally cease trading. In such cases, the period to closure will be longer than the two-year limit proposed by other studies (Meyer and Goldstein, 1961) and in some cases, as in Instrutec and OptiSensor, may take up to 10 years.

A Typology of the Founding and Early Development

Considering similarities and differences in the development of the aspects a typology of the founding and early development process can be created. In this context there are types related to how difficult the aspects are to develop to the high level. The typology illustrates among other things to what degree the situation at founding determines whether the firm will remain vulnerable or not.

In Figure 5.1, a distinction is made between aspects marked D, representing the aspects which are difficult to develop to the high level (idea, market and organisation), and aspects which are easy to develop or are there from the start, marked E. The situation at founding is given on the left-hand side of the figure, and on the right-hand side there is the probable situation when the aspect has stagnated. The positive sign shows that the aspects are relatively well developed, and the minus sign shows that they are poorly developed.

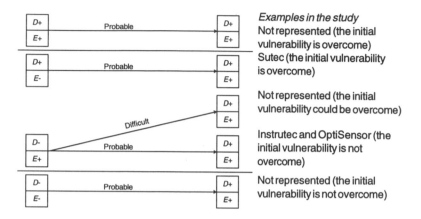

Figure 5.1   Types of development process

If the difficult aspects are well developed at founding (*D*+) the firm will overcome its early vulnerability. When the market aspect is well developed the poorly developed aspects stand a good chance of being improved. When the situation is *D*– at founding it is probable that the firm will not overcome its early vulnerability and become a more stable firm with an increased chance to survive and develop.

CONCLUSIONS AND IMPLICATIONS

This chapter has focused on critical aspects on the early development of technology-based firms. Eight such aspects have been defined, representing three areas covering the development of the firm *per se* (four aspects), key corporate actors (two aspects) and external relations (two aspects). These aspects are more or less difficult to develop and they can be categorised into three groups: difficult aspects, easy aspects and those which were already there from the start.

The concept of a business platform has been discussed, and a micro-level approach was used which allows analyses of the single firm and the criteria necessary to overcome early vulnerability and attain a business platform. The results show that it is possible to identify the existence of a business platform. A business platform is attained when a firm has become viable enough to continue its existence through internal financing. The findings indicate that a business platform is mandatory for long-term survival and growth. If a firm has not established its business platform within two or three years of its founding, there is a considerable risk that it will eventually fail and disappear from the market arena.

It has been shown that it is possible to ascertain the existence of a business platform by measuring the maturity level of the eight essential aspects of achievement. Minimum requirements can be defined for each aspect. Researchers of early development processes and managers of young firms should be aware of the importance of using a holistic approach when studying or managing a firm. This chapter addresses eight aspects where all are of equal importance and one aspect cannot compensate for failings in another.

This study is concerned with only one type of platform: the business platform. Do other types of platforms exist? In Klofsten (1987), a hypothesis on a so-called launching platform is discussed. This describes the firm's situation at the time of founding, focusing on the aspects of market definition, accumulation of knowledge and the existence of business networks. Commercial activity need not have started at this stage. An important note is that a business platform is not the final destination in a development process. The study at hand has not discussed the events occurring after a business platform is established. An analysis model designed for a post-business-platform stage might prove fruitful.

Another significant topic for further research is what distinguishes early development processes in technology-based firms and in other firms? The findings discussed here may be compared to other types of firm to discern differences and similarities. Certain aspects could be of more or less importance and the levels of the aspects necessary for the firm to attain a business platform may differ from those levels discussed here. It would be interesting to repeat the study with empirical material representing some other category of business firm.

The establishment of new business firms and the stimulation of young firms is of high priority in contemporary society. The early development process is a significant topic for both the public and private sectors, including banks and other financial institutions, business firms serving as vendor or customer, venture capitalists, government agencies and managers of science parks. The findings presented here can be put to practical use in many ways. The aspect model can be used to diagnose early corporate health at different checkpoints in time. Benefits could, for example, include the following :

(a) individuals who wish to found and operate a business firm get an idea of the requirements necessary for success;

(b) young firms with development problems can use the model as an instrument to review weak points;

(a) financial backers and banks can be aided in their decision as to whether to stake a new firm;

(d) government agencies in the support network can gain vital information about what resources are needed to take effective action.

Early development processes, have therefore been an interesting topic for many actors in the public and private sectors, including banks and other financial institutions, business firms serving as supplier or customer, venture capitalists, state agencies, managers of science parks and others. This chapter shows that access to capital is not the most problematical development aspect, and that having sufficient capital at an early stage does not solve all problems. More energy should be spent in resolving 'soft' issues, such as definition of the business idea and market. (the former is particularly difficult to develop).

6 Success Strategies in High Growth Small and Medium-Sized Enterprises

Colm O'Gorman

INTRODUCTION

During the 1980s, researchers and policy-makers became increasingly interested in understanding the processes of enterprise development and growth. Encouraged by Birch's (1979) evidence that job creation in the USA was only occurring in the small business sector, policy-makers began to champion the cause of the small business. For the first time, most European governments recognised the significant role new and small businesses play in employment and wealth creation. In Ireland, policy-makers sought to maximise the rate of start-up of new businesses and to protect existing small businesses by minimising the burdens resulting from government bureaucracy.

However, despite generous financial incentives in the form of non-repayable and interest-free grants from the state, the start-up rate and the survival rate of new businesses is no better in Ireland than in other European states (Task Force on Small Business, 1994). This indifferent performance of new and small businesses caused many researchers to question the usefulness of the policy of state support for new venture creation. Research evidence from Ireland and the UK has suggested that high growth is the exception for SMEs (Gallagher and Miller, 1991; Kinsella *et al.*, 1993; Storey, 1994). This research work suggests that for any given sample of start-ups, growth will be restricted to a very small percentage of businesses. The evidence suggests that for every 100 start-ups, a decade later *only four businesses* will account for over half the surviving jobs created. For many researchers and policy-makers this evidence confirmed the doubts as to the wisdom of generous state financial support for all new start-ups.

Researchers and policy-makers recognised that these few fast growth businesses had a disproportionate impact on job creation. The emphasis of this research is on those businesses that achieve high growth. Having survived the environmental and organisational challenges of early life these small businesses must identify what strategies will allow them achieve high growth. By targeting state support towards those businesses that seek growth, the state may be able to have a much more significant impact on the rate of wealth and employment creation.

RESEARCH QUESTION

In this chapter, the strategy literature is used to explain the growth of those few SMEs characterised by sustainable high growth. It is argued that this is a productive approach to researching high growth businesses for several reasons. First, the strong tradition of cross-industry research in the strategy literature would suggest that the findings should be applicable across industries and across national boundaries. There are significant differences in the business context of the different European countries: for example, there are significant differences in terms of the size of local markets; the stage of industrial development; the productivity of the workforce; the competence and expertise of management; and the transport infrastructure. Despite these differences there is evidence that, in terms of business level competitive strategies, businesses of similar size and stage of strategic development have more in common than in difference. Therefore it is argued that the general business strategies lessons to be learnt from a high growth food manufacturer in Ireland should be applicable to a high growth instrument manufacturer in Denmark or a high growth textile business in northern Italy. Second, by focusing on the strategies pursued by high growth businesses, the results should be of direct benefit to individual owner-managers.

The key question for discussion in this chapter is whether we can identify the business strategies of high growth businesses. From a review of the literature on 'success' strategies in SMEs, a list of strategies are developed that are hypothesised to characterise high growth companies. This is followed by the results of a survey that compared high growth and low growth indigenous Irish companies. Case evidence from two businesses in the wholesale sector is then presented to illustrate the results. Finally, conclusions are drawn and recommendations made for researchers, policy-makers and managers of SMEs seeking high growth.

ALTERNATIVE EXPLANATIONS OF THE CAUSES OF HIGH GROWTH

Can we explain how high growth businesses achieve their success? Researchers have studied whether growth is driven by management choices or by environmental forces (Smallbone *et al.*, 1991; Murray and O'Gorman, 1994). Previous research by this author suggests growth is determined both by environmental forces and by managerial choices. In the cases described later in this chapter, the growth of one of the companies appears to be driven *exclusively* by growth in the environment: that is, the choice of a high growth market resulted in high growth for the business. In contrast to this, the other company achieved growth rates much higher than market growth rates, which suggests that the decisions of managers and the resource endowments of the business also impact on growth levels. Other research has suggested that periods of high demand conditions, such as industry growth and industry maturity, increase the chances of organisational survival (Carroll and Delacroix, 1982; Romanelli, 1989) and the growth prospects of businesses (Eisenhardt and Schoonhoven, 1990).

The choice of environment is often a key determinant of the growth potential of a business. However, this is of little value to the individual entrepreneur for two principal reasons.

1. The decision that a founder faces is whether to enter an industry rather than which industry to enter. The choice of environment is constrained by the entrepreneur's past experience and does not appear to be an active decision variable (Eisenhardt and Schoonhoven, 1990). Furthermore, having chosen an environment it can be difficult for a business to move to a new environment. Murray (1984) argues that founders 'set very powerful rules concerning acceptable and "proper" strategic moves' (1984:9) and consequently may limit the future strategic choices of the business.
2. Aaker and Day (1986) have demonstrated that the choice of a high growth market is not a sufficient condition for growth. Not all businesses in high growth environments are successful and for many resource-constrained businesses the demands of a high growth environment may result in organisational failure.

In the small business and entrepreneurship literature, many researchers have suggested that process models are the most useful way of studying how organisations grow (Greiner, 1972; Normann, 1977; Churchill and

Lewis, 1983; Kazanjian, 1988). These process models set out to highlight the various stages businesses progress through as they grow. Each stage is characterised by a number of problems relating to management style, organisation structure, and so on. However, these stage models have a number of difficulties:

(a) these models are purely descriptive and consequently are of little use to the manager of a growing business;
(b) the models suggest that structural and managerial style variables are common to each stage of growth, but the nature of organisations is such that they all progress at different rates;
(c) significantly, not all organisations progress through the various stages of these models, with the vast majority of small businesses appearing not to progress beyond the early stages of these models.

Therefore these process models do not explain how businesses achieve high growth.

Growth may be the outcome of the differing ability of managers to exploit opportunities (Eisenhardt and Schoonhoven, 1990). This ability appears to be a function of the make-up of the top management team and its ability to interact and work together. In the organisational behaviour literature, growth is explained in terms of the motives of managers (Starbuck, 1965; Rhenman, 1973; Child and Kieser, 1981). Benefits such as increased resources and increased influence on external stakeholders motivate managers to pursue growth. However, neither of these explanations really tells us how managers achieve high growth.

The question remains, how best can we explain how high growth businesses achieve their success? The environmental explanation, the process explanation and the behavioural explanation do not provide adequate answers to this question. The environmental explanation of growth is inadequate in that its prescriptive advice is to choose a high growth market. However, in the context of most businesses, the current market position is the result of, and is constrained by, prior decisions. Furthermore, changing market position is a resource- and time-consuming process and therefore is often not a viable strategic proposition for a resource-constrained SME. The process explanation of growth is inadequate in that it is essentially descriptive. The behavioural explanation suggests that the motive to grow determines the likelihood of growth. This does not help to explain how managers pursue these growth objectives. These limitations lead us to explore the strategy literature for clues about how businesses achieve high growth.

THE STRATEGIC ATTRIBUTES OF HIGH GROWTH BUSINESSES

Strategy is about two questions: 'What business(es) should we be in?' and 'How do we compete in a given business?' (Hofer, 1975). This research seeks to address the second of these questions for high growth SMEs. There are various difficulties in using existing strategy content literature to develop hypotheses about high growth SMEs.

1. Strategy researchers traditionally focus on large organisations (Aldrich, 1985). Differences in resource endowments and organisation structure between large businesses and SMEs might mean that strategy prescriptions are not transferable from large companies to their smaller competitors.
2. Within the strategy content literature, growth is rarely used as a dependent variable. Market share position, size and profitability are the preferred dependent variables. Many researchers have focused on 'successful' companies, using a composite measure of existing competitive position and the change in this position over time. It can be difficult, and perhaps unwise, to separate the strategies associated with growth from those associated with competitive success.

Accepting these constraints, a number of hypotheses will be developed which will describe the strategic attributes of high growth SMEs (see Figure 6.1). The assumption will be made that managers of high growth SMEs make similar strategy choices across a wide range of industry contexts.

Market Niches

The prescriptive advice from the strategy literature is that small businesses should focus on market niches. The early strategy content literature attempted to identify strategies associated with different size businesses. Katz (1970) suggested strategy prescriptions for both large and small businesses, the thrust of his suggestions being that the small business must focus and conserve its resources while the larger competitor must play to the advantages of its size by planning activities carefully to ensure resources are allocated to activities in relation to their contribution to the business.

This theme was repeated by Porter who suggested that a focus strategy is most appropriate for smaller companies (1985). According to Porter, the focuser competes by selecting a segment or group of segments in its industry and by tailoring its strategy to serving these segments to the exclusion of others. By optimising its strategy in the target segments, the focuser achieves a competitive advantage even though it does not possess a competitive advantage for the whole market.

High growth strategy of SMEs	Studies
Characterised by a *focus strategy*: that is, their activities are restricted to a limited number of market segments	Hannan, 1976; Hammermesh, Anderson and Harris 1978; Porter, 1980; Vesper, 1990; Kuhn, 1982; MacMillan, Hambrick and Day, 1982; Cavanagh and Clifford, 1983; Solem and Steiner, 1989; Macrae, 1991; Kinsella *et al.*, 1993; Storey, 1994.
They compete on the basis of a *differentiated strategy*	Abbanat, 1967; Porter, 1980; Kuhn, 1982; Cavanagh and Clifford, 1983; Sandberg, 1986; Sandberg and Hofer, 1987.
The source of the uniqueness that drives the business's differentiation strategy is *innovation*	Abbanat, 1967; Cohn and Lindberg, 1972; Scherer, 1980; Buzzell and Wiersema, 1981; Hambrick, 1982; MacMillan and Day 1982; Cavanagh and Clifford, 1983; Buzzell and Gale, 1987; Boeker, 1989; Phillips and Kirchhoff, 1989; Cambridge Small Business Research Centre, 1992; Kinsella *et al.*, 1993; Wynarczyk *et al.*, 1993.
They are characterised by superior performance on a *number of competitive devices* such as product quality, premium prices and the introduction of new products	Hambrick, MacMillan and Day, 1982; Anderson and Zeithmal, 1984; Buzzell and Gale, 1987.
They are characterised by a propensity to invest in *future oriented expenses*, such as marketing, the building of distribution channels, product R&D, product availability, and in capacity increases through new plant and equipment	Buzzell and Wiersma, 1981; Hambrick, MacMillan and Day, 1982; Anderson and Zeithmal, 1984.
They grow by building on existing strengths and by emphasising *corporate relatedness*	Channon, 1973; Rumelt, 1974, 1979; Woodward, 1976.
The choice of market position and competitive strategy is the result of *corporate flexibility* in that successful high-growth companies are characterised by an ability to change their market position and/or competitive strategy. This often manifests itself in increased export activity	(Abbanat, 1967; Katz, 1970; Cohn and Lindberg, 1972; Kuhn, 1982; Smallbone, Liegh and North, 1993a, 1993b). (Cavanagh and Clifford, 1983; Cambridge Small Business Research Centre, 1992; Kinsella *et al.*, 1993).

Figure 6.1   Summary of common high growth strategies from the literature

Research on small businesses has suggested that there is evidence supporting a market niche strategy in high growth small businesses. The essence of a market niche strategy in the context of many small businesses appears to be the avoidance of direct competition with both larger and smaller competitors. The evidence from the studies of fast growth businesses in Ireland and the UK suggests that, despite attempts in the research to control for sector influences on growth by choosing 'matched pairs', high growth companies rarely competed directly with low growth companies (Kinsella *et al.*, 1993; Storey, 1994). Abbanat (1967) concluded, with reference to his comparison of the strategies of small companies with the strategies of large companies, that 'if there was a pattern to the results, it was a pattern of difference and in this sense the impression that small manufacturing companies compete directly with large corporations is erroneous. Rather these companies probed for soft spots and gaps in the market.'

Studies of successful medium-sized companies have suggested that a market niche strategy is an important characteristic of these companies. Cavanagh and Clifford (1983:10) concluded that 'most winning companies are leaders in market niches, often in markets they have created through innovation'. Research evidence from the UK suggests that market position is an important characteristic of fast-growth businesses (Solem and Steiner, 1989; Macrae, 1991). This research suggests that while the choice of overall sector may influence profitability and growth, the choice of specific market position is more important to the performance of an individual enterprise.

The empirical identification of a market niche strategy in small businesses is fraught with operational and definitional difficulties. It is difficult for researchers to precisely define the product-market a business is competing in. How does a small food manufacturer producing speciality frozen deserts for supermarkets delineate its product-market arena? Such a business could define its business very narrowly as 'a producer of premium frozen deserts for supermarkets', or more broadly as 'a dessert producer'. The classification of its competitive strategy will be a function of the choice of business definition and, more importantly, this definition may broaden as the business seeks to grow and expand.

Neither Kalleberg and Leicht (1991) nor Westhead and Birley (1993) were able to provide conclusive evidence of market niche strategies among fast growth small businesses in the UK. Furthermore, Biggadike (1976) compared the relative attractiveness of a niche strategy and an aggressive market share-seeking entry strategy and suggested that the latter is the more appropriate for new ventures seeking to establish themselves.

He suggested that the poor performance of many new ventures is the direct consequence of limiting market focus at the time of entry.

Despite this inconclusive empirical evidence, the prevailing wisdom in the strategy literature is that small businesses should optimise the use of their limited resources by competing in a limited market niche. In the literature on small businesses the prescriptive advice is that the best way to avoid direct competition with larger competitors is to pursue a niche strategy (Hannan, 1976; Vesper, 1990). This suggests our first hypothesis: H_1 – *High growth SME's focus on market segments.*

Generic Competitive Strategies

Having chosen what market to compete in the SME must then choose how it is going to compete within this market. Porter (1985) identified two types of competitive advantage, which he termed cost leadership and differentiation. Based on these two advantages and on the competitive scope of the business, which he classified as either industry-wide or focused, he developed three generic competitive strategies. The three generic strategies are cost leadership, differentiation, and focus (Figure 6.2). According to Porter, businesses must choose one of these generic strategies, since failure to do so results in below-average profitability. Porter prescribes a focus strategy, whether it be based on a cost advantage or a differentiation advantage, for small and medium-sized businesses. Sandberg and Hofer

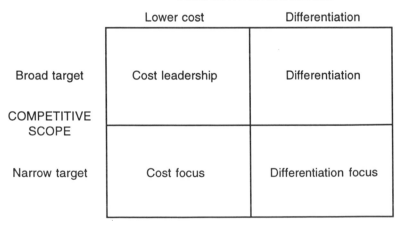

Figure 6.2   Porter's generic competitive strategies
Source: Porter (1985), p.12.

(1987) suggest that a differentiation strategy is the most appropriate strategy for new ventures. Sandberg (1986) concluded that new ventures pursuing undifferentiated strategies performed less well than new ventures pursuing differentiated strategies.

Porter (1985) proposes that a business differentiates itself from competitors by being unique at something which is of value to buyers. To be sustainable, a business's differentiation must perform unique activities that impact on the customers' purchasing criteria. Porter (1985:152) identifies several methods that a business can employ to enhance its differentiation. These are:

- enhance its sources of uniqueness
- make the cost of differentiation an advantage
- change the rules of competition to create uniqueness
- reconfigure the value chain to be unique in entirely new ways

Kuhn (1982) studied the strategies of 128 successful mid-sized companies, and concluded that successful mid-sized companies compete by being unique. Uniqueness was defined as aspects of the business's interaction with the external environment which set it apart from competitors, and was achieved by differentiating both the company and its products from those of competitors. Kuhn included:

- market segmentation by product uniqueness
- market segmentation by geographic specificity
- market segmentation by customer/industry specificity
- evidence of corporate uniqueness
- dependence on brand names as measures of uniqueness

A finding which surprised Kuhn was that successful mid-sized companies were product oriented. The companies in the study emphasised product quality, product brand name, and product value to customers as essential elements of their strategy. According to Kuhn, the corporate claims of product leadership were 'vigorous, persistent and widespread among our sample' (1982:170). In addition, Cavanagh and Clifford (1983) later concluded that successful mid-sized companies competed on value. Therefore the second hypothesis is: H_2 – *High growth SMEs pursue strategies of differentiation and uniqueness.*

Innovation

It is not clear whether mid-sized businesses produce a higher or lower level of innovation than their larger and smaller counterparts. The literature on innovation is fraught with definitional and measurement problems. A consistent argument in work based on better performing mid-sized companies is that they do rely on innovation, although this finding is not exclusive to this size of firm. Peters and Waterman (1982) argued that innovation is also a characteristic of successful large companies.

The traditional literature on innovation spends a lot of its time trying to establish links between levels of innovation and business size, an area that is important in determining public policy towards small businesses. A different perspective to take is to compare the level of innovation with business profitability, growth and survival. To the extent that this has been done, mostly indirectly by studies examining the characteristics of better performing companies in a particular size/industry sector, it appears that there does exist a link between better performance and a higher measure of innovation (Kuhn, 1982; Peters and Waterman, 1982; Cavanagh and Clifford, 1983). Scherer (1980:422) concluded that:

> what we find . . . is a kind of threshold effect. A little bit of bigness – up to sales levels of $250 million to $400 million at 1978 price levels – is good for invention and innovation. But beyond the threshold further bigness adds little or nothing, and it carries with it the danger of diminishing the effectiveness of inventive and innovative performance.

Cavanagh and Clifford (1983), in a study of the strategies of successful mid-sized companies, concluded that innovation was 'a way of life' among the top performing mid-sized growth companies. Most of their survey respondents achieved their first major success with either a unique product or a distinctive way of doing business. On average 25 per cent of sales in the companies came from products which were not offered in the previous five years.

In the context of small, rapidly growing businesses, the evidence suggests new product introductions are related to growth (Cambridge Small Business Research Centre, 1992; Kinsella *et al.*, 1993; Wynarczyk *et al.*, 1993). Other evidence suggests that those businesses that are technically more sophisticated or technologically more innovative are likely to grow faster (Boeker, 1989; Phillips and Kirchhoff, 1989). However, it may be that these technically more sophisticated sectors are experiencing faster growth.

Buzzell and Wiersema (1981) used the PIMS database to test what strategies were characteristic of businesses that were increasing their market share position. They found that the strategic factors generally involved in market share gains included increases in new product activity, increases in relative product quality and increases in sales promotion, relative to the growth rate of the served market. Cohn and Lindberg (1972) also concluded that the key advantage of small businesses is their flexibility in relation to customer service and making product changes.

Overall it would appear that SMEs are at no particular disadvantage when it comes to innovation; in fact, some studies would suggest that they have an advantage over larger competitors within a fixed range of potential innovations, certain innovations being outside the scale of their resources. Therefore, innovation appears to offer SMEs a potential competitive weapon. This leads to the third hypothesis: H_3 – *High growth SMEs are characterised by innovation.*

Competitive Devices

Studies by Hambrick *et al.* (1984) and Macmillan *et al.* (1982) used the PIMS database to compare businesses in different cells of the Boston Consultancy Group (BCG) portfolio. By definition, 'stars' and 'wildcats' are businesses in high growth markets (Figure 6.3). The BCG portfolio can be used to compare businesses in high growth markets, (those businesses located in the top half of the portfolio), to businesses in low growth markets (those businesses located in the lower half of the portfolio). Alternatively, successful high growth businesses, 'stars', can be compared to less successful growth business, 'wildcats'.

The findings of a comparison of 'star' and 'wildcat' businesses with 'dog' and 'cash cow' businesses, and the comparison of 'star' businesses with 'wildcat' businesses, suggest the following.

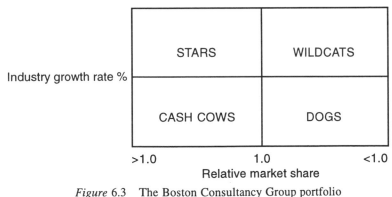

Figure 6.3   The Boston Consultancy Group portfolio
Source: Henderson (1973)

1. Successful high growth companies have superior competitive devices in terms of superior product quality, premium prices, greater value added and higher sales from new products.
2. High growth companies require high levels of resources to invest in future oriented expenses. Investment is required for R&D, new plant and equipment, and for high levels of current assets (inventories and trade credit).
3. High growth businesses should focus on a narrow domain by producing a narrow breadth of product for a relatively homogeneous customer group.
4. That high growth businesses should ensure a high level of product availability. This can be achieved by investing in capacity and inventory.
5. That high growth companies should emphasise revenue-increasing activities rather than efficiency in production measures. This is because efficiency is not as important when demand is high.
6. That profitability is associated with a high value-added to revenue ratio, a low manufacturing costs to revenue ratio, a low capital intensity (these three prescriptions apply to all businesses), and high capacity utilisation.

One explanation for the differences between 'stars' and 'wildcats' is that the businesses may be at different stages of the growth cycle. Star businesses have a dominant market share position, suggesting that they have successfully penetrated their market. Wildcats, on the other hand, may be at an earlier stage of development in the growth cycle, and may still be trying to penetrate the market. Alternatively, it is possible that 'wildcats' are inferior competitors. The most important conclusion of the work by Anderson and Zeithmal (1984), Macmillan, Hambrick and Day (1982), and Hambrick, Macmillan and Day (1982) is that the critical strategic focus in growth businesses is ensuring that the business is well positioned for industry maturity.

Buzzell and Gale (1987) examined the factors that followers in a market change when they are gaining market share. Table 6.1 shows the types of change made by market followers that gained share, as compared to those that stayed even or lost share. The basic conclusions are that followers who gained share typically improved quality, and maintained or increased all categories of marketing expenses at rates faster than the growth rate of the served market. Buzzell and Wiersema (1981) argue that in order to make gains in a market share position businesses must increase new product activity, increase relative product quality and increase sales promotion activity. Therefore, hypotheses four and five are: H_4 – *High growth SMEs are characterised by superior competitive devices;* H_5 – *High growth SMEs invest in their future.*

Growth Strategies

Rumelt (1974, 1979) and Channon (1973) tried to test whether particular corporate growth strategies are more profitable than others. Rumelt's (1974) study of the relationship between business diversification and business performance in 250 of the top 'Fortune 500' companies found that those businesses that diversified to some extent but restricted their range of activities to a central skill or competence showed a higher rate of profitability and growth than businesses that diversified into unrelated areas. Of the nine categories of businesses that he identified, the two constrained categories, 'dominant constrained' and 'related constrained', were almost always superior in profit performance. The outcome of Rumelt's (1974, 1979) and Channon's (1973) work suggests that related diversification is the most profitable of all diversification strategies. Do these results also apply to high growth SMEs?

High growth SMEs must change market focus in order to grow. Cavanagh and Clifford found that only 2 per cent of their sample still sold a single product to a single market, attributing this to the fact that over time the original niche does not offer the necessary growth opportunities (1983). This ability to grow and develop from an initial market niche is often referred to as strategic flexibility. The literature on SMEs suggests that greater flexibility is a key advantage of smaller sized businesses (Abbanat, 1967; Katz, 1970; Cohn and Lindberg, 1972). Smallbone, Leigh and North (1993a, 1993b) suggest that the ability to respond to market changes is an essential prerequisite for the growth of a small business. Kuhn concluded that flexibility was an important success strategy for mid-sized companies (1982).

This ability to move from an initial market position is often reflected in the SMEs propensity to engage in exporting or in export markets. The literature on small businesses suggests that most small businesses do not export. Both Storey (1994) and Kinsella *et al.* (1993) suggest that exporting is an important characteristic of high growth small businesses and in Ireland, the ability to export appeared to be a critical necessity for small businesses with growth aspirations due to the small size of the local market. Further research evidence suggests that high growth SMEs are likely to be exporters (Cambridge Small Business Research Centre, 1992), with Cavanagh and Clifford (1983) reporting that 73 per cent of the successful mid-sized companies were successful exporters.

The evidence of whether growth is an appropriate objective for small businesses is conflicting, with Storey (1994) suggesting that most small businesses do not have growth as an objective, and that growth in employment appears to be correlated with growth as an objective. However, seeking growth as a goal in itself is not necessarily the most appropriate strategy. Woodward (1976) identified three principal areas of weakness in small businesses, each of which is a function of management actions and goals. The first weakness was a desire for growth for growth's sake, where management in these small companies did not consider growth in terms of the market and competitors, but rather viewed growth as a goal in itself. Hammermesh, Anderson and Harris (1978), in their examination of three low market share companies which competed against larger companies, also concluded that the smaller companies should avoid growth for the sake of growth. In terms of their growth orientation, Kuhn concluded that successful mid-sized companies do actively pursue growth, not for growth's sake, but for what he termed 'business sake'. Kuhn argues that mid-sized companies should evaluate the growth-profit trade-off carefully, and if the company is in a strong market position, it should market its products forcefully. However, if the business's market position is weak, it should value profits more than growth.

Table 6.1   Strategic changes by market followers that lost, held or gained market share

Strategic changes	Market share change(%)		
	Losers	*Holders*	*Gainers*
Relative product quality	−0.6	+0.6	+1.8
New products, (% of sales)	−0.5	+0.1	+0.1
Price, relative to major competitors	+0.2	+0.2	+0.3
Marketing expenditures *(adjusted for market growth)*			
Sales force	−8	0	+9
Advertising			
Consumer products	−9	+1	+13
Industrial products	−14	−6	−1
Promotion			
Consumer products	−5	+5	+13
Industrial products	−10	−1	+7

Source: Buzzell and Gale (1987:190).

Therefore, changing market focus is often a necessity for high growth SMEs. In studies of medium-sized business both Hammermesh, Anderson and Harris (1978) and Woodward (1976) suggest that small businesses should grow by competing in areas in which their particular strengths are most valued. This leads to the sixth and final hypothesis, which is:

H_6 – *High growth SMEs grow in related areas of business by building on their existing strengths.*

Therefore the various themes associated with growth in the literature were recast as a list of strategic attributes which, it is hypothesised, characterise high growth companies.

H_1: High growth SMEs focus on market segments.

H_2: High growth SMEs pursue strategies of differentiation and uniqueness.

H_3: High growth SMEs are characterised by innovation.

H_4: High growth SMEs are characterised by superior competitive devices.

H_5: High growth SMEs invest in their future.

H_6: High growth SMEs grow in related areas of business by building on their existing strengths.

These various proposed explanations and correlates of growth are, in general, plausible and carry some evidence of empirically-based relationships. However, the general thrust of the literature is such that it is not always clear whether the suggested strategic correlates are uniquely associated with growth in companies as distinguished from success in a more general sense. The issue of whether and how specific correlates of successful growth can be separated from correlates of success without growth remains clouded. It is clear that some of these measures are associated with the business's existing competitive position. Some of the measures relate to how the business develops and exploits new product-market positions. It is through the dynamic interplay of these strategy themes that some businesses achieve sustainable high growth.

RESEARCH METHODOLOGY

The six hypotheses were tested using a sample of small and medium-sized indigenous industrial Irish companies. The size range of the companies studied was a turnover of between IR£6 million (US$10 million) and IR£1.2 billion (US$2 billion), though the sample was skewed towards the lower size restriction. Within this size range, there are 317 indigenous Irish companies in the manufacturing, distribution, wholesaling, retailing, farming co-operative and service sectors (with the exception of companies operating in financial services). A two-page questionnaire was posted to these 317 companies. The questionnaire required the respondent companies to compare the strategies and the strategic position of their core business with those of their leading competitor. Descriptive information and performance measures such as return on sales, growth in turnover, percentage of turnover exported, and size of markets was collected.

Of the 317 companies in the sample 131 valid responses were received, a response rate of 41 per cent. Despite there being a wide discrepancy in the growth rates and the size of the population, the respondent companies were representative of this wide spread (Tables 6.2 and 6.3).

Table 6.2   Respondents are representative of the growth spread of the total population

Growth in sales	Number of companies in population	Number of responses	Percentage of responses
<15%	74	29	24
15% to <37%	73	37	31
37% to <77%	73	29	24
77% to 1688%	74	26	21
Total	294	121	100

Table 6.3   Respondents are representative of the size spread of the total population

1989 sales (million)	Number of companies in population	Number of responses in sample	Percentage of all responses
£50–£1371	79	31	24
£21–£50	80	23	18
£10.5–£21	79	39	30
£6–£10.5m	81	37	28
Total	319	130	100

The respondent companies were divided into four growth quartiles on the basis of growth rate of the core business for the 1984–9 period (Table 6.4). The high growth quartile of sample companies was compared to the low growth quartile (the comparison consisted of calculating mean, median, percentile values, cross tabulations with Pearson's x^2 values and correlation coefficients). To eliminate expected frequency errors in the cross-tabulations, it was necessary in many cases to reduce the number of answer options from five-point answer scales to two categories, usually a 'better' or 'higher' category and a 'same','no difference','lower' or 'worse' category.

Table 6.4   The responding companies divided into quartiles based on growth rate

	Core business growth rate(%)	No. of companies
Bottom quartile (low growth business)	−50–22	32
Lower middle quartile	24–49	31
Upper middle quartile	50–100	32
Top quartile (high growth businesses)	112–2000	32

RESEARCH FINDINGS

H_1: High Growth SMEs Focus on Market Segments

The mean Irish market size for high growth companies was IR£226 million. This compares to a mean for low growth companies of £486 million and a sample mean of IR£357 million (a correlation coefficient of −0.17 suggests no correlation). While high growth SMEs appear to be focusing on a more focused market, the research evidence suggests that they are more likely to have a wider product range. Of the high growth companies, 77 per cent classified themselves as 'several' or 'many' product companies, compared to 32 per cent for low growth companies (chi square significant at a 0.03 confidence level). This result was unexpected because it was thought that as part of their focus strategy high growth companies would be characterised by a narrow product range (as suggested by, for example, Hambrick, Macmillan and Day, 1982).

Therefore, the hypothesis that high growth SMEs pursue focus strategies is rejected. High growth SMEs appear to pursue broad-based product lines in their target markets. The evidence suggests that these markets *may* be more tightly defined. A possible explanation for this result is that the small size of the Irish market requires Irish companies to cover all product options in their niche. This evidence seems to support Biggadike's (1979) findings that aggressive broad-based entry strategies are more successful than focused strategies.

H₂: High Growth SMEs Pursue Strategies of Differentiation and Uniqueness

The analysis suggested that high growth companies are more likely to have products that are differentiated from competitors (this was chi-square significant at a 0.013 confidence level). Customer differentiation was measured by the respondents comparing the 'kind of customers' they sold to with those of their competitors. High growth companies are not different from low growth companies in terms of customer differentiation, although customer differentiation may have been insignificant because the respondent companies were comparing themselves to competitors and the definition of competitors is often based on the kind of customers sold to. Therefore, the hypothesis that high growth companies pursue differentiation strategies is accepted on the basis that this differentiation is product-based.

The results also suggested that high growth companies differentiate themselves in terms of their personnel policies (chi-square significant at a 0.0023 confidence level). The other functional areas, marketing, production, finance, R&D and distribution did not differentiate between the two groups.

H₃: High Growth SMEs are Characterised by Innovation

Innovation was measured by the percentage of the company's sales that came from new products. Relative to competitors, high growth companies have a higher percentage of new products: the mean percentage of sales coming from new products in high growth companies was 38 per cent compared to 15 per cent for low growth companies and a total sample mean of 23 per cent (correlation coefficient of 0.51 and significant at a 0.000 confidence level). Relative to low growth companies high growth companies have a core product that is much younger. The mean response for high growth companies was 1975. This compares to 1950 for the low growth quartile (weak correlation coefficient for this variable of 0.29 but significant at a 0.013 confidence level). For the variable 'percentage of sales from products introduced within the previous five years', 70 per cent of high growth companies responded in the 'much higher' and 'higher' categories compared to 36 per cent for low growth companies (chi-square significant at a 0.011 confidence level). The variables 'first to introduce the product' and 'offered unique benefits' did not discriminate between the two groups. Therefore, this hypothesis is accepted.

H₄: High Growth SMEs are Characterised by Superior Competitive Devices

Product quality, customer service and the percentage sales accounted for by new products each discriminated between the high growth and low growth groups. Relative to competitors, high growth companies are more likely to sell higher quality products: 87.5 per cent of high growth companies responded in the 'much higher' and 'higher' categories versus 61 per cent for the low growth companies (chi-square significant at a 0.016 confidence level). Relative to competitors, high growth companies are more likely to have a higher customer service reputation: 91 per cent of high growth companies responded in the 'much higher' and 'higher' categories compared to 54 per cent for low growth companies (chi-square significant at a 0.002 confidence level). As noted above, the new product variables differentiated between the high growth and low growth groups. Selling prices did not discriminate between the high growth and low growth groups. Therefore, this hypothesis is accepted in terms of product quality, customer service and the percentage sales accounted for by new products.

H₅: High Growth SMEs Invest in their Future

Relative to competitors, high growth companies had a much higher percentage growth in capacity over the previous five years as 87.5 per cent of high growth companies responded in the 'much higher' and 'higher' category compared to 28 per cent for low growth companies (chi-square significant at a 0.00001 confidence level). Relative to competitors, high growth companies have newer plant and equipment (72 per cent of high growth companies responded in the 'much higher' and 'higher' category compared to 41 per cent for low growth companies, chi-square significant at a 0.016 confidence level). This hypothesis is therefore accepted.

The measure used to test for product development was the ratio of R&D expenditure to sales. This did not successfully discriminate between the two groups, although the outcome of R&D expenditures – new products – did discriminate between the two groups. Market development expenditure was measured by 'advertising and promotion to sales ratio', and 'stocks to sales ratio' (a measure of investment in stocks). The outcome of market development was measured by both the 'number of distribution channels used' and the 'penetration of distribution channels'. None of these four variables discriminated between the two groups. High growth companies spend on capacity expansions and on new plant and equipment, but there was no direct evidence that they spend on market and product development.

H$_6$: High Growth SMEs Grow in Related Areas of Business by Building on their Existing Strengths

Each company was asked to indicate which growth path described their business for the 1984–9 period and to rank the six options. High growth companies stated that they grew by 'expansion in Irish market', by 'related product diversification', and by 'expansion in overseas markets', whilst low growth companies described their growth direction as 'retrenchment', and 'related new product diversification'. Primary growth direction differentiated between the two groups when compared for the top four choices (retrenchment, expansion in Ireland, overseas expansion, related new products). Around 61 per cent of responses for the top four categories were in the 'expansion in Irish market' option for the high growth group compared to 13 per cent for the low growth group (chi-square significant at a 0.001 confidence level). Therefore, this hypothesis is accepted.

It was argued that strategic flexibility was an essential characteristic of high growth SMEs. As a measure of the business's ability to change focus, the 'growth direction' variable was considered. For both the high growth and the low growth group, over 50 per cent of the respondents chose either 'expansion in the Irish market' or 'retrenchment in the Irish market' as their primary growth direction for the 1984–9 period (59 per cent for the low growth group and 53 per cent for the high growth group). A comparison of the distribution of the responses for the second choice indicates that for the low growth group, 50 per cent of the responses were in categories that did not involve a change of focus ('expansion in the Irish market' and 'retrenchment in the Irish market') compared to 19 per cent for the high growth group. This evidence suggests that the high growth SMEs in this study were characterised by strategic flexibility.

The analysis also suggested that, relative to low growth companies, high growth companies have a higher level of exports. Mean exports for the high growth group was 33 per cent compared to 24 per cent for low growth companies, and a total sample mean of 24 per cent (the analysis suggested a weak correlation coefficient of 0.34, which was significant at a 0.003 confidence level).

Is Growth Profitable?

Using published profit and growth figures, a correlation was found between growth and profitability (the 'business and finance' data reported in Table 6.5 suggest that profits and growth are correlated. Correlation coefficients of 0.54, 0.53 and 0.56 at 0.010, 0.008 and 0.010 levels of significance for the 'business and finance' profit variable for 1989, 1988 and 1987 supported this finding). Relative to their competitors, high growth companies are more likely than low growth companies to have a higher percentage return on sales. About 70 per cent of high growth companies responded in the 'much higher' and 'higher' category compared to 38 per cent for low growth companies (chi-square significant at a 0.013 confidence level for two categories of answer options). Mean returns are at least 80 per cent higher for high growth companies (Table 6.5). However, the correlation coefficients for both the core profit variables and the total profit variables for each of 1985 to 1989 would suggest no correlation between growth and profitability.

Table 6.5   Core business profits as a percentage of sales

Year	High growth		Low growth		Total sample	
	Mean	Std	Mean	Std	Mean	Std
1989	10.7	8.1	5.9	4.9	7.7	6.9
1988	9.7	7.7	5.3	4.3	6.8	6.6
1987	9.2	7.0	4.0	2.8	6.1	6.4
1986	8.2	6.0	4.2	3.3	5.8	5.3
1985	8.3	5.9	4.6	3.6	5.6	6.6

Std = Standard.

SUMMARY OF THE RESULTS OF THE QUESTIONNAIRE SURVEY

Therefore, the results of the questionnaire suggest that high growth SMEs:

(a) do not necessarily pursue focus strategies, but do pursue a strategy of a broad product line which may be in a narrower product-market niche;

(b) pursue strategies of differentiation and uniqueness by differentiating their products from those of their competitors;

(c) are characterised by innovation, and continually introduce new products, (in addition, over a period of five years they will significantly change and improve their product portfolio);

(d) compete by emphasising product quality, customer service and by introducing new and improved products;
(e) invest in their future by expanding capacity and by up-dating plant and equipment;
(f) grow in related areas of business by building on their existing strengths, and are likely to be involved in exporting or in export markets;
(g) combine profitability and growth.

CASE ANALYSIS

The survey results provided a 'snapshot' of the strategies being pursued by high growth SMEs. This 'snapshot', however, could not tell the whole story as growth is by definition a process that occurs over time. Casual observation suggested that growth in many SMEs was not sustained and that the relative growth performance of competing SMEs often differs significantly. The survey results did not fully explain the differences between those businesses that have sustained growth over a period of, say, 20 years and those that experienced either very slow growth or an initial period of growth followed by a period of stagnation. In a follow-up to the questionnaire survey, two in-depth case studies were carried out in order to provide a longitudinal study of the growth process.

Table 6.6   Growth rates achieved by Regional Ltd and City Ltd
(turnover in IR£ 000s)

	1971	1979	1990
Regional Ltd			
Delivered wholesale			
(franchised stores)	2 700	11 500	229 000
Cash-and-carry	1 500	31 000	143 000
Other business	4 800		
Total	9 000	42 500	372 000
City Ltd			
Cash-and-carry	< 4 000	8 200	15 200

One high growth and one low growth case were chosen from the respondents to the questionnaire survey. The case research was based on interviews with the founder and/or the CEO and a review of company plans, grant submissions and other relevant company documentation. The two case companies operate 'cash-and-carry' wholesale operations: that is, a business where the retailer comes to the wholesaler's warehouse, picks the range of merchandise required, pays in cash and then 'carries' the goods away. The companies, Regional Ltd and City Ltd, were founded in the 1880s and the 1940s respectively. Both grew rapidly during the 1970s and early 1980s as the 'cash-and-carry' concept replaced many of the more traditional wholesalers who delivered directly to the retail outlet and provided credit. While both of these companies considered that they performed very successfully in this market Regional Ltd clearly out-performed City Ltd during the period of the analysis (1970–90: see Tables 6.6 and 6.7). In aggregate, the grocery wholesale industry grew at approximately 15½ per cent compound during the 1970s and 1980s.

Regional Ltd is a family owned business carrying dry grocery goods. The company operates two divisions, a 'cash-and-carry' wholesaler that sells predominantly to newsagents and grocery stores, and a wholesale business that sells to its own franchise supermarkets. During 1970 to 1979, the company grew by 375 per cent and by a further 775 per cent during 1980–9. City Ltd is also a family owned and run 'cash-and-carry' operation. The company's sales consist of dry grocery goods sold to small family owned newsagents and food stores from their premises in Dublin, Ireland's capital. The company experienced steady and significant growth and achieved a market share ranking of third in the Dublin market. During the period 1970–80, the company grew by 105 per cent and by a further 85 per cent during 1980–9. During the period of analysis, both companies were profitable. The rate and direction of growth of these two companies is described briefly below.

Table 6.7   Growth in capacity in the Dublin region: additional square foot of cash-and-carry premises

	Additions to capacity		Total capacity 1991	
	1972	*1982*	*Dublin*	*Ireland*
Regional Ltd	90 000	110 000	200 000	628 000
City Ltd	4 000	8 000	16 000	16 000

Regional Ltd

In 1972, Regional Ltd introduced the concept of large-scale 'cash-and-carry' operations to an industry sector which was facing shrinking market demand due to the development of supermarkets. During the 1960s, the company diversified away from their traditional wholesale business by acquiring companies in areas such as tea blending and distribution, confectionery manufacturing and hotel management. Although these acquisitions resulted in significant growth in company sales, profitability levels remained very low.

In 1971, management reacted to these low levels of profitability by refocusing the company's business in the wholesale sector, with the objective of achieving a leadership position in national food wholesaling. The vehicles of expansion would be 'cash-and-carry' operations and wholly-owned supermarkets. To fund this growth the company decided that the diversifications undertaken during the 1960s would be disposed of and that no new diversifications would be undertaken. The company had successfully introduced the 'cash-and-carry' concept to one region of Ireland during the 1960s. Management believed that if they replaced their small wholesale operations with large sized 'cash-and-carry' sites (100 000 square feet), they would get sufficient economies of scale and purchasing power to allow them to underprice competing services. This concept required locating in large centres of population so that demand would be high enough. The consequence of this was that the company, which had traditionally operated exclusively in a regional market, would have to move to new locations. The company opened its first large 'cash-and-carry' in Dublin in 1972 and, following the success of this store, the company located outlets in the major population centres of Ireland during the remainder of the 1970s. Management operated these new stores separately from their traditional wholesale delivery business.

The company grew rapidly and by 1980 was the leading 'cash-and-carry' wholesaler in Ireland. In parallel to these developments the company began to operate its own supermarkets. However, these were unprofitable and were disposed of in 1977. The 'cash-and-carry' business continued to grow during the 1980s, though growth was at a slower rate than the 1970s. The growth in the 1980s was primarily the result of further geographical expansion as Regional Ltd developed a new site in a new geographical location and acquired a regional-based wholesaler.

City Ltd

City Ltd is a family run 'cash-and-carry' based in Dublin. The company was founded by the father of the current management team who developed a small shop into a wholesale business in the 1960s. He introduced the 'cash-and-carry' concept to Dublin from these new premises, though he continued to operate the traditional wholesale service. His strategy was one of very low margins to persuade customers to switch from a delivery service. Management increased the size of the company's warehouse in 1968 and sold off some of its transport.

In 1974, competition increased when Regional Ltd opened their 'cash-and-carry' in Dublin, reducing prices and trying to persuade Dublin retailers to switch from their existing wholesaler. In response to the threat of Regional Ltd opening a second location in Dublin in 1978, City Ltd expanded existing premises by doubling their size. In addition, several areas within the warehouse were extended and up-graded during the latter half of the 1980s; new customers were targeted (in particular pubs and restaurants), and a new range of toy products was added. In addition, the company leased out a small space in the car park to a greetings card supplier operating a greetings card wholesale operation. Overall, the product range was adapted during the latter half of the 1980s to reflect the products being sold by convenience stores. During the 1980s, the company sponsored the creation of nine 'neighbourhood' franchise stores, which were deals arranged with individuals that were personally known to management. However, due to limited management time, the company felt that they would not expand further in this area.

The company's sales continued to grow during the 1980s, with turnover increasing by 30 per cent from 1984 to 1989, with a 1988 product range very similar to that sold in 1983. Despite the premises being overcrowded, the company did not expand to a second site because they believed that the success of their business was the result of personal contact between the family and customers.

DISCUSSION

The cases highlighted several factors which may account for these differences in performance. First, the case analysis suggests that the companies played different roles in developing the market in which they were competing. The case evidence suggests that the growth in the size of the 'cash-and-carry' sector reflected the growth of Regional Ltd: that is, as Regional Ltd expanded and opened new outlets, the 'cash-and-carry' sector expanded. It appears that growth in the company led the growth in the sector. The implication of this is that the competitive strategy choices of the firm may in fact have been driving the growth of the sector rather than the growth in the market driving the growth of the venture.

However, during the 1970s and 1980s, City Ltd achieved a growth rate that was lower than the growth rate for the sector and lower than the growth rate achieved by Regional Ltd (Table 6.8). The dominant role that

Regional Ltd played in developing and expanding the market meant that the growth rate of the market reflected the high growth rate of Regional Ltd. It seems appropriate, therefore, to conceptualise the growth in the market as the driving force behind the growth in City Ltd.

Table 6.8   How the case companies performed relative to the growth of the wholesale sector

	Total	Per annum	Total	Per annum
	1971–77		1977–88	
Wholesale grocery sector	+226%	21%	+275%	12%
	1971–79		1977–90	
Regional Ltd*	+912%	33%	+775%	22%
	1970–80		1980–89	
City Ltd	+100%	7.5%	+85%	7%

* Only wholesale operations are included.

Second, the cases suggest that the difference in growth rates was the direct result of Regional Ltd pursuing a strategy of multiple locations in comparison to City Ltd, which developed in only the one location. Since success depends on independent retailers travelling to the 'cash-and-carry' site to select, purchase and take away their merchandise, short travel distances might reasonably be considered a key success factor. Several reasons could be suggested for the difference in strategy. For example, it is plausible to hypothesise that the difference is a function of the different motivations and goals of senior management. However, the case analysis suggests a different explanation, highlighting the larger resources that Regional Ltd developed to finance its development. Initially they sold a range of unrelated businesses to fund their first large site. Subsequently, through careful attention to the management of this business, the company continued to generate resources to finance further outlets. The case suggests that Regional Ltd:

(a) was better at managing;
(b) had a higher quality product in terms of the range of goods offered (e.g., 25 000 lines as compared to 16 000 lines in City Ltd);
(c) had better layout of the physical premises (larger premises with wider aisles, etc.);
(d) had better stock control (computerised stock control systems);
(e) had higher purchasing power and therefore better margins;
(f) had better marketing and promotion.

In comparison, City Ltd operated on very tight margins and failed to develop significant profitability. Clearly City Ltd has survived and been successful, though it appears that the quality of its product is inferior.

A second explanation which may account for Regional Ltd developing multiple locations and City Ltd focusing on one location is that management in each company identified different factors and competitive strategy variables as being associated with success. The 'success formula' adopted by management at Regional Ltd was to compete by developing large outlets with large volumes, lower prices and better margins. In comparison, management at City Ltd attributed the success of their venture to the close contact between members of the owners' family and customers. Consequently, management at City Ltd saw no necessity to advertise but rather relied on 'word-of-mouth'. Management were very proud that many customers had done business with several generations of their family. By conceptualising their advantage in terms of loyalty and relationships, it appeared inappropriate to set up a second location because they believed customer attention in the first location would deteriorate and they would not be able to attend sufficiently to new customers in a new location. As growth in 'cash-and-carry' is directly related to customers' travel distance and therefore to the development of multiple locations, City Ltd cut itself off from market growth anywhere but in the travel zone around their traditional site. Their company growth was not only driven by market growth but limited to a geographically constrained segment of that market's growth. This problem of not being able to identify the factors that are associated with success may be termed causal ambiguity (Lippman and Rumelt, 1982).

In addition to the above explanations for the different levels of performance between the two companies, the cases highlighted the fact that Regional Ltd expanded into new business which further increased the growth of their wholesale business. This was achieved by developing franchise stores which were required to purchase a significant percentage of their produce from the company (a strategy of vertical integration). Interestingly, City Ltd also developed a number of these stores but did not grow them into a significant business because management believed that it would take up too much of their time. The ability to expand the core business by developing vertically into a related area had a significant impact on maintaining high growth rates in Regional Ltd after the growth of the 'cash-and-carry' market began to fade. This corporate flexibility (Abbanat, 1967; Katz, 1970; Cohn and Lindberg, 1972; Kuhn, 1982), appears to be central to their sustained growth. The case analysis suggests that an ability to change market position and/or competitive strategy is essential if growth is to be sustained over a long period.

DO THE CASES SUPPORT THE SURVEY FINDINGS?

Both companies achieved significant growth in a high growth market in the 1970s and early 1980s. However, within this high growth market the companies fared very differently in a number of ways. The companies differed in terms of sales volume growth, geographical expansion and the degree of vertical integration.

1. In terms of absolute growth rates, Regional Ltd grew at a much faster rate; by 1990, its 'cash-and-carry' business was nine times bigger than City Ltd. Regional Ltd achieved this higher growth by developing multiple locations whereas City Ltd concentrated on the development of a single location.
2. Regional Ltd developed larger sites and expanded into more sites. By 1990, Regional Ltd had six sites compared to the one site of City Ltd. Furthermore, the average size of each Regional Ltd site was six times the size of City Ltd's site.
3. Most significantly, during the 1980s, management at Regional Ltd expanded their wholesale business beyond the 'cash-and-carry' concept by developing the concept of franchised convenience stores and franchised small, neighbourhood supermarkets. This new business built on their existing wholesale strengths as the franchise agreements required the stores to purchase a significant percentage of their supplies from the wholesale operation. This business added 50 per cent to total business turnover. In comparison, City Ltd pursued a very modest level of forward vertical integration.

The case analyses supports the findings of the questionnaire survey. The questionnaire survey suggested that high growth SMEs do not necessarily pursue focus strategies. From the outset Regional Ltd sought to dominate the 'cash-and-carry' market and pursued a strategy of complete market coverage, although their initial market entry strategy was focused on one geographical location. However, having established a presence in this market they moved to new geographical locations. In comparison, City Ltd restricted their market coverage by not pursuing a strategy of geographic diversification. While the strategy at City Ltd could be described by management as a 'focus' strategy, the case evidence suggests that there is no market rational for 'focusing' on one geographic area and that this strategy hampered the growth potential of City Ltd.

The results of the survey suggested that high growth SMEs pursue strategies of differentiation and uniqueness by differentiating their products from those of their competitors. Additionally, the results suggested that high growth SMEs emphasise product quality and customer service. These findings clearly differentiated between the two case companies in terms of size of premises, breadth of product range, presentation of premises and merchandise, and overall prices. Regional Ltd out-competed and out-performed City Ltd.

The survey suggested that high growth SMEs are characterised by innovation and that they continually introduce new products. The nature of the 'cash-and-carry' business is such that new products are determined by manufacturers and suppliers. However, Regional Ltd offered a significantly broader range of products and a wider choice for any given product line.

Regional Ltd grew in related areas of business and by building on their existing strengths. They pursued this strategy by developing multiple locations and larger stores, whilst City Ltd did not develop beyond their initial location. Regional Ltd also exhibited strategic flexibility when they moved into developing and supplying 'franchise stores' in the 1980s. Neither Regional Ltd nor City Ltd entered export markets during the case analysis, though Regional Ltd were considering plans to invest outside Ireland. The expansion at Regional Ltd involved the development of additional capacity. In comparison to City Ltd, Regional Ltd invested in its future by expanding capacity and by up-dating plant and equipment throughout the 1970s and 1980s (Table 6.7). The survey also suggested that high growth SMEs combine profitability and growth. Both case companies were successful in this market and were profitable. Despite its very high growth rate, Regional Ltd remained profitable.

CONCLUSIONS AND IMPLICATIONS

This chapter argues that there are strategies common to high growth companies independent of their industry sector and that these strategies discriminate between high growth and low growth SMEs. Owner-managers of SMEs who seek high growth must decide *where to compete* and then must make key choices and commitments relating to *how they will compete*. It is the combination of these decisions that results in sustained growth.

In an attempt to understand why growth is not necessarily achieved and sustained by all SMEs in similar product-market environments, two cases were presented. The cases highlighted the importance of the choice of market in determining the growth rate of a company. The results presented in this chapter confirm for both the owner-manager and for policy-makers that the choice of market is not the sole determinant of a company's growth. In the short term, the choice of a high growth market may result in high growth for individual SMEs, although if this growth is to be sustainable the SME must grow at a rate higher than market growth rates. As a result, high growth SMEs must penetrate their markets at a faster rate than their competitors. The period of growth observed in the low growth case was attributed to the growth in the market, with the low growth SME actually losing relative market share during this period of growth. The higher rate of market penetration in the high growth SME was the result of superior competitive strategies. Therefore, the survey suggested a number of superior competitive strategies.

1. The SME competes with differentiated products. The source of this differentiation appears to be an emphasis on innovation. Innovation manifests itself in terms of the development of a stream of improved and new products. These products are of high quality and are delivered with an emphasis on customer service.
2. The SME grows by emphasising its existing strengths and by growing in related areas. This growth requires continued investment in capacity expansion and new plant and equipment.
3. Growth often necessitates a change in market focus, which may be the result of introducing new products or of entering export markets. The high growth SME must be able to identify and make the necessary changes in product-market positioning.

Sustainable growth is built by good management and a strong commitment to the future. Policy-makers must, therefore, encourage SMEs to develop strategies that are fundamentally sound and robust. The results suggest that the traditional advice of 'focus, focus, focus' which many researchers and policy-makers offer SMEs may be misplaced and may restrict the growth potential of the SME. Broad-based market strategies appear to be associated with high growth.

The findings suggest that researchers must explore the issue of market focus in more detail. A first step towards this would be the development of a typology of the competitive scope and the competitive strategies of SMEs. Having identified in this research the strategies associated with growth, the logical next step is to identify how some SMEs develop these strategies and what is preventing all SMEs from pursuing these strategies.

7 New Technology-Based Firms in Innovation Networks

Erkko Autio

INTRODUCTION

This chapter develops and applies a systemic approach to research on NTBFs. It will be contended that the traditional body of research on NTBFs essentially reflects a linear model of the spin-off process of these firms (e.g., Roberts, 1991b). This linear model, for its part, is largely based on the obsolete linear sequential model of technological innovation. The linear model of the spin-off process of NTBFs can be summarised as follows:

(a) a technology-based idea is generated;
(b) a new firm is established to exploit the new idea;
(c) the new firm starts to amass resources, both human and financial, and starts developing a prototype based on the new idea;
(d) if the business idea turns out to be viable, the new firm embarks on a rapid growth path.

The linear model of the spin-off process of NTBFs is in contrast to the developments made in innovation theory during the last decade (Rothwell, 1992; Soete and Arundel, 1993). Indeed, modern innovation theory essentially contends that the process of technological innovation is a complex, iterative, often systemic one, in which a number of factors exercise an important influence on the outcomes of the process, such as:

(a) the creation of positive externalities (Wade, 1995);
(b) the maturity of the technological system (Carlsson and Stankiewicz, 1991);
(c) the transferability and symplectic character of the technology in question (Autio and Hameri, 1995);
(d) patterns of local and global accumulation of technologies (Allen, 1990; Hameri, 1993);

(e) emergence of technological trajectories (Dosi, 1982) and guideposts (Sahal, 1985);
(f) the modularity of the system (Langlois and Robertson, 1992; Garud and Kumaraswamy, 1995);
(g) the structuring of the network (Debackere *et al.*, 1994; Grandori and Soda, 1995) and of the organisational population (Hannan and Freeman, 1989).

Essential for the modern view of the innovation process is that the process is viewed as a systemic, irreversible phenomenon (Pavitt, 1990), during which the environment shapes the innovating firm as the firm shapes its environment (Amendola and Bruno, 1990), not as an isolated, sequential, goal-oriented project.

The modern view of the technological innovation process has many important implications for research on NTBFs, implications that arguably have not been given sufficient attention so far. Recent research emphasises the importance of technology as a factor shaping and regulating the evolution of business systems and of individual (technology-based) firms in particular (Nelson, 1994; Suárez and Utterback, 1995). Acs and Audretsch, in particular, present evidence supporting the suggestion by Nelson and Winter (1982) that different technological regimes offer different opportunities for the survival of small and large firms (Acs and Audretsch, 1990; Audretsch, 1995).

NTBFs are firms that essentially base their business idea on the exploitation of their internal storage of technological competencies, or their internal technological competence pool. The present study takes the view that such firms are essentially concentrations of technological competencies. It is thus reasonable to expect that NTBFs are, to a greater extent than many other types of firms, affected by the characteristics of the technological system (Carlsson and Stankiewicz, 1991) of which they constitute one part.

Technological innovation constitutes one essential characteristic and one dominating activity of NTBFs. As the dominant mode of technological innovation is becoming increasingly systemic in character, it is necessary to study how such a development is reflected in the behaviour and evolution of NTBFs. The modern view of the technological innovation process largely remains to be implemented in research on such firms. The present study strives to contribute towards this end, and is structured as follows. First, growth studies and empirical findings are discussed. Then, a model depicting possible niches for NTBFs is constructed. The model is empirically tested by using data from three populations of NTBFs:

namely, spin-off firms of the University of Cambridge, spin-off firms of Stanford University, and spin-off firms of the Technical Research Centre of Finland. Finally, implications of the empirical findings are discussed.

THE GROWTH MYOPIA

The traditional body of research on NTBFs arguably suffers from growth myopia. This means that an important fraction of the traditional studies on such firms focuses on picking the winners, assuming that practically all new firms are growth-oriented, interpreting success as rapid organic growth and related amassing of resources, and recommending strategies whereby the success of NTBFs can be increased: that is, more rapid organic growth can be induced (Roberts and Wainer, 1966; Roberts, 1968; Feeser and Dugan, 1989; Feeser and Willard, 1990; Roure and Keeley, 1991). The new venture is expected either to grow or to die. Absence of growth is viewed as stagnation. If a trade sale occurs, (i.e., the control of the new venture is sold to an established industrial firm), this is considered as a kind of failure: the entrepreneur has failed to live up to the myth of the heroic entrepreneur.

The above characterisations are, of course, over-simplifying. Yet, there is a clear discrepancy between the frequently recurring contentions and the results of many empirical studies on NTBFs. Empirical studies suggest that rapid organic growth is both rare and often even unwanted among NTBFs. The median size of these firms has been found to be approximately 10–20 employees, and the mean size less than 50 employees, independent of the environment in which the study has been conducted (Rodenberger and McCray, 1981; Doutriaux and Peterman, 1982; Tyebjee and Bruno, 1982; Gould and Keeble, 1984; Keeble and Kelly, 1986; Oakey, Rothwell and Cooper, 1988; Autio *et al.*, 1989). The median sales of Finnish, Canadian and American NTBFs have been found to be practically the same, approximately one million Finnish Markka (5 Finnish Markka = US$1) after approximately four years (Rodenberger and McCray, 1981; Tyebjee and Bruno, 1982; Doutriaux and Peterman, 1982; Autio *et al.*, 1989). An increasing number of follow-up studies carried out in various science parks in Europe support the conclusion that the primary contribution of NTBFs to economic dynamism may be realised through other mechanisms than through rapid organic growth (Monck *et al.*, 1988; Autio and Kauranen, 1992; Kauranen *et al.*, 1990). On the basis of extensive surveys, Storey points out that as few as 4 per cent of all new independent ventures create as much as up to 50 per cent of the total direct employment created by these ventures (Storey, 1994; Westhead, 1994; Westhead and Cowling, 1994). The 35-year longitudinal survey of the spin-off firms of the Chalmers University reveals that the majority of these firms employs less than 15 employees (Wallmark and Sjösten, 1994).

The absence of growth is not confined to realised growth only. Importantly, there is an absence of growth aspirations. In Finland, over 60 per cent of NTBFs do not perceive rapid or even moderately rapid organic growth as a feasible way to develop their activities (Kauranen *et al.*, 1990). Even more modest growth aspirations have been cited for small information technology firms (Kellock, 1992; Courtney and Leeming, 1994). In Finland, a national survey focusing specifically on high-potential NTBFs, selected regionally by expert panels, reported relatively low means of expected growth rates, with the mean expected annual growth rate in company sales being estimated at approximately 15 per cent (Lumme, 1994b; Oakey, 1994). Reflecting on a large number of studies on NTBFs, Oakey concludes that: 'NTBF's [*sic*] were not a simple panacea for the industrial ills of the United kingdom', and that 'it is a gross oversimplification to argue that all (or most) NTBF's [*sic*] have rapid growth potential' (Oakey, 1994:2–6).

In spite of the extensive empirical data pointing to the conclusion that most NTBFs do not grow and do not even want to grow, growth studies continue to dominate research on such firms. There is an important body of literature focusing on the problem of inducing growth among NTBFs, in spite of the fact that small size is an essential part of the *modus operandi* for the majority of such firms (Hull and Hjern, 1989; Poza, 1989; Barber, Metcalfe and Porteous, 1990; Flamholtz, 1990; Slatter, 1992). For such firms, inducing growth through incentives is often like pushing with a rope. There is a need to understand the reasons underlying the low growth orientation among NTBFs.

THE MODEL

The discrepancy between expectations and reality pertaining to growth among NTBFs is largely due to the rather over-simplifying contentions assumed in many studies. The NTBFs is viewed as operating in a market environment, being influenced by the 'Porterian' (Porter, 1980) forces shaping industry competition. Being predominantly viewed as a combination of financial resources and entrepreneurial spirit, the NTBF is assumed to be able to freely position itself in relation to its operating environment.

The main task of the management team has been viewed as formulating the right strategy (in terms of product-market-organisation combination) that would maximise the opportunities for success: that is, for rapid growth.

What such studies largely fail to perceive is that the NTBF is also influenced by other external forces than the traditional forces driving industry competition. Examples of such forces have been identified by economists. Following the Marshallian (Marshall, 1890) tradition, geographical economists emphasise the importance of agglomeration benefits, using the industrial district, or the local milieu (Crevoisier and Maillat, 1991), as their reference point. Innovation theory and organisation ecology have produced concepts such as dominant designs, technological trajectories, structuring of organisational populations, and, for example, creation of positive externalities, all of which can be used as reference points in attempting to understand the patterns of emergence and survival of NTBFs. The present study continues on this track, attempting to see whether niches can be found for NTBFs in terms of their functional relationship with technology transformation processes in innovation systems.

Construction of the Model

The view of NTBFs as concentrations of technological and economic competencies leads to a natural focus on links between the NTBF and its environment. The external technological resource base represents the external source of technologies that such a firm can draw upon. It is reasonable to expect that the characteristics of this resource base, as proposed by Håkansson (1989), or the knowledge base, as proposed by Balconi (1993), or the technological system, as proposed by Carlsson and Stankiewicz (1991), tend to be reflected in the characteristics of the NTBF.

An NTBF links with its external resource base in various ways in order to derive benefits from it (Covin and Prescott, 1991; Rothwell, 1991). As one conceptual basis for the analysis of such phenomena, the concepts of technological articulation, as proposed by Clark and Juma (1987), and basic technologies, as proposed by Stankiewicz (1990), will be used. Technological articulation refers to the process by which generic scientific knowledge is transformed into application-specific technological knowledge. During this transformation process, the transforming knowledge can take the form of basic technologies, as defined by Stankiewicz. A systemic depiction of the technological innovation process is presented in Figure 7.1.

Figure 7.1 illustrates the point that within an innovation system, or an innovation network, several types of knowledge transformation processes may be under way at any point in time. Rather than running sequentially, these processes can be expected to run in parallel. This is in contrast with the old linear sequential view of the process of technological innovation, a view that is reflected in the linear view of the spin-off process of NTBFs.

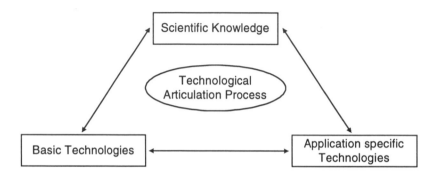

Figure 7.1   Systemic view of the interaction between scientific knowledge, basic technologies and application-specific technologies

If NTBFs are viewed as concentrations of technological competencies, it is reasonable to expect that the hierarchy depicted in Figure 7.1 should be reflected in their technology behaviour. The parallel technological transformation processes can be expected to offer niches according to which NTBFs can adapt their operations.

The present study expects that at least two technological niches can be found for NTBFs in innovation systems. These two technological niches are characterised as those characteristic of science-based firms on the one hand, and those characteristic of engineering-based firms on the other. It is expected that science-based firms are relatively more active in transforming scientific knowledge into basic technologies and application-specific technologies. It is also expected that engineering-based firms are relatively more active in transforming basic technologies into application-specific technologies. The two technological niches and the related transformation roles characteristic to science-based and engineering-based firms are depicted in Figure 7.2.

According to the model depicted in Figure 7.2, science-based firms should be attached to two transformation processes: the ones by which scientific knowledge is transformed into basic technologies and also into application-specific technologies. The shading in the box depicting the niche of science-based firms illustrates the expectation that science-based firms should be relatively more active in transforming scientific knowledge into basic technologies than in transforming scientific knowledge into application-specific technologies.

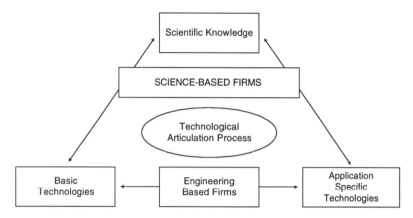

Figure 7.2   Technological niches occupied by science-based and engineering-based firms

The categorisation depicted in Figure 7.2 emphasises the point that science-based firms also develop practical applications. The very concept of technological norm, as defined by von Wright (1987), requires that a practical application for any technology must be found. In this respect, the difference between science-based and engineering-based firms is a relative one. Science-based firms can crudely be categorised as firms developing the first practical applications concerning certain physical phenomena or theoretical constructs. Engineering-based firms can crudely be categorised as firms expanding the scope of use of these first practical applications. However, this categorisation is not very clear-cut.

Verification of the Model

Pointers for the verification of the model depicted in Figure 7.2 can be derived from the discussion on the nature of basic technologies, as provided by Stankiewicz (1990). Stankiewicz suggests that basic technologies are essentially identified by the character of the natural phenomena they exploit, not by their functions or applications, as such. Technical systems-in-use, of which basic technologies make one part, can be analysed in terms of the functions that they are designed to perform. The performance of a technical system-in-use is realised by a set of applications that pertain to the set of functions which the system-in-use is designed to perform. The applications are based on the set of basic technologies that the technical system-in-use exploits.

The above discussion suggests that basic technologies should, in general, be more generic in nature than application-specific technologies. An example of basic technologies is, for example, the application of scientific knowledge concerning semiconducting materials into developing a generic purpose micro-processor. It is expected that differences can be found between firms developing generic purpose micro-processors and firms tailoring micro-processor technology into specific uses. It is expected that while science-based firms are essentially technology driven, engineering-based firm tend to be relatively more market driven (Chidamber, Shyam and Henry, 1994). Science-based firms are expected to be relatively more active in exploiting scientific breakthroughs, while engineering-based firms are expected to be relatively more active in exploiting market opportunities.

The scope of application can, in general, be expected to be broad for basic technologies. Here, the breadth of scope is evaluated in relative terms: the scope of applications should be broader for basic technologies than for application-specific technologies. The relatively broader scope of application of basic technologies follows naturally from the more generic nature of them.

The present study has chosen to ground the categorisation between science-based and engineering-based firms on a qualitative analysis of the free-form business descriptions given by the firms themselves. An NTBF cannot be expected to perceive itself and its functions in terms of the framework depicted in Figure 7.2. The judgement of whether an NTBF should be categorised as a science-based firm or an engineering-based firm thus should not be left to the firm. On the other hand, an NTBF can be expected to be able to provide an accurate description of the business in which it is active. If the model depicted in Figure 7.2 reflects reality, it is reasonable to expect that the distinction between science-based and engineering-based firms is reflected in their free-form business descriptions. If NTBFs are essentially concentrations of technological competencies, as the present study contends, it is reasonable to expect that the type of technological transformation process to which an NTBF is attached should be reflected in its business description.

The discussion concerning the differences between basic technologies and application-specific technologies provides pointers concerning the type of qualitative differences that can be expected in the free-form business descriptions of science-based firms and engineering-based firms. The qualitative differences are listed in Table 7.1. The expected differences listed in Table 7.1 are based on free-form descriptions. The numbering of characteristics indicates the relative importance attached to each differentiating characteristic when making the categorisation of the firms. In cases of conflicting characteristics, the categorisation of the firm is made on the basis of the relatively more important differentiating characteristic.

Table 7.1 Summary of qualitative differences in the business descriptions of science-based firms and engineering-based firms

Science-based firms	Engineering-based firms
1. Product or service of the firm is described in terms of some natural phenomenon	1. Product or service of the firm is described in terms of some specific application
2. Product or service of the firm is described in terms of some theoretical construct	2. Product or service of the firm is defined in terms of some customer need
3. Product or service of the firm is generic in nature	3. Product or service of the firm is application-specific in nature
4. The scope of application of the product or service is (relatively) broad	4. The scope of application of the product or service is (relatively) narrow
5. (Generic) technical features of the product or service are emphasised in the business description	5. Market needs and features of the market niche are emphasised in the business description
6. The business description conveys the impression of a technology-push mode of technology transfer; exploitation of technological opportunities is emphasised	6. The business description conveys the impression of a market-pull mode of technology transfer; exploitation of market opportunities is emphasised

The selected approach to making the categorisation between science-based and engineering-based firms provides the following setting for the empirical verification of the model depicted in Figure 7.2. The setting is outlined in Table 7.2. The technology behaviour of NTBFs is evaluated using three groups of dependent variables. As the focus of the present study is on the systemic technology impacts delivered by NTBFs in innovation networks, emphasis is placed upon variables pertaining to external technology interaction. The three main sets of dependent variables are:

(a) technology contributions derived from various internal and external sources of technology;

(b) the use of various technology transfer mechanisms in external technology interfaces;
(c) functional contributions provided by the NTBFs.

The first set of dependent variables relates to the composition of pool of technological competencies possessed by NTBFs. The second set of dependent variables relates to the type of technology flows catalysed by NTBFs in technological systems. The third set of dependent variables makes it possible to evaluate the systemic contributions provided by NTBFs in functional terms.

Table 7.2   Research setting for the empirical verification of the model of science-based and engineering-based firms

Independent variable	Dependent variables
• Categorisation to science-based and engineering-based firms, based on the free-form business description provided by the firm	• Technology contributions derived from various internal and external sources of technology
	• Use of various technology transfer mechanisms in external technology interfaces
	• Functional contributions provided by the firms to their customers

EMPIRICAL SAMPLES

The empirical data analysed in the present study has been collected from NTBFs in three different regions. These regions are the Cambridge area in the UK (Lumme *et al.*, 1992), Finland (Autio, 1993a), and the Silicon Valley area in the USA (Leone, Keeley and Miller, 1992; Geust and Autio, 1994). The three databases were compiled in several stages between 1991 and 1994, with the aim of ensuring the maximum degree of compatibility between them.

The survey of the spin-off firms of the Stanford University focused on a population of 313 Stanford University spin-off firms identified in an earlier survey (Leone, Keeley and Miller, 1992). The survey produced 82 usable replies. The database of the Technical Research Centre of Finland spin-off firms contains usable data from 29 of the 43 spin-offs identified in earlier surveys (Hyvärinen and Ahola, 1989; Ahola, 1990; Autio, 1993b). The database of the University of Cambridge spin-off firms contains

usable data from 19 of the 45 spin-off firms surveyed in an earlier survey
(Lumme *et al.*, 1992; Lumme, Kauranen and Autio, 1994).

The basic characteristics of the three sets of firms are summarised
in Table 7.3. The three rows at the bottom of Table 7.3 show the *p*-values
of pair-wise comparisons between individual distributions. The *p*-values
have been calculated using *t*-tests for unpaired groups.

Table 7.3   Background characteristics of the Stanford, Cambridge, and
Technical Research Centre of Finland (VTT) distributions

	Number of firms	*Mean age*	*Number of employees (mean)*	*Sales revenue (FIM*)*
Stanford	82	10.5	98.4	n.a.
Cambridge	19	9.0	13.1	1 020 000
VTT	29	5.0	4.3	406 500
p (Stanford, Cambridge)	n.a.	0.23	0.16	n.a.
p (Stanford, VTT)	n.a.	0.004	0.03	n.a.
p (Cambridge, VTT)	n.a.	0.13	0.002	0.03

* US$1 = FIM5.
n.a. = not applicable.

The small size of the Technical Research Centre of Finland firms
is partly due to their young age. The large mean size of the Stanford firms
is due to three outlier firms employing from 600 to 1400 employees.
The existence of these firms in the Stanford database is a sign of the
maturity of the spin-off phenomenon among the Stanford firms as well as
the extraordinarily favourable conditions of the Silicon Valley area.

The division between science-based and engineering-based technology groups is presented in Table 7.4. The bulk of the firms in the three
databases represent engineering-based technology groups. The largest technology groups in the three databases combined are software application,
technical consulting and electronics (communication). The share of firms
belonging to science-based industry groups is approximately 21 per cent
of the total. This share is surprisingly similar in the three groups. No statistically significant differences could be observed between the Stanford,
Cambridge and Technical Research Centre of Finland databases in terms
of the relative shares of science-based and engineering-based firms.
No statistically significant differences could be observed between science-
based and engineering-based firms in terms of their size, age or customer
profile.

ANALYSIS OF THE EMPIRICAL DATABASES

The empirical analysis is structured following the order of dependent variables, as listed in Table 7.2. First, the composition of the technology pool of science-based and engineering-based firms is analysed. Second, the intensity of technology flows catalysed in external technology interfaces is analysed. Third, the type of functional contributions provided by these firms to their customers is analysed.

Table 7.4   Science-based and engineering-based technology groups in the Stanford, Cambridge, and Technical Research Centre of Finland databases

Industry group	Number of firms	Classification
Aquaculture	1	Engineering-based
Electronics (automation)	1	Engineering-based
Electronics (basic)	4	Engineering-based
Electronics (communication)	19	Engineering-based
Electronics (computer-related)	7	Engineering-based
Electronics (measurement)	4	Engineering-based
Electronics (optoelectronics)	1	Engineering-based
Electronics (other)	5	Engineering-based
Laboratory services	1	Engineering-based
Manufacturing (basic)	1	Engineering-based
Metal processing	1	Engineering-based
Software application	34	Engineering-based
Technical consulting	23	Engineering-based
Training services	1	Engineering-based
Biotechnology	7	Science-based
Chemicals	1	Science-based
Electronics (IC related*)	2	Science-based
Electronics (microwave)	1	Science-based
Electronics (photonics)	5	Science-based
Electronics (semiconductor-related)	3	Science-based
Electronics (SQUIDs†)	1	Science-based
Geotechnical	1	Science-based
Medical	4	Science-based
Pharmaceutical	2	Science-based
Engineering-based altogether	103	
Science-based altogether	27	

* IC = Integrated circuit.
† SQUID = Superconductive quantum inference device.

Composition of the Technology Pool

In the databases, the composition of the technology pool (Tiler, Metcalfe and Connell, 1993) of the firms was evaluated with regard to a number of both internal and external sources of technology, and two different periods (the time of founding the firm and the time of survey or interview). This made it possible to monitor the evolution of the technology pool during the early years of the firm.

The existing literature gives some indications of the possible changes in the composition of the technology pool of NTBFs over time. The importance of the incubating organisation has already been demonstrated by Roberts (Roberts and Hauptmann, 1986; Roberts, 1991a). Von Hippel's studies on the importance of customers as a source of innovations suggest that the customer can be an important source of technological know-how

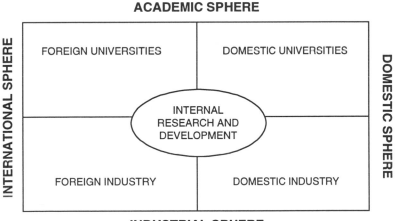

Figure 7.3   Different categories of internal and external sources of technology

for NTBFs (von Hippel, 1976, 1988). Von Hippel also points out that it is not unusual for technology-based firms to share technology with their suppliers and sometimes even with their competitors (von Hippel, 1986a). The same is also suggested by the numerous studies focusing on technological collaboration (Hagedoorn, 1989).

The internal and external sources of technology can be divided into different categories, as depicted in Figure 7.3. The external sources of technology are classified along two continuums: the academic–industry continuum and the domestic–international continuum. The academic–industry continuum also represents a continuum from publicly distributed to privately controlled technology, a distinction emphasised, for example,

Table 7.5 Comparison between science-based and engineering-based firms: use of external sources of technology

Source of technology	Mean(%) (Eng-B)	Mean(%) (Sc-B)	Mean diff.	DF	t-value	p-value
Parent, establishment	27.8	34.1	-6.30	115	-0.76	0.4507
Parent, present	12.1	13.6	-1.49	117	-0.34	0.7322
Internal R&D, establishment	39.9	35.0	4.88	115	0.56	0.5758
Internal R&D, present	59.2	53.8	5.42	117	0.75	0.4564
Customers, establishment	10.4	7.0	3.47	115	0.71	0.4789
Customers, present	12.3	7.0	5.21	117	1.20	0.2320
Domestic academic, establishment	4.6	9.7	-5.07	115	-1.54	0.1259
Domestic academic, present	2.4	10.3	-7.89	117	-3.78	0.0002***
Domestic industrial, establishment	7.2	11.1	-3.91	115	-0.80	0.4236
Domestic industrial, present	6.0	7.8	-1.85	117	-0.48	0.6324
Foreign academic, establishment	0.7	0.5	0.16	116	0.24	0.8148
Foreign academic, present	0.9	0.8	0.11	117	0.16	0.8747
Foreign industrial, establishment	3.8	0.0	3.83	114	1.23	0.2203
Foreign industrial, present	4.2	6.7	-2.51	117	-0.80	0.4266

Eng-B = Engineering-based.
Sc-B = Science-based.

For Tables 7.5–7.10.
Significance levels. >* = 0.05 level (5%); >** = 0.01 level (1%); >*** = 0.001 level (0.1%);
† = significance level of 0.05–0.1

by Nelson (Nelson, 1987). Science-based NTBFs are expected to be more closely connected with the academic sphere, while engineering-based NTBFs are expected to be more closely connected with the industrial sphere. The domestic–international continuum gives some insight into the international character of the particular technological system in which an NTBF operates. At the centre of the illustration of technology sources is the internal R&D activity of the firm, which is the main tool in developing firm-specific technological competencies.

Table 7.5 shows the differences between these two groups of firms in terms of the use of external sources of technology over two periods: the time of establishment of the firm and the time of interview. In calculating the statistical significance level of the differences shown, the *t*-test for un-paired groups was used. The results were checked with the Mann-Whitney U test for unpaired groups. The means are indicated as percentages of the whole.

The comparison between science-based and engineering-based firms in terms of the use of external sources of technology reveals only one statistically very significant difference between these two groups of firms. Science-based firms rely relatively more heavily on the domestic aca-demic sphere as a technology source than do engineering-based firms. Im-portantly, no difference was found between these two types of firms at the time of start-up. The absence of such differences confirms that the study did not start by analysing two different groups of firms. The difference in Table 7.5 can thus be interpreted as reflecting the different technology transformator roles of the firms, thus supporting the model depicted in Figure 7.2.

To check the generality of the finding in Table 7.5, the two largest tech-nology groups categorised as science-based were analysed separately. First, biotechnology firms were compared with the group of engineering-based firms. Second, science-based and engineering-based electronics firms were compared with each other. The results of the generality checks are shown in Table 7.6. Only statistically significant differences are shown.

The generality checks yield strikingly similar results to those revealed by the comparison between science-based firms and engineering-based firms. The generality check using biotechnology firms only gives exactly the same difference as observed for all science-based and engineering-based firms. The generality check using electronics firms also confirms the same finding. The generality checks suggest that the divisions between science-based and engineering-based firms are quite universal ones, ap-plying consistently to different sectors of technology.

Table 7.6 Results of generality checks

	Difference between groups	t-value	p-value
Biotechnology firms versus all engineering-based firms			
Domestic academic, present	23.3 %	7.16	< 0.0001***
Science-based versus engineering-based electronics firms			
Domestic academic, establishment	10.0 %	3.16	0.0027**
Domestic academic, present	3.7 %	2.71	0.0093**

Two further generality checks were carried out. The science-based and engineering-based firms were compared within the Stanford and Cambridge databases. The comparison yielded a result similar to that in Table 7.5. In the combined Stanford and Cambridge database, science-based firms had received a relatively more significant contribution from the domestic academic sphere at the time of interviews (this difference was statistically very significant at the significance level $p = 0.0002$). This check run provides evidence that the division between science-based and engineering-based firms is a quite universal one also in geographical terms.

Use of Various Technology Transfer Mechanisms in External Technology Interfaces

The composition of the technology pool of an NTBF can be altered through the use of various technology transfer mechanisms in external technology interfaces. Through these links, NTBFs catalyse technology flows in innovation networks. The results of the comparison between science-based and engineering-based firms in terms of technology interaction with their customers are shown in Table 7.6. The intensities of technology flows were evaluated using a five-step Likert scale from 1 (non-existent) to 5 (very intensive). The p-values in Table 7.6 indicate the statistical significance of the difference between the means of both distributions (they have been calculated using the t-test for unpaired groups and confirmed using the MannWhitney U test).

Table 7.7 supports the general hypothesis concerning the different domains occupied by science-based and engineering-based firms in innovation systems. The technology transfer patterns of the two groups of firms differ from each other, and the differences are in line with the model. The technology transfer mechanisms between engineering-based firms and their customers are clearly 'harder', or replication-intensive, in nature when compared with those of science-based firms. The technology transfer mechanisms between science-based firms and their customers seem to be more R&D-intensive in nature when compared with those of engineering-based firms.

For engineering-based firms, the most important technology transfer mechanism in the technology interaction with customers is the sale or purchase of products and services. This mechanism is emphasised statistically significantly more by engineering-based firms. The sale or purchase of products and services seems to be accompanied by training and consulting, with both mechanisms emphasised statistically almost significantly more by engineering firms. The relatively greater development-intensive customer interaction of science-based firms is signalled by the statistically significant greater emphasis given by science-based firms to joint research programmes with their customers. This conclusion is supported by the statistically almost significant difference in terms of co-operation in basic research.

Table 7.7 Means of the maximum intensities of technology flows generated by different technology transfer mechanisms between the firms and their customers

Technology transfer mechanism	Mean (SB)	Mean (EB)	p (SB,EB)
Subcontract product development	2.74	2.61	0.7266
Consulting	2.26	2.97	0.0501[†]
Joint research programmes	2.75	2.09	0.0286[*]
Patenting and licensing	2.14	1.72	0.1990
Transfer of documents	2.30	2.39	0.8126
Sale or purchase of products and services	3.27	4.04	0.0424[*]
Informal discussions between colleagues	3.29	3.28	0.9656
Training	2.22	2.87	0.0684[†]
Transfer of people	1.65	1.41	0.2694
Co-operation in basic research	1.83	1.40	0.0599[†]
Co-operation in applied research	2.50	2.06	0.1663
Co-operation in product development	3.29	3.18	0.7308

SB = Science-based.
EB = Engineering-based.

The differences observed in Table 7.7 are essentially qualitative in nature: different technology transfer mechanisms are used in science-based and in engineering-based firms. Whereas science-based firms tend to involve their customers in relatively more development-intensive interaction, engineering-based firms are able to utilise more replication-intensive mechanisms. In this sense, science-based firms can be viewed as operating in the 'development zone' of technological systems. This difference becomes even more evident when the technology interaction with the parent organisation is analysed. The breakdown of the interaction between science and engineering-based firms and their respective parent organisations is shown in Table 7.8a and b.

Table 7.8 reveals a clear, quantitative difference between science-based and engineering-based firms in terms of technology interaction with their respective parent organisations. Science-based firms seem to out-interact engineering-based firms over the whole range of technology-transfer mechanisms. This finding is consistent with the finding that science-based firms derive greater technology contributions from the domestic academic sphere, as depicted in Table 7.5. A similar difference could not be observed for customers, presumably because of the qualitative nature of the differences between science-based and engineering-based firms in terms of technology interaction with customers.

It is interesting that in the case of technology co-operation with the parent organisation, the patterns of technology transfer of science-based and engineering-based firms almost exactly mirror that of customers. When technology interaction with customers was concerned, sale or purchase of products and services was emphasised significantly more by engineering firms, with the difference in consulting being statistically almost significant. In the case of technology co-operation with parent organisations, it is the science-based firms that put more emphasis on these mechanisms.

Similar checks were carried out to examine the generality of the division between science-based and engineering-based firms. First, the bio-technology firms were compared against all engineering-based firms. Second, science-based and engineering-based electronics firms were compared with each other. These generality checks are shown in Table 7.9.

On the whole, the generality checks provide only weak support for the generality of the division between science-based and engineering-based firms in terms of technology interaction with customers. No statistically significant differences were observed between science-based and engineering-based electronics firms in terms of technology interaction with customers. On the other hand, the biotechnology firms depict a relatively more research-intensive co-operation with their customers than do all science-based firms when compared with all engineering-based firms.

The diffusion in terms of technology interaction with customers was expected. In different areas of technology, the forms and mechanisms of customer interaction can depict broad differences. Biotechnology, for example, is well known for R&D-intensive links between suppliers and customers (Forrest and Martin, 1992). Electronics, on the other hand, is well known for its often modular character. It is thus not surprising to find different patterns among firms active in these sectors of technology.

Table 7.8 Generality checks for the technology interaction with customers and parent organisations: means of the maximum intensities of technology flows generated by different technology transfer mechanisms between (a) the firms and their customers and (b) the firms and their parent organisations

(a)

Technology transfer mechanism	p (SB, EB) electronics firms	p (SB, EB) biotechnology firms	p (SB, EB) all firms
Subcontract product development	n.s.	n.s.	n.s.
Consulting	n.s.	n.s.	0.0501†
Joint research programmes	n.s.	0.0921†	0.0286*
Patenting and licensing	n.s.	0.0023**	n.s.
Transfer of documents	n.s.	n.s.	n.s.
Sale or purchase of products and services	n.s.	n.s.	0.0424*
Informal discussions between colleagues	n.s.	n.s.	n.s.
Training	n.s.	n.s.	0.0684†
Transfer of people	n.s.	n.s.	n.s.
Co-operation in basic research	n.s.	0.0259*	0.0599†
Co-operation in applied research	n.s.	0.0278*	n.s.
Co-operation in product development	n.s.	n.s.	n.s.

SB = Science-based.
EB = Engineering-based.

(b)

Technology transfer mechanism	p (SB, EB) electronics firms	p (SB, EB) biotechnology firms	p (SB, EB) all firms
Subcontract product development	0.0126*	n.s.	n.s.
Consulting	0.0028**	>0.0001***	0.0006***
Joint research programs	n.s.	0.0355*	n.s.
Patenting and licensing	n.s.	0.0048**	n.s.
Transfer of documents	n.s.	0.0661†	n.s.
Sale or purchase of products and services	0.0012**	n.s.	0.0179*
Informal discussions between colleagues	0.0070**	0.0067**	0.0101*
Training	n.s.	n.s.	n.s.
Transfer of people	n.s.	n.s.	n.s.
Co-operation in basic research	n.s.	0.0028**	n.s.
Co-operation in applied research	n.s.	0.0697	n.s.
Co-operation in product development	0.0743†	0.0403*	0.0720†

SB = Science-based.
EB = Engineering based.

On the other hand, the generality checks for the technology interaction with parent organisations (belonging to the domestic research sphere) provide reasonably good support for the generality of the model. All of the statistically significant and statistically almost significant differences in the overall distributions are supported by at least one of the two generality checks.

These checks therefore provide reasonably good support for the generality of the division between science-based and engineering-based firms, especially where technology interaction with parent organisation is concerned. As expected, the results emerging from generality checks concerning technology interaction with customers yield a more ambiguous picture. In a way, this finding seems natural. The technology interaction with customers can be expected to be relatively more exposed to market forces than is the technology interaction with parent organisations belonging to the domestic academic sphere. Even the development-intensive links between NTBFs and their customers can be expected to be more likely to be competitive stage arrangements. The development-intensive links with parent organisations belonging to the domestic academic sphere can be expected to be more likely to be pre-competitive stage arrangements.

Table 7.9   Means of the maximum intensities of technology flows generated by different technology transfer mechanisms between the firms and their parent organisations

Technology transfer mechanism	Mean (SB)	Mean (EB)	p (SB,EB)
Subcontract product development	1.65	1.42	0.3707
Consulting	2.43	1.45	0.0006***
Joint research programmes	1.91	1.49	0.1334
Patenting and licensing	1.52	1.25	0.2029
Transfer of documents	1.52	1.35	0.3775
Sale or purchase of products and services	1.67	1.22	0.0179*
Informal discussions between colleagues	2.91	2.06	0.0101*
Training	1.57	1.41	0.4747
Transfer of people	1.48	1.35	0.5587
Co-operation in basic research	1.76	1.37	0.1172
Co-operation in applied research	2.00	1.58	0.1397
Co-operation in product development	1.77	1.37	0.0720†

SB = Science-based.
EB = Engineering-based.

Functional Contributions Provided to Customers

In the present study, a functional contribution refers to the type of product or service delivered by a firm to its customers. The frequency of nine types of functional contributions was analysed. The comparisons between science-based and engineering-based firms are shown in Table 7.10. The percentage of firms indicating each functional contribution is shown for the overall distributions. In addition, the statistical significance of pair-wise comparisons for each functional contribution is shown.

Table 7.10 Functional contributions provided by the firms to their customers

Type of functional contribution	SB (%)	EB (%)	p (SB, EB)
Functional contributions related to production			
Increasing customer's efficiency of production through a consulting service	13.6	35.0	0.0741[†]
Increasing customer's efficiency of production through a physical product	50.0	51.5	>.9999
Offering subcontract manufacturing services, OEM production	27.3	9.7	0.0365[*]
Functional contribution related to administration and logistics			
Increasing the administrative or distribution efficiency of customers	4.3	24.5	0.0433[*]
Functional contribution related to marketing			
Serving as a marketing or distribution channel	18.2	7.0	0.1103
Functional contributions related to infrastructure			
Providing test, measurement, or calibration services to customer	9.1	22.5	0.2408
Acting as an external maintenance, installation, or repair resource	4.5	15.7	0.3032
Functional contribution related to R&D			
Acting as an external development resource for customers	59.1	36.9	0.0608[†]
Stand-alone functional contribution			
Developing own products and marketing them to end users	68.2	55.9	0.3461

OEM = Oringinal Equipment Manufacturer.
SB = Science-based.
EB = Engineering-based.

In Table 7.10, the final column lists the statistical significance of comparisons between science-based and engineering-based firms. Column SB shows the relative shares of science-based firms indicating each functional contribution, while column EB shows the relative shares of engineering-based firms indicating each functional contribution.

Table 7.10 shows that engineering-based firms are relatively more active in increasing the administrative or distribution efficiency of customers than are science-based firms. Engineering-based firms are also relatively more active in increasing customers efficiency of production through a consulting service. Science-based firms, for their part, are relatively more active in offering subcontracted manufacturing and original equipment manufacturing services than are engineering-based firms. Science-based firms are also relatively more active in acting as an external development resource for customers than are engineering-based firms.

These findings therefore support the model. Increasing the administrative or distribution efficiency of customers is a functional contribution that can be achieved by developing new applications for existing basic technologies. It seems reasonable to consider this kind of transformation as more commonplace than one in which new basic technologies would be developed for a similar purpose. Increasing the customer's efficiency of production through a consulting service can also be considered as a functional contribution that is more often achieved by applying existing basic technologies than by developing new ones for this purpose. Offering subcontracted manufacturing and original equipment manufacturing services can also be expected to be more typical for science-based firms, as defined above. An examination of the free-form business descriptions given by science-based firms reveals that those services provided by science-based firms are not standard manufacturing subcontracting services. The difference in Table 7.10 is not indicative of the provision of standard assembly services or other manufacturing services based on the use of excess manufacturing capacity. The manufacturing services provided by science-based firms demand specialised technical competencies that are not available elsewhere. The products produced often complement the existing product line of customers. It is also more typical of science-based than of engineering-based firms to function as external development resources.

In general, the findings listed in Table 7.10 indicate a relatively stronger link between engineering-based firms and the replication-intensive functions of their customers, when compared with science-based firms. Compared with science-based firms, engineering-based firms seem to be relatively more active in developing applications of basic technologies in order to render the replication-intensive and administrative processes of their customers more efficient.

These results also suggest a relatively stronger link between science-based firms and the development-intensive functions of their customers, when compared with engineering-based firms. Compared with engineering-based firms, science-based firms seem to be relatively more active in complementing the technology pool of their customers through the development and application of new basic technologies. Science-based firms thus seem to provide a relatively direct channel through which scientific and technological knowledge is extracted from the public research sector, refined to basic technologies, and further injected into the development-intensive activities of the customers of science-based firms.

The generality checks did not provide consistent support for the model in terms of the type of functional contributions provided to customers. After the analysis presented above, this was not even expected, as the functional contributions related to customer interaction.

CONCLUSIONS AND DISCUSSION

The present study has contended that some of the basic assumptions of the traditional body of research on NTBFs do not reflect reality very well. The Roberts (Roberts, 1991a) view of the spin-off process of such firms, the present study argues, largely reflects the linear sequential view of the process of technological innovation. The Roberts type of high-technology entrepreneur is an opportunistic individual who recognises opportunities, amasses resources, and pursues rapid growth. The success of the new firm is often interpreted as organic growth.

A different picture emerges from the present study. The analysis of external technology links suggests that high-technology small firms are quite tightly embedded in their operating environment. This embeddedness is largely technological in character. The technological embeddedness of high technology small firms has some important implications that do not match with the traditional view of NTBFs as stand-alone units of economic activity that aggressively pursue organic growth.

First, measuring the effectiveness and contributions of high-technology small firms by looking only at their product sales, innovation outputs and employment generation may understate their contribution. The present study reveals an important contribution by NTBFs to systemic innovation processes. The picture emerging from the present study emphasises the catalysing role of NTBFs' innovation networks. Ultimately, the most important economic impact delivered by NTBFs may well be a catalysing one, delivered through technology interactions between the firms and their operating environment. Importantly, NTBFs are not merely active in technological innovation and in technology transfer; they are also active in technology transformation and diffusion.

Second, if flexibility, small size and the exploitation of technological synergies constitute the very *modus operandi* of the high-technology small firm, the pursuit of growth would imply altering its very reason of existence. The traditional life cycle (Webster, 1976; Kazanjian, 1983; Scott and Bruce, 1987; Churchill and Lewis, 1993) models of small firms thus do not apply well to the majority of NTBFs. The evolution of such firms is not predominantly one of growth in size. Their evolution is rather an evolution of technological competencies. NTBFs should be viewed as unique concentrations of technological competencies, whose mission, motivated by survival, is to maintain their technological leadership. Thus the present study suggests that success among high-technology small firms should be defined more broadly than it has been in the traditional body of research on such firms. In addition to defining success of an NTBF as the amassing of resources, it should also be defined as continued technological leadership (Raffa, Zollo and Caponi, 1995).

Third, an important fraction of the technological competencies stored in the high-technology small firm is carried by a few individuals only, including the high-technology entrepreneur himself or herself. Consequently, in addition to conducting the 'classical' profit-seeking entrepreneurial activities, we see many a high-technology entrepreneur active in exploiting technology diffusion opportunities opened by the changing dynamics of the industrial innovation process (Kline and Rosenberg, 1986). These opportunities often present themselves in the form of dynamic complementarities between small and large firms in innovation (Rothwell, 1983). NTBF may achieve innovation efficiency through specialisation, flexibility and speed. Such advantages often constitute a complementary match to the predominantly resource-based advantages of large firms, thus creating a positive dynamic complementarity. The analysis of the present study supports the conclusion that the existence of such dynamic complementarities may provide an explanation for the existence of an important fraction of NTBFs.

Finally, the model constructed in the present study receives support from the analysis of empirical data. The empirical evidence shows, for the first time, that NTBFs are not only active in exploiting external sources of technology and information, as shown, by Gibbons and Johnston (1974) and Faulkner and Senker (1994). The model constructed in the present study identifies niches for NTBFs in a novel way that complements the model of Pavitt (1984). The present study suggests that it is possible to identify niches for such not only in terms of the technological dynamics of industry sectors, but also in terms of their functional relationship with the articulation process of basic technologies. In other words, the present study provides evidence, for the first time, that stable niches can be identified for NTBFs in systemic innovation processes.

The model constructed in the present study contributes to the discussion of the roles of small and large firms in innovation and in the production of new technologies. According to the model, small and large firms should not be seen as alternative, mutually exclusive producers of new technologies. Instead, they should be seen as mutually complementary producers of new technologies, with large firms often steering the process, and small technology-based firms contributing to it by providing specialised technology inputs. These findings provide a complementary match with recent research on innovation in large firms. Patel and Pavitt show compelling evidence of the trend toward a higher diversity in the technological competence portfolios of large (Fortune 500) firms (Patel and Pavitt, 1994). According to the findings reported by Pavitt, almost all Fortune 500 firms have increased the number of technology sectors in which they apply for patents. The average number of sectors, in which patents are applied by each Fortune 500 firm, has substantially increased.

The trend discussed above reflects the general trend towards increasingly modular, complex, multi-technology product systems and is likely to be enhanced by the increasingly symplectic character of basic technologies. It also provides a good piece of evidence against the notion of core competencies, as proposed by Hamel and Prahalad in their widely-cited *Harvard Business Review* article (Prahalad and Hamel, 1990). What researchers such as Patel and Pavitt are witnessing is a trend towards increased diversity, not towards concentration on core competencies, as proposed by Hamel and Prahalad. The new industrial paradigm seems to favour the emergence of complex product systems (Hobday, 1995), in which inputs representing several basic technologies are integrated. The rapid increase in the number of NTBFs, we believe, can at least be partly explained by the influence of this trend on industrial organisation. To understand this development, it is necessary to study factors underlying the high degree of technological embeddedness (Autio, 1995) that characterises many an NTBF.

Technological embeddedness is the result of the process by which an NTBF becomes immersed in the business system in which it operates. The process of becoming immersed in a business system often involves adaptive context-specific adjustments in the competence pool of the firm. In order to provide the best possible fit with the business system, the firm often adjusts its routines and operations, acquires context-specific information and knowledge, makes context-specific investments, comes to know customers' systems, products, and processes, develops trust, expands its contact network and enhances its reputation. Many such assets are more or less context-specific and not easily implemented into new contexts as such. Thus the process of becoming tightly embedded often also means that many assets of the firm become idiosyncratic, with little of no value outside the context in which they have been created.

The findings by Pavitt can be partly explained by the phenomenon of technological embeddedness. Even though the customer would outsource technology inputs from the NTBF, it is necessary for it to maintain matching technological competencies in-house in order to be able to manage its technology sourcing interface effectively. The firms analysed by Pavitt can be interpreted as systems integrator firms. Such firms often maintain networks of external technology suppliers, locked into the network by the competencies that are allocated in each customer interface. The occurrence of such arrangements is particularly high in so called 'network industries', characterised by a particularly high occurrence of NTBFs (Garud and Kumaraswamy, 1993; Tidd, 1995).

One essential implication of the above trends for the research on NTBFs is that the evolution of the embedded firm is largely regulated by the innovation system of which the firm constitutes one part. The present study provides evidence that, in such cases, the technological evolution of the NTBF assumes increased importance, presumably sometimes even dictating the organisational evolution of the firm.

The present study has implications also in the area of technology and industrial policy. The popular 'throughput' perception of science parks, for example, assumes that science parks should act as 'linear accelerators' through which new ventures could be launched on rapid growth trajectories. The dominant perceptions concerning the role of science parks are still dominated by the following features.

(a) the linear view of the spin-off process of NTBFs, reflecting the obsolete linear model of technological innovation;
(b) the technology push orientation, in which public sector research organisations are perceived as reservoirs of technologies that need to be transferred to commercialisation stage;
(c) excessive focus on one type of actor only (namely, on NTBFs).

Throughput activity has not been much in evidence in surveys of science parks. Even if science parks are populated by NTBFs, there is often not much traffic by firms moving into the park or out from it, at least not because of the need to find more space to accommodate the rapidly growing new venture. The empirical analysis and the related discussion of the present study suggests that this should not even be expected. Rather than expecting that science parks should act as hotbeds for growth, they should rather be viewed as 'headquarters of innovation networks' (Autio, 1995), accommodating some development-intensive activities of such networks. Such arrangements are not very likely to witness immediate economic returns based on rapid organic growth by the tenants. The main impact of such arrangements is likely to be a catalysing one.

8 Informal Networks of Relationships in Successful Small Firm Innovation

Steve Conway

INTRODUCTION

In recent years a great deal of research effort has been directed towards identifying, mapping out, understanding and rationalising the formal interactions and relationships of innovative organisations (Håkansson, 1989; Håkansson and Johanson, 1990; Lawton-Smith, Dickson and Lloyd Smith, 1991; Hagedoorn and Schakenraad, 1992). However, while research has also indicated the importance of informal relationships to the innovation process, both within and outside such formal frameworks as joint ventures and technology agreements (von Hippel, 1988; Kreiner and Schultz, 1993; Shaw, 1993), this has largely been anecdotal in nature. This view is supported by Freeman (1991:500–2), who argues that 'although rarely measured systematically . . . informal networks are extremely important, but very hard to classify and measure'.

This chapter reviews the literature concerning the identification of the external sources of inputs in the development of successful technological innovation, and the nature of the channels and mechanisms through which these are sourced by innovative organisations. A conceptual framework is then discussed: the *focal innovation action-set* (Conway, 1994). This framework aids the systematic study of the multiple sources and pluralistic patterns of interaction typical of the innovation process. The research project is then introduced. The original study (Conway, 1994) investigated 35 awarding-winning technological innovations. In this chapter results concerning the 12 small-firm innovations are extracted and discussed. Particular emphasis is placed on the role and importance of informally derived inputs into the innovation process that have been sourced from outside the innovating firm. The role of a variety of external actors, such as users and suppliers, is then discussed in relation to these small firm innovations.

Such research is of particular relevance to small innovative firms. Johannisson and Peterson (1984:1) note the apparent paradox of entrepreneurship: while on the one hand 'the entrepreneur personifies individualism and independence', on the other 'he is . . . very dependent on ties of trust and co-operation'. Indeed, research has indicated the importance of boundary-spanning links to the innovation process of entrepreneurs (Johannisson and Peterson, 1984; Leonard-Barton, 1984; Birley, Cromie and Myers, 1991) and SMEs (Rothwell, 1991; Rothwell and Dodgson, 1991). With this in mind, Aldrich and Zimmer (1986:9) argue that 'comprehensive explanations of entrepreneurship must include the social context of behaviour, especially the social relationships through which people obtain information, resources and social support'.

THE SOURCES OF STIMULI IN SUCCESSFUL TECHNOLOGICAL INNOVATION

A number of studies since the 1960s have attempted to determine the nature and source of the stimuli leading to the initiation of successful technological innovation (Myers and Marquis, 1969; Utterback, 1971; Rothwell *et al.* [Project SAPPHO II], 1974; Baker, Green and Bean, 1985). This research has indicated that between two-thirds and three-quarters of innovations are *need-stimulated*, as opposed to *means-stimulated*. However, variations do exist between industrial sectors and between types of innovation: for example, Baker, Green and Bean (1985) found that customers in the USA were more likely to suggest new product projects than process projects, a situation that was reversed for in-house R&D staff. Utterback (1971) and Rothwell *et al.* (1974) found a positive correlation between need-stimulated innovation and commercial success.

The Sources of Inputs in Successful Technological Innovation

The origins and sources of inputs in technological innovation have also been a subject of interest in many studies since the 1950s. Early concerns focused on the utility of basic science to technological innovation (Sherwin and Isenson [Project Hindsight], 1967; Illinois Institute of Technology [TRACES], 1968; Gibbons and Johnston, 1974) and the importance of sources external to the innovative firm (Carter and Williams, 1957; Myers and Marquis, 1969; Achilladis, Robertson and Jervis [Project SAPPHO], 1971; Langrish *et al.*, 1972). However, whilst this research suggested that external sources account for between one-third (Gibbons and Johnston, 1974) and two-thirds (Langrish *et al.*, 1972) of the inputs important to the innovation process, evidence of the utility of basic science to technological innovation was mixed.

Variations in the importance of external sources to the innovative firm have been identified between industrial sectors (Myers and Marquis, 1969; Easingwood, 1986; Sowrey 1989), between product and process innovations (Baker, Green and Bean, 1985), between large and small firms (Allen, Hyman and Pinckney, 1983), between the idea-generation and problem-solving stages of the innovation process (Myers and Marquis, 1969; Utterback, 1971; Allen, 1977), and between *basic* or *radical* innovations, and major and minor improvements, termed *re-innovation* (von Hippel, 1988; see also Rothwell and Gardiner, 1985; Shaw, 1985; Rothwell, 1986).

Research has also shown that a variety of external organisations may contribute during the development of successful innovation, including users, suppliers, academia, competitors, distributors, and government research laboratories. Studies have shown that users in particular, but also suppliers, play an important role in the innovation process (von Hippel, 1988; Vanderwerf, 1990; for a summary see Conway, 1993), as well as the continuing significance of the independent inventor as a source of innovative ideas leading to successful innovations in larger firms (Udell, 1990; Whalley, 1991). However, cross-sector studies (e.g., Langrish *et al.*, 1972) have suggested the limited importance of academia as a source of inputs.

The Channels or Modes of Linkage with External Sources

Empirical studies of successful technological innovation have consistently found that 'multiple sources of information and pluralistic patterns of collaboration were the rule rather than the exception' (Freeman, 1991: 500). A number of typologies have been developed to express the diversity of external relationships that may be employed in the innovation process. Freeman (1991) distinguishes between the following:

- joint ventures and research corporations
- joint R&D agreements
- technology exchange agreements
- direct investment motivated by technology factors
- licensing and second-sourcing agreements
- subcontracting, production-sharing and supplier networks
- research associations

- government-sponsored joint research programmes
- computerised data-banks for technical and scientific interchange
- informal or personal networks

DeBresson and Amesse (1991:364) argue that 'because interactions between firms . . . are iterative and broad in content, time and space, what matters is the complete set of relationships'.

With reference to studies undertaken since the mid-1980s concerning the changing patterns of R&D collaboration in the last decade or so, Freeman (1991:507) argues that 'in quantitative terms there is abundant evidence of a strong upsurge of various forms of research collaboration [the first five categories], especially in the new generic technologies . . . involving extensive international collaboration as well as national and regional networks. There is also ample evidence of a qualitative change in the nature of the older networking relationships [the next three categories].' A number of innovation studies have also highlighted the importance of informal boundary-spanning relationships as a means of sourcing ideas and information during the development process (Allen, Hyman and Pinckney, 1983; Lawton-Smith, Dickson and Lloyd Smith, 1991; Kreiner and Schultz, 1993; Shaw, 1993). However, in relation to informal exchange, this research has typically been anecdotal in nature. This view is supported by Freeman (1991:500–2), who argues that 'although rarely measured systematically . . . informal networks are extremely important, but very hard to classify and measure'. More in-depth and systematic studies of informal interaction in the innovation process do exist (e.g., Conway, 1994)

The Mechanisms or Modes of Transfer of Innovation Inputs

Research has identified a number of mechanisms for the transference of ideas and information across the organisational boundary, including: the hiring of new staff, termed *boundary-crossing* (Aldrich, 1979); the use of scientific and technical journals, and trade publications, termed *formal* literature (Allen, 1977), and in-house publications, termed *informal* literature (Allen, 1977); formally established meetings and conferences; fieldtests; and informal person-to-person modes of communication such as telephone conversations, correspondence and visit-s, that may be broadly termed *boundary-spanning* interactions. Kelley and Brooks (1991) dichotomise these mechanisms into *active*, referring to those modes of transfer involving personal interaction, and *passive*, referring to textual material.

Burns (1969:12) has argued that 'the mechanism of technological transfer is one of agents, not agencies; of the movement of people among establishments, rather than the routing of information through communication systems'. This view has received some empirical support, most notably from Langrish *et al.* (1972) in their study of award-winning UK innovations. In this study they found that the major mode of transfer was via a person joining the company, accounting for 20 per cent of the key ideas obtained from external sources. In addition, studies by Roberts and Wainer (1971) and Roberts (1969), concerning spin-offs from research at the Massachusetts Institute of Technology, found that the displacement of academic staff was crucial to the success of technology transfer to the commercial sector.

However, a number of other studies have indicated the importance of personal boundary-spanning contacts and formal literature, particularly in relation to idea-generation rather than problem-solving, where internal sources were found to be more important (Myers and Marquis, 1969; Utterback, 1971; Allen, 1977). In addition, research by von Hippel (1976, 1977) into manufacturer-user relationships placed most emphasis on *multiple* and *continuous* interaction, while Shaw (1985:290) notes the 'dominance of personal contact . . . within a very efficient informal and formal networking system', in relation to his study of medical equipment innovation in the UK.

An interesting study by Menzel (1962), on the information-gathering behaviour of biochemists, chemists and zoologists in an American university, revealed a variety of unplanned mechanisms through which ideas and information came to light accidentally in informal discussion. A further study of 430 engineers and scientists within a large American electrical corporation by Rosenbloom and Wolek (1970), found that in one-third of the instances where useful technical information was obtained from outside an individual's division, the acquisition had occurred by chance. These studies reinforce the importance of personal contact and serendipity in the innovation process.

Innovation as an Ensemble of Inputs

Innovation should not be viewed as resulting from a single idea, but from a *bundle* or *ensemble* of ideas, information, technology, codified knowledge and know-how, which may or may not be embodied within the product or process. Previous research has also clearly demonstrated that new ideas seldom appear fully formed and articulated from a single source (Myers and Marquis, 1969; Utterback, 1971; Allen, 1977; Allen, Hyman and Pinckney 1983). For example, Allen, Hyman and Pinckney (1983: 201) found in their study of technological change in 102 SMEs in Ireland, Spain and Mexico, that 'Bits and pieces of what eventually becomes a new idea arrive from a variety of sources . . . The individuals who introduce the new idea to the organisation, integrate these messages and in that way make their own creative contribution to the process.'

The Nature and Complexity of Informally Exchanged Transaction Content

From their study of industry-academia links in emerging technologies, Senker and Faulkner (1993:26) conclude that 'we suspect that much of the knowledge transferred through personal networks is tacit, and our evidence is suggestive in this regard'. Menzel (1962) also reveals the *tacitness* of much of the information transferred in unplanned ways during personal contact. In addition, Freeman (1991:502) argues that 'informal networks . . . have a role somewhat analogous to *tacit knowledge* within firms'. However, it should not be assumed, simply because tacit knowledge tends to flow through personal contact, that this mechanism is not also a useful mode of transfer for other types of transaction content, such as codified knowledge or equipment and materials, for example. On this point, Steward and Conway (1993:4) argue that 'It is extremely important to maintain a clear analytical distinction between network relationships and the type of knowledge being conveyed through these relationships . . . While there may be a strong connection [between channel and transaction content], this should not be assumed *a priori*.'

The complexity of a message is also likely to influence the mechanism of exchange employed. Wolek (1970:233), for example, argues that 'the probability that a communication will involve interpersonal interaction between source and receiver varies directly with the complexity of the message communicated'. This is because the flexibility of interpersonal communication allows the sender and receiver to adopt mutual coding schemes, to focus on uniquely relevant relationships and to vary the format of communication in order to tackle more complex messages (Committee on Information in the Behavioural Sciences, 1967; Horowitz, 1968; Wolek, 1970).

However, McLaughlin, Rosenbloom and Wolek (1965) also note that while the first impulse may be to ask somebody, when a precise answer is required the first impulse may be instead to look it up in the literature. With this in mind, Wolek (1970:239) argues that since science is a structured body of knowledge, which 'permits scientists to break down many ideas and observations into messages of low complexity', scientists may be expected to be less reliant on interpersonal communication than technologists or engineers.

The Personal Network of Entrepreneurs

The personal or focal networks of entrepreneurs can be seen to play a number of important roles: to generate social support for the actions of the entrepreneur; to extend the strategic competence of the entrepreneur in relation to the identification of opportunities and threats; and to supplement internal resources to resolve acute operating problems (Johannisson and Peterson, 1984). Thus, the personal network should be viewed as an important, and sometimes critical, resource of the entrepreneur. Leonard-Barton (1984:113) argues that 'entrepreneurs who, for geographic, cultural or social reasons, lack access to *free* information through personal networks, operate with less *capital* than do their well-connected peers'.

In relation to the individual linkages of the entrepreneurial network, Johannisson and Peterson (1984:3) argue that they 'are multi-stranded involving unique syntheses of instrumental, affective and moral [bonds]', in contrast to the bureaucratic desire 'to separate the strands and in particular to focus in on instrumental [bonds] only'. Gibson (1991:117–18), however, contends that 'the more extensive, complex and diverse the web of relationships, the more the entrepreneur is likely to have access to opportunities, the greater the chance of solving problems expeditiously, and ultimately, the greater the chance of success for a new venture', whereas Birley, Cromie and Myers, (1991:58) state 'networks do not emerge without considerable endeavour'.

BUILDING A CONCEPTUAL FRAMEWORK FOR STUDYING INNOVATION

The *rules of inclusion* (of actors, links and flows) adopted in a research project are inextricably linked to the research question. The social network literature was employed to build an appropriate conceptual framework for studying discrete instances of output-orientated innovative activity.

The Total Network versus Partial Networks

Mitchell (1969:12) conceptualised what he termed the *total* network of a society as 'the general ever-ramifying, ever-reticulating set of linkages that stretches within and beyond the confines of any community or organisation'. Thus, Mitchell (1969) argues that the researcher must always select particular aspects of the total network for attention; he termed these *partial* networks. This process of selecting partial networks for further study is commonly termed *abstraction* (Scott, 1991). There are two key decisions to be taken in abstraction: the first focuses on the rules of inclusion based on the attributes and/or participation of the actors themselves, known as the *definitional* focus (Laumann, Marsden and Prensky 1983); the second relates to the manner in which the abstraction is *anchored* or *centred*, which may be around a particular actor or group of actors (Scott, 1991). This may be termed *nodal-anchoring* (Conway, 1994). A third decision for focal-nets is also required with respect to the 'cut-off' distance (i.e., maximum number of links away) of actors not directly linked to the focal-actor.

Abstraction and Definitional Focus

Laumann, Marsden and Prensky (1983) identify three sets of components, or what they term *definitional foci*, for establishing the rules of inclusion of actors in a network: actors, relationships and activities. In establishing the *partial network* to study, network analysts may select one or more of these three sets of components. However, Laumann, Marsden and Prensky (1983:22) argue that 'the choice of a definitional focus is of importance in that it fixes certain features of the network while leaving the remaining features free to vary'.

The first and most commonly employed definitional focus is the use of an inclusion rule based on some attribute or characteristic of the actors in the network under study. This approach is used to construct *attribute* networks. Fombrun (1982:280) defines attribute networks as those that link actors who share a commonality. The second definitional focus often adopted is that of selecting actors on the basis of their participation in some specified type of social relationship. This approach is used to construct *transaction* networks. In addition, Fombrun defines transaction networks as those which focus on the exchanges that occur among a set of actors. The third definitional focus is one that adopts an inclusion rule based on some event or activity. In this approach, participation in the event or activity serves to select individual actors and the social relationships among them. This method may be employed to construct what are termed *action-sets*. Mitchell (1969:39–40) argues that the action-set 'is delineated in terms of the specific transaction that brings it into being . . . An action-set may be looked upon as an aspect of a personal network isolated in terms of a specific short-term instrumentally-defined transactional content: the personal network itself is more extensive and more durable.'

Abstraction and Nodal-Anchoring

Scott (1991) argues that there are two bases on which such abstraction can then proceed: 'First, there is abstraction which is *anchored* around a particular individual so as to generate *ego-centred* networks of social relations of all kinds. Second is abstraction of the overall, *global* features of networks in relation to a particular aspect of social activity: political ties, kinship obligations, friendship or work relations.' A review of the science and technology studies literature indicates that the socio-centred approach is far more commonly used than ego-centred approaches in researching inventive and innovative activity (Crane, 1972; Allen, 1977; Hagedoorn and Schakenraad, 1992).

In the first approach the researcher focuses on the relations of a single actor in the network population, referred to as the *focal-actor*. Ego-centred networks or *focal-nets* may be termed *personal* networks at the level of the individual (Rogers and Kincaid, 1981) or *organisation-sets* at the level of the organisation (Evan, 1965). Aldrich (1979:279) also notes that: 'Many of the dimensions used for structural analysis of networks can be applied to organisation-sets. Size, density, diversity and stability all tap different features of an organisation-set that are useful for comparing organisation-sets of different organisations or of the same organisation over time.'

The second approach identified by Scott (1991) focuses on a population of actors rather than a single actor. This is sometimes referred to as a *socio-centred* approach. Such a network is constructed by first identifying the presence of a specified type of tie defined by the researcher, such as friendship or joint-venture, between each of the actors in the population under study. The identified links are then mapped out between the actor population.

Since this research was based on the investigation of the development process of a series of discrete innovations, it was felt that the most appropriate definitional focus for the inclusion of actors was one that selected actors by their participation in the specified event or activity. Thus the action-set approach was selected. As the innovations were to be investigated from the perspective of the award-winning innovator, a focal or ego-centred nodal-anchoring approach was chosen. The resulting network may be termed a *focal action-set*. An example from the study is presented in Figure 8.1 below.

With respect to such an approach, Aldrich and Whetten (1981:386) argue that 'focusing on resource flows or boundary-role interaction avoids the problem of mixing transitory or ephemeral relations with enduring or consequential ones'.

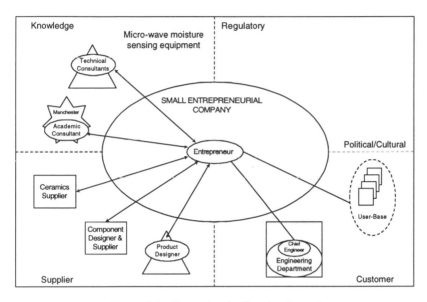

Figure 8.1   Example of a Focal action-set

Setting the Boundaries of the Network

Aldrich and Whetten (1981:400) also note that 'a problem related to the linkage-identification issue is how far investigators should go in recording and analysing indirect, as opposed to direct, ties'. Clearly some limit must be placed on the network under study otherwise it becomes co-extensive with the total network. Mitchell (1969:40) argues that 'this difficulty is resolved by fixing the *boundary* of the network in relation to the social situation being analyzed . . . There can be no general rule.'

As the original study focused on 35 innovations, resource constraints were certainly seen as an important factor in limiting the investigation primarily to direct links during data collection. However, because of the interest in the role of liaisons, bridges and link-pins in the innovation process, indirect links were pursued if they existed in relation to channels providing important inputs into the innovation project under study. In this way a clear picture was obtained as to the manner in which the focal innovation action-set was embedded in the innovator's environment.

Researching Focal Innovation Action-Sets

In building focal innovation action-sets the researcher must not only collect information on the sources of external inputs, such as the types of actor involved (e.g., users, suppliers, universities), but must also gather data concerning various dimensions of the linkages between the innovator and these external actors, and the nature of the flow through these linkages. The resulting focal action-sets may also be analysed according to a number of dimensions.

The Dimensions of Relationships

Individual relationships or dyads may vary along a number of *dimensions* (Aldrich, 1979). The most relevant dimensions of dyadic links with regard to this research project are outlined below.

1. *Formalisation.* Aldrich (1979) distinguishes between what he terms *agreement formalisation* and *structural formalisation.* The former refers to the extent to which a transaction between two organisations is given official recognition. The latter refers to the linkage between two organisations, which is considered formalised where it is embodied in a written contract.
2. *Intensity.* The intensity or strength of a link is indicated by the frequency of interaction and flow of transaction content between two actors over a given time period (Tichy, Tushman and Fombrun, 1979).
3. *Reciprocity.* The reciprocity or symmetry of a relationship refers to the balance of flow over time of transaction content between two actors through a given linkage. The underlying structure of the link is termed *asymmetric* or *unilateral*, where the flow is one-way, and *symmetric* or *bilateral*, where the flow is two-way. Asymmetric linkages tend to imply some form of inequality in the power relations between two actors (Boissevain, 1974).
4. *Multiplexity.* At the level of the individual, multiplexity identifies the degree to which two actors are linked by multiple role relations (Tichy, Tushman and Fombrun, 1979). It is also contended that the greater the number of role relations linking two actors the stronger the linkage (Tichy, Tushman and Fombrun, 1979). Boissevain (1974:30)

also argues that 'there is a tendency for single-stranded relations to become many-stranded if they persist over time, and for many-stranded relations to be stronger than single-stranded ones, in the sense that one strand role reinforces others'.

5. *Origin*. This dimension refers to the identification of the events leading to the origin of a linkage. It is intended to incorporate factors such as the context in which the relationship originated and the initiator of the relationship.

6. *Motives*. Giddens (1979) points out that the functional significance of networking does not qualify as a convincing explanation of its occurrence. In addressing this issue, Kreiner and Schultz (1993:201) argue that 'one must determine the motives and perspectives of the actors who reproduce such patterns'.

Transaction Content

Kadushin (1966) refers to *transaction content* as the *flow* between actors, to emphasise that something is being exchanged or is passing through a relationship. Dyadic relationships and networks of exchange can be categorised according to the transaction content that flows through them. Tichy, Tushman and Fombrun (1979) distinguish four types of transaction content:

(a) *affect* – the exchange of friendship between actors;
(b) *power* – the exchange of power and influence between actors;
(c) *information* – the exchange of ideas, information and know-how between actors;
(d) *goods* – the exchange of goods, money, technology or services between actors.

The perceived value of the transaction content, both received and transmitted by each of the actors in a given relationship, is termed the *exchange value*. The exchange value of transaction content may be measured in terms of discrete units within specific exchange events, or as the cumulative value of exchanged units within a series of exchange events over time.

The Dimensions of Networks

Networks also vary along a number of *dimensions* which may be analysed by the researcher. The most relevant network dimensions, with regard to this research project, are shown below.

1. *Size*. This dimension simply refers to the number of actors participating in the network (Tichy, Tushman and Fombrun 1979; Auster, 1990). However, the potential size of the network under investigation is most often dictated by some arbitrary boundary set by the researcher.
2. *Diversity*. This network characteristic refers to both the number of different types of actor, which may be measured along a number of dimensions (Auster, 1990), and the number of different types of linkage in a given network (Burt *et al.*, 1983).
3. *Stability*. Tichy, Tushman and Fombrun (1979:508) define this dimension as 'the degree to which a network pattern changes over time'. Auster (1990) expands on this, by referring to the frequency and magnitude of change of the actors and linkages in a given network.
4. *Centrality*. Tichy, Tushman and Fombrun (1979:508) define this network characteristic as 'the degree to which relations are guided by the formal hierarchy': that is, the proportion of the links in the network which may be viewed as formal.
5. *Openness*. This network dimension is defined by Tichy, Tushman and Fombrun (1979:508) as 'the number of actual external links in a social unit': that is, the number of links between a given network and other networks.

THE RESEARCH PROCESS

The Sample of Innovations Investigated

Having decided upon a multiple-site case analysis approach, the next critical step was to determine the manner in which an appropriate sample of innovations could be selected. Miles and Huberman (1994:29–30) argue that 'multiple-case sampling . . . has to be thought through carefully. An explicit *sampling frame* is needed. It will be guided by the research questions and conceptual framework . . . random sampling will not help.' To aid in this process, Miles and Huberman (1994) provide a broad typology of sampling strategies available to the *qualitative* researcher. The typology may be applied to either within-case (single-site) or across-case (multiple-site) sampling decisions. These sampling strategies are not mutually exclusive, but may be combined to focus the sample.

A wide variety of sampling techniques have been employed by earlier innovation studies to select innovation samples:

(a) award-winning innovations – *criterion* (Utterback, 1971; Langrish *et al.*, 1972);

(b) innovations selected from industry trade journals (Shaw, 1985);
(c) innovations selected by recourse to industry experts – *reputational* (von Hippel, 1976; Vanderwerf, 1990);
(d) innovations representing complete or partial new product development portfolios of selected companies – *comprehensive* (Spital, 1979);
(e) innovations selected by the respondents themselves (Sowrey, 1989);
(f) radical innovations – *extreme* (Jewkes, Sawers amd Stillerman, 1969).

It was decided that the innovation sample would be selected with reference to recent winners of two high-profile UK innovation award schemes: the Queen's Award for Technological Achievement and the British Design Award. Both awards emphasise commercial achievement or potential as well as novelty, and are cross-sector and nation-wide schemes generating a combined annual sample of around 50 innovations. This approach may be classified as drawing upon three sampling strategies: *criterion*, through its focus on winners of specific awards representing instances of successful innovation; *reputational*, as these award-winners were selected by a panel of industry experts; and *quota*, since the award panels selected the innovations to represent a breadth of industrial categories (explicitly with the Design Award).

Data Collection

Semi-structured interviews were undertaken with one or more of the key individuals involved in the development process for each of the innovations investigated. Each innovation was viewed as deriving from a *bundle* or *ensemble* of ideas, information, technology, knowledge and know-how, that had been accumulated, configured and reconfigured by the project team, from a diversity of actors and through a variety of relationship types and mechanisms. The interview process first sought to identify the multiplicity of inputs or *flows* into the development of the product or process. The role (impetus, concept, feature, solution or testing), origin and importance (*exchange value*) of these inputs or *transaction content* (the content of what is exchanged between actors) was then obtained. Information was then sought concerning a number of dimensions of the source-recipient relationship, including: the nature of the dyadic link (i.e., the exchange of friendship, power, information or goods); the degree of formalisation; the degree of reciprocity or *symmetry*; the extent of *multiplexity* (i.e., single or multiple links); and the strength or intensity of the relationship. Therefore, the task of each interview was to gather as much information as possible concerning the three components of those intra- and inter-organisational boundary-spanning dyadic relationships found to be contributing to the innovation process: the source actors, their relationship with the innovation project team, and the nature and flow of transaction content between these actors.

Data Reduction

Miles and Huberman (1994:10) define *data reduction* as the process of 'selecting, focusing, simplifying, abstracting, and transforming the data that appear in written-up field notes or transcriptions'. In the instance of this investigation, brief *contact summary sheets* (Miles and Huberman, 1994) were written shortly after each interview in order to record the main themes and personal reflections relating to the case material. In addition, rough action-sets were drawn to accompany the text. Each interview was tape recorded and transcribed at a later date; the process of transcription yielded around 500 A4 sheets of text. Due to the large volume of transcribed text relating to the innovations under investigation, a systematic process of data reduction was employed.

The first stage of data reduction undertaken involved the process of *coding*, to allow for the retrieving and organisation of data (Miles and Huberman 1994). Words, phrases, sentences and chunks of text were tagged with *codes* to assign meaning. The codes in this instance were focused very clearly around the well-formed research questions and hence related to actors as sources of inputs to the innovation process, the inputs themselves, and the nature of the links between innovators and external actors.

Subsequent stages of data reduction involved the categorisation of data concerning actors, dyads and transaction content, and the use of matrix data displays to present this categorised information. This process was undertaken initially on a *within-case* basis and latterly on a *cross-case* basis. A number of important classifications were employed in order to allow for the analysis of the case-material. Transaction content was classified, for example, with respect to: the exchange value of the flow, which was categorised as *critical* (fundamental to the innovation, which could not have proceeded without the input), *important* (major input to one or more core elements of the innovation); *useful* (constructive input into one or more elements of the innovation), or *minor* (minor or no input into the innovation process); and the nature of the flow, which was categorised as cognitive, material or service. In addition, dyads were classified with respect to: the nature of the relationship (i.e., instrumental, affective or moral); the formalisation of the link (i.e., formal or informal); or whether the link had been established prior to, or during, the project under investigation.

SUMMARY OF CASE-STUDY FIRMS AND INNOVATIONS

Amethyst

Amethyst is an expert system for the automatic on-line diagnosis of rotating machinery faults through the analysis of their vibration patterns. It achieves in a matter of minutes what previously took four to eight hours as a manual process undertaken by highly skilled engineers. This innovative software product was developed by a small company based near Edinburgh that specialises in the application of expert system technology. The package was awarded the Queen's Award for Technological Achievement in 1991.

Backlite

Backlite is the first system to enable the heating elements of a standard heated rear windscreen of a car to be used as a radio antenna, and is capable of meeting the requirements of FM/VHF reception at all wavelengths as well as AM on long, medium and short waves. The device was developed and commercialised by a small start-up company based in Swinton, despite failed attempts by a number of large companies such as Lucas Industries and Pilkington Glass plc. Launched in the early 1980s, sales through licence had reached approximately one million units per annum by the year it received the Queen's Award for Technological Achievement in 1991.

The DVA-4000

The DVA-4000 provides for the combination of video and graphic signals on the display screen of a personal computer, alongside synchronised audio signals. By utilising digital techniques the DVA-4000 has overcome the problems experienced by the low resolution analogue systems which it replaces. Principal among these problems was the difficulty in synchronising the graphics signals from the computer and the signals generated by the various video standards, such as cable broadcasts, camcorders and video cassette recorders. The initial development work was undertaken in the mid-1980s when the company was a small start-up enterprise employing a handful of highly skilled engineers and video production staff. The innovation was awarded the Queen's Award for Technological Achievement in 1992, and this has enabled the company to play a major role in the European multi-media industry.

Elektra

Elektra is a software package for the analysis of electro-magnetic frequencies generated by high technology devices. The innovation was awarded the Queen's Award for Technological Achievement in 1992, and was developed by a small software/consultancy company based in Oxford. The company includes a number of highly regarded electro-magnetic scientists who were previously employed by the prestigious Rutherford Appleton Laboratory. This highly innovative and technical software is an important aid in the design of high-technology electrical equipment, and is in use in many areas requiring the analysis of electromagnetic frequencies to very high tolerances, including: Magnetic resonance imaging body-scanners, medical diagnostic equipment, super-conductivity, and electrical machines, such as motors, generators and transformers.

Hydro-Probe

The Hydro-Probe sensor is used to measure moisture in a variety of process industries, the largest of which are the pre-cast and ready-mix concrete markets for the construction industry. The product is totally innovative in its design, and provides the most accurate and cost-effective method for on-line measurement of moisture in sands and aggregates. The innovation embodies state-of-the-art microwave knowledge and comprises two main elements: the sensor itself and the control equipment that provides the interface between the sensor and the user. This very small (presently two employees) entrepreneurial company was founded in 1982 specifically to develop and commercialise the use of microwave technology in accurate moisture measurement. It won the British Design Award for this innovation in 1992.

Linear Actuator

The linear actuator is a unique integrated mechanical device designed for use on boats to move the rudder in response to commands from an autopilot. This development was undertaken by a small well-established engineering company based in Devon, which already produces an extensive range of valves and pumps for a variety of applications. The innovation gained the British Design Award in 1991. The major design innovation of the product is its containment of all the hydraulic circuit components within a single sealed unit: valve block, actuator cylinder, pump, motor assembly, and oil reservoir. This design avoids the common problem of an ingress of air and dirt during operation, thereby minimising the risk of failure and allowing the actuator to be fitted anywhere, even underwater for the first time. This innovation represents a totally new design approach to an established technology, and offers the possibility of promising valuable applications beyond the marine world, such as providing greater mobility for the disabled.

The On-Line Tape Certification System

This innovation allows for the automatic on-line certification of digital magnetic tapes at 1600 and 6250 bits per inch simultaneously. Developed by a small recently founded control equipment company based near Manchester, this certification system won the Queen's Award for Technological Achievement in 1992. The on-line tape certification system employs specially coated ceramic reader heads and air bearings which have been developed to float the tape over these heads. The whole operation previously employed manual intervention and required two hours in order to certify 50 tapes. The new certification system undertakes the same operation entirely automatically and in just ten minutes.

Polifold

Polifold is an incremental innovation in roofing for transport vehicles. The innovation, which was awarded the British Design Award in 1992, was developed by a small well-established engineering company based in Hertfordshire. Polifold is a PVC sheet folding roof for transport vehicles, which uses polypropylene leaf springs to produce an automatic concertina effect to maximise the roof opening and hence facilitate loading by overhead crane. The roof system was originally developed for glass transportation vehicles, where the maximisation of the roof opening is required by virtue of the indivisibility of glass, and its weight which dictates loading by crane. The Polifold roof is water-tight, gives 90 per cent roof opening, and is easier to operate single-handed, maintain and repair than previously existing roof systems on the market.

Synon/2

Synon/2 is a software package that helps programmers to write new programmes. The software development was undertaken by a small start-up software company based in London. The product has seen exponential sales growth since its launch in the late 1980s, and was awarded the Queen's Award for Technological Achievement in 1991. The unique feature of this innovation is its data modelling facility which enables applications to be designed correctly from the outset. The application generator then aids the process of programme writing by automatically generating standard chunks of programme code and inserting these into the application.

The Town and Country III

The Town and Country III is an incremental innovation in electric-tricycles for the disabled and elderly. Winner of a British Design Award in 1992, the product was developed by a small family company (a father-son partnership), now considered to be the world leader in electric-tricycle design. The Town and Country III incorporates a number of innovative features which have reinforced the company's reputation in the market-place: down-hill speed control, emergency-braking, rear-wheel drive, puncture-proof tyres, maintenance-free batteries, lights and indicators. Industrial design has also been employed to improve the ease of use, the aesthetics, and the manufacturability of the product.

The Xenos Pain Management System

Xenos is an electronic pain relief device based on the proven drug-free method Transcutaneous Electrical Nerve Simulation (TENS), and is employed in conditions such as spinal injury, arthritis and post-operative pain. TENS works by applying a low frequency current to the pain area, whereby pain impulses are intercepted and attenuated within the spine on route to the brain. Launched in 1989, the Xenos rapidly established itself as the UK market leader and won the British Design Award in 1991. Though much of the development work was undertaken externally, the innovation was envisaged, realised and commercialised internally by a small entrepreneurial Norfolk company of around ten employees. Although an incremental innovation, the Xenos offers a number of new improvements over existing TENS devices, and incorporates a state-of-the-art Application Specific Integrated Circuit (ASIC) microchip, which lies at the heart of the product.

The Yeoman Marine Navigator

The Yeoman Marine Navigator provides for the automatic plotting of positional data, obtained from navigation equipment, on to conventional navigation charts. This replaces the traditional process of manually plotting positional data. Developed by a small company specialising in marine navigation equipment, the innovation was awarded the British Design Award in 1991. This innovative electronic plotter has been designed for use in leisure craft, of which there are some four million world-wide. The impetus for the development arose from the company chairman who, like a number of his employees, is an experienced yachtsman. The Yeoman offers sophisticated technology at a low price, and combines smart functional industrial design with high levels of accuracy. These features have steered the company into a commanding position in the leisure craft navigation market.

RESEARCH RESULTS

This chapter focuses on two areas of the results from the original study: the role and importance of informal boundary-spanning (external) relationships during the development of the award-winning technological innovations; and the source of these external inputs.

The Role and Importance of Informal Boundary-Spanning Relationships

One of the first tasks during the interviews was to identify the various inputs into the innovation process and to determine whether they had been sourced internally or externally. Interviewees were then questioned about the nature of the boundary-spanning relationships with the various external sources that were identified as contributors to the innovations under investigation.

Table 8.1   The importance of external inputs during the innovation process

	Small-firm sample ($n = 12$)	
	No. of projects	*% of projects*
Critical	4	33
Important	3	25
Useful	4	33
Minor	1	8

Input from external sources was found to have been critical to the development of one-third of the innovations (Amethyst, Hydro-Probe, Xenos, and Yeoman) and important in a further three cases. Only one of the projects was found not to have benefited, or to have benefited to only a minor extent, from external inputs (see Table 8.1). With respect to the formality of this external sourcing of inputs, it was revealed that informal exchange played a critical or important role in three of the innovations (Backlite, Hydro-Probe and Yeoman). In addition, informal external sources provided useful inputs in a further six (50 per cent) of the projects (see Table 8.2).

However, further analysis revealed that the importance of external inputs was seen to vary between the different stages of the innovation process; for example, external inputs were of greater importance during field-testing than during problem-solving (solution inputs) or idea-generation (inputs concerning the features, functionality and specifications of the innovation). The following pages take a closer look at the role of informal boundary-spanning activity by analysing the importance of informally sourced external inputs in stimulating the innovation project, and aiding the idea-generation, problem-solving and field-testing processes.

Table 8.2   The importance of informal inputs during the
innovation process

	Small-firm sample ($n = 12$)	
	No. of projects	*% of projects*
Critical	1	8
Important	2	17
Useful	6	50
Minor	3	25

The Formalisation of Project Stimuli

Four of the developments were found to have been stimulated by an explicit market-need (the linear actuator, the on-line tape certification system, Polifold and the Town and Country III). The other eight projects were stimulated by various internal processes, such as internal needs, perceived external needs, in-house technology, or the recognition of the potential application of existing technology developed externally. In assessing the formalisation of the stimuli of these four externally triggered projects, it was found that two (the linear actuator, and the on-line tape certification system) arose from a formal approach by an external actor. The other two projects were triggered by external stimuli of a more casual and informal nature. In the case of Polifold, the innovator was spurred into action following mounting customer complaints concerning existing market solutions, which it installed but did not manufacture.

The Formalisation of Idea-Generation Inputs

During idea-generation, external sources were found to be critical in only one case (Amethyst) and important in one other (the Town and Country III). External sources proved useful in generating ideas in a further seven cases (see Table 8.3). Typical of the innovations which received useful input from external sources is Elektra. With reference to the development of this software package, it was recalled that: 'The basic concept and ideas are all [internal] . . . The gloss on it is from the users, who have allowed us to tidy it up' (Elektra interview).

Table 8.3   The exchange value of external idea-generation inputs

	Small-firm sample (n = 12)	
	No. of projects	*% of projects*
Critical	1	8
Important	1	8
Useful	7	58
Minor	3	25

Informally derived external inputs were not found to be critical or important in any of the small firm projects, though were considered useful in seven of the developments. Thus, informal mechanisms of exchange were considered unimportant in five of the cases, compared to three for external inputs in general (see Table 8.4).

Table 8.4   The exchange value of informal idea-generation inputs

	Small-firm sample (n = 12)	
	No. of projects	*% of projects*
Critical	0	0
Important	0	0
Useful	7	58
Minor	5	42

Much of the informally derived external input into the idea-generation process of these projects was both *tacit* and *incomplete*. In addition, a good proportion of this external input was obtained on an *ad hoc* basis from a large number of actors with whom the innovator had only a transitory relationship. However, a smaller set of long-term personal relationships (in which friendship played an important part) were found to be instrumental in promoting the two-way flow of ideas, thus allowing ideas to take form in a more interactive manner over time.

The Formalisation of Problem-Solving Inputs

In relation to problem-solving, the analysis of the case material revealed that external inputs were critical in one-quarter of the cases (Hydro-Probe, Xenos and Yeoman) and important in one other development (see Table 8.5).

Table 8.5   The exchange value of external problem-solving inputs

	Small-firm sample (n = 12)	
	No. of projects	% of projects
Critical	3	25
Important	1	8
Useful	5	42
Minor	3	25

However, while many of the useful external inputs into the problem-solving phases of the projects were informal, most of the critical and important inputs were sourced formally (see Table 8.6). This was linked to the fact that many of the useful inputs during the problem-solving process were cognitive and tacit in nature. In contrast, the important and critical external inputs were seen to be largely tangible components or materials, resulting from a formal approach by the innovator to a supplier. In the development of the Yeoman, this critical external input provided the *enabling* digitising technology; while in the Xenos project, the entrepreneur formally commissioned a technical consultancy to undertake the development of the critical electronic components.

Table 8.6   The exchange value of informal problem-solving inputs

	Small-firm sample (n = 12)	
	No. of projects	% of projects
Critical	1	8
Important	0	0
Useful	6	50
Minor	5	42

The Formalisation of Field-Testing Inputs

Many of the innovators were found to mobilise external linkages during the field-testing phase of the project. In half of the cases this input was found to play either a critical (Amethyst) or important role, with only three cases indicating that external sources played only a minor role (see Table 8.7). This high incidence of external interaction was accounted for by many of the interviewees in terms of the limitations of testing an innovative product in an artificial or laboratory environment.

Table 8.7   The exchange value of external field-testing inputs

	Small-firm sample (n = 12)	
	No. of projects	% of projects
Critical	1	8
Important	5	42
Useful	3	25
Minor	3	25

In contrast to the results concerning the formality of external inputs in idea-generation and problem-solving, informally derived external inputs were found to be important during field-testing in one-third of the developments (Backlite, Elektra, Hydro-Probe and Yeoman), although critical in none. Useful inputs were also found to be derived informally in a further two projects, although considered as minor in the remaining six cases (see Table 8.8).

Table 8.8   The exchange value of informal field-testing inputs

	Small-firm sample (n = 12)	
	No. of projects	% of projects
Critical	0	0
Important	4	33
Useful	2	17
Minor	6	50

Typical of the informal nature of external field-testing input is this quotation from an interview with Elektra:

'We have strong connections with . . . ten firms that we use . . . They're lead-users, where we know the people who are using the software in the companies and have a high level of expertise . . . They're friends . . . We tried to establish [formal] beta-test sites where we get feed-back and it just didn't work, so we just work with individuals that we're friendly with.'

Also of interest is the field-testing of the Yeoman:

Hugh and I sailed on a friend's yacht . . . to San Tropez and tested it [the first prototype] . . . Although we'd worked a lot on the software in the office, it's not until you take a product like that to sea that you really find what you've got . . . And we were able to change the software dynamically on board the vessel as I had it all on a lap-top computer . . . The second prototype we took to sea extensively. It was still a top-secret project then . . . We selected friends we trusted and we used to take it out in their boats and get their comments, their feed-back . . . This was the first attempt to crack the user-interface between man and machine. (Yeoman interview)

Thus, in the field-testing of the Elektra software package the utilisation of relationships reinforced by friendship allowed Elektra to obtain more reliable feed-back, while in the cases of Xenos and the Yeoman, the motivation for mobilising friends in field-testing was primarily one of retaining the secrecy of the project.

These results not only illustrate the exchange value of informal boundary-spanning inputs into the field-testing process of innovative products, but also the importance of friendship between particular individuals in the innovating organisation and those outside, often within 'user organisations'.

External Product Champions

Interestingly, the analysis also highlighted the incidence of informal product championing by individuals outside the innovating organisation. Interviewees in a third of the small-firm cases explicitly referred to external individuals who had played a role analogous to the so-called *product champion* (Amethyst, Backlite, Hydro-Probe and Synon/2). For example, in the testing of early prototypes of the Synon/2 software package, 'The DP Manager there [City Bank], who knew us, believed in our ideas, was prepared really to risk quite a lot' (Synon/2 interview).

The Hydro-Probe interviewee recounted in detail the important role played by an individual within English China Clays both in the field-testing of the Hydro-Probe and in developing their basic understanding of the technology:

We didn't understand the relationship of the output signals of the sensor. My colleague didn't even realise the relationship is different for different materials . . . We fairly early on met somebody from English China Clays, on the technical side, and they were very interested in the product . . . He had one of the first ones we made . . . He had a little laboratory down there and he actually built a silo so he could test our product out with a variety of different materials . . . He did some curves for us [voltage/moisture] on different materials . . . The sort of work we couldn't have done. He did it for his own interest . . . So that was a totally informal relationship . . . When you get a big company with an enthusiastic technical employee, they can do wonders for a small company . . . He championed the product! (Hydro-Probe interview)

Furthermore, the Amethyst interviewee noted that they consciously scan the market for potential external product champions prior to initiating development projects: 'In all these product developments there's always been a couple of key [external] individuals that make it all work. . . In every case there is a [external] product-champion. And we've found these guys initially through this market-survey sweep process, where it emerges who's really keen and who isn't' (Amethyst interview).

A number of the interviewees also commented explicitly on the informal role played more generally by lead-users and the professions in the adoption and diffusion of the innovations (Elektra, Synon/2, Xenos and Yeoman). In relation to the role of lead-users in the adoption of the Synon/2 software package, it was noted that:

Certainly in the early sales in the States and Europe, you saw . . . people in companies who were interested in things state-of-the-art . . . I would say they were literally adopting for the sake of adopting, to make their lives more interesting, but without them, certainly, I don't think we would have got very far. (Synon/2 interview)

Behind Every Formal Link

The case material provides many references, both explicit and implicit, regarding the importance of informal boundary-spanning relationships between individuals in supporting formally established links between organisations. That is, there exists much evidence to corroborate the contention of Freeman (1991:503) that 'behind every formal network, giving it the breath of life, are usually various informal networks . . . Personal relationships of trust and confidence . . . are important both at the formal and informal level.' The importance of friendship in collaborating with external partners was noted by a number of the interviewees: for example, 'We have very close relationships with the groups that we collaborate with ... It is the friendships ... It is important. It develops a level of under-standing which you wouldn't get otherwise' (Elektra interview).

Since the combining of formal and informal relationships appears to be an important element of successful collaboration, the origin of this dual-ism or multiplexity is of interest. Boissevain (1974:30) argues that 'there is a tendency for single-stranded [uniplex] relations to become many-stranded [multiplex] if they persist over time'. This begs the question of whether informal relationships precede formal relationships, or *vice versa*. The analysis of the case-material reveals that both of these pro-cesses are in evidence. For example, in relation to the formation of friend-ships which developed within the framework of a formal collaboration with a lead-user during beta-tests, it was noted that: 'We made some very good friendships among some of the developers [at City Bank during the beta-test] ... Of course, if you're working on something new with some-one it's a good environment to make friends' (Synon/2 interview).

Conversely, the importance of previously existing friendships was stres-sed in the decision to involve Philips in the Elektra project: 'The group at Rutherford got heavily involved with ... Philips, STC, GEC ... to form a big [EEC] project ... Friendships were formed in that original project, which carried forward. You learnt who it was good to work with, who you could rely on' (Elektra interview).

In summary, the analysis of the case-material revealed the importance of informal friendship-based boundary-spanning relationships in *breath-ing life* into formal collaborations. This supports the contention of Cun-ningham and Homse (1984:17) that 'social bonds between organisations are an important element of many successful [formal] relations'.

The Source and Nature of Informally Derived External Inputs into the Innovation Process

The following pages look at the role played by users, suppliers, research establishments, consultants and industrial designers, distributors, the pro-fessions and competitors in the development of the 12 small-firm innova-tions studied.

The Role of Users

Users were seen to play only a minor role in stimulating new innovation projects. However, the analysis did identify users as *the* major external source of inputs into idea generation: that is, the process of defining the features, functionality and specifications of the innovations studied. Users were seen to provide important inputs into the idea generation process of two of the innovations: Amethyst and the Town and Country III. Interestingly, in both of these cases user involvement was particularly evident during *reinnovation*: that is, the modification of earlier models (Rothwell and Gardiner, 1985). Indeed it was noted that, in subsequent versions of the Amethyst software package, 'The substantial number of changes have come from the users . . . We try and be really careful about putting our own ideas in unless a user agrees with it' (Amethyst interview).

In addition, users were also seen to represent *the* major external source for the pre-commercialisation field-testing of the innovations, playing a critical role in the Amethyst project and an important role in a further five (Backlite, Elektra, Hydro-Probe, Synon/2 and Yeoman). This adds support to Habermeier's (1990) hypothesis that product characteristics and user requirements can often only be discovered if the innovation is actually used, sometimes for long periods of time. It is also worth noting that in most of these cases field-testing was undertaken by what von Hippel (1986b) has termed *lead-users*. Field-tests were seen not only as an important test-bed for the technical performance of the innovations, but also for the suitability of the embodied features and functionality. However, it is also true to say that a fair amount of what may be considered as post-commercialisation *field-testing* was highlighted by the research. That is, a number of the innovating companies either consciously or unwittingly commercialised rather *rough and ready* versions of their innovations, which were subsequently tested by users in a commercial situation. This led directly to new product versions that incorporated debugging and/or much improved functionality. This point was expressed quite openly in relation to the development of the Hydro-Probe: 'I suppose at the back of your mind you're realising that you're doing development, to a certain extent, maybe, on your customers' (Hydro-Probe interview).

This form of *field-testing* may occur for a number of reasons: for example, it had occurred consciously in relation to the development of Xenos largely because of the lack of financial resources:

> [larger competitors] can afford to produce a thousand pre-production prototypes and put them out to all sorts of people . . . And they'll have all the [feedback] that comes in. We are not able to do that. So we have to take our best bet . . . and do a certain amount of development afterwards once it gets out into the field. (Xenos interview)

Although the principal identified role of users concerns their input into the features and field-testing of the innovations, users were also seen to provide information and equipment to aid in the problem-solving process (e.g., the on-line tape certification system), as well as adapting and modifying the innovation to local needs (e.g., Backlite).

A good proportion of the messages entering the idea-generation process were found to be sourced informally from transitory relationships with users. The principal mechanisms mentioned by the interviewees in this respect include: exhibitions (the Town and Country III); customer-site visits (the on-line tape certification system); person-to-person contact over the phone or on-site (Elektra, Hydro-Probe, Polifold and the Town and Country III). The development of friendships with those in other organisations promoted this informal boundary-spanning interaction. In the development of Xenos, for example, it was noted that: 'We didn't do too much with customers, partly through security ... [However] we were using about half a dozen different people to assess the benefits and the bugs ... from friendships built-up over the years' (Xenos interview).

Although the exchange value of much of this input into the idea-generation process was classified as only useful or minor, the Town and Country III interviewee, for example, argued that it served to avoid the commercial pitfalls of so-called *engineer-solutions*. Typical examples of informal user input channelled through these mechanisms include the positioning of the rechargeable plug and adoption of puncture-proof tyres in the development of the Town and Country III. With respect to the user inputs to the Yeoman: 'They were largely in-house ideas with some feed-back from other yachtsmen and friends and journalists. And good feed-back too. Although there weren't that many changes to the original idea, so we had it pretty well right the first time. The changes were subtle' (Yeoman interview).

Semi-formal user-groups were reported to have played a useful role in the Elektra project, while in the development of the Town and Country III, the innovating firm plugged into existing groups, such as local branches of the Polio and MS (Multiple Sclerosis) societies, for ideas and user feed-back. The Elektra user-group meetings, for example, were described thus:

> It's essentially one or two days. Some sort of social event in the evening, to start it off and to encourage people to come, and also you get people talking outside of the formal atmosphere of the lecture room. Then a series of lectures by Elektra people who are involved ... A report on the existing products, the sort of problems that people have had. A report on the next releases which are coming out, and developments which are coming for the future. That takes roughly half a day and the rest of the time is users talking about the product, reporting problems with the software. (Elektra interview)

Thus, user-group meetings provided a suitable forum for the two-way flow of information and the establishment of longer-term friendship-based relationships between individual users and engineers, alongside already existing formal organisational links.

In summary, informal input from users was found to be particularly evident in idea-generation and the field-testing of the innovations, with the exchange value being greater in the latter. The analysis revealed a plurality of informal mechanisms through which this informal input was channelled and highlighted the importance of friendship between engineers and users in the exchange process.

The Role of Suppliers

The analysis highlighted the supplier as *the* major external source of solution inputs into the innovation process, playing a critical role in a quarter of the innovations. In these three cases (Hydro-Probe, Xenos and Yeoman), the supplier was seen to have developed one or more of the critical components of the innovation in response to specific requests from the innovator. In the development of the Hydro-Probe and Xenos, for example, the respective technological entrepreneurs essentially played the role of project co-ordinator rather than developer, orchestrating a series of developments by innovative suppliers; in the development of the Yeoman, however, suppliers were commissioned to develop the enabling technology (i.e., large-scale digitising technology). Suppliers were also found to have provided important inputs through their development of one or more of the core components in a further two of the innovations: the ceramic reader-head for the on-line tape certification system, and the speed control system for the Town and Country III.

The cases therefore provide illustrations of both the 'complementary' (the on-line tape certification system, the Town and Country III and the Yeoman) and the 'substitutive' (Hydro-Probe) nature of external sources of technology in relation to indigenous innovative activity in small firms.

In contrast to the informal nature of much of the input from users, supplier input into the innovation process was found to be largely formal. However, the importance of friendship and informality was stressed by a number of the interviewees with respect to the nature of the formal relationships that existed between the innovator and their suppliers in the projects studied. The innovative nature of the components required of the suppliers in these developments necessitated frequent interaction and the resultant development of good-will, informality and friendship at the engineer-level.

The Role of Research Establishments

Research establishments played a role in half of the developments (Amethyst, Backlite, Elektra, Hydro-Probe, Synon/2 and Xenos). However, in many of these instances the input was considered peripheral rather than core to the innovation process (i.e., useful but not important or critical). Research establishments were found to have been formally commissioned to undertake consultancy work in two of these six cases (Backlite and Xenos). In the Backlite project, this consultancy work was employed to help optimise in-house technical solutions. More typical were informal approaches to universities, and the tapping into, or membership of, broad research networks. The most common manner in which these networks were operationalised was through informal face-to-face contact at technical conferences. This informality is well illustrated by reference to the Elektra project: 'We have a good understanding with university groups who have research in the areas that are important, or could be important, to Elektra . . . Friendship is very important in this respect' (Elektra interview).

Interviewees noted that they more frequently employed universities in exploratory research rather than in product development. This occurred because of the variance between commercial and research organisations with respect to time-scale expectations and ways of working. The following comment was typical:

> We've had CASE [Phd] awards with universities, which were OK . . . which were cheap, but we didn't actually get anything from them. I think we quickly learnt that the direction that a postgraduate student takes forms no relation to what we are interested in. It was too easy for them to get deflected onto something of interest . . . The Teaching Company Scheme . . . is much more related to our work . . . and we can use them for speculative things . . . [that] involve a lot of research . . . The Teaching Company Scheme is allowing us to find out about what are the fields which could be important. (Elektra interview)

To a lesser extent, knowledge and information were also found to flow from research establishments to innovative small firms via scientific and technical journals. Scientific literature was explicitly mentioned as playing a role in providing information and ideas in two of the cases (Amethyst and Synon/2). In the case of Synon/2, it was felt that academic journals had been 'very valuable' in post-rationalising the ideas of the development team: 'We worked out our fundamental ideas more or less intuitively from the patterns that we'd seen from writing systems for the City . . . In theoretical academic papers we found the rationale for what we had arrived at . . . It was very valuable finding the theoretical underpinning' (Synon/2 interview).

In summary, the analysis of the cases found that while research establishments seldom played an important or critical role in the innovation process, they frequently provided useful cognitive input into problem-solving. A great deal of intangible and tacit cognitive transaction content was found to flow between research establishments and innovators primarily via *active* (person-to-person), but also *passive* (literature) mechanisms.

The Role of Consultants and Industrial Designers

Technical consultants were utilised in two of the projects (Elektra, and the on-line tape certification system). This consultancy work was seen to cover a variety of functions, but on the whole was used on an *ad hoc* basis to provide information or advice for specific problems that needed addressing in the problem-solving process, or for the evaluation of the performance of components or prototypes. With respect to product design, industrial design consultants were employed in one-third of the projects (Hydro-Probe, the Town and Country III, Xenos and Yeoman). These design consultants were invariably commissioned to undertake a specific piece of work on a formal basis. In each of these cases, the design consultancy work focused on both aesthetics and the sensitising of the product to the end-user. Although in relation to the technical solutions and functionality embodied within an innovation the aesthetics and ergonomics may not be considered as a core input, the industrial design may provide the vital differentiator in terms of commercial success. This point was articulated in relation to a number of the above innovations; for example, with reference to Xenos: 'It's important that a product not only should work and look good, but actually feel good. At the beginning it [Xenos] looked as though it was going to come out far too light, and if it was we were going to weight it!' (Xenos interview).

The analysis also revealed that these formal inputs, particularly in relation to product design, were largely undertaken at *arm's-length*. As a consequence, friendship rarely developed from these work relationships. This arm's-length approach is also well illustrated by the example provided by the Xenos project, concerning the product and circuit design:

> I ended up going to Cambridge Consultants. I laid down a specification of what I wanted . . . the minimum size, and that sort of thing. They came back with these concept drawings and none of them were really ideal . . . I set them a challenge . . . Having worked on some [more] drawings . . . they came up with a mock-up. (Xenos interview)

Thus, it was found that it was most common for consultants to undertake work on a formal and arm's-length basis.

The Role of Distributors

Only two instances were located in the case-studies of a distributor playing any role in the innovation process. However, in one of these cases (Amethyst) the distributor was found to have played a critical role in both providing the features and functionality of the product, and in co-ordinating the beta-testing of the software package with its own customers. It was noted, with respect to the role of the supplier in the development of Amethyst, that:

> When we built it [Amethyst], they [IRD, the distributors] told us what to do. So although we built the expert system, we took their market knowledge and their knowledge of what was needed, and used that to build a successful product . . . They decided on the colour scheme. They decided on all the functionality. They knew what their users would need. That's a classic case of where we are a technology-provider. (Amethyst interview)

However, it was also pointed out that in relation to the roles of the distributor and end-user that: 'It's hard to know [the end-user's role], because they [user comments and feedback] were all consolidated before they got to us [by IRD, the distributor]. So I think there were some pretty major [user] inputs, but we can never really separate them out' (Amethyst interview).

Although this relationship was formal, the intensity of the interaction during this development and the consequent need for good communication meant that personal ties were also forged:

> The programmer guys have never met, but they have worked extremely well for several years now . . . They'd talk on the phone and tell jokes, and have a good time, and try and build that repartee up . . . but it is quite remarkable that you could build such a successful product, without the programming teams meeting . . . But the link was not that far, it was just a modem and fax machine away! . . . He [the IRD new product manager] was a very friendly and very easy going guy. Real friendly. And we got on really well . . . Certainly it was critical that we had a really good flow of information. They could specify what they wanted and we could respond . . . Certainly without the good communications, we

would never have got the product right in the first place. (Amethyst interview)

The second instance is provided by the Town and Country III project. With respect to this development, a number of the features and specifications (including the introduction of lights, indicators and maintenance-free batteries) were driven by the firm's Dutch distributor, which services a sophisticated user-base. The flow of information was unstructured, largely one-way, and informal, with the distributor acting primarily as a conduit for the user needs and demands of an overseas market out of reach of the small innovator.

The Role of the Professions

Professionals, such as doctors and educationalists, were not seen to play a critical or important role in any of the small-firm innovations investigated, though doctors were found to play a useful role in the development of Xenos. In this project, doctors and physiotherapists provided general information and the names of patients willing to test new medical products:

We've built up a lot of contacts with doctors who run the pain-clinics . . . A lot of good friends. We don't have a sales-force, unlike all of our competitors. Our sales-force *is* the doctors and the physios themselves, because they recommend it to one another and the word gets about . . . With professional people, once you've built up your reputation and a relationship with them, they are very loyal . . . They're happy to then pass on their patient into your care, and this is effectively what's happening. (Xenos interview)

These relationships and the flow of information were primarily informal and often reinforced by friendship. However, a small number of these professionals were sometimes paid for their services.

The Role of Competitors

Competitors were rarely mentioned explicitly in relation to providing inputs into the innovation process, either with respect to interacting with competitors or in analysing their products. In fact, only two of the interviewees indicated that information concerning the features, functionality and specifications of competitors' products had in some way influenced their innovations (the Town and Country III and Xenos); this information was collected generally without direct interaction, through product marketing literature.

CONCLUSIONS AND POLICY IMPLICATIONS

The sources of innovation have been a subject of continued interest amongst researchers since the 1950s (Carter and Williams, 1957; Myers and Marquis, 1969; Achilladis, Robertson and Jervis [Project SAPPHO], 1971; Langrish *et al.*, 1972; von Hippel, 1988; Conway, 1994). Wolek and Griffith (1974) argue that much of this research has been encouraged by the search for ways to stimulate science and technology, and as such has received extensive support from policy-makers. However, prior to the recent government White Paper entitled 'Realising Our Potential' (Chancellor of the Duchy of Lancaster, 1993), Allen, Hyman and Pinckney (1983:208) had contended that 'the overwhelming dominance of personal contact in technology transfer has been replicated in study after study, yet it is consistently ignored by policy-makers'. Yet, for policy-makers to implement policies to encourage informal transfer they need first to have a clearer understanding of the channels and mechanisms through which the process occurs. This need is articulated by Wolek and Griffith (1974:420), who argue that 'for policy-makers to effect improvements and changes in the flow of information, they must have a firm understanding of the existing and desired relationships which bind groups of professionals into productive communities'.

Through employing a network perspective and a systematic approach to the study of linkages and flows, this research has sought to reveal and build upon our knowledge of the informal channels and mechanisms through which ideas enter the innovation process. The value of undertaking such research lies in the belief that 'the social structure revealed by network analysis is generally invisible to the participants in the system of study' (Rogers, 1987:8).

The original study from which this data has been extracted (Conway, 1994) indicates that external inputs are of greater importance for the small firm than for the large firm during the innovation process. Although important in both small-firm and large-firm innovation, external inputs were more frequently sourced informally by small firms; this was particularly evident in relation to the pre-commercial field-testing phase of small-firm innovation projects. Informal boundary-spanning relationships therefore represent a valuable mechanism through which external inputs enter the innovation process in small firms and, as such, are an important intangible organisational resource. The focal innovation action-sets studied and mapped out were often found to be large, predominantly informal, localised, and diverse, stretching *upstream* along the supply chain to suppliers, *downstream* to various users and distributors, and incorporating other individuals such as university academics. Personal trust was important and, as a consequence, such small-firm networks were centred more on relationships with particular individuals within external organisations, rather than more formal, bureaucratic, faceless linkages at the level of the organisation. It is also important to note that the network of external relationships built, nurtured and mobilised by this sample of innovative small firms was frequently found to be centred largely around one individual: the entrepreneur.

Evidence from the study indicates that not only is informality in the sourcing of external inputs favourable to the process of successful small-firm innovation, but it is also the favoured mode of boundary-spanning interaction by the entrepreneurs themselves. Informality would appear to have an important role to play in allowing entrepreneurs to overcome the apparent paradox of entrepreneurship that was raised in the introductory section: that while on the one hand 'the entrepreneur personifies individualism and independence', on the other 'he is . . . very dependent on ties of trust and co-operation' (Johannisson and Peterson, 1984:1).

While entrepreneurs appear to be more at ease with informality, such 'off-the-books' interaction is not only more problematic for the managers of larger firms, it is also 'sometimes interpreted as a sign of weakness and the need for better *formal* systems' (Wolek and Griffith, 1974:411); their concerns centre around the following issues (Conway, 1995):

- the unpredictable nature of informal interaction
- the competitive cost of information leakage
- the difficulty of managing and controlling informal interaction
- the reliance and over-dependence on a small number of boundary-spanning employees

With the continuing proliferation of information, knowledge, and scientific and technological specialities, in the post-war period (Allen, 1977; Badaracco, 1991), it is likely that innovative firms will become increasingly dependent on external sources during the innovation process. Indeed, Rogers and Kincaid (1981:343–4) argue that 'information overload is often handled by the structuring of interpersonal network links by individuals. *Knowwho* thus begins to replace *knowhow* as one of the main determinants of individual effectiveness.' It follows that know-who is likely to become a critical intangible resource for innovative organisations, in particular for SMEs which have limited internal resources at their disposal (Rothwell, 1991).

Plugging into or forming networks of relationships between organisations with complementary skills can be a way in which SMEs can maximise their innovative output from limited R&D resources. However, 'networking' is not a panacea to the human, technical and financial resource problems of SMEs. The deficiency of innovative capacity in SMEs is unlikely to be overcome by simply substituting indigenous R&D activity by externally developed technology and know-how; in-house R&D not only generates new information but also develops a firm's capacity to identify, assimilate, and exploit external technology and know-how (Cohen and Levinthal, 1989). Indeed, Freeman (1991:501) argues that 'the successful exploitation of imported technology is strongly related to the capacity to adapt and improve this technology through indigenous R&D'. It would appear, then, that the innovative capacity of SMEs is best served by a balance between developing the technical and network assets of the enterprise, rather than on a reliance on one or the other.

In the last decade, policies have emerged and evolved at both the level of the nation-state and the European Union (in particular through the SPRINT programme) which recognise the importance and interdependence of external networking and internal capacity to the innovation process of SMEs. These actions involve a complementary mix of policies aimed at:

(a) improving the technology absorption capacity of SMEs: for example, through the MINT initiative (Managing the Integration of New Technologies) under the SPRINT programme, and the 'Business Links' programme in the UK, which offers a range of consultancy advice and support;

(b) supporting and encouraging technology transfer to SMEs through intermediaries: for example, through the Inter-firm Mini Networks Action Line under the SPRINT programme;

(c) the formation of technology and task-orientated networks that explicitly encourage the incorporation of SMEs: for example, the Specific Project Action Line (also under the SPRINT programme), aimed at building task-orientated networks for the adaptation and transfer of specific innovations and technology across regions and industrial sectors.

However, Bessant (1995:268) argues that 'networks are a comparatively new addition to the policy-maker's tool-box, and there is considerable excitement about their potential; this carries the risk that they will be used widely and not always appropriately. There is a need to explore further the strengths and weaknesses of this new approach.' One potential tension does stand out and requires further investigation: on the one hand, research highlights the importance to small-firm innovation of informal, personal, trust-based relationships established and nurtured over time, and the preference of entrepreneurs for such informality; while on the other, the 'reliance [on informal interaction] is somewhat troublesome, for it is formal channels which seem to be much more amenable to control and institutional support' (Wolek and Griffith, 1974:412).

9 Technological Interweavement: A Means for New Technology-Based Firms to Achieve Innovation Success

Peter Heydebreck

INTRODUCTION

Research on efficient innovation management was focused on intra-organisational topics until at least the beginning of the 1980s. Then the research on industrial procurement and on industrial marketing began to show that it is not meaningful to study isolated players in homogeneous markets, because '[f]irms are not islands but are linked together in patterns of co-operation and affiliation' (Richardson, 1972:895). The interweavement of actors demands an analysis of dyadic relationships and complex networks. This insight holds true not only in respect to the mere procurement and distribution of products but also in regard to innovation management.

Empirical studies have made it clear that technological interweavement is not a phantom but a very real phenomenon (Håkansson, 1987; Hagedoorn and Schakenraad, 1990a,1990b; Herden, 1992; Hahn *et al.*, 1995). There is a lack of empirical evidence, though, when it comes to the impact technological interweavement has on the innovation success and on the growth of a company. This has inspired the study to deal with three basic questions.

1. Are there forms of technological interweavement (i.e., types of partners) that are particularly apt for increasing the technological product and process innovation success of a company and for transforming a technological innovation success into a commercial success?
2. Is the impact of technological interweavement on success dependent on context factors: that is, is there an overall ideal pattern of network structure or is the effectiveness of a type of interweavement dependent

on a firm's size, age, industry, location, corporate strategy or other context variables? In this contribution, the analyses are limited to the possible interaction effect between corporate strategy and interweavement.

3. Are there possibilities for helping companies, especially NTBFs, to intensify their networking and to manage their relationships more efficiently? Particular attention is given to two types of 'fosterers' of NTBFs, namely seed capitalists and science parks. The focus on NTBFs is due to two reasons: First, it is assumed that the potential of growth is particularly large for NTBFs compared with other companies; Second, despite the high need for an efficient network, NTBFs face massive barriers of interweavement. For a discussion of such barriers see Gemünden and Heydebreck (1994c).

Technology-oriented relationships with external partners serve a wide variety of functions that, on the one hand, create stability and increase the efficiency of routine processes and, on the other hand, stimulate innovation success (Gemünden and Heydebreck, 1994a; Heydebreck, 1996). The most important functions of stimulating innovation success are the following:

(a) the function of learning stimulates the technical innovation success and comprises the functions of information as well as development;
(b) the function of information and the function of diffusion (which stimulates commercial innovation success).

The Function of Learning

Technology-oriented relationships fulfil a function of information by serving as communication channels through which external know-how on new technologies or new challenges (for example, by new laws) can be acquired. The knowledge need not necessarily be on an abstract level but might very well be problem-specific. It might be that the partner himself possesses the information needed or, alternatively, that he has to access it via his partners.

Relationships with external partners (particularly with customers) constitute a means of receiving critical information of a much higher quality than can be bought from, for example, market research institutes. This is the direct result of the higher motivation and capability of partners to serve each other compared with interactions with anonymous actors.

The partners are highly motivated to communicate their momentary and future needs early and correctly, because they want their partners' support in satisfying them. In contrast to pure market interactions, long-term relationships offer the opportunity to exchange confidential information, because the partners can judge whether or not they can trust each other. This is crucial because information is only valuable if it is correct, and if the recipient can be sure that it is correct.

Partners are well-acquainted; adjustments of organisational routines allow an efficient flow of information (with a low risk of misunderstandings and protractions due to, for instance, harmonised codes and computer systems). Thus, the partners receive relevant information without explicitly asking for it, since their partners know which information is valuable for them. At the same time, the risk of an information overload is eliminated.

Relationships are not only a means of transferring know-how that already exists but can even be a means of developing new knowledge jointly. They serve a function of development. Exploiting the inherent synergy potentials by combining the complementary knowledge of two or more partners can lead to numerous advantages:

- a speeding-up of processes
- increasing the probability of a successful development
- gains in quality
- reduction and split of costs of development
- reduction of uncertainty

The Function of Information and the Function of Diffusion

In addition to technological know-how, relationships constitute a valuable channel through which market information can be exchanged. In particular, bonds with customers (be they institutionalised in the form of Customer Advisory Boards or Customer Development Teams or not) lead R&D activities away from technical gimmicks towards customer needs, at the same time securing market demand for the innovative product.

Business relationships are not one-way streets by which means information and other resources are acquired; instead, they serve as a mode of target-oriented diffusion of information, in order to foster the commercial innovation success as well. Diffusion of information about future products to customers prevents customers from buying competitors' products today and allows them to make the necessary preparations for using the new product (e.g., training of employees).

Suppliers can only help to speed up innovation processes if they know about their tasks in the innovation process (such as development of new components) as early as possible. Diffusion of innovation-relevant information and property rights to competitors (e.g., by cross-licensing agreements) is an instrument for creating new norms and standards. In addition, the distribution can be enlarged by alliances: first, this is achieved by combining distribution forces, and second, the users will tend to overcome their scepticism against a new product more easily if several companies guarantee its superiority against traditional products.

DEVELOPMENT OF HYPOTHESES

The basic assumption of this chapter is that the general competitiveness of a company (and its innovativeness, in particular) are determined not only by internal resources but also to a large extent by its access to complementary know-how and resources via technology-oriented relationships.

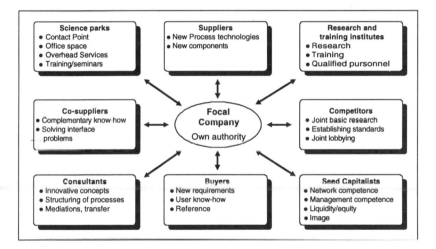

Figure 9.1 Innovation partners and their resources
Source: Based upon Gemünden, Heydebreck and Herden (1992:360).

In order to develop specific hypotheses and to verify them empirically, the complex construct interweavement is broken up into several actor specific dimensions. Figure 9.1 illustrates the most important types of external partners and the kind of resources they can offer. In addition to those actors mentioned in Figure 9.1, for example, public bodies and distributors can have a positive impact on a firm's innovation success (Gemünden, Heydebreck and Herden, 1992). Therefore many different types of actors can contribute to a company's innovation success. However, in this contribution, the analysis is limited to those types of partner which the companies themselves believe to be the most important: customers, suppliers, research institutes and universities (defined here as Research and Technology Organisations, or RTOs) as well as consultants. In NTBF-specific analyses, the focus is on relationships with seed capitalists and science parks. Each of these relationships will be considered in turn, and hypotheses derived from the discussion.

Customers

The companies themselves regard customers as their most important partners. This judgement is shared by most researchers and holds particularly true in regard to innovation processes (Dertouzos, Lester and Solow, 1990). Customers want to take an active part in the innovation process in order to ensure that the results meet their targets, and the study tests the following hypotheses with respect to the impact of collaboration with customers on innovation success. This leads to the first hypothesis:

Hypothesis 1a – Customers help their suppliers to achieve different forms of innovation success: technological product innovation success, commercial product innovation success, technical process innovation success and economic impact of a process innovation.

By simply threatening not to buy the supplier's existing product in the future, customers force their suppliers to develop and deliver products of improved quality. Thus, they help the innovation promoters in the supplier company, for example, to get access to more financial resources for performing R&D. Customers possess user know-how. They know about the weaknesses of existing products and how other companies have tackled them. Quite often, they have even worked on further developments themselves. Therefore, they can technically contribute to their suppliers' innovation processes. For example, manufacturers can get access to their customers' knowledge by visiting them regularly (Bailetti and Guild, 1991) or by developing concepts for new products in joint workshops (Herstatt and von Hippel, 1991). This leads to hypothesis 1b:

Hypothesis 1b – The commercial product innovation success. Customers help their suppliers to innovate in fields that are commercially relevant. They always want their current needs to be satisfied better. In addition, new needs arise continuously. Customers are highly motivated to inform manufacturers that they trust will be able and willing to develop the products about their needs.

The ideas of the customers are typically superior to those resulting from brainstorming activities in the manufacturers' marketing department, because they result from real needs and are uttered by actors who are willing to pay for need satisfaction in general and the focal manufacturer in particular. It is up to the manufacturer to consider complaints about existing products and demands for improvement as stimulation for product innovation and not as something evil that should be ignored or even opposed.

Given a level of technical innovation success, customer involvement in the product innovation process increases the commercial innovation success. In case the customer has invested in joint product development with a selected supplier (be it ideas, time or money), the new product is also the customer's 'baby'. The not-invented-here (NIH)syndrome becomes less relevant. Instead, a change of partners at the time of the buying decision would create exit costs in the form of, for example, costs for the search for new partners and the danger of being regarded as a non-trustworthy co-operation partner by third parties.

Technological co-operation with customers not only helps to sell the new product to the partner directly; in addition, a customer that uses the new product creates a pressure of innovation for other companies. This holds particularly true in those cases where the customer uses the product as a crucial component in a larger system. The automobile industry is a classic example of this behaviour: the introduction of new safety measures (e.g., new brakes, new airbags, new side impact systems) is emphasised in promotion campaigns by the first buyer of the innovative component, which creates an enormous pressure on the other car producers. Whereas the customer simply accepts her reference role in this case, she can even actively recommend the new product to other companies. Therefore, the next hypothesis is:

Hypothesis 1c – The efficiency of the production processes. Customers continuously demand lower prices, shorter delivery cycles, higher rates of perfect orders and so on. This forces their suppliers to increase the efficiency of their production and distribution processes.

Suppliers

Customers often possess know-how that can be used to make the processes of their suppliers more efficient. They hand it over to those partners with whom they maintain close relationships in order to receive better results. Some firms (such as Honda) go as far as sending their own personnel to their suppliers for several weeks or even months to increase their partners' efficiency. The suppliers only pay for this help by handing over the majority of the efficiency gains in the relationship with Honda but they can keep all the profit otherwise gained as a result of higher efficiency.

A technology-oriented relationship between supplier and user offers potential gains not only for the supplier but also for the customer. The gains might be more efficient production processes or superior products. Japanese companies realised the potential of collaborating with suppliers long before their European or US competitors. 'Loyalty has been conspicuously absent from the US auto industry in recent decades ... However, loyalty has been a powerful force for promoting voice-based supplier relations in Japan' (Helper, 1990). The pent-up demand of Western companies has significantly decreased since the late 1980s, though (Cusumano and Takeishi, 1991; Helper, 1991).

Burt, Nordquist and Anklesania (1990:viii) even speak of a revolution that is taking place in American industry: 'A ... revolution is taking place in the relations with outside suppliers. No longer are suppliers seen as "the enemy" or "necessary evils". At several progressive firms, suppliers are seen as "Partners in Progress". These partners bring technology, design and manufacturing expertise, and managerial skills to the partnerships.' This leads to the hypothesis:

Hypothesis 2 – Technology-oriented relationships with suppliers will increase the process innovation success of a manufacturing company. In particular, it will increase the productivity of the machinery, reduce lead times, lead to savings of material and energy and allow the reduction of human input per unit produced.

Research and Technology Organisations

RTOs possess outstanding technical knowledge, have access to external know-how via world-wide collaboration with other research organisations and are particularly experienced in developing new knowledge. They therefore constitute a valuable source of external technological know-how. Research organisations are competent partners both for product and for process innovations. For them, it makes no difference whether the technologies and products they develop are used by their industrial partners directly (process innovation) or whether the industrial partners sell them to their customers (product innovation). Furthermore, research organisations do not typically pursue commercial goals, so that there will be no disputes regarding how the new knowledge is going to be exploited commercially. This leads to two further hypotheses:

Hypothesis 3a – Collaboration with research institutes and universities is a means of increasing a firm's technical product innovation success.

Hypothesis 3b – Collaboration with research institutes and universities is a means of increasing a firm's technical product innovation success and the efficiency of its production processes.

Consultants

Consultants identify weaknesses in existing structures and processes and motivate their clients to eliminate them. This is not unique to consultants because even other actors do so: customers complain about weaknesses in products in order to receive better quality and suppliers point out possibilities for improving the efficiency of processes in order to sell their newest equipment. However, in contrast to suppliers and customers, consultants are neutral advisers (although some people claim that consultants advise in such a way as to secure future consultancy products). Consultants have their client companies' overall success in mind when they design and implement measures. This means that those process innovations which consultants initiate should have a significant positive impact on the company's bottom line. They consider not only the direct costs of, for example, new machinery, but also take into account the costs of necessary organisational adjustments. Therefore, using innovation-oriented consultancy services is one way of integrating external experience, creativity and network competence into a firm's innovation processes. From this analysis, two hypotheses are derived:

Hypothesis 4a – Using innovation-oriented consultancy services is a means of increasing the efficiency of production processes.

Hypothesis 4b – Using innovation-oriented consultancy services is a means of increasing the economic impact of technical process innovation success.

Technological leaders and customer-focused developers base their competitive advantage on technology. They face a much higher necessity to achieve innovation success than companies which sell their products due to other features (price, tradition, fashion and so on). Companies can only gain from relationships with RTOs if they are capable of clearly defining what their needs are and if they understand the contributions of the external partners, and are able to adjust the results to fit their individual needs and further develop them. The study assumes that technological leaders and customer-focused developers are much more capable of efficiently interacting with research organisations than companies with other strategies. The study will therefore only test one hypothesis:

Hypothesis 5 – Technological leaders and customer-focused developers do gain more from technology-oriented relationships with RTOs than companies pursuing other strategies: that is, cost leaders, specialists and companies without a clear-cut strategy (dissipaters).

Seed Capitalists as Promoters of New Technology-Based Firms

SMEs in general (and NTBFs in particular) can substantially gain from maintaining relationships with external partners (Roberts, 1980; Yip, 1982; SIND, 1985; Jarillo, 1989; Landström, 1990; Müller-Böling and Klandt, 1993; McGee and Dowling, 1994). Singh, Tucker and House (1986) regard lack of relationships as the number one reason for NTBF failure. Still, empirical studies have shown that they are less intensively interwoven than larger, established companies. Seed capitalists help their portfolio companies to overcome the NTBF-specific barriers of interweavement: lack of motivation, lack of reputation and lack of resources. They encourage and enable their portfolio companies to build up more technology-oriented relationships with external partners than NTBFs would otherwise.

They motivate their portfolio companies to collaborate with external partners by illustrating the potentials and synergies of relationships with individually selected partners to the entrepreneurs. This is necessary because many entrepreneurs have founded their companies in order to become independent. They do not want to replace their former superiors by too powerful external actors (Klandt, 1990). Seed capitalists transfer their positive image to their portfolio companies: an investment by a highly reputed actor signals that the firm has high potential and is unlikely to become a flop. Thus, investing in relationships with the firm is not a risky business. There are two main reasons for this judgement:

(a) external actors trust the expertise of an experienced evaluator with commercial interests;
(b) third parties know that the seed capitalist will help its portfolio companies to become commercially successful.

Indeed, the selection argument is over-emphasised by both practitioners and researchers. It is by no means evident that seed capitalists would be capable of picking winners, because entrepreneurs regard seed capital as the most expensive capital that is available. They prefer loans to selling equity. This means that only companies which do not get money otherwise address seed capitalists. It is therefore assumed that supporting the selected companies is a more crucial success factor than selecting the 'right' ones. As Plosila and Allen (1987:529) put it: 'No firms are proven winners at this stage, all are untested.'

NTBFs are typically founded by scientists without any experience in the management of business relationships. Seed capitalists help their portfolio companies by actively searching for matching partners and bringing them together with the NTBF. It is assumed that seed capitalists promote high growth rates of their portfolio companies indirectly via innovation success, by increasing the intensity of their technological interweavement and by helping them to exploit external technological resources efficiently. In addition, a direct impact is also assumed because seed capitalists possess know-how which is highly complementary to that of the typical NTBF, which has its competitive advantage in technical expertise.

Seed capitalists provide their portfolio companies with equity and liquidity, enabling them to invest into growth. They invest themselves, they mediate loans from banks and they find customers who are willing to pay for products even before they are fully developed. In addition, they help entrepreneurs to cope with the challenges of growth, by actively participating in the management of the company and guiding the implementation of management techniques. From this evidence, the following two hypotheses will be tested:

Hypothesis 6a – NTBFs in the portfolio of a seed capitalist are more intensively interwoven with external partners than independent companies. Hypothesis 6b – NTBFs in the portfolio of a seed capitalist grow faster than independent companies.

Science Parks as Promoters of New Technology-Based Firms

Science parks host NTBFs that are in quite similar situations as regards their needs for external resources and know-how as well as in respect to their strategic goals. This, together with the fact that all companies are located within coffee-break distance, fosters a feeling of belonging. Trust grows among the member-firms. Positive experience from co-operation with park-internal firms helps to overcome barriers of collaboration with park-external firms. The closeness of a nearby university stimulates contacts between the NTBF and the on-site university, which in turn motivates the NTBFs to interact with other RTOs as well. In addition to the positive impact on an NTBF's technological interweavement, the management of a science park provides on-site companies with training seminars (such as marketing or project management), offers overhead services (reception desk and so on) and advisory services regarding the raising of public funds. Therefore, the two final hypotheses are:

Hypothesis 7a – NTBFs that are located in science parks are more intensively interwoven with external partners than independent companies.

Hypothesis 7b – NTBFs that are located in science parks grow faster than independent companies.

METHODOLOGY

The Sample

The study bases the statistical tests of the hypotheses on a series of quantitative empirical studies. Table 9.1 provides an overview of the different studies. In addition to the quantitative analyses, some 30 cases were analysed by performing face-to-face interviews with the focal company and its most important external partners. This has been done in order to check the extent to which statistically significant correlations can be interpreted as causal mechanisms.

Operationalisation of Constructs

In order to test the hypotheses, four constructs need to be operationalised:

- corporate growth
- innovation success
- technological interweavement
- context

DEFINITIONS

The following illustrates the basic steps of operationalisation (for a more comprehensive documentation, see Heydebreck, 1996).

Table 9.1   The quantitative database

Study	Target population	Sample	Project design
Lake Constance	Totality of all 4564 manufacturing firms in the Lake-Constance area with at least six employees.	848 companies answered the questionnaire.	The project performed jointly by the FhG-ISI; the ITEM and the IBU on behalf of BIGA. A standardised questionnaire sent to the managing director by mail; one reminder.
High Tech			The project was performed by the IBU on behalf of the BMBW
Biotechnology	Totality of all 157 German bio-tech firms which perform R&D.	104 firms answered the questionnaire.	All companies were called in advance to learn whom to address and to motivate him to answer a mailed questionnaire; one reminder.
EDP	490 EDP companies located in Bavaria, Baden-Württemberg and Saarland	68 companies answered the questionnaire.	All companies called in advance in order to learn whom to address and to motivate him to answer a mailed questionnaire; one reminder.
Medical instruments	All 174 German companies which are members of medical instruments group of association of precision mechanics and optical industry.	34 companies answered the questionnaire.	All companies were called in advance in order to learn whom to address and to motivate him to answer a mailed questionnaire; one reminder.
Micro electronic	213 young German firms locaed in science parks plus control group of 50 randomly selected	30 companies answered the questionnaire.	All companies were called in advance in order to learn whom to address and to motivate him to answer a mailed

Table 9.1   Contd.

Study	Target population	Sample	Project design
	micro-electronic firms.		questionnaire; one reminder.
Sensor	716 German sensor companies.	95 companies answered the questionnaire.	A standardised questionnaire was sent to the managing director by mail; one reminder.
NTBF	223 Swedish NTBFs:52 out of the portfolio of seed capitalists, 86 located in science parks and 85 independent companies.	79 companies responded: 16 portfolio of seed capitalist; 29 science park; 34 independent firms.	A standardised questionnaire was sent by mail to the contact person provided by Landström one reminder.

FhG-ISI – Fraunhofer Institute of Systems and Innovation Research, Karlsruhe.
ITEM – Institute for Technology Management at the Hochschule St Gallen.
IBU – Institute for Applied Business Administration and Corporate Strategy at the
   University of Karlsruhe.
BIGA – Bundesamt für Industrie, Gewerbe und Arbeit, Bern.
BMBW – Bundesministerium für Bildung, Wissenschaft, Forschung und
   Technologie (German Federal Ministry of Education, Science, Research and
   Technology).

Corporate Growth

This is the percentage of growth in turnover during a three-year period (this
indicator has only been calculated for companies with a minimum age of
five years).

Innovation Success

Four different types of innovation success have been identified.

   1. *Development of a new product or technical improvement of an existing
product (technological product innovation success).* In the Lake Constance
study (Table 9.1), the respondents rated their company's technological
product innovation success on a three-point rating scale. Around 19 per cent
of the companies answered that they had not realised any product innovation
at all, 46 per cent said that they had done so to a limited extent and 35 per

cent said they had considerable technological product innovation success. This quite rough measurement was refined in the high-tech studies and the NTBF study. The companies were asked to give the exact number of:

(a) product improvements;
(b) developments of new products during a period of three years for the NTBF study and five years for the high-tech studies.

These figures have been related to the companies' total number of products.

2. *Getting paid for the new product (commercial product innovation success).* Commercial product innovation success has been operationalised as the share of turnover that a company makes with improved or new products (R.G. Cooper, 1984, 1985; Brockhoff, 1985; Scholz, 1989). In the Lake Constance study and the high-tech studies, the respondents were offered answer categories (such as 'less than 10%', '10–30%', '30–50%' and 'more than 50%'), whilst in the NTBF study no answer categories were given.

3. *Technical improvement of a process in regard to, for example, costs, time, reliability and flexibility (technical process innovation success).* Process innovation success has been measured by a range of indicators on a five point scale in the high-tech studies and on a six point rating scale in the NTBF study the indicators correlate highly. Therefore, factor analyses (using principal component analysis) have been performed to reduce the indicators to one factor. Table 9.2 illustrates the factor loadings of the resulting factors for the High-Tech studies and the NTBF study.

Table 9.2   Matrix of factor loadings for the technical process innovation success

	Technical process innovation success (high-tech studies)	Technical process innovation success (NTBF study)
Reduction of labour time	0.73	0.88
Increase of productivity	0.78	not measured
Reduction of lead times	0.81	0.92
Savings of material and energy	0.74	0.82
Increase of production flexibility	not measured	0.92
Reduction of defect rate	not measured	0.91
Explained variance (%)	58.7	79.4
Kaiser-Meyer-Olkin criterion	0.72	0.78
Cronbach's a	0.75	0.93

4. *Economic relevance of a technical process innovation success to the company in terms of higher profit or faster growth (economic process innovation success).* This dimension of innovation success has been operationalised exclusively in the high-tech studies. Three indicators (all measured on five-point rating scales) were reduced to one factor. Table 9.3 shows the factor loadings.

Table 9.3   Matrix of factor loadings for the economic process innovation success

Relevance of the technical process innovation success for:	Economic relevance of the process innovation
• Survival of the company	0.85
• Profit of the company	0.92
• Growth of the company	0.90
Explained variance (%)	80.1
Kaiser-Meyer-Olkin criterion	0.72
Cronbach's a	0.88

Technological Interweavement

In the NTBF study, the companies were asked to rate the intensity of their technological interweavement with other companies on a five-point rating scale. In the Lake Constance study and the high-tech studies, technological interweavement was measured by a large variety of indicators. It is assumed that it is most plausible that the dimensions of technological interweavement should be defined as actor-specific, and this assumption is supported by exploratory factor analyses. Therefore, uni-factorate factor analyses were performed on the following dimensions of interweavement:

- technological co-operation with RTOs
- technological co-operation with suppliers
- technological co-operation with customers
- technological co-operation with consultants

Tables 9.4 and 9.5 illustrate the factor loading matrices for the Lake Constance study and the high-tech studies. If not stated otherwise all indicators have been operationalised on five-point rating scales (1 means of no importance, 5 means necessary).

Table 9.4 Dimensions of technological interweavement (Lake Constance study)

	RTOs	Suppliers	Customers	Consultants
RTOs as discussion partners	0.88	xx	xx	xx
R&D co-operation with RTOs	0.86	xx	xx	xx
Contact with RTOs	0.85	xx	xx	xx
Contracting out R&D	0.77	xx	xx	xx
Suppliers as discussion partners	xx	0.83	xx	xx
Suppliers: source of innovative know-how	xx	0.73	xx	xx
Procurement of new materials/components	xx	0.68	xx	xx
Customers as discussion partners	xx	xx	0.84	xx
Customers: source of innovative know-how	xx	xx	0.84	xx
Consultants as discussion partners	xx	xx	xx	0.85
Using consultancy and information services	xx	xx	xx	0.85
Explained variance (%)	70.8	56.2	70.3	72.3
Kaiser-Meyer-Olkin criterion	0.81	0.59	0.50	0.50
Cronbach's a	0.86	0.61	0.58	0.62

Context

In all multi-variate analyses, selected context variables are controlled simultaneously. These are size (operationalised as the *logarithmus naturalis* of the number of employees), age (operationalised as the *logarithmus naturalis* of the number of years the company exists) and industry. However, the context variable which is of the highest importance to the study is the firm's business strategy. The literature offers a variety of different concepts to operationalise strategy. For example, ideal-type strategies were defined by Miles and Snow (1978) and Porter (1980, 1985), whilst real-type strategies based on empirical evidence have been formulated by Brockhoff and Chakrabarti (1988), Miller and Roth (1994) and Weisenfeld-Schenk (1994). In addition, a further typology of real-type strategies was developed, based upon previous data (Gemünden and Heydebreck, 1994b, 1995c; Heydebreck, 1996). Consequently, information was collected on a wide range of different strategic activities of the companies. Explorative factor analyses were used to identify the dimensions of business strategy. These dimensions are similar but not identical in the manufacturing sample (Lake Constance study) and the high-tech sample and, as a result, cluster analyses on the strategy dimensions resulted in slightly different strategy types. The next section will discuss these types of strategy in more detail.

Table 9.5   Dimensions of technological interweavement (high-tech studies)

	RTOs	Suppliers	Customers	Consultants
RTOs as discussion partners	0.93	xx	xx	xx
Type of contact with RTOs	0.93	xx	xx	xx
Suppliers as discussion partners	xx	0.68	xx	xx
Importance of suppliers for generating new product ideas	xx	0.79	xx	xx
Importance of suppliers for product conceptualisation	xx	0.86	xx	xx
Importance of suppliers for product development	xx	0.87	xx	xx
Importance of suppliers for testing newproducts	xx	0.82	xx	xx
Customers as discussion partners	xx	xx	0.71	xx
Importance of customers for generating new product ideas	xx	xx	0.76	xx
Importance of customers for product conceptualisation	xx	xx	0.77	xx
Importance of customers for product development	xx	xx	0.68	xx
Importance of customers for testing new products	xx	xx	0.71	xx
Consultants as discussion partners	xx	xx	xx	0.88
Engineering companies as discussion partners	xx	xx	xx	0.88
Explained variance (%)	85.7	65.1	52.7	77.7
Kaiser-Meyer-Olkin criterion	0.50	0.80	0.77	0.50
Cronbach's a	0.83	0.86	0.77	0.71

DIMENSIONS OF NTBF BUSINESS STRATEGY

Lake Constance Study

Four factors have been identified, as outlined below.

1. *Variety-orientation*: This factor loads on breadth/width of product range and novelty of products. There is a substantial negative loading on developing products to the needs of specific customers, indicating inflexibility in regard to individual demands of customers.
2. *Customer-orientation*: This factor loads highly on flexibility in regard to customer requests and on developing products to the needs of specific customers as well as on keeping delivery dates.
3. *Technological innovation orientation*: This factor shows high positive loadings on R&D intensity and a substantial positive loading on the

technological standing of a company's products. At the same time, there are very negative loadings on price, which may be explained by the fact that a company that strives for technological innovation typically can and must sell its products at premium prices.

4. *Total quality orientation*: This factor loads highly on quality and technological standing and substantially on keeping delivery dates and customer service.

Cluster analysis results in five strategy types. Table 9.6 characterises them by their mean values of the strategy dimensions.

Table 9.6   Real-type strategies (Lake Constance study)

	Variety	Customer	Total quality	Technology/ innovation
Technological leader (85 cases)	0.39	−0.65	0.57	0.88
Customer-focused developer (75 cases)	−0.08	1.02	0.98	0.48
Cost leader (112 cases)	0.65	−0.10	−0.88	0.14
Specialiser (79 cases)	−1.24	0.07	−0.63	0.20
Dissipater (100 cases)	−0.02	−0.15	0.27	−1.41

High-Tech Studies

The strategy dimensions are similar to those which have been identified for manufacturing companies in general, although there are some differences. The variety factor could not be identified because the novelty of products means technical improvements in high-technology industries, whereas it might very well mean changes due to fashion in other industries. Instead, the technological innovation factor has split up into innovation and price, which is also plausible. Table 9.7 shows the resulting strategy types from a cluster analysis on the four strategy dimensions.

Table 9.7   Real-type strategies (high-tech studies)

	Price	Customer	Total quality	Innovation
Technological leader (65 cases)	−0.54	−0.19	0.45	1.06
Customer-focused developer (63 cases)	−0.16	1.42	−0.13	−0.08
Cost leader (50 cases)	0.86	−0.74	−0.14	0.28
Specialiser (81 cases)	0.35	−0.11	0.42	−0.87
Dissipater (37 cases)	−0.71	−0.85	−0.19	−1.29

The real-type strategies in the high-tech studies are surprisingly similar to those identified in the Lake Constance study. Therefore, the corresponding clusters were labelled identically. Both studies showed empirical evidence of the following five strategy types.

1. Technological leaders are giving technological innovation the highest emphasis compared with all other strategy types. They develop technologies for markets, not for individual customers. Product quality is leading, price is of minor importance.
2. Customer-focused developers serve as problem-solvers for individual clients. They offer custom-made concepts.
3. Cost leaders market standardised products of below-average quality in homogenous market (segments). Price is their most important marketing instrument.
4. Specialisers focus on a very narrow product range. No additional joint characteristics can be seen.
5. Dissipaters do not show a clear strategy.

RESULTS

Technological Interweavement and Innovation Success

Technology-oriented relationships with external partners are a powerful means of complementing a firm's internal resources, thus increasing a firm's innovation success. However, not all forms of interweavement are equally suited to reaching different forms of success. The next section will report and discuss the regression functions resulting from multiple linear regression analyses for the different forms of innovation success.

In both samples, a strong positive impact of maintaining technology-oriented relationships with customers on technological product innovation can be identified (Table 9.8). Therefore, hypothesis 1a – that customers help their suppliers to achieve different forms of innovation success – is fully supported.

The results in regard to a collaboration with RTOs are less clear. Whilst hypothesis 3a is supported by the findings from the Lake Constance study, no significant effect could be measured in the high-tech studies. This is quite surprising because the high-tech companies themselves regard RTOs as important partners, whilst most companies in the Lake Constance area do not.

Most high-technology firms collaborate with RTOs and show a high technological product innovation success, which is consistent with hypothesis 3a (that collaboration with research institutes and universities is a means of increasing a firm's technical product innovation success).

Table 9.8   Determinants of technological product innovation success

Technical product innovation success = (Lake Constance study)	0.26* customer ($p = 0.00$) + 0.18* RTO ($p = 0.00$) + 0.20* R&D co-operation ($p = 0.00$) − 0.11* age ($p = 0.03$) corporate strategy ($p − 0.01$)
Technical product innovation success = (high-tech studies)	0.15* customer ($p = 0.04$) − 0.49* age ($p = 0.00$).

Notes: All regression coefficients are standardised; technological leaders ($\beta = 0.24$), customer-focused developers ($\beta = 0.20$), cost leaders ($\beta = 0.15$) and dissipaters ($\beta = 0.14$) have a significantly higher technological product innovation success than specialisers.

Significance of the F-test: 0.00; $R^2_{ADJ} = 0.30$. Industry, size and interweavement with suppliers, and consultants were simultaneously tested, none of these variables shows a significant impact on technological product innovation success in a multi-variate analysis.

Significance of the F-test: 0.00; $R^2_{ADJ} = 0.25$. In the high-tech studies, there is a substantial correlation between age and size. Therefore, a stepwise regression leads to the fact that only age or size is included in the model. If one eliminates age from the regression function, size is included with a β of −0.38 ($p = 0.00$). Corporate strategy, industry and interweavement with suppliers, RTOs and consultants were simultaneously tested; none of these variables shows a significant impact on technological product innovation success in a multi-variate analysis.

Therefore, the study has tested whether the lack of significance is due to a lack of variance of collaboration intensity with RTOs. This was done by simultaneously analysing the data from the Lake Constance study and the high-tech studies. Due to differences in operationalisation this is only possible to a limited extent. The interweavement with RTOs is measured by a single indicator (importance of RTOs as discussion partners), and product innovation success was operationalised dichotomously (companies with substantially improved or new products and companies without substantial technological improvements of their products). Therefore, the result fully supports hypothesis 3a.

In spite of the quite rough operationalisation, the standardised correlation coefficient between collaboration with RTOs and technological product innovation success increases from $r = 0.29$ (Lake Constance study) to $r = 0.33$ (joint sample). Apart from customers and RTOs, no other single type of actor seems to show a significant impact on a firm's technological product innovation success. However, particularly intensive forms of co-operation (R&D co-operation with other companies) also demonstrate a significant impact.

To summarise, the hypothesis that specific types of technological interweavement are appropriate means of increasing the technological product innovation success is supported by the data. This finding holds true even if one simultaneously controls context variables. This means that technology-oriented relationships increase the technological product innovation success for technological leaders as well as for companies with considerable pent-up demand.

Commercial Product Innovation Success

Bivariate analyses show a high correlation between different types of technological interweavement and commercial product innovation success. However, when simultaneously controlling technological product innovation success, no significant impact caused by any form of technological interweavement can be found to be had on the commercial product innovation success. This 'non-finding' supports Gemünden, Heydebreck and Herden (1992) but is in contrast to hypothesis 1b. This has motivated the study to operationalise the commercial innovation success, not only by the share of turnover with new products, but also as the share of product innovation processes which were commercially satisfying the focal company. This has been done in the high-tech studies, measuring the share of efficient product innovation processes for three different types of product innovations: product improvements, new product development for known customers and new product development for new customers. The empirical findings are documented in Table 9.9.

The findings show that the integration of customers into product innovation processes leads to a higher degree of success in achieving objectives. This is partly due to a more realistic definition of goals and, in particular, it is due to a higher efficiency of the innovation processes. RTOs turn out to be actors that are capable of helping their partners to reach their commercial goals in new product development.

Furthermore, there is an interesting finding concerning the influence of age and size of the firm on the efficiency of innovation. Whereas the data shows that small and young companies innovate more intensively than well established larger ones, older and larger firms innovate more efficiently. An explanation for this might be the higher potential of larger firms to market their technical innovations successfully, due to their higher experience in distribution and marketing, a trustworthy image and established relationships with loyal customers.

Table 9.9 Determinants of the efficiency of product innovation processes

Efficiency of product improvements =	0.20* customer ($p = 0.00$) + 0.18* size ($p = 0.01$)
Efficiency of new product development for known customers =	0.14* customers ($p = 0.02$) +0.23* RTOs ($p = 0.00$) industry ($p = 0.03$)
Efficiency of new product development for new customers =	0.15* customers ($p = 0.02$) +0.20* RTOs ($p = 0.00$).

Notes: If one eliminates size from the equation, age becomes a significant determinant of the efficiency of a firm's product innovation processes ($\beta = 0.19, p = 0.00$).

Significance of the *F*-test: 0.00; $R^2_{ADJ} = 0.10$. Industry, strategy and interweavement with suppliers, RTOs and consultants were simultaneously tested; none of these variables shows a significant impact in a multi-variate analysis. Sensor companies are particularly successful in developing new products for known companies.

Significance of the *F*-test: 0.00; $R^2_{ADJ} = 0.08$. Age, size, strategy and interweavement with suppliers and consultants were simultaneously tested; none of these variables shows a significant impact in a multi-variate analysis.

Technical Process Innovation Success

On a bivariate level, one finds a positive correlation between all investigated forms of technological interweavement and process innovation success. On a multi-variate level, this holds true only for the collaboration with customers (Table 9.10). Therefore while hypothesis 1c is confirmed, hypotheses 2, 3b and 4a are not. In summary:

(a) customers will continuously demand lower prices, shorter delivery cycles, higher rates of perfect orders and so on, which forces their suppliers to increase the efficiency of their production and distribution processes;

(b) technology-oriented relationships with suppliers will *not* increase the process innovation success of a manufacturing company;

(c) collaboration with research institutes and universities is *not* a means of increasing a firm's technical product innovation success and the efficiency of its production processes;

(d) using innovation-oriented consultancy services is *not* a means of increasing the efficiency of production processes.

Interweavement with suppliers, RTOs and consultants was simultaneously tested, and none of these variables shows a significant impact in a multi-variate analysis. It might seem surprising that even corporate strategy seems to have no impact on process innovation success, although one could assume that cost leaders reach a higher level of process innovation success. There are two explanations for this 'non-finding'.

Table 9.10 Determinants of the technical process innovation success

Technical process innovation success =	0.14^* customer ($p = 0.04$)
	$+ 0.15^*$ size ($p = 0.03$)
	industry ($p = 0.00$)

Notes: If one eliminates size from the equation, age becomes a significant determinant of technical process innovation success ($\beta = 0.13, p = 0.05$).
Biotechnology companies rationalise significantly above average, EDP companies significantly below average.
Significance of the F-test: 0.00; $R^2_{ADJ} = 0.15$.

1. Cost leaders do not primarily achieve an increased efficiency of their processes by internal R&D but by integrating external know-how (e.g., acquisition of new equipment). If interweavement is simultaneously controlled, there is no additional effect of strategy.
2. Process innovation success has been operationalised as improvements of existing processes. In case cost leaders were cost leaders in the past as well, it would take an effort out of all proportion to increase efficiency by the same percentage as non-cost leaders.

It is expected that consultants concerned with efficiency would contribute to rationalisation activities to a significant degree. However, this assumption is not supported by a multi-variate regression analysis. One explanation could be that consultants are experienced networkers, who efficiently introduce their client companies to adequate external partners but who do not typically possess technical problem-solving know-how themselves. Holding constant the interweavement with other partners, no significant contribution from the consultants remains.

In respect to collaboration with suppliers and RTOs, there is a definite need for additional research. It might be that it is typical of high-tech companies for suppliers and RTOs not to play an important role in increasing the efficiency of production processes, or that the impact becomes statistically significant only when differentiating between, for example, equipment and components suppliers.

Economic Process Innovation Success

The economic process innovation success is primarily determined by the technical process innovation success (Table 9.11). There is also a direct positive impact of a collaboration with consultants, which confirms hypothesis 4b (i.e., that using innovation-oriented consultancy services is a means of increasing the economic impact of technical process innovation success).

Table 9.11   Determinants of the economical process innovation success

Economic process innovation success =	0.15^* consultant $(p = 0.03)$
	$+ 0.15^*$ RTO $(p = 0.06)$
	$+ 0.40$ technical innovation success $(p = 0.00)$
	industry $(p = 0.00)$

Notes: Biotechnology firms achieve the highest degree of technical process improvement but the economic relevance is significantly below average $(\beta = -0.38)$. Significance of the F-test: 0.00; $R^2_{ADJ} = 0.21$. Age, size, strategy and interweavement with suppliers and customers was simultaneously tested; none of these variables shows a significant impact in a multi-variate analysis.

Furthermore, the data suggests that those process innovations which are realised in collaboration with RTOs have a higher impact on the firms' overall success than others. However, the study was more conservative when formulating the hypotheses – there was no expectation in finding a significant impact – and consequently, it is proposed that this aspect needs additional research. A possible explanation would be that RTOs are – like consultants – neutral advisers and supporters in increasing the efficiency of processes, leading their clients to innovate in those areas which have the highest potential for them, whereas customers and suppliers are primarily interested in their need satisfaction.

Technological Interweavement and Corporate Strategy

The study assumed that technological leaders and customer-focused developers gain more from technology-oriented relationships with RTOs than companies with other business strategies (hypothesis 5). The companies themselves also believe this, which can be seen from the fact that technological leaders have the highest degree of collaboration with RTOs of all strategy types, and customer-focused developers show a degree of interaction which is above average.

These findings have encouraged a test for an interaction effect between corporate strategy and collaboration with RTOs on corporate growth, using a two-factor analysis of variance. Two groups of strategies were identified:

(a) technology-based strategies: (technological leaders and customer-focused developers);
(b) other strategies: (cost leaders, specialisers, dissipaters).

This grouping is necessary because it is almost impossible to confirm significant effects for groups of considerably different sizes (Stone-Romero, Alliger and Aguinis, 1994). This would be the case if one strategy was tested against all others. Collaboration with RTOs is dichotomised: negative factor values are interpreted as a below-average intensity of collaboration with suppliers, positive factor values as above-average intensity.

The analysis of variance on the basis of the data from the Lake Constance study provides some support for hypothesis 5 but not at a significant level (Gemünden and Heydebreck, 1994b). The same analysis for the high-tech firms shows a significant result: The primary effects are significant (strategy: $p = 0.00$), collaboration with RTOs: $p = 0.10$) and the interaction effect between strategy and interweavement is significant as well ($p = 0.06$). Technological leaders and customer-focused developers profit sig-

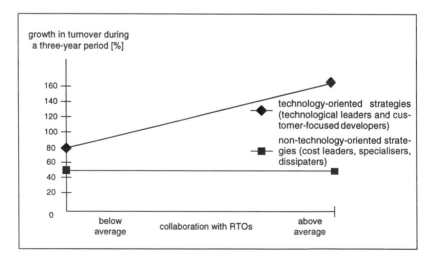

Figure 9.2   Interaction between strategy and collaboration with RTOs

nificantly from collaborating with RTOs, but for companies following other strategies no effect could be detected. This finding is illustrated by Figure 9.2.

Figure 9.2 illustrates that technology-based companies in high-technology industries grow faster than companies which are not technology-based. They not only have more links with RTOs but also gain substantially from these relationships which firms not based on technology seem unable to do. Technology-based firms which collaborate with RTOs to more than an average extent show an increase in turnover during a three-year period of 176 per cent, whereas the less co-operating firms 'only' grow at a rate of 78 per cent. The firms which are not technology-based show a growth rate of about 50 per cent, regardless of whether or not they maintain close links with RTOs.

Science Parks and Seed Capitalists: Fosterers of New Technology-Based Firms

Science parks and seed capitalists successfully support NTBFs in their efforts to initiate, maintain and co-ordinate technology-oriented relationships (Figure 9.3). Companies in the portfolio of seed capitalists, and

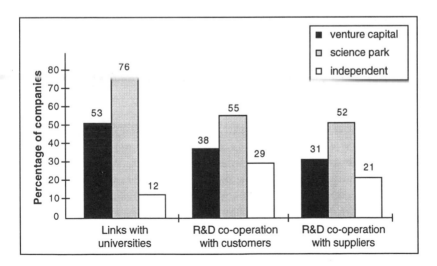

Figure 9.3   Science parks and seed capitalists as fosterers of technological interweavement
Source: Gemünden and Heydebreck (1995b)

particularly those which are located in science parks, are significantly more intensively interwoven than independent companies. This confirms both hypotheses 6a and 7a, namely that:

(a) NTBFs in the portfolio of a seed capitalist are more intensively interwoven with external partners than independent companies;
(b) NTBFs that are located in science parks are more intensively interwoven with external partners than independent companies.

No significant impact of age, size and industry on the intensity of the technological interweavement could be identified in a multi-variate regression analysis. This is due to the sample being very homogeneous and the low variance in context variables which results from this homogeneity. Type of company (independent verus portfolio of seed capitalist verus on-site company) alone explains 25 per cent of the variance in technological interweavement (significance of the F-test: 0.00). It turns out that companies which are located in science parks have a higher intensity of technological interweavement than those which are in the portfolio of a seed capitalist (β for science parks: 0.60; β for seed capitalists: 0.24). This is due to the philosophy of most seed capitalists which regard the technical competence of their portfolio companies as a precondition for picking them. They therefore, focus on providing assistance in the search for paying customers instead of looking for external technological know-how, whilst the closeness of a science park to nearby RTOs primarily stimulates technology-oriented relationships.

By increasing the technological interweavement of NTBFs, science parks and seed capitalists indirectly promote commercial product innovation success (at a level of significance of $p = 0.01$, technological interweavement and commercial product innovation success correlate with $r = 0.32$), which in turn is the single most important determinant of corporate growth for NTBFs ($\beta = 0.45$, $p = 0.00$). In addition to this indirect effect, there also is a highly significant direct effect, meaning that seed capitalists and science parks help their clients to turn innovation success into growth: innovative companies which have received support from seed capitalists have grown in turnover by 97 per cent during a three-year period compared with growth rates of 72 per cent for companies in science parks and only 28 per cent for independent companies. Therefore, hypotheses 6b and 7b are confirmed, namely:

(a) NTBFs in the portfolio of a seed capitalist grow faster than independent companies:

(b) NTBFs that are located in science parks grow faster than independent companies.

CONCLUSIONS AND IMPLICATIONS

The empirical analyses have shown that relationships with external partners can contribute significantly to increasing a firm's process and product innovation success. At the same time, no best network pattern exists which can be made available to companies as if it were an extract taken directly out of a textbook. Instead, it is necessary for each individual company to develop a network strategy which suits its strategic targets, its context and its internal resources.

NTBFs have a high need for external management and network know-how although, at the same time, they face high barriers of interweavement which they very often cannot overcome without assistance. Therefore, in conclusion, in order to stimulate product and process innovation success and, for example, fight unemployment, it is necessary that public bodies support SMEs in general, and NTBFs in particular, by giving access to complementary external resources. Seed capitalists and science parks have demonstrated the meaning of supporting NTBFs in their network management, but they only reach a very limited number of companies.

This approach should definitely be demand-oriented and network-oriented. That means the starting point of public support must be a study of the companies' needs for external know-how and resources and an analysis of the barriers preventing the companies from exploiting external sources. This insight is not new, but has been widely ignored by public policy: traditionally, policy aims are oriented towards supporting intra-organisational R&D processes financially or towards marketing the new technical knowledge which is generated in publicly-sponsored research institutes and universities.

Presently, the Commission of the European Communities (DG XIII and DG XVI) is running a project in close collaboration with regions throughout the Community namely the Regional Innovation and Technology Transfer Strategies (RITTS) and Regional Innovation Strategies (RIS) programmes), which aims to increase and exploit the innovative potential of these regions. This initiative is an action study: based upon a thorough analysis of the regional companies' needs and the existing innovation support offered an action plan is then developed in order to overcome barriers to efficient technological interweavement. This initiative is still in its pilot phase but some results seem to have repeated themselves in most of the regions which have been investigated so far.

Companies' Needs for External Technological Resources are often Met by a Sufficient Regional Offer

Unsatisfied needs for external technological resources and know-how are typically due to a high intransparency of the regional offer. There is lack of focal entry points which could serve as guides to the companies. In particular, NTBFs are completely unaware of the available offers. The high intransparency of the existing supply of innovation support resources must be addressed (e.g., by stimulating networks between innovation support actors).

Companies' Needs for Market-Related Services are not Given the Necessary Attention

Whereas established companies have both the experience and the financial resources to make use of consultants and market researchers, NTBFs neither have the money to pay for market analyses nor do they know whom to contact. Many NTBFs are highly competitive in technical aspects but very inexperienced in management. Public bodies should attempt to overcome their fear of getting too close to the market. A possible means of achieving this might be to subsidise market studies performed by approved experts for some 50 per cent of the consultancy fees.

There is a Distinct Lack of Entry Services (Low Cost, Low Risk) Aiming Towards Finding Solutions for Smaller Problems which have been more Precisely Defined by Companies

In small first-step projects, the companies can learn about the potential of a wider collaboration with technology providers and intermediaries without having to risk a lot of money and a lot of time. The staff of the industrial companies become familiar with the individuals from the external partner, personal bonds are established, and levels of trust develop which is necessary for overcoming both cultural and language barriers between highly sophisticated and specialised researchers and managers facing ordinary business challenges.

The author would like to thank DG III of the European Commission for support in the completion of the research.

10 Infant Multinationals: Internationalisation of Small Technology-Based Firms

Maria Lindqvist

INTRODUCTION

During the last few years, the relatively few large multinational corporations dominating Swedish industry have, whilst increasing their international activities, dramatically reduced domestic employment within their organisations. As a result, there has been a focus by policy-makers on the development of small technology-based firms, mainly because it is frequently argued that such firms have an important role in creating opportunities for new employment and stimulating industrial growth. However, since opportunities in a small home market are limited to niche-oriented, technology-based firms, Swedish firms have traditionally been forced to direct their activities abroad at a relatively early stage (Carlson, 1975). This trend is perhaps even more important today, with the globalisation of markets and an increased speed and complexity of technology development. At the same time, small firms are particularly dependent upon their home market, since the time and resources required for successful international activities – such as access to managerial competence and extensive funds – are limited. Consequently, the process of internationalisation may be complicated for small firms and many may favour a more localised growth strategy.

The purpose of this study is to describe the international behaviour of small technology-based Swedish firms, and analyse the conflicting impact of a limited size and high-technology characteristics. The process will be analysed in terms of speed of internationalisation, pattern of foreign market selection and selection of foreign entry approach (with a focus on direct export, local agents or distributors, and subsidiary establishment).

THEORETICAL BACKGROUND

The Internationalisation Process

Following the traditions of behavioural theory of the firm (Simon, 1947; Aharoni, 1966) and the theory of the growth of the firm (Penrose, 1956), a model of the internationalisation of firms was developed by researchers at Uppsala University in Sweden during the 1970s (Hörnell, Vahlne and Wiedersheim-Paul, 1973; Carlson, 1975; Johanson and Vahlne, 1977; Johanson and Wiedershiem-Paul, 1974). In 1977, Johanson and Vahlne presented a model in which the firm gradually increased its commitments to foreign activities as knowledge about foreign markets and operations was developed. A basic idea is that market knowledge is acquired through experience: as experience is accumulated during foreign business activities, market uncertainty is reduced and firms become willing to invest more abroad.

As a result, foreign involvement tends to proceed in small steps. Activities in a particular country are likely to follow an established pattern, whereby the firm initially has no regular exports, then starts exporting via independent representatives, later through a sales subsidiary and eventually establishes a manufacturing subsidiary. While following such an pattern, market knowledge increases successively and the firm becomes willing to commit more resources to the market. Similar observations have been made by other empirical studies (Bilkey and Tesar, 1977; Newbould, Buckley and Thurwell, 1978; Utterback and Reitberger, 1982).

The pattern of market selection also tends to proceed in stages. While firms prefer to initiate activities in markets with similar conditions to the home market, increased experience makes the firm willing to enter new markets of successively greater 'economic distance'. The concept is defined in terms of differences in geographic as well as psychic distance such as language, culture and business traditions which are all factors that complicate foreign activities. (Hörnell, Vahlne and Wiedersheim-Paul, 1973). A similar observation was made by Davidson (1980), who found that the impact of cultural distance was greatest during early stages of internationalisation.

The Technology Factor

Using the arguments of gradual commitment, one could expect small firms, with restricted resources and limited experience of foreign activities, to be particularly inclined to follow a sequential process of internationalisation.

However, technology factors may have a completely different impact on the process. For a niche-oriented, technology-based firm with a narrow customer segment and high R&D expenditures, a process of rapid internationalisation may be essential to achieve the necessary sales volumes before the technology becomes obsolete or imitated by others.

Besides, several research studies have stressed the information properties of firm-specific advantages based on investments in know-how, such as product innovation, process technology, patents or human capital. Valuation difficulties, transmission problems – for example, a high tacit content restricting codification and standardisation, and a character of 'free goods' – make it difficult to capture the returns of an investment in know-how in the market place (Arrow, 1962; Williamson, 1975; Magee, 1977; Calvet, 1981; Teece, 1983). To avoid imitation and diffusion of new technologies, firms are expected to exploit their proprietary knowledge in-house, using wholly-owned subsidiaries based on acquisitions or green-field investments, rather than using market channels such as indirect exports, independent representatives or licensing.

In addition, previous empirical studies also indicate that the propensity to internalise a technology is particularly high during early stages of the technology cycle (Magee, 1977) and amongst firms with high R&D intensity (Contractor, 1984; Telesio, 1984; Davidson and McFetridge, 1985). The resulting technology-intensive products with a high tacit content are so complex that technological evaluation becomes difficult.

THEORETICAL FRAMEWORK

Based on the theoretical arguments above a general framework, including the main explanatory variables related to limited firm size and high technology characteristics, as well as contextual variables, (such as industry structure and local market characteristics) was developed (Figure 10.1)

The objective of this study was to analyse the internationalisation behaviour of small technology-based Swedish firms in order to assess the conflicting impact of a limited size (favouring a sequential process due to restricted resources and limited experience of foreign activities) and high technology characteristics (indicating a need for rapid internationalisation and internalisation). The process of internationalisation will be described in three dimensions:

- speed of foreign market entry
- pattern of foreign market selection
- choice of foreign entry form

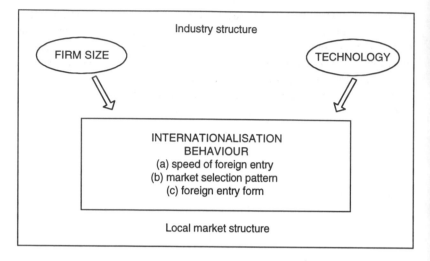

Figure 10.1   A general theoretical framework

The focus of this chapter will be on the two latter dimensions (which is where foreign activities take place) in terms of what countries are entered and in what order, and how these activities are organised: whether through direct export, representatives, licensing or foreign subsidiaries. The motives for entering certain markets will also be briefly examined.

METHODOLOGY

The Sample of Firms

The study upon which this chapter is based was presented by Lindqvist (1991). Data was collected during an interview study and a mail survey. The selection criteria of firms to be included was guided by the aim of studying the early internationalisation of small technology-based Swedish firms. All firms included in the sample were established as independent firms between 1965 and 1985, had at least some in-house R&D and a minimum of 20 per cent turnover generated from foreign sales.

Using the Swedish Export Directory and the business catalogue Kompass, 15 firms fulfilling these criteria were selected for the interview study (Table 10.1). After the initial contact, all firms agreed to participate. Interview data was collected during semi-structured interviews, usually with the president, who was often also the founder of the firm. As a

complement, primary material in written form as well as secondary information sources were used. The selected firms differed in terms of size,
product type and level of internationalisation.

Table 10.1   Firms included in the interview study

	Instruments	Electronics	Number of firms
		Industry	
0–19 employees	5	2	7
20–49 employees	0	1	1
50–employees	3	4	7
Total	8	7	15

Since firms fulfilling the inclusion criteria were generally of limited
size, public registration of these firms was rather incomplete, and several
alternative sources were used to identify potential candidates for inclusion
in the mail study:

(a) members of the Swedish Association of Electronics Industries 1987;
(b) firms listed in the Swedish Export Directory (1987);
(c) Swedish export companies listed in Liber (1985);
(d) several non-systematic sources, including the Kompass business cata-
    logue, newspaper articles, interviews and the Swedish Telephone Di-
    rectory (1987).

The difficulty of assessing export intensity made it hard to establish the
size of the actual population. However, based on the sources above, 434
firms were identified as potential sample members. By applying the selection criteria above during initial contacts, the number of firms was further
reduced, resulting in 148 candidates for the mail survey. After an initial
mailing and two reminders, 85 complete responses were received. In an attempt to increase the response rate further, an abbreviated version of the
questionnaire was distributed, resulting in another 10 responses. After
this, an overall response rate of 64 per cent, representing 95 respondents,
was achieved.

An analysis of non-respondents indicated that their distribution in age,
size and industry was similar to the respondents. During telephone contacts with 18 non-respondents, their export shared turned out to have the
same distribution as the respondents. Overall, there appears to be no systematic difference in general firm characteristics between respondents
and non-respondents.

The firms included in the mail study varied slightly in terms of size, ownership structure, and R&D intensity (Table 10.2) An average of almost 25 per cent of the workforce, excluding production, were engaged in R&D functions and average R&D expenditures were 8.6 per cent of turnover, which indicates a relatively high level of R&D intensity among the firms. Four main industries were represented by these firms: non-electrical industrial machinery, electrical products, instruments/optics and chemistry.

Table 10.2   General firm characteristics

	Number of firms	%
Number of employees		
0–19 employees	42	46
20–49 employees	21	23
50+ employees	28	31
Ownership		
privately owned	42	50
mixed ownership	21	25
corporate ownership	21	25
Industry		
non-electrical industrial machinery	33	37
electrical products	23	26
instruments/ optics	15	17
chemistry	10	11
others	9	10

Operationalisation of Variables

The questionnaire developed for this study included a large number of variables. The key question, concerning the internationalisation process, indicated the year of first entry (using either direct exports, local representatives or a subsidiary) into the 20 'economically' closest countries to Sweden. The main reason for using this format was to facilitate comparisons with the results developed by the researchers at Uppsala University during the 1970s. The list was also expanded to include other markets of particular importance to individual firms.

To analyse the impact of firm and technology characteristics, the descriptive presentation of internationalisation behaviour among the firms included in the mail study was complemented by several multi-variate analysis, of which two are presented in this chapter. Due to difficulties in including the complete concept of establishment sequence and establishment chain in single variables, two proxies were used to permit multi-variate analyses. The first dependent variable was entry into the US market. This, on the one hand, is a market one expects to be entered relatively late, due to economic distance, but, on the other hand, it is an important market for many advanced technology-based products. In the sample, 59 firms had attempted to enter the USA. Over time, however, more than 10 per cent of these firms terminated their activities in USA, yielding one of the highest termination rates (together with Canada and South Africa). The second dependent variable used as a proxy for an establishment chain was the time lag between first foreign activities and first establishment of a foreign subsidiary. Altogether, 42 firms had established foreign subsidiaries, within an average of 5.5 years from establishment.

In the multi-variate analyses, four categories of explanatory variables were included:

(a) general firm characteristics, including firm size and ownership structure;
(b) firm experience (previous experience of management regarding the industry as well as foreign activities);
(c) product characteristics (level of technology, level of innovation, marketing requirements, market niche size and level of customer awareness);
(d) R&D intensity, based on number of patents, R&D expenditure per employee as well as a percentage of turnover, and number of R&D employees as a percentage of the total workforce, excluding production.

The explanatory variables were originally measured either on an interval or ordinal scale (using a 5-point Likert scale), except for ownership structure, which was measured on a nominal scale (firms with purely private ownership and firms with at least some corporate ownership). In order to reduce the number of variables for the multi-variate analyses, a number of factor analyses were undertaken. For a complete specification of variables employed, see Table 10.3. The first analysis conducted was a logit analysis, since the dependent variable was measured on a nominal scale. However, in the second analysis, a multiple regression analysis was permitted.

THE PROCESS OF INTERNATIONALISATION

When looking at actual internationalisation behaviour among small technology-based Swedish firms, a number of observations were made. This section therefore describes, in general, internationalisation behaviour among these firms in terms of when, where and how foreign activities take place.

Table 10.3   Variables included in the multivariate analysis

Variable	Name	Explanation
Size	SIZE	Factor based on turnover (+), number of employees (+)
Ownership	OWTYPE	Dummy 0 = private; 1 = corporate
Experience		
Industry	IEXP	Factors based on: local representative contacts (+), general industry knowledge (+)
Foreign	FEXP	local market experience (+)
Technology intensity		
R&D intensity	INTENS	Factors based on: R&D-costs/turnover (+), R&D-costs/employee (+), percentage of R&D employees
Number of patents	PATENT	number of patents
Technology level	HIGH	Level of product technology (1 = low, 5 = high)
Innovation level	INOVA	Level of product innovation (1 = low, 5 = high)
Marketing requirements		
Educational needs	EDUCATE	Factors based on: importance of technological sales personnel (+), customer education (+)
Local adaptation	ADAPT	importance of local adaptation (+), credit (+), low price (+)
Image creation	IMAGE	importance of after sales services (+), brand name (+), low price (+)
Industry structure		
Stage of development	STAGE	Factors based on: number of competitors (+), level of customer awareness (+), market growth (−)
Market potential	POT	number of applications (+), number of end users (+), market growth (+)

Overall, the sample varies in terms of foreign experience, with the number of years of foreign activities ranging between one and 19 years, and export shares between 20 and over 90 per cent of turnover, with an average export share of 60 per cent of turnover (Table 10.4).

Table 10.4   Export shares

Export shares	Number of firms	%
20–49 per cent of turnover	29	33
50–74 per cent of turnover	36	38
75 per cent or more of turnover	30	32

Speed of Foreign Entry

Unfortunately, there are no statistics available to make direct comparisons of speed of foreign entry with previous studies of internationalisation. However, in this study, small technology-based firms were found to initiate foreign activities at a relatively early stage. The average age of the firms at first foreign entry was slightly over 3 years in the sample as a whole, and as many as 43 per cent of the firms had sales activities in at least five foreign markets within 3 years of their first foreign sales. To a certain extent, this may be an outcome of the selection criteria, since young firms had not been included unless they had at least 20 per cent foreign sales. Nevertheless, it gives an indication of the importance of foreign activities among small technology-based firms.

During the interviews, one explanation for rapid internationalisation was the chance to take advantage of the international experience of Swedish multinational corporations. For example, by entering co-operative sales agreements with Swedish multinationals, such as SKF and Fläkt, some firms quickly managed to establish foreign representations in a number of important markets all over the world. In other cases, the firms acted as subcontractors for large Swedish or foreign OEM (Original Equipment Manufacturer) customers. These observations agree with the previous findings of Carlson (1979), which showed that Swedish firms have traditionally been willing to enter co-operative agreements. Sometimes, the international tradition of Swedish industry contributed indirectly simply by providing a positive attitude towards internationalisation: in several firms, it was possible to identify 'an international vision' or ambition to go outside the Swedish market at an early stage (e.g., by entering co-operative development projects with foreign customers).

Another observation during the interviews concerned the importance of previous experience of foreign activities among managers. Firms established as spin-offs from established firms could sometimes make use of existing contacts in foreign markets, thus speeding up the search for potential customers or representatives. In university spin-offs, the founder often had an international contact network, established during international seminars and symposia, which could be expected to contribute to an international outlook.

Pattern of Market Selection

The most commonly entered foreign markets, using either direct exports, local representatives or subsidiaries, were found to be the geographically closest markets of Finland, Norway and the Denmark, and large industrialised countries, such as Germany, the UK, France and the USA (Table 10.5).

Table 10.5   The most commonly entered foreign markets

Country	Number Of firms	%
Finland	81	85
Norway	81	85
Denmark	77	81
Germany	72	76
UK	66	69
Netherlands	66	69
France	65	68
USA	58	61
Switzerland	56	59
Italy	50	53
Belgium	49	52
Austria	44	46
Canada	44	46
Australia	39	41
Spain	38	40
Japan	26	27
Portugal	25	26
Brazil	12	13
Argentina	10	11
South Africa	9	99

In terms of perceived importance to the firms, however, the list was slightly different (Table 10.6). Large markets, like Germany, the USA and Japan, received higher rankings, while smaller European markets, like Finland, Denmark, the Netherlands and Belgium, received lower ones. One explanation could be found in the motives for entering these markets, as indicated by the firms in Table 10.7.

The dominating motives turned out to be market potential and access to advanced customers. However, actual motives differed between markets. The Scandinavian markets were often entered in response to perceived opportunities (e.g., low geographic distance, limited competition, orders received, established market contacts or access to advanced customers). In large industrialised countries, such as Germany, the USA, France, the UK and Japan, the single most important motive was market potential, followed by access to advanced customers. In Germany, it was considered important to be close to other competitors while, in France, limited competition was indicated as an important motive. One explanation for this may be that France is frequently considered by Swedish firms as a difficult market, partly due to language problems. If there are competing firms active in the market, the difficulties may be perceived as too great by many firms.

Table 10.6 Number of firms considering specific market (in which the firm is active) to be one of the three most important markets as a percent of all entries into that market

Country	Number of firms considering this an important market	Number of entries into this market	%
Germany	41	64	64
USA	28	54	52
UK	25	57	44
Norway	28	72	39
France	18	58	31
Finland	21	71	29
Japan	6	23	26
Italy	9	45	20
Denmark	11	69	16
Switzerland	7	51	14

Table 10.7 Motives for entering the three most important markets

Motives	Number of entries	%
Large market potential	169	25
Access to advanced customers	109	16
Established market contacts	74	11
Limited geographic distance	70	10
Limited competition	65	10
Orders received	60	9
Presence of advanced competitors	45	7
Language knowledge	34	5
Limited cultural distance	34	5
Considerable geographic distance	16	2
Total	676	100

In order to investigate the sequence of market selection, a ranking based on mean establishment rank (MR) of each market was established. The concept was defined by Hörnell, Vahlne and Wiedersheim-Paul (1973), in an empirical study of foreign subsidiary establishment among Swedish firms. In this study, the measure is not based only on subsidiary establishments, but on market entry using either direct exports, local represent-atives or a subsidiary. A Spearman rank correlation coefficient of 0.777 between the traditional ranking, established by the internationalisation process researchers in Uppsala, and the ranking developed in this study, indicated a relatively limited change in pattern of market selection.

Table 10.8   Mean establishment rank (MR) of foreign markets, using direct exports, local representatives or subsidiary

Country	Present rank	Economic distance	Difference	MR	Number of firms
Norway	1	2	+1	2.02	81
Denmark	2	1	−1	2.21	76
Finland	3	3	0	2.41	82
Germany	4	4	0	3.11	72
France	5	12	+7	3.22	64
UK	6	5	−1	3.29	65
Switzerland	7	9	+2	3.39	56
USA	8	8	0	3.47	58
Netherlands	9	6	−3	3.58	66
Belgium	10	7	−3	3.69	49
Japan	11	16	+5	3.77	26
Austria	12	11	−1	3.81	43
Argentina	13	19	+6	4.10	10
South Africa	14	18	+4	4.20	10
Brazil	15	17	+2	4.33	12
Australia	16	29	+13	4.44	39
Canada	17	10	−7	4.48	44
Italy	18	13	−5	4.56	50
Spain	19	14	−5	4.68	37
Portugal	20	15	−5	5.20	25

Notes:
MR = sum WiRi/sum Wi.
Ri = establishment rank (1st, 2nd, 3rd, etc.).
Wi = no. of establishments of each rank/market.
sumWi = total no. of establishments/market.

In the first half of the list, few variations from previous research are found (Table 10.8). The main exception is France, with a considerably higher position in this ranking. In the second half, on the other hand, a number of distant markets (such as Japan, Argentina and Australia) have advanced, while some European markets, (Italy, Spain and Portugal) have lost their positions. Still, one has to be careful when interpreting the re-sults, since the actual differences in MR-measure between countries is limited, as is the number of observations in certain countries. Besides, many firms were found to enter more than one foreign market during each year, further complicating the interpretation of market selection sequences.

Another interesting observation was a tendency among firms initiating activities in markets other than the Nordic ones, such as Germany, France or the USA, to continue to follow a less traditional sequence of market selection.

Forms of Foreign Entry

In terms of organising foreign activities, by far the most important form of entry was independent local representatives – agents or distributors – used by 87 per cent of the firms in the sample. Direct exports were used by 68 per cent and foreign subsidiaries by 44 per cent of the firms (Table 10.9) Concerning other entry forms, the results are not directly comparable for methodological reasons.

Table 10.9   Forms of foreign entry used

Entry Method	Number of firms	%
Foreign agents/distributors	83	87
Direct exports	65	68
Subsidiary	42	44
Licensing	10	11
Piggybacking	7	7
Export co-operation	3	3

The propensity to use different forms differed between markets. In some markets – such as Australia, Austria and Spain – agent or distributor agreements represented more than 70 per cent of all entries, and the remaining entries were basically direct exports. A lower share of representative agreements was found in markets with a large number of export entries – particularly in relatively distant or restricted markets such as Brazil, South Africa and Italy – and in markets with many subsidiary establishments (mainly large industrialised countries such as the USA, the UK and Germany).

The major problem concerning internationalisation, indicated by 58 per cent of the firms in this study, was the difficulty of finding suitable local representatives. Still, a number of different methods were used to identify and evaluate potential representatives. The most common included personal contacts and requests from interested firms (Table 10.10), which were used by 79 per cent and 73 per cent of the firms, respectively. Approximately 45 per cent of all firms indicated that they had been able to use

Infant Multinationals

managers' previous contacts with local representatives or general knowledge about foreign markets during internationalisation. Another method
was participation during trade shows/fairs and travelling abroad; official
offices were less frequently used. To study how well these different alternatives had functioned, firms were asked to evaluate them on a 5-point
Likert scale from 1 (very bad) to 5 (very good).

Table 10.10   Contact alternatives and evaluation

Contact alternatives	Number of firms	%	Evaluation
Personal contacts	67	79	4.3
Travelling abroad	47	55	4.2
Requests	62	73	3.6
Trade shows/fairs	50	59	3.5
Export Chambers	26	31	2.6
The Swedish Export Council	25	26	2.6

According to this evaluation, the best methods required close contacts
with potential representatives, such as personal contacts or travelling
abroad. Most firms agreed that personal contacts had been particularly
important during first foreign entries, indicating the great importance of
previous experience of foreign markets during the early stages of internationalisation. This, in turn, agrees with the expectations of the internationalisation process theory.

In an attempt to investigate the relevance of the establishment chain, the
percentage of firms using different sequences of foreign entry forms in individual markets were studied. Within the sample, a total of 968 foreign
market entries, using direct exports, local representatives, subsidiaries or
a combination of the three, were indicated (Table 10.11).

Table 10.11   The establishment chain

Entry sequence	Number of entries	%
Only direct export	166	17
Only foreign representative	515	53
Only subsidiary	50	5
Combination export/representative	192	20
Combination export and/or representative before subsidiary	34	4
Other sequences	11	1
Total	968	100

In most cases, firms used only one single method of entry in each market, usually local representatives. This seems reasonable, since these are

small (as well as young) firms, which are still active during the early stages of internationalisation. However, among firms with foreign subsidiaries, it is interesting to note that as many as 65 per cent of all establishments were not preceded by direct exports and/or local representatives.

The propensity to follow a traditional establishment chain seems to differ between countries. In large, distant markets such as Japan and the USA, a higher level of uncertainty could explain the more traditional sequence, which was via direct exports and/or local representatives (75 per cent and 60 per cent of all subsidiary establishments, respectively). In the UK and Germany, on the other hand, subsidiaries were usually established without any preceding stages (67 per cent and 62 per cent of the cases). One interpretation may be that the 'home market' of Swedish managers has expanded to include other parts of Western Europe as the perceived 'economic distance' to these markets has decreased.

Influencing Factors

In order to test the combined impact of explanatory variables put forward by internationalisation process researchers and internalisation theorists, two multi-variate analyses were undertaken. As an initial step, all explanatory variables were included simultaneously. In the second step, only variables with statistically significant, or almost significant, t-values were retained. First, a logit analysis was used to investigate whether firms active in the US market differed from other firms (Table 10.12).

The goodness of fit of the model was reasonably good, with high chi-square values and pseudo R^2-values indicating that approximately 30 per cent of the variance in the dependent variable was 'explained' by the explanatory variables. (The pseudo R^2-value was based on the following formula, proposed by Aldrich and Nelson (1984): Pseudo $R^2 =$ chi-square/(N + chi-square).)

Looking at the results, firms entering the USA differed slightly from others in certain respects. They were often corporately owned firms, providing innovative products for a narrow market niche. Contrary to what could have been expected, using an internalisation approach, R&D intensity was lower among these firms than among others. One possible explanation could be that these firms are spin-offs from other firms or university research, where a large part of R&D expenditure has been invested prior to the establishment. Another, and perhaps more likely, explanation is that these firms enter the USA at an early stage when considerable R&D investments in close co-operation with advanced customers have yet to be made.

Table 10.12   Logit analysis: entry into USA

Explanatory Variables	Initial Analysis		Second Analysis	
	Estimates	t-values	Estimates	t-values
CONSTANT	1.089	0.632	1.292	0.772
SIZE	0.315	0.382		
OWTYPE	1.389	1.718*	−1.457	−2.076**
IEXP	−0.483	−1.397	−0.532	−1.574
FEXP	−0.048	−0.133		
INTENS	−1.317	−2.496**	−1.206	−2.535**
PATENTS	−0.380	−0.524		
TECH	0.566	1.459	0.484	1.321
INOVA	0.677	2.302**	−0.631	−2.358**
EDUCAT	0.482	1.345	0.513	1.500
ADAPT	0.401	1.000		
IMAGE	0.136	0.358		
STAGE	−0.711	−1.345	−0.527	−1.136
POT	−0.822	−2.172**	−0.742	−2.133**
Chi-square value (df)		29.81 (13)***		28.287 (8)***
Pseudo R^2-value		0.302		0.291

Notes:
Dependent variable:
1 = Entry into USA; 2 = No entry into USA
*** = 0.5% level of significance
** = 2.5% level of significance
* = 5.0% level of significance

In the second multi-variate analyses (Table 10.13), a regression analysis was made in an attempt to identify any differences in timing of foreign subsidiary establishment (this model received a relatively high explanatory value, with an R^2-value of 0.667 and an adjusted R^2-value of 0.430 at the initial step).

The results indicate a more rapid establishment of foreign subsidiaries among larger firms with corporate ownership. This agrees with the expectations of Johanson and Vahlne (1990), that access to resources may reduce the importance of a slow, sequential process of internationalisation. Firms indicating a high importance of creating an image around their products – by providing after-sales services and establishing a brand name – are quicker to establish their own subsidiaries, which seems intuitively correct. The analyses also indicated that subsidiaries were established earlier when the level of competition was low.

Strangely enough, firms whose managers had previous foreign experience were slower to establish foreign subsidiaries, which is contrary to what could be expected. One explanation may be that these managers hesitate to establish foreign subsidiaries since they are aware of the possible difficulties. Another explanation may be that they already have established contacts with foreign customers or representatives, favouring a rapid internationalisation based on direct exports or representatives' agreements. The expected results, using an internalisation argument, could not be supported since firms with high R&D intensity were found to be slower to establish subsidiaries abroad.

Table 10.13 Regression analysis: timing of subsidiary establishment

Explanatory variables	Initial analysis		Second analysis	
	Estimates	t-values	Estimates	t-values
CONSTANT	2.955	0.718	5.252	5.891***
SIZE	−2.921	−2.845**	−2.583	−2.718**
OWTYPE	−5.438	−3.030***	−4.272	−2.727**
IEXP	1.190	1.163		
FEXP	2.096	2.499**	1.943	2.764**
INTENS	3.639	2.207**	5.087	4.167***
PATENTS	2.375	1.711*	2.024	1.559
TECH	0.716	0.800		
INOVA	0.553	0.818		
EDUCAT	−1.519	−1.559		
ADAPT	1.132	1.165		
IMAGE	−1.793	−1.841*	−1.831	−2.173**
STAGE	2.171	2.161**	2.889	3.466***
POT	−1.285	−1.412		
F-value		2.743		4.818
R^2-value		0.677		0.595
Adjusted R^2		0.430		0.471

Notes:
Dependent variable: number of years from first foreign entry
*** = 0.5% level of significance
** = 2.5% level of significance
* = 5.0% level of significance

DISCUSSION

The main purpose of this study was twofold:

(a) to describe the international behaviour of small technology-based Swedish firms in terms of speed of internationalisation, pattern of market selection and choice of foreign entry form;
(b) to analyse variations in internationalisation behaviour in an attempt to understand what factors might explain these variations.

It was expected that a limited size and certain technology characteristics – for example, a high level of R&D intensity and an innovative or 'high-technology' product – would influence internationalisation behaviour. To some extent, these expectations were supported.

Description of International Behaviour: A Summary

Among firms included in this study, the speed of internationalisation was relatively high. This may partly be an outcome of the selection criteria used, but it is likely to reflect the need for rapid internationalisation among technology-based firms, which are active in small market niches. The result may also be affected by a general increase in the speed of internationalisation, due to a reduced economic distance over time, as markets becomes more similar due to improved communication technologies and a homogenisation of demand (see the discussion in Nordström, 1991). Unfortunately, methodological differences do not allow for a direct comparison with previous studies.

In terms of foreign market selection, the observed pattern did not differ considerably from the traditional entry sequence of Hörnell, Vahlne and Wiedersheim-Paul (1973), which was based on 'economic distance'. However, in terms of 'most important' markets, large industrialised markets such as Germany, the USA, the UK and Japan were selected as a result of strategic considerations, such as market potential, access to advanced customers and competitive situation, while the Scandinavian markets were selected in response to perceived opportunities, such as limited geographic distance, limited competition, orders received and access to local market contacts.

The propensity to use different forms of foreign entry varied between markets. Overall, the most commonly used method of entry was to appoint local representatives. In distant or restricted markets, such as Brazil and South Africa, the propensity to use direct exports was relatively higher, which could be the result of difficulties in identifying and evaluating suitable representatives in these markets. The propensity to use subsidiaries was relatively higher in large, industrialised markets, such as the USA, the UK and Germany. In these countries, market size may support a subsidiary establishment. Besides, a subsidiary is an important way of transfering tacit knowledge during early application development in close co-operation with advanced customers and of providing after-sales services.

When analysing the entry sequence, as many as 65 per cent of all subsidiaries were established without any prior experience of the market via exports or local representatives. The propensity to establish direct subsidiaries was highest in markets of limited 'economic distance', such as the UK and Germany. Due to an increased economic integration, establishing a subsidiary in these countries may not be considered a great international step, but rather an increased commitment within an extended 'home market'. However, in large, distant markets, such as the USA and Japan, a high level of uncertainty still seems to favour a sequentially increased market commitment.

Overall, the results indicated that foreign activities had been rather successful for most firms. About 46 per cent of the firms indicated a good or very good perceived profitability of foreign operations, while only 15 per cent had a low or very low profitability. Almost 30 per cent of the firms had reached a higher-than-expected profitability, and 95 per cent of the firms expected to increase foreign sales further in the future.

Analyses of Variations in Internationalisation Behaviour

When looking at the impact of size, one may argue that this would be of limited importance in this study since all the firms included are either small or medium-sized. However, there are considerable differences between firms with ten employees and those with 150 employees in terms of access to internal resources, such as management competence and financing. This may explain some of the variations observed.

One type of internal resource which turned out to influence the process of internationalisation was access to the previous experience of managers. Firms established as spin-offs from established firms or universities seemed more likely to have international contact networks, thus speeding up the internationalisation process. Established contacts – such as with local representatives – simultaneously influenced the pattern of market selection and choice of foreign entry method. Another important question related to access to resources concerns external ownership. About 50 per cent of firms were (at least partly) owned by external corporate owners. One important motive for inviting in external owners is to increase internal resources, and therefore it is not surprising to note that firms with external owners were more likely to enter the USA and to rapidly establish foreign subsidiaries.

This study gives limited support to the idea of internalising investments in proprietary knowledge measured as R&D intensity. However, in terms of product characteristics, the expected relationship was supported. Foreign subsidiaries appear to be motivated by a need for close customer contact during development, rather than by a need to internalise R&D investments. The propensity to enter the USA was also higher among firms providing innovative products or 'high-technology' products. The results agree with the previous discussion of the USA as a market of high strategic importance, with sophisticated customers and a large market potential, where direct customer contacts are necessary for customer adaptation and training before a new technology is accepted.

The results of this study were later supported by a Nordic study by Forsström, Eskilenen and Lindmark (1994), where small export companies were compared with home market-oriented companies. The relative share of active exporters – with an export share above 20 per cent – was higher among Swedish companies than among Finnish or Norwegian companies, which was explained by a stronger export tradition in Sweden. Active exporters were found to be larger, and have higher levels of technology and automation, more internal division of labour, and managers with higher levels of education, language knowledge and more experience from working with foreign companies or companies in other industries.

IMPLICATIONS FOR RESEARCH

The results presented in this study have theoretical implications related to three different schools of thoughts; behaviouristic theories, internalisation theories and network theories.

First, the study gives some support to the behaviouristic theories, indicating a sequential process of internationalisation. Using data from the case studies, the basic mechanisms of learning seem to explain the observed change from an opportunistic selection of foreign markets, during the early stages of internationalisation, to a more strategically-based selection process in later stages. Similarly, the selection of local representatives varies over time, with an initial *ad hoc* selection – often based on established contacts or orders received – followed by a more careful selection and evaluation in later stages. Over time, many of the initial representatives are replaced as companies accumulate more knowledge about foreign activities. There is also a greater propensity to follow a traditional establishment chain in 'economically distant' markets than in closer markets, indicating the greater importance of successive learning in markets with which companies are less familiar.

Second, if R&D intensity is used as a measure of level of proprietary knowledge, this study gives limited support to the idea of internalisation of such investments. However, in terms of product technology, the expected relation is – at least partly – supported. The character of product technology and marketing requirement seems more likely to influence internationalisation behaviour than the amount of resources invested. For small firms providing innovative products, it is more important to develop close customer contacts in order to develop the product and increase general customer awareness than to worry about future imitation and competition.

Third, this study gives some support to a network approach. Initial internationalisation has often been facilitated by the relation to other firms. Network contacts have not always provided the optimal solutions for the firms (initial contacts have often been replaced by more strategically selected alternatives over time), but they have made it possible to speed up the process.

IMPLICATIONS FOR PRACTITIONERS

The observations presented above indicate that there is potential for small technology-based firms to succeed internationally. One way to speed up the process is to make use of the contact network available to the firm, and even if these contacts do not immediately provide the optimal solutions – as indicated above – they may facilitate and speed up the initial entry process, since the main problem was often to identify foreign representatives. Over time, however, it is important to make an extensive evaluation of foreign activities.

In order to avoid any mistakes, one has to remember that the bulk of the empirical data on which this study is based was collected towards the end of the 1980s, when interest in Eastern Europe was limited among most Swedish firms. Besides, Sweden was not yet a member of the European Community. Today, one could expect a greater interest in Eastern Europe as well as an even higher propensity among the firms to regard other European countries as an 'extended home market'.

IMPLICATIONS FOR POLICY-MAKERS

The main problem during internationalisation, as indicated by the firms in this study, was to identify suitable foreign representatives. The second most important problem was to get local market knowledge. Consequently, these are areas where many small technology-based firms may need support. Since a good representative relationship is often characterised by the development of close personal relationships, the main topic for policy-makers would be to provide these firms with an arena for developing such relations.

Interestingly enough, only 24 per cent of all firms indicated problems with financing their international activities. However, the financial situation during the end of the 1980s, was considerably more positive for smaller firms than during the early 1990s, when financial crises in the Swedish bank sector made it exceedingly difficult to finance technological development as well as international activities.

Therefore, many small technology-based firms still face many different challenges, including:

(a) developing their technology to meet international standards (e.g., in quality and environmental protection areas);
(b) developing the company, often with limited management experience, few specialists and restricted financial resources;
(c) initiating international activities, which requires considerable investments in time as well as resources to evaluate representatives and develop personal relations.

11 Spin-Off and Acquisition of Small Technology-Based Firms

Åsa Lindholm Dahlstrand

INTRODUCTION

In a large technology-based firm, technology and innovations can be developed internally, although they can also be acquired from external sources, such as small technology-based firms. In addition, technology and innovation can be spun off from one organisation to another, perhaps from a large technology-based firm to establish a new spin-off firm. Nevertheless, innovation researchers, as well as policy-makers, have traditionally focused strongly on whether large *or* small firms are the most frequent, effective and/or efficient innovators, rather than on the interaction between these firms. Earlier studies have, for example, shown that small firms often have advantages in the early stages of the innovation process, while large firms have advantages in the later stages of scaling up innovations, and large and small firms can interact in several ways, such as through ownership changes. This chapter concentrates on ownership changes in the forms of acquisition and spin-off of small technology-based firms.

The research presented here is based on the work of Lindholm (1994), analysing growth and innovativeness in (mainly) Swedish technology-related ownership changes. This work has, to some extent, a theoretical origin in Williamson's (1975:196–207) discussion of a 'systems approach' and proposition of a 'systems solution by classical specialisation'. Even though Williamson introduced what he called the 'systems solution' over 20 years ago, the idea is still quite unexplored. Williamson's argument is that small firms are frequently high performers when it comes to product innovation, and often have advantages in the early stages of the innovation process, as well as in less expensive and radical innovations. On the other hand, large firms have an advantage in the later stages of scaling up innovations, with large scale or size often found to be a determinant of malfunctioning in the earlier and creative stages of the innovation process. Therefore, as Williamson (1975) proposed, the 'systems solution by classical specialisation' may be an efficient innovation process. He hypothesised that, because of the large firms' innovative disabilities in the early stages, an efficient procedure by which to introduce new products would be to allow the initial stages of the innovation process to be performed by independent innovators and small firms. The successful companies would then be acquired for subsequent development by a large firm.

Large technology-based firms also have potential as sources of innovation, usually encompassing several technologies within existing product areas, and may have a potential advantage in a relatively large amount of technology development. The technologies can also have a potential for innovation outside the existing product areas of the large firm. It is, however, usual that a large firm does not encourage potential innovations outside its existing product areas and may therefore have (often neglected) potential as a source of radical new innovations. By spinning off this potential for external development, the large firm can act as an important source of innovation (Lindholm, 1994).

By combining the process of large firm acquisition of small technology-based firms with the process by which parent firms 'spin off' small technology-based firms, this chapter will propose an 'extended systems approach' as an extension of Williamson's initial ideas. It will therefore argue that an economic system where large and small firms interact through technology-related ownership changes can, under certain conditions, be highly conducive to overall innovativeness and long-term growth. This study seeks an improved knowledge about technology-related ownership changes, in the forms of spin-off and acquisition of small technology-based firms. Lindholm (1994) found that even though there are a large number of studies, and a considerable amount of literature about acquisitions in general, technology-related acquisitions are seldom analysed (some exceptions are: Chakrabarti and Souder, 1987; Chakrabarti, 1990; Granstrand and Sjölander, 1990b; Lindholm, 1990, 1994; Garnsey and Roberts, 1992; Chakrabarti, Hauschildt and Süverkrüp 1994). In addition, the existing literature includes very few systematic, empirical studies of technology-related spin-offs. Also, in the literature on spin-offs, either divestments (Duhaime and Grant, 1984; Thomas, 1986; Rizzi, 1987; Woo, Willard and Daellenbach, 1992), or entrepreneurial spin-offs (Roberts 1968, 1991a, 1991b; Roberts and Wainer, 1968; Cooper, 1971a, 1973, 1984; Smilor, 1987; Dietrich and Gibson, 1990; Granstrand and Alänge, 1995) are analysed, but never both together. Further, empirical studies made of entrepreneurial spin-offs most often focus on university spin-offs, while very few analyse corporate spin-offs.

INTERACTION BETWEEN LARGE AND SMALL TECHNOLOGY-
BASED FIRMS

The Role of Small and Large Firms in Technological Innovation

One of the first modern (twentieth-century) economists to focus upon the dynamics of economic development and technological change was Joseph Schumpeter. In his view, the key development process was the 'carrying out of new combinations', or innovations, which, in turn, would mean the competitive elimination of the old (Schumpeter, 1934, first published in 1912). He perceived the entrepreneur as being the one to carry out the new combinations, reaping an entrepreneurial profit, with other producers following him. Further, the entrepreneurial profits depend upon the time which elapses before competitors are established and the temporary monopoly of the entrepreneur is destroyed. Thus, Schumpeter saw the entrepreneur as an important means of revitalising an economy. However, in his later work, Schumpeter (1976) recognised the increasing importance of innovations through large-sized firms, arguing that 'The perfectly bureaucratised giant industrial unit not only ousts the small or medium-sized firm and "expropriates" its owners, but in the end it also ousts the entrepreneur.' (Schumpeter, 1976:134, first published 1942). Therefore, whilst recognising that large firms, because of size advantages such as economies of scale in management, marketing, finance and R&D, are able to quickly exploit inventions on a large scale, he did not recognise the potential positive interplay that could exist between the large and the small firm, or the organisational limits of the large firm, including among other things the problems of bureaucratic commitment and entrepreneurial incentives, which were later highlighted by authors such as Williamson (1975). Therefore, it seems clear that both the newly established entrepreneurial small firm and the large-sized firm can have their respective advantages in the progress of technological development and change. This is also one important ingredient in Williamson's recommendation of a 'systems solution by classical specialisation'.

In their criticism of the neo-classical growth theories, Nelson and Winter (1982) stressed that in an evolutionary theory of economic change, consideration has to be given to the mechanisms operating in Schumpeterian competition. They argued that Schumpeterian competition is a process that tends to produce winners and losers, and that some firms exploit emerging technological opportunities, experiencing prosperity and growth, while others are less successful, suffering losses and decline.

Nelson and Winter did not discuss the work of Penrose (1959), where she dealt with the theory of the growth of the firm. She argued that:

> when a firm's strength is not closely related to its technological strength, but rests primarily on a dominant position in important markets, it is more difficult for the firm to move into entirely new basic areas of specialisation. Not only is such a firm unlikely to develop abilities that would give it a substantial technological advantage in an entirely new field, but it is also handicapped in the acquisition of other firms in fields where technology is substantially different. (Penrose 1959:118)

While Penrose used terms like technological strength and advantage, Teece (1980:233) instead argued that a firm's competitive advantage is defined in terms of capabilities, rather than in terms of products, and that 'The firm is seen as establishing a specialised know-how or asset base from which it extends its operations in response to competitive conditions.' In addition, the technology base of a company is essentially the asset of the technological competence and capacity that a company possesses, and as an asset it can be built up, maintained and exploited in various ways or contractual forms. Since technology is becoming more complex, with increased possibilities of combinations, it might include completely changing the rules of established business (Granstrand and Sjölander, 1990a).

Many studies have reported that established firms tend to misperceive the importance of a new technology. This is because they are inclined to view it by the values and criteria applicable to the old technology. Cooper and Schendel (1976) found that the traditional firm responds to technological threats in two different ways. The first is to improve the old technology, while the second includes commitments to develop products utilising the new technology. When the established firm continues to improve the existing technology, very few firms succeed in this.

In the often cited paper by Hayes and Abernathy (1980), the authors suggested that a long-term focus is needed for development of new products and processes, and that a certain amount of risk-taking is needed to exploit new innovations. However, the authors found indications of US firms focusing on financial short-term returns. Also, Utterback and Reitberger (1982) argued that the firms who make creative and lasting investments in technology have a potential for survival, and that these firms might be able to acquire and integrate the new innovative firms successfully. In addition, Ansoff (1965) had earlier claimed that mergers which complement strong and weak sides, and permit integration of the companies' technical know-how, have the best opportunities for success.

Acquisition of Small Technology-Based Firms

From the point of view of the large firm, acquisition of small firms allows a higher degree of integration and control and can therefore be an efficient method for large firms to acquire new technology quickly. However, if the acquiring firm has a limited technological competence, these acquisitions can cause difficulties. According to Penrose (1959), a firm will be less able to acquire other firms with a substantially different technology, partly because the management is unlikely to have great confidence in its ability to operate in fields entirely alien to its own experience, and partly because it will in general be more difficult for a firm with no special advantage in a new field to acquire firms with specific technical qualifications at a profitable price.

External growth through acquisition and internal development (i.e., growth through new investments) are the two methods of growth for the firm (Penrose, 1959; Kumar, 1984). Penrose argued that the firm can often make more profitable use of its resources over a period of time by spreading production over a variety of products. The expansion is then made through diversification, either by internal development or by acquisitions. The studies by Granstrand and Sjölander (1990a) and Oskarsson (1990) also demonstrated that the degree of technological diversification is important for the growth of firms.

In 1969, Marquis argued that since no firm can perform more than a very small proportion of the innovative activity in any technology area, serious attention must be paid to technology sources outside the firm (Marquis, 1969). For this purpose, Granstrand and Sjölander (1990a) presented a typology of technology sourcing and exploitation strategies including, on the one hand, internal R&D as well as purchasing of licences and innovative firms, and, on the other, the selling of licences and spin-offs. The sourcing strategies discussed by Granstrand and Sjölander are similar to the strategies for entering new product markets, as examined by Roberts and Berry (1985). When key parameters for success in a new business field cannot easily be duplicated via internal development, acquisitions are even more attractive. It was also suggested that acquisitions are attractive because of their higher speed and lower initial cost, a conclusion which was reached in many other studies as well (e.g, Penrose, 1959; Salter and Weinhold, 1979).

In many studies, the small firm is supposed to have an advantage in the earlier stage of the inventive work, and in less expensive and radical innovations, while large firms have an advantage in the later stages of scaling up innovations and in efficient marketing (Freeman, 1974; Williamson,

1975; Roberts and Berry, 1985; Rothwell, 1994b). Successful commercialisation of an innovation requires several complementary assets (Teece, 1986), including resources for continued R&D, large-scale production, international marketing, after-sales support, and overall management. To acquire these resources on separate markets and integrate them takes time and effort on the part of the small firm. Besides, any hampering imperfection on the capital market, commonly encountered by small innovation companies, may jeopardise the whole venture. In other words, the transaction costs involved in acquiring complementary assets are likely to be high for the small firm. The alternative of having the whole innovation process internalised in a large firm with a more complete set of resources available from the outset will economise on transaction costs but is likely to give relative disadvantages, such as dulled entrepreneurial spirits, bureaucracy, internal procurement bias, and various innovation barriers (Williamson, 1975; Granstrand, 1982).

Under these circumstances the firms might gain from co-operation. Venture capital, nurturing and the 'new-style' joint ventures (Roberts and Berry, 1985) are, together with the technology-related acquisitions, important because they all make this co-operation possible. Furthermore, instead of being acquired in full, the small firm could also license out its technology or engage in joint ventures. The latter could contractually be designed to come arbitrarily close to an acquisition, and so from a theoretical point of view only pure licensing needs to be considered. Licensing out is in fact an unbundling of the small firm's resources, which involves transaction costs. Besides, small innovative firms typically contain nontradable complementarities in the form of, for example, entrepreneurial skill, tacit knowledge and key customer relations. To acquire the whole firm rather than just a license for its technology is, then, a way to make a package deal that again economises on transaction costs. However, if the market for acquisitions does not offer candidates for sufficient resource fits, licensing might be a superior option.

Even though Penrose paid no attention to the respective advantages of small and large firms, she suggested that the selling of small firms is suitable under certain circumstances. As the small firm grows, Penrose argued, it will reach a point where a change in its managerial structure must take place because of the necessity of subdividing the managerial task. In addition to the management problem, the small firm has problems of raising capital. Thus, the small firm may find substantial advantages in selling to a large firm. It is then near at hand to advocate a transaction whereby a large firm with complementary assets acquires the small, innovation-based firm at a suitable stage. This is what Williamson suggested in his 'systems solution by classical specialisation' (Williamson, 1975:196–207). There is still a transaction cost involved in the acquisition, but to the extent that there is a resource fit between the large and the small firm, everything else being equal, the transaction cost will be lowered.

The Spin-Off Phenomenon

Biggadike (1979) found that new ventures need, on average, eight years to reach profitability, and that the big losers are those ventures with the smallest entry scale. This finding further underlines the importance of some sort of systems solution, where small ventures and large-sized firms are able to co-operate to the mutual benefit of both organisations. The development of different kinds of new venture organisations, as methods of dealing with the rapidly changing environment, and as a sort of systems solution, has been focused upon by various researchers (Fast, 1979). Burgelman (1983, 1985) examined internal entrepreneurship and various ways of integrating the entrepreneurial organisation into the overall corporate structure. He describes the methods as ranging from direct integration, to establishment of new product/business departments, to special business units, to micro new venture departments, to new venture divisions, to independent business units, to nurturing plus contracting and to full outside contracting, to a complete spin-off of the new entrepreneurial organisation (Burgelman, 1985).

As was discussed above, the spin-off mechanism allows a potential innovation, with its origin in a large firm, to be further developed within a small firm. This may be of special importance when the potential innovation is outside the existing product areas of the large firm, which then does not want to continue the development. In today's rapidly changing environment, firms continuously have to deal with new technologies. In addition, if technology is becoming more complex, this increases the possibilities of combining technologies into new products (Granstrand and Sjölander, 1990a). From the point of view of the company, this will result in decisions about how to deal with both the growth and technology base of the firm: that is, how to conduct R&D and innovation, either internally or by various external alternatives. Possibly, an increased technological complexity and development will include an increasing number of potential innovations within large firms in the future, and then an increased importance of (perhaps quasi-integrated) technology-related spin-offs. By spinning off the potential innovation, the technology development need not be delayed or discontinued. Hence the technology related spin-off mechanism is likely to contribute to an increased innovativity and long-term growth.

There are several reasons for believing that the acquisition and spin-off of small technology-based firms would be efficiency-inducing, and that they are also complementing each other.

1. As hypothesised by Williamson, there are the small firm's early-stage advantages, the large firm's advantages in scaling up innovations, and the advantages of combining the small and large firms after acquisition.

2. There are advantages in spinning off small technology-based firms from parent firms. Such advantages may include the above mentioned development of potential new innovations which lies outside the scope of the parent firm.

Additionally, it can be argued that, because of the early-stage innovation disadvantages of the large firm, there is a potential benefit in developing such new innovations in newly created 'firms' within the large firm. Thus these new units may be decreasingly integrated with the large firm, with the opportunity to change ownership and capital structure being possible to varying degrees. They may be jointly owned by the large firms and the inventors, or spun off as fully independent new firms. They may also later be reintegrated by the large firm, or acquired by another large firm, in order to benefit from large firms' advantages in scaling up the innovations. The extended system will therefore consist of a population of large firms that acquire and spin off small technology-based firms, and a population of small firms, independently established or spun off from parent firms, subsequently acquired by, and perhaps re-spun off from, the large firms.

Both acquisitions and spin-offs could be made gradually, and with varying degrees of integration. Moreover, large firms can be linked together by, and interact through, jointly owned small firms. Thus, operating on the market for corporate control, the extended system could be considered as a collection of large firms with a cluster of small firms attached to them in a dynamically changing quasi-integrated manner. In this system a market for technology-based firms is created as a supplement to other forms of technology markets.

METHOD

In the empirical research of Lindholm (1994), upon which this chapter is based, three different empirical substudies were included:

(A) the STBF (small technology-based firm) study – a cross sectional study focusing on technology-related acquisitions of small techno-logy-based firms;

(B) the ESO study – a cross-sectional study focusing on entrepreneurial spin-offs among small technology-based firms;

(C) the LTBF (large technology-based firm) – case studies of two large corporations illustrating both of the two major processes of technology-related ownership changes: that is, acquisitions and spin-offs.

In this chapter, the results from (A) and (B) will be focused upon. A few findings from the two LTBF case studies will also be included here (for a full description and analysis of the LTBF case studies, see Lindholm, 1994).

The STBF Study

The STBF study was carried out in order to analyse both the growth, and the explanatory variables influencing the growth, in technology-related acquisition. The STBF study is cross-sectional, and includes data collected from 106 small technology-based firms. The interviews were made by telephone, based on a prepared questionnaire.

The sample of firms in the STBF study consists of three different sub-samples. The first of these is the 'WMcQ' sample. This sample includes the 20 new firms established from the 100 major innovations in Sweden during 1945–80, as identified by Wallmark and McQueen (1983, 1986). The second sub-sample is the 'CPA' sample, which consists of 60 NTBFs established in Sweden during 1965–80, a sample used by Utterback and Reitberger (1982). They estimated that approximately half of the firms in the engineering industry in Sweden meeting their criteria were included in the sample. Their selection criteria included (a) the firms should have partly or wholly developed their own major products (b) they should be wholly and independently owned within Sweden, and (c) they should have at least SEK5 million in sales and 20 employees in Sweden in 1980. (Note: a few firms were included in the sample – by Utterback and Reitberger – even though they did not meet all these criteria.)

The third subsample is the 'CTH' sample, which includes all the 39 manufacturing firms spun off from Chalmers University of Technology before 1988. In total, this adds up to 119 firms, but the sample size is reduced to 111 firms because eight are included in more than one sample. Furthermore, three firms have been liquidated, and for an additional two firms data are missing. Therefore, the number of firms analysed is 106. Of these firms, 50 were acquired and 56 were not acquired, in 1989.

In the STBF study, it is possible to analyse whether growth is increasing because of acquisition, but also whether acquired firms are growing faster than non-acquired firms, before and after acquisition, as well as during their total lifetime. In the statistical analysis of the cross-sectional study, attempts are made to find a growth model explaining the different growth patterns of acquired and non-acquired firms, as well as the post-acquisition growth in the acquired firms.

The ESO Study

In the ESO study, entrepreneurial spin-offs were analysed, focusing on growth and inventiveness in technology-related (entrepreneurial) spin-offs, and explanatory variables influencing growth and inventiveness. The ESO study does not include any divestments; only newly established firms are included (i.e., entrepreneurial spin-offs and non-spin-offs). The sample used in the ESO study is identical to one of the subsamples of the STBF study above, namely the CPA sample, identified and used by Utterback and Reitberger (1982). It consists of 60 NTBFs established between 1965 and 1980. In the selection of firms, Utterback and Reitberger eliminated those with ownership either outside Sweden or by larger publicly held firms in Sweden. Hence the 60 NTBFs in the sample cannot be divestments or joint ventures. There is also a risk that some 'sponsored spin-offs'– for example, firms where the spin-off parent holds a minority share – are under-represented in the sample, even though other kinds of sponsored spin-offs can be assumed to have been included.

Not least important in the selection of the CPA sample are the time and resource advantages of using a sample analysed earlier. Also, in the ESO study, the coded answers of the interviews made in the Utterback and Reitberger study were available. Some of these answers could be directly used in the ESO study, while others helped in the formulation of a questionnaire. In addition to these two earlier studies, new information was collected in the ESO study. In 54 of the 60 firms, supplementary telephone interviews were made. Among the missing six firms, two had been liquidated earlier and four did not want to participate. In two other firms, the answers were incomplete due to lack of knowledge (founder ill). Nevertheless, by including the data from the two earlier studies, the missing data were limited and basic information about all firms is available.

The interview data was complemented by publicly available information about the growth and patents of the firms. This information, including the patent frequency and economic information about sales and number of employees, was collected from the Swedish Patent and Registration Office. It was not possible, within the time and resource limits of the ESO study, to collect information about new products or innovations and the sales from new products. Instead, the patent frequency was used as an indicator of the inventiveness of the 60 firms. In turn, the inventiveness can be used as an approximation of the potential innovativeness. A complete picture of the variables included in the analysis is given in Lindholm (1994).

GROWTH AND INVENTIVENESS IN ACQUIRED AND SPIN-OFF FIRMS

In this section, the empirical results of the STBF and the ESO studies will be presented. In the first part of this section, the growth and inventiveness in technology-related acquisitions, as well as variables influencing these effects, are analysed. Here, the cross sectional STBF study is providing some findings about the technology-related acquisitions within Swedish industry. In the second part of this section, characteristics of Swedish entrepreneurial spin-offs, including the effects on growth and inventiveness, are analysed.

The STBF Study: Acquisition of Small Technology-Based Firms.

The Effect of Acquisition on the Growth of Small Technology-Based Firms

Regarding the effects on growth in technology-related acquisitions, the study analysed whether the acquired firms had grown differently before as well as after acquisition, and whether the growth had increased after the acquisition (where the growth of the small technology-based firms is measured as the growth in sales). As stated earlier, 106 firms were examined in the STBF study, of which 50 were acquired by 1989. An earlier analysis of this sample by Granstrand and Sjölander (1990b) found that the post-acquisition growth of the small technology-based firms is significantly higher than the pre-acquisition growth. In addition to this analysis, the growth of the small technology-based firms may be separated into the pre- and post-acquisition growth for both the acquired and the non-acquired firms. In Table 11.1, the average annual increase in sales is presented for both the acquired and non-acquired firms.

Table 11.1   Annual increase of sales among acquired and non-acquired firms

Average annual increase of sales	Acquired Firms			Non-acquired Firms			Significance Level
(change in MSEK/year)	n	Mean	Std. dev.	n	Mean	Std. dev.	Prob. > F'
Total growth	46	7.5	17.9	54	2.4	5.2	0.05
Pre-acquisition growth	45	5.7	12.6	54	1.4	3.5	0.02
Post-acquisition growth	43	16.2	47.9	48	2.7	6.2	0.05

Std. dev. = Standard deviation
Notes:
The growth is measured for three different time periods: total growth = from the year of foundation until 1987, pre-acquisition growth = from the year of foundation until 'acquisition age'; and post-acquisition growth = from 'acquisition age' until 1987. Year ten was used as an approximation for 'acquisition age' in all of the non-acquired firms, because around half of the acquired firms (24 out of 50) were acquired within their first 10 years.

Table 11.1 shows that the total growth rate has been significantly higher (by over 200 per cent) for acquired firms than for non-acquired firms. The pre-acquisition growth rate is even higher for acquired firms than for non-acquired firms. During this period, the annual growth is about three times as high in the acquired firms. Post-acquisition growth rate is also significantly higher among acquired firms. Though the non-acquired firms increased their growth rate after the 'acquisition age', the acquired firms still grew five times as fast during this period. The acquired firms increased their growth by 184 per cent after acquisition, while the corresponding increase in the non-acquired firms was 93 per cent.

The Effect of Acquisition on the Inventiveness of Small Technology-Based Firms

Measuring effects on innovativeness can be complex, and it is often easier to measure the inventiveness (indicated by, for example, the patent frequency) as an approximation of a potential innovativeness. For the 60 firms of the CPA sample of the STBF study, the patent frequency has been compared for the acquired and the non-acquired small technology-based firms. First, whether the acquired small technology based firms had a higher patent frequency than the non-acquired small technology-based firms was analysed, and whether the patent frequency in the acquired small technology-based firms changed after acquisition. In Table 11.2, the mean patent frequencies (totally, as well as before and after acquisition) are presented for the acquired and the non-acquired small technology-based firms.

Table 11.2   Patent frequency in acquired and non-acquired small technology-based firms

	Acquired firms (n = 40)	Non-acquired firms (n = 20)	Significance level
Patent frequency:			
mean value: number per firm	5.58	1.50	0.04
mean value: number per firm and year	0.23	0.07	0.04
Patent frequency before acquisition:			
mean value: number per firm	3.4	1.0	0.08
mean value: number per firm and year	0.20	0.08	0.08
Patent frequency after acquisition:			
mean value: number per firm	2.2	0.5	0.07
mean value: number per firm and year	0.18	0.06	0.09

Together, as a group, the 40 acquired small technology-based firms have 222 patents, while the 20 non-acquired small technology-based firms have only 30 patents. Thus it can be argued that, as a group, the acquired small technology-based firms have been more inventive than the group of non-acquired small technology-based firms. Also, during its total lifetime, as indicated in Table 11.2, the acquired small technology-based firm is (on average) significantly more inventive than the non-acquired small technology-based firm. Table 11.2 also indicates that the acquired small technology-based firms are more inventive (significant at the 0.10 level) than the non-acquired small technology-based firms, before as well as after the acquisition. However, the decreasing patent frequencies after acquisition, of both the acquired and the non-acquired small technology-based firms, are not significant. It can be argued that the patent frequencies do not decrease as the firms get older. Additionally, the inventiveness is not significantly changed after an acquisition, becaue the average acquired firm continues to be inventive after acquisition.

Furthermore, there is a correlation between the growth and the inventiveness in the technology-related acquisitions (the Pearson correlation coefficient is 0.55, and significant at the 0.01 level). Thus, it may be assumed that high inventiveness contributes to high growth, but also that high growth generates possibilities for innovative work, and thereby high inventiveness. Moreover the high pre-acquisition patent frequency among the acquired small technology-based firms indicates that highly inventive firms are becoming acquisition targets. Hence, rather than being acquired because of a high pre-acquisition growth (as indicated in Table 11.1), it can be speculated and argued that the high growth firms are more likely to be acquisition targets because of successful and complementing technology, and because successful technology is usually perceived as leading to high future growth.

Variables Influencing the Post-Acquisition Growth and Inventiveness of Small Technology-Based Firms

In the STBF study, tentative linear growth models were tested (for further details, see Lindholm, 1994). Included in the analysis were both a model of growth among the small technology-based firms (acquired as well as non-acquired) and a model of post-acquisition growth. Below, the findings of the analysis of the post-acquisition growth in the STBF study will be presented. The STBF study did not include any analysis of variables influencing the inventiveness, but some indications can be found in the two LTBF case studies analysed by Lindholm (1994).

In the STBF study, the integration of planning and control systems and the integration of operating systems were not found to contribute significantly to growth. Similarly, the financial and managerial synergies were not found to contribute significantly to post-acquisition growth. The analysis shows that post-acquisition growth is affected significantly by the fulfilment of the sellers' and buyers' primary motives, and by the synergy effects in technology. This result seems reasonable, since the matching of the buyers' and sellers' motives, together with the matching of the firms' technology resources, ought to be of great importance in technology-related acquisitions. Moreover, a growth model with only these three significant variables was formulated and tested (this analysis shows that all three variables contributed significantly to post-acquisition growth and yielded an R^2 of 60.6 per cent).

It is worth noting here that in the STBF study, obtaining capital for development was the main reason for selling Swedish firms. Nevertheless, in several acquired firms it was demonstrated that financial security is especially important for improving growth when the small firms has large customers who are dependent on this security. For example, in one of the acquired firms it was estimated that the firm had grown by an additional 25 per cent because of the financial security and the higher risk-taking that became possible.

It is also worth noting that, in small firms, administration is often minimised and the staff is often accustomed to a great deal of flexibility and freedom. In the STBF study it was demonstrated that, after acquisition, there was often an increase in administration and the staff experienced a loss of freedom. If the degree of integration in administration is high, this might cause dissatisfaction and loss of motivation among the employees, affecting the growth (and the fulfilment of potential synergies) negatively.

In the post-acquisition growth model of the STBF study, the fulfilment of the seller's motive contributes negatively to growth. It is possible that when a seller has a non offensive motive – for example, to free capital for private consumption – this will incline him to behave opportunistically and thus damage the post-acquisition growth. In the STBF study, two firms with a very low level of growth both had non-offensive motives for selling their businesses; in one firm the founders wanted capital for private consumption, and in the other firm, the founders were simply not interested in running it. Additionally, internationalisation was quite often facilitated by the fact that the small firm used personal contacts and relations belonging to the acquiring firm. Only in one case were the synergies found in the mutual use of an international sales organisation. More common was the large firm helping the smaller firm with personal contacts, in finding both foreign customers and other foreign partners.

Among the synergy effects, realised synergies in R&D were (together with synergies in production) the least common among the various areas of synergies; in only 26 per cent (13 out of 50) of the acquisitions were R&D synergies realised. The important technology synergy effects were found to arise from:

- increased R&D resources
- R&D co-operation
- complementary key knowledge in products and processes
- economies of scale such as the mutual use of R&D equipment
- the mutual use of external and internal experts

An additional synergy effect was sometimes found in an increased motivation among the R&D personnel: for example, when the acquired firm received additional resources and encouragement to continue its own R&D.

One conclusion in the STBF study is that synergies in R&D can be difficult to realise but, when this has been achieved, these synergies are important for post-acquisition growth.

In order to realise synergies in production and marketing, there is a need for the firm to have ready-developed products. If the firm is young or the technology is complex, the firm might not have such products at the time of acquisition. The complexity of the acquired firm's technology is very important for realising different synergies after an acquisition (e.g, in production and marketing). In the acquired firms with a low degree of technology diversification, there are more realised synergy effects in production and marketing than in acquired firms with a high degree of technology diversification.

To summarise, the study has made the following findings regarding the growth and inventiveness of acquired small technology-based firms.

1. The acquired small technology-based firms showed significantly higher growth than the non-acquired firms, totally as well as before and after the acquisition. The growth of the acquired small technology-based firms is higher after acquisition.
2. The acquired small technology-based firms showed significantly higher patent frequency (indicating inventiveness) than the non-acquired small technology-based firms. The patent frequency is not significantly different before and after an acquisition.
3. For post-acquisition growth, the fulfilment of the buyers' and sellers' motives, along with the realisation of technological synergies, are most important. However, fulfilment of the seller's (non-offensive) motive contributes negatively to growth. The results of this study also indicate that, in acquired firms with complex technology, the products were not sufficiently developed in order to fully realise other potential synergies.
4. The high correlation between growth and inventiveness must be remembered, as the two variables influence each other, and are naturally important for the outcome of the technology-related acquisitions.

The ESO Study

In this section, some characteristics of Swedish entrepreneurial spin-offs will be presented, followed by an analysis of the effects on growth, the inventiveness, and the variables influencing the performance of the 60 technology-related firms in the ESO study. Originally, these firms were selected to be included in a study of NTBFs in Sweden (Utterback and Reitberger, 1982; Utterback *et al.*, 1988), but not specifically in order to analyse spin-off firms. Utterback and Reitberger (1982) estimated that the sample (the CPA sample) represented 50 per cent of all NTBFs in the engineering industry in Sweden which were established between 1965 and 1980.

In the ESO study, firms have been categorised as spin-off firms if the original product idea, which led to the establishment of the firm, originated in the previous employer of the founder (such as universities or industrial firms). Adopting this criterion, it was found that, out of the 60 firms in the sample, 30 could be considered as entrepreneurial spin-off firms. Since the sample is estimated to cover approximately 50 per cent of all the new Swedish small technology-based firms, and the distribution can be considered as representative, it can be estimated that half of all new Swedish small technology-based firms are entrepreneurial spin-offs. In addition, as illustrated in Table 11.3, the previous employer was a private firm in the majority of the spin-offs; in fact half of the incubators were manufacturing firms, and an additional seven firms (23 per cent) originated in other private firms.

Table 11.3   Origin of (product) idea that led to the establishment of the 60 small technology-based firms

	Entrepreneurial spin-off	Non-spin-off
University	5 (17%)	3 (10%)
Private firm	22 (73%)	7 (23%)
Other organisation	3 (10%)	–
External inventor	–	5 (17%)
Founder alone	–	15 (50%)
Total	30 (100%)	30 (100%)

Table 11.3 also shows that only a minority of the spin-offs originated in a university. The remaining spin-offs originated in other kinds of organisation, but none of them in a governmental organisation or institute. Almost 75 per cent of the entrepreneurial spin-offs were corporate spin-offs, and 18 per cent university spin-offs. Therefore, it can be argued that private industrial firms in Sweden play a major role as a breeding ground for new firms. In addition to these figures, several of the non-spin-offs originated in ideas generated within other external corporations and universities. A quarter of the non-spin-offs were initiated by ideas originating in private firms (mainly earlier customer contacts) and 10 per cent from universities, with some firms established by external inventors introducing the idea. However, approximately half of the non-spin-offs were based on the founder's own idea. In total, out of the 60 firms, half were spin-

offs, a quarter were established on the founder's own idea, and the remaining quarter were established on external ideas.

In order to understand the spin-off phenomenon, it is important to understand the relationship between the previous employer and the newly established firm, and whether or not there are differences between spin-offs and non-spin-offs. Therefore, the degree of disintegration from the previous employer can be analysed, which in turn is important for potential externalisation disadvantages caused by the spin-off. In Table 11.4, the degree of technology transfer, the degree of competition, and the degree of co-operation between the firms are presented.

Table 11.4   Relation between the previous employer and the new firm

	Entrepreneurial spin-off	Non-spin-off	T-test: Prob. > T
Degree of technology transfer from previous employer (scale 0–4, 0 = none, 4 = direct)	2.79 (n = 29)	2.17 (n = 29)	0.08
Competition with previous employer (scale 0–4, 0 = none, 4 = direct)	1.29 (n = 28)	1.14 (n = 28)	0.62
Co-operation with previous employer (0 = no, 1 = yes)	0.28 (n = 29)	0.16 (n = 25)	0.31

The only significant (at 10 per cent level) difference in the relation with the previous employer, between the spin-offs and the non-spin-offs, is the degree of technology transfer. The spin-offs have enjoyed a higher degree of technology transfer than the non-spin-offs. This seems quite natural, since all entrepreneurial spin-offs have been established on ideas originating from the previous employment. However, no significant differences exist between the two groups of firms when the competition and co-operation with the previous employer are compared. It is notable that among the spin-offs, 28 per cent have developed an on-going relation with the former employer, and that 16 per cent of the non-spin-offs have also developed such a relation. In other words, in almost a third of all the spin-offs studied, the externalisation disadvantages of spin-offs have been curbed by co-operation between the spin-off firm and the spin-off parent.

It is natural for a newly established firm to use the contacts developed in previous employment. In addition, it could rightly be assumed that a significantly higher degree of co-operation and actual contributions should have been found among the spin-offs: since they originated in the business sector of the previous employer, they also ought to be more closely connected with the contacts in this business sector. The results are notable and surprising, as they indicate that the potential advantages of the spin-off process, in an extended systems approach, seem to be utilised neither by the spin-off itself nor by its parent. Nevertheless, it might be that this potential co-operation is destroyed when the spin-off firm and the spin-off parent become competitors, which happens in about a third of the cases.

The ESO Study: The Effect of Spin-Offs on the Growth of Small Technology-Based Firms

As a group, the entrepreneurial spin-offs have grown more rapidly than the non-spin-offs. Neither of the two groups had any significant growth before 1970, when the majority of the firms were established. Not until 1980, at the age of approximately 10 years, did the spin-offs start to outperform the non-spin-offs. After 1980 the mean annual growth in the entrepreneurial spin-offs was 66 per cent, whereas in the non-spin-offs it was only 7 per cent. That is, the annual growth after 1980 was significantly higher (probability $T = 0.001$) in the spin-offs than in the non-spin-offs. Furthermore, in 1991 the mean annual sales in the spin-offs were more than double the sales in the non-spin-offs, as in the entrepreneurial spin-offs it was SEK185 million and in the non-spin-offs it was SEK74 million. It is consistent with the literature (Biggadike, 1979) that significant increases are found first after approximately 10 years, as it often takes this long for a product or a venture to be fully developed and showing signs of growth on the market. One may speculate that when the firm finally starts to grow, the spin-off, as compared to the non-spin-off, will have a potential advantage in developing an ongoing relation with the spin-off parent, taking benefit from a limited disintegration, or quasi-externalisation.

The ESO Study: The Effect of Spin-Offs on the Inventiveness of Small Technology-Based Firms

In the ESO study, the granting of patents is used to represent the invention frequency – inventiveness – which might indicate a future innovation potential of the firms. The analysis shows that there are small differences in the patent frequency between the spin-offs and the non-spin-offs, but also that the entrepreneurial spin-offs show higher inventiveness during a few years after 1978. In the time period after 1978, there is also a positive correlation between growth and inventiveness in the spin-offs. Table 11.5 summarises the differences in patent frequency and total number of patents between the two groups.

There are no significant differences in inventiveness between the spin-offs and the non-spin-offs. On the contrary, the firms show quite similar patent performance. The total number of patents is somewhat higher among the spin-offs, as is the patent frequency after 1978. These differences are, however, so small that they may be disregarded.

Table 11.5   Inventiveness in the entrepreneurial spin-offs and non-spin-offs: patent frequency and total number of patents

Mean values	*Entrepreneurial spin-off*	*Non-spin-off*	*Prob.* > *T*
Patent frequency (patents/year)	0.11	0.12	0.92
Total number of patents/firm	2.73	2.64	0.94
Patent frequency after 1978	0.17	0.16	0.82
Total number of patents after 1978	2.40	2.18	0.83

Entrepreneurial Spin-Offs: Variables Influencing the Growth and Inventiveness

Variables influencing the differences in growth and inventiveness can be found in, and classified into, two groups:

- pre-spin-off variables
- post-spin-off development variables

The first group of variables is used to analyse whether the background or origin of the firms is important for the subsequent growth and inventiveness of the spin-offs, and whether there are different variables – because of the origin of the product idea – influencing spin-offs and non-spin-offs. The pre-spin-off variables include several factors, such as:

(a) the circumstances at the previous employer causing the founders to establish the new firms;
(b) why no development of the idea was made within the previous employment firm;
(c) the kind of parent company;
(d) the personal motives of the founders;
(e) the technology transfer from the previous employer;
(f) the arising competition and co-operation with the previous employer.

It can be speculated that spin-off motives cause different effects on growth depending on whether they are offensive or defensive: for example, if the firm is established because the founder sees an opportunity ('pull') or if he is 'pushed' away because of problems within his employment. Additionally, whether the previous employer was a private firm with market contacts, or a university without such contacts, can be assumed to influence the growth of the firm. To some extent, the degree of technology transfer, along with co-operation and competition, characterises the dependence and similarity between a spin-off firm and its parent. It can be speculated that, the higher the degree of transfer, the more familiar the spin-off will be with the industry or the market which, in turn, may enhance growth.

However, in a test made of a linear growth model of pre-spin-off variables explaining growth, none of the variables above could explain the differences in growth. Several attempts were made but no variables proved significant, as they could not explain anything at all of the growth of the firms. Thus, it can be concluded that the pre-spin-off variables (presented above) analysed within this study have no direct influence on the growth of the firms investigated.

Neither could a linear model of pre-spin-off variables explain inventiveness in any detail. Also, it is further underlined that the inventiveness is not affected by whether the firm is a spin-off or not. In the pre-spin-off model, only one of the variables in the model has a significant influence on inventiveness: when the founder is 'pushed' away because his ideas are not utilised within his previous employment, this has a serious negative effect on the inventiveness. This indicates either that the founder was unsuccessful in utilising his own ideas, or that the ideas were actually no good or not patentable. As also speculated in earlier studies (e.g., Roberts, 1991b), founders with defensive motives are not likely to take advantage of new technology and business opportunities.

However, it is possible that there exists an influence from the previous employment which will affect the later post-spin-off development of the firms, and that several of the potential explanatory variables in the post-spin-off development can be affected by the previous employment. For example, a founder of a spin-off may feel more familiar and comfortable working in a large company, so that he later wants to sell the firm instead of managing it himself.

In the statistical analysis, it was found that the growth of spin-offs is positively affected in firms that have divested minority shares at a low age. Possibly these spin-offs were financially and managerially helped by their minority investors, and thus able to invest and enhance growth. Whilst the number of foreign subsidiaries explains almost all of the growth in the spin-offs, it could not explain any of the growth in the non-spin-offs. Also, early internationalisation (low age when the first foreign subsidiary was established), which was made possible by contributions from the minority investors, contributed to the growth of the spin-offs. However, whilst the number of own acquisitions affects the growth negatively, if the firm has made technology-related acquisitions this contributes positively to the growth. It may be that the spin-offs, because of the high technology transfer from the previous employer, are more technically sophisticated, and thus better able to manage a technology-related acquisition. Technologically sophisticated products often focus on small market niches, which makes internationalisation necessary for the firm to grow. In consequence, it is logical that the number of foreign subsidiaries and early internationalisation are important for the growth of the spin-offs.

It should also be remembered that there was a delay of several years before the inventiveness and the growth of the spin-offs began to increase. This may be due to the fact that the spin-offs benefited from earlier inventive work undertaken for the previous employer, and thus the initial inventive work in the spin-offs may not be focused upon to the same extent as in the non-spin-offs. Only in later product generations do the spin-off firms increase their inventiveness. If this is so, it is natural that the spin-offs enjoy an advantage over the non-spin-offs, since the spin-offs will then initially be able to focus on marketing and growth instead of product development.

Therefore, it can be concluded that, after a 10-year period, the entrepreneurial spin-offs were growing significantly more than the non-spin-offs, but there was no difference in inventiveness between the two groups of firms. The pre-spin-off variables could not explain the growth differences in the firms, and neither were they important for explaining the inventiveness. Rather, the growth was influenced by variables in the post-spin-off development phase.

The inventiveness was negatively affected when the founder had a defensive motive for establishing the firm. It was assumed that the entrepreneurial spin-offs had an indirect advantage in the inventive work, with initially more developed products, allowing them to focus on the growth of the firm.

DISCUSSION

In the first two parts of this section, the empirical findings on the acquisitions and spin-offs will be discussed and compared to the findings of earlier research. The final part of this section is based on Lindholm's (1994) proposition of an extended system. An economic system, including both technology-related acquisitions and spin-offs, is outlined and presented.

Technology-Related Acquisitions

In this century, a huge body of literature concerning acquisitions and the outcome of acquisitions has been produced. From the research, it is clear that there is a need to distinguish between different kinds of acquisitions and different motives. Nevertheless, technology-related acquisitions are rarely analysed: instead, the classification within earlier research tends to be based on Rumelt's (1974) definition of diversification relatedness. However, a further qualification of the classification, with emphasis on technology-related acquisitions and spin-offs, has been made by Lindholm (1994). Despite this, the focus of earlier research on acquisitions will make it difficult to compare the technology-related acquisitions of this study with the earlier findings of related or unrelated acquisitions.

Acquisition performance

The findings of this study demonstrate that the growth in the acquired firms was significantly higher than in the non-acquired firms. The acquired firms also had higher growth prior to, as well as after, acquisition, and their growth increased after acquisition. These findings support the suggestion that acquired technology-based firms outperform independent businesses, something Gallagher and Miller (1989) could not prove. The findings are in line with Granstrand and Sjölander (1990b), who found that acquired small technology-based firms increased their growth after acquisition. Therefore, the finding of Lipsey and O'Connor (1982) regarding decreased post-acquisition growth is not supported for technology-related acquisitions.

Additionally, despite the growth of the acquired small technology-based firms being higher before acquisition, it can be argued that this is not the reason for their acquisition. In relation to the acquiring firm, the size and pre-acquisition growth of a small technology-based firm are often negligible. Instead, it can be argued that small technology-based firms are acquired because of future potential in their products and technology. In this study, it was also found that the acquired small technology-based firms had a higher patenting rate than the non-acquired small technology-based firms, and that the acquired firms continued to be innovative after acquisition. This may indicate that the acquiring firm acquires innovative firms and (often) successfully manages them in a way that allows continued innovativeness.

Variables Influencing the Performance of Acquired Small Technology-Based Firms

The acquisition performance is influenced by several explanatory variables, and can be affected by the actions taken after an acquisition. Some of these variables are very different with respect to technology-related acquisitions, as compared to other acquisitions, with several of the explanatory variables in the pre-acquisition phase, identified by earlier research (see Lindholm, 1994), proving to be essential for the performance of the technology-related acquisitions. The acquisition initiative and the motives, as well as the transaction times used for evaluation of the candidate, are all important ingredients of an acquisition strategy. In earlier studies, both the length of the transaction time and the use of an 'earnout' formula were found to be important for the acquisition outcome. The importance of the acquisition strategy was discussed in several earlier studies, and is further underlined in this study.

In line with the findings of Ansoff *et al.* (1971), it was demonstrated that technological synergies are seldom realised. However, when they do occur, they are highly important for growth. Technology-related acquisitions can be assumed to differ from other acquisitions, and the value of the realised technology synergies might be higher in technology-related acquisitions. Additionally, when compared to Kitching's (1967, 1973) findings of pay-off from synergies, the financial synergies might indeed be the ones that are most easily realised in technology-related acquisitions as well. However, in general, the financial synergies do not contribute to performance in the technology-related acquisitions. Indeed, despite the fact that lack of capital was the most usual reason for selling a small Swedish technology-based firm, the most important of the financial synergies after the acquisition was the financial security of having a large owner, not the financial resources and contributions from the parent. It can be argued that for the post-acquisition performance of technology-related acquisitions, the value of the realised financial synergies is less important than that of the realised technology synergies.

In the STBF study, it was argued that the higher initial growth of the acquired firms is correlated with a successful technology, and that firms with a successful or promising technology are more likely to become acquisition targets. It was also speculated that when the degree of technology complexity is high, the product development will be more difficult, will take longer to develop and, consequently, the small firm is sold in order to receive capital for further development. In those cases, the firm might not yet have ready-developed products or a proven technology at the time of acquisition. The timing of an acquisition is crucial for successfully combining the advantages of the large and the small firm: without ready-developed products, complementary assets of the small and the large firm will be of less importance, and the potential synergy effects are hard to realise. This would imply that the more complex and unproved the technology of the acquisition target, the higher the risk for the acquiring firm and the longer the time needed before synergies can be realised. Additionally, when the acquired firms had ready-developed products, the marketing synergies were found to be important for the growth of these acquisitions.

As argued above, the realisation of marketing synergies is dependent on whether the acquired firm has any ready-developed products. But the marketing synergies seem to enhance a future inventiveness, and since the inventiveness is correlated to the growth there seems to be a 'snowball effect' for the marketing synergies. A further qualification of the importance of the marketing synergies is that they seem to be especially important for inventiveness when the realised financial synergies are low (Lindholm, 1994). As was argued above, contrary to the pre-acquisition beliefs of the seller, the financial synergies did not contribute to the post-acquisition growth; rather the ambition of the acquired firm was sometimes lowered when all its financial needs were fulfilled after the acquisition. In addition, for marketing synergies to be realised, a low integration of the managerial systems is also important.

In technology-based firms, the managers and key technological personnel are often the same people. Losing key personnel can seriously damage the firm, and result in a loss of motivation among the remaining personnel (Lindgren, 1982; Jacobsson, 1984; Shirvastava, 1986). The continued motivation of personnel is important for the post-acquisition performance, and the loss of key personnel after acquisition can have grave indirect effects, both on the motivation of the personnel (and thus the realisation of the marketing synergies) and on the technological diversification.

Technology-Related Spin-Offs

Existing literature on spin-offs is by no means as extensive as the literature on acquisitions. As was pointed out earlier, the spin-off concept includes both divestments and entrepreneurial spin-offs, while the existing literature most often deals with one of these. Also, in this study the corporate spin-offs are focused upon before university spin-offs. In this section, the empirical findings on the spin-offs will be discussed and compared to the findings of earlier research.

The Spin-Off Frequency

In the ESO study, whilst the sample consisted of mainly independently established firms, all the spin-offs found in this sample are entrepreneurial spin-offs. There were more than four times as many corporate as university spin-offs. However, if the number of employees in universities is compared to the number of employees in private firms, it is possible and can be hypothesised that the frequency of spin-offs per capita is higher from the universities than it is from the private firms.

The distribution of corporate and university spin-offs can be compared to the findings of Cooper (1971a), who in his first study found only 3 per cent of the spin-offs to have been spun off from non-profit organisations, while the corresponding figure in a second study was 25 per cent (Cooper, 1984). Cooper compared this to the findings of Roberts (1968), and argued that in the Boston area, the proportion of university spin-offs seemed to be higher. However, one important distinction between Roberts's findings, and those by Cooper and this study, is that in Roberts's study, every firm with a founder who had ever worked for the university laboratory is included in the data: that is, Roberts does not analyse the proportion of founders who had been employed in an industrial firm and possibly gained additional key knowledge within that firm. When only the last previous employer is analysed, the finding of 17 per cent university spin-offs in this study supports Cooper's low figures.

Nevertheless, the universities may have an important indirect role for spin-offs. Among the non-spin-off firms in the sample, 10 per cent had gained their idea for start-up from a university. It can be hypothesised that the combination of a university employment followed by an industrial employment causes a higher proportion of spin-offs. Under such circumstances the possibilities for the founder to have both technological, as well as industrial and business knowledge, increases.

Additionally, the literature reveals conflicting views of what size of company creates the higher share of spin-offs. In some studies, the large firms are argued to be more favourable to the formation of spin-offs. In others, small businesses are found more likely to spin off new firms (Cooper, 1971a, 1973, 1984; Bollinger, Hope and Utterback, 1983; Dorfman, 1983; Bruno and Tyebjee, 1984). Dorfman (1983) argued that, besides universities, a main source of technology-related spin-offs is other technology-related spin-offs, although in contrast, Granstrand and Alänge (1995) found large industrial corporations as incubators in more than half of the start-up companies in Sweden. Primarily, this underlines the importance of the employment and training within a large firm (an indirect and contributory incubator) rather than the importance of the large firm as a direct or main incubator.

In the ESO study, half of the corporate spin-offs are spun off from industrial manufacturing firms and, of these, two-thirds of the founders had previously worked in a small company. Therefore, although the sample is limited, it supports the suggestion that small firms are the main source of direct entrepreneurial spin-offs. However, the importance of different incubator systems, including constellations of 'main' and 'contributory' incubators, has not been analysed. Also, spin-off frequencies are only measured as absolute frequencies, and not as relative frequencies (such as 'spin-offs per capita'). It is possible to hypothesise that entrepreneurial spin-offs from a small firm are most common, but that the most efficient spin-off procedure occurs when this is coupled with the earlier positions (in different kinds of organisations) of the spin-off founders, all contributing as incubators. There is therefore a need for additional research in which the roles of incubators are more fully developed and analysed.

The Spin-Off Motives

An entrepreneurial spin-off may take place no matter what the opinion or motive of the spin-off parent. For example, if an entrepreneur is not satisfied with his employment and instead wants to start a business of his own, he might do this without regard to the wishes and ambitions of his employer. Under such circumstances it is possible that the spin-off will be hostile, and that the parent and the spin-off will become competitors developing the same technology. On the other hand, divestments are often made as a result of the parent's business strategy; when the parent organisation has decided to divest a certain business or development project, the wishes of the single entrepreneur (or key personnel) are likely to be of less importance. Under such circumstances – where the ideas of the entrepreneur might not be taken care of – it is possible that the entrepreneur will leave the parent organisation and establish a spin-off.

In earlier research on entrepreneurial spin-offs, the motives of the founder are often discussed in terms of 'offensive-pull' or 'defensive-push' motives (Cooper, 1973; Smilor, 1987, Dietrich and Gibson, 1990). In the examples above, the entrepreneur leaving because of the divestment could be considered as having a 'defensive-push' motive, while the classification of motive in the other example (of the entrepreneur in the hostile spin-off) will depend upon whether his dissatisfaction or future ideas could be considered as most important. Lindgren (1982) found defensive motives to be more usual than offensive ones. In the ESO study, more than half of the spin-off founders have a defensive motive, and are 'pushed' away from the earlier employment. Here, three different reasons are equally frequent for pushing the founder to leave:

- employer closed down
- employer bought up or was thinking of selling
- an internal crisis within the firm

However, these 'defensive motives' were similarly important for founders of non-spin-offs leaving their earlier employment. Despite this, 13 of the 30 spin-offs' founders had left their previous employment because their ideas were not utilised, whilst this was the case in only one-sixth of the non-spin-off firms.

Relation Between Spin-Off Firm and Spin-Off Parent

Of additional interest, indicating a future potential of both the spin-off firm and the parent, is the relation that develops between the two firms after the spin-off. This is something that has only been analysed to a limited extent in the literature (e.g., by Smilor, 1987). In the two case studies of large technology-based firms, both divesting and spinning off units, Lindholm (1994) found that after a divestment – where the firm received a new owner – a continued co-operation between the spin-off parent and the firm was unusual. However, among the entrepreneurial spin-offs, an ongoing relation, including different kinds of co-operation, was most often developed. In several cases, the continued co-operation was established by formal contracts. However, even when the spin-off parent had no ambition to co-operate with the spin-off and no contracts were established, informal contacts and co-operation were often developed. Personal contacts between the spin-off founder and his earlier colleagues continued to be important after spin-off, and sometimes resulted in other employees establishing small firms for 'moonlight consulting' in the spin-off firm. Further, in the ESO study it was indicated that in one-third of the spin-offs, an ongoing relation develops after the spin-off event. Yet this was not significantly more than in the non-spin-offs, where an ongoing relation with the former employer was developed in 18 per cent of the cases. On the other hand, it is as unusual for the spin-offs to become competitors with their former employer as it is for the non-spin-offs.

As was also found by Roberts (1991b), there is a higher degree of technological transfer from the earlier employer to the entrepreneurial spin-offs than there is to the non-spin-offs. The higher degree of technological transfer indicates that the spin-off and the parent are often, at least initially, developing similar technology, but possibly for different applications. This could show a higher potential for (technology) co-operation between the parent and the spin-off, a potential that is currently not always taken advantage of. In the LTBF case studies (see Lindholm, 1994), it was indicated that the spin-off firm, but not the spin-off parent, was often well aware of the advantages (for both firms) of a continued relation with its spin-off parent. It can be speculated that it is often the parent's low interest in a continued relation that hinders more substantial co-operation. The only time when entrepreneurial spin-offs seemed to be encouraged within the parent firm was when personnel reductions became necessary. It seems that, rather than co-operating with their own spin-offs, such as in sponsored spin-offs, parents often favour acquisitions of, or minority investments in, external technology-based firms.

The negative attitude towards spin-offs may need to change in order to benefit more from potential synergies between spin-offs and spin-off parents. For example, in the works by Roberts, he changed his earlier view (1968) that an incubator would suffer from spin-offs, to encourage the potential incubator to produce spin-offs (1991b), arguing that the spin-off firm is more often formed from general technological skills (tacit knowledge) than from specific proprietary knowledge. His argument is supported by the findings of the ESO study (for further details, see Lindholm, 1994): very few of the entrepreneurial spin-offs bring (or steal) any proprietary knowledge or assets from their previous employers. Apart from the degree of technology transfer, there is surprisingly little difference between spin-offs and non-spin-offs with regard to the different contributions from the earlier employer. Possibly, the lack of substantial contributions (in the entrepreneurial spin-offs) may be an additional result of the large firm's negative attitude towards spin-offs.

Spin-Off Performance

Few studies analysing the total performance of either the growth, or the inventiveness, of entrepreneurial spin-offs have been found, even though several authors have found the spin-offs themselves to have both a high survival rate and high growth, as well as a high degree of technology transfer (Roberts, 1968; Roberts and Wainer, 1968; Cooper, 1971a; Utterback, 1974; Dietrich and Gibson, 1990). Nevertheless, Roberts (1968), Dietrich and Gibson (1990) and Smilor, Gibson and Kozmetsky (1988) have examples where the incubator firm is spinning off new firms, which some years later are (together) more than double the size of the parent. These examples can only serve as illustrations of the potential importance of the performance in entrepreneurial spin-offs. The studies do not analyse the impact on the spin-off parent, and neither do they compare the growth of the spin-offs to the growth of other new firms. Additionally, they do not conclude what conditions have caused the firms to grow, and whether these conditions are different in spin-offs as compared to non-spin-offs. Naturally, it is hard to demonstrate any effects of spin-offs upon the growth of the spin-off parents, since the spin-offs are so much smaller.

In the ESO study, the growth of the spin-offs was compared with the growth of the non-spin-offs. It was demonstrated that the two groups had about the same (low) growth for the first 10 years of their lifetime. However, after this time, the relative annual growth was significantly higher within the entrepreneurial spin-offs. After an additional period of about 10 years, the mean value of the sales within the spin-offs was approximately twice as high as the sales of the non-spin-offs. That it took so many years for the differences to emerge further underlines the need to include a relatively long time period when analysing technology-based firms. Considering the conclusion by, for example, Biggadike (1979) that a new venture needs 8 years to reach profitability, it seems natural to find the first growth difference (between the spin-offs and the non-spin-offs) after a period of about 10 years.

Variables Influencing the Spin-Off Performance

Naturally, the performance in the entrepreneurial spin-offs is influenced by several explanatory factors. However, there is little evidence, from previous studies, of the identification of the pre-spin-off variables which can affect the performance of the subsequent spin-off firms. Instead, researchers have focused on discussing different circumstances which can be efficiency-inducing, rather than on analysis of specific explanatory variables; one exception is the work of Kudla and McInish (1988), which indicated that the size of an equity in a spin-off directly affects its subsequent performance. The ESO study also found that the performance of spin-offs could not be explained by pre-spin-off variables, and that variables in the post-spin-off development were much more important for the growth of the firm.

The suggestion by Bruno and Tyebjee (1984) that the firm would benefit from outside minority investment is supported by the findings of the ESO study. However, that the spin-off should benefit from the technology transfer from the source organisation (Roberts, 1968; Roberts and Wainer, 1968) is not supported in terms of increased growth. The higher growth of the entrepreneurial spin-offs (as compared to non-spin-offs) emerges only 10 years after the establishment of the firm, and it seems that this increase is not (directly) influenced by either the spin-off decision or the spin-off parent. Still, it is possible that the earlier employment within the spin-off parent has indirectly influenced the performance in the entrepreneurial spin-off.

In the ESO study, the technology transfer from the earlier employment was higher for the spin-offs than for the non-spin-offs. Additionally, the spin-off firms were found to have a higher degree of newness of the technology employed within the firm. It is therefore possible that, rather than having a direct influence on the performance, this would suggest that the spin-offs to be better equipped for developing new inventions. However, in comparing the spin-offs with the non-spin-offs, both types of firm have approximately the same inventiveness, with no difference in either the number of patents per year or in the total number of patents.

Above, it was argued that the spin-off firms have the initial advantage of more developed products as a result of technology transfer from their earlier employment. Therefore, these firms would initially not have to undertake much of the initial inventive work and could developed a marketable product more quickly, which then can contribute sooner to increased growth. Also, the comparatively lower need for initial innovative work could free resources, which can then be used in the business's development and the growth of the firm. The non-spin-offs would have to devote relatively more resources to the initial inventive work before they could start to expand the business and growth of the firm. Hence the degree of technology transfer from the spin-off parent can be assumed to contribute indirectly to the development and growth of the spin-off.

A System Of Ownership Changes

In the introduction to this chapter, the idea of an 'extended systems approach' was presented, which was initially proposed by Lindholm (1994), and partly based on Williamson's (1975) systems approach and the 'systems solution by classical specialisation' of an efficient innovation process. Williamson hypothesised that since large firms may have early-stage disadvantages (but later-stage advantages) in the innovation process, an efficient procedure is to have innovations initially carried out within small firms (or by independent innovators), subsequently acquired by large firms, despite transfer difficulties and transaction costs. Even though Williamson has continued to focus on contracting and transaction costs, he himself has not especially developed his proposed systems solution.

Instead, Granstrand (1982) qualified Williamson's hypothesis, concluding that there are intermediate quasi-integrated forms of R&D organisation, and that these are the most conducive to technological innovation. He further hypothesised that there is a movement towards employing quasi-integrated forms of organisation, while the use of pure market structures and totally integrated structures is being reduced. Examples of quasi-integrated organisations include the acquisition of small innovative firms by large firms, and also small firms which are 'spun off from larger ones as new business development units or exist as a permanent semi-autonomous innovation company for the purpose of acquisition and early stage development of internal and/or external ideas for transfer or divestment in some form at a later stage' (Granstrand, 1982:198). Thus, in the extended systems approach, large and small firms interact through acquisition and spin-off of small technology-based firms. Further, these ownership changes can be made gradually, and thus the firms are interacting in a dynamically changing quasi-integrated (extended) system. By spinning off small technology-based firms for subsequent acquisition, a market for technology-based firms is created as a supplement to other forms of technology markets: that is, on a market for corporate control where both acquisitions and spin-offs are made. When functioning, this market is (under certain conditions) conducive to innovation and technology-based business development.

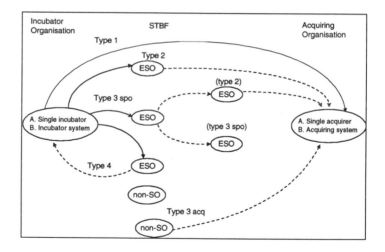

Type spo = spin-off
type acq = acquisition
STBF = Small Technology-Based Firm,
ESO = Entrepreneurial Spin-Off, non-SO = non-spin-off

Figure 11.1   Spin-off and acquisition system of interaction between
technology-based firms: the 'extended system'
(*Source*: Lindholm 1994:232).

Lindholm (1994) introduced an extended system (see Figure 11.1) including four types of (technology-related) ownership changes:

Type 1   *Acquisition of a divestment*: The acquisition of another firm's divestment.

Type 2   *Acquisition of an entrepreneurial spin-off*: The acquisition of a (entrepreneurial) spin-off (including a spin-off of a previous spin-off) by another large firm.

Type 3 (acq) *Acquisition of an independent firm*: The acquisition of an independently established firm (non-spin-off).

Type 3 (spo) *Spin-off of a new firm*: Or the establishment of a new (entrepreneurial spin-off) firm.

Type 4   *Acquisition of own spin-off*: The acquisition of an earlier spin-off firm from one's own organisation, including internal spin-offs.

The technology-related spin-offs are of four different kinds:

(a) a direct divestment;
(b) the creation of a new firm (entrepreneurial spin-off), subsequently acquired by another firm;
(c) continuing as independent;
(d) creation of a new firm that is later re-integrated into the spin-off parent organisation.

Similarly, the acquisitions can be made as:

(a) direct acquisition of other firms' divestments
(b) acquisition of other firms' independently established spin-offs
(c) acquisition of independent non spin-off firms
(d) acquisition of an earlier spin-off from one's own organisation

Furthermore, as indicated above, all ownership changes can be made gradually, and as a result it is possible for a small firm to have several large firms as minority owners (e.g., both an earlier spin-off parent and a future owner).

On empirical grounds (see Lindholm, 1994), it can be concluded that the majority of all acquisitions of small technology-based firms in Sweden are made up of earlier spin-off firms. The frequencies of Type 2 and Type 3 acquisitions are approximately the same, and in addition to these are Type 1 and Type 4 acquisitions. Moreover, it has been estimated that about half of all independent small technology-based firms are entrepreneurial spin-offs (Type 3 spo), and that more than half of all small technology-based firms are later acquired (Types 2 and 3 acq). That is, more than one-quater of all Swedish small technology-based firms are going through both types of ownership changes (spin-off and acquisition): they are established as spin-off firms, and after some years as independent firms, are later acquired by another firm. Therefore, in a systems approach or a systems solution by classical specialisation, the acquisition of earlier spin-offs must be an important complement to the acquisition of independently established small technology-based firms. The procedure by which large firms are spinning off small technology-based firms must then be incorporated into 'extended systems', in which the population of small technology-based firms available for acquisition is increased.

Lindholm (1994) concluded that actually more than half of all technology-related acquisitions consisted of earlier spin-off firms (divestments, entrepreneurial spin-offs, or own/internal spin-offs). From this, it could be hypothesised that the population of technology-based firms available for acquisition by a large firm mostly consists of spin-offs from other firms or organisations. Additionally, among the entrepreneurial spin-offs, the corporate spin-offs are more common than the university spin-offs, and the divestments are, naturally, also spin-offs from other corporations. Therefore, the importance of private existing firms, both small and large, as a source of new technology-based firms for later acquisitions, is underlined.

It has also been concluded that entrepreneurial spin-offs, when compared to non-spin-offs, had a significantly higher growth after the age of 10 years. It was also concluded that technology-related acquisitions increase the growth of the small technology-based firms, and can be important for the growth of the acquirer. Hence the empirical findings indicate that an efficient method within the extended system is to have large and small technology-based firms (or other private firms) spinning off firms which, after being developed and growing independently for about 10 years, are acquired by another firm.

Since both the acquisition frequency and the importance of making technology-related acquisitions are increasing (Lindholm, 1994), the demand for technology-based firms is growing. If the number of firms available for acquisition is not increased, there is an increased risk of opportunism because of a small-numbers situation and, consequently, the transaction costs might increase. Indeed, a small-numbers situation (few available acquisition candidates) can cause a risk of increased acquisition prices and shortened transaction times and, together with opportunism, this will increase the risk of acquisition failures. Since more than half of all technology-related acquisitions originate from the population of spin-off firms, an increased spin-off frequency is (apart from other spin-off benefits) highly important for increasing the population of acquisition candidates, and thus indirectly for reducing the transaction costs of the extended system.

The findings of Cooper (1971a), Dorfman (1983) and Bruno and Tyebjee (1984) suggest that the main source of technology-related spin-offs are other small technology-related spin-offs. Hence it can be argued that previous evidence of entrepreneurship makes future entrepreneurship more likely, with both Cooper and Dorfman indicating the importance for future entrepreneurs of knowing other founders who had taken this step. Therefore, a high spin-off frequency can cause even further spin-offs to take place.

In line with this discussion, successful technology-related acquisitions can also contribute to an increased (entrepreneurial) spin-off frequency. In a successful technology-related acquisition, the potential spin-off entrepreneur in the large technology-based firm will come to know of the successful entrepreneur or founder of the acquired firm. It is also possible to assume that the spin-off frequency would increase because of internal competition and NIH effects, caused by externally acquired technology and firms, which may lead the potential spin-off entrepreneur to leave the parent firm. On the other hand, as argued by Granstrand (1992), an efficiently functioning extended system will include a suitable acquisition mechanism, which might compensate for a possibly too high or misdirected spin-off propensity and too much fragmentation of industry. In other words, when the extended system is functioning, it will be self-regulating in a way that will allow the supply and demand of small technology-based firms to be in balance.

CONCLUSION AND IMPLICATIONS

The specific purpose of the present study has been to analyse the impact of ownership changes, in the form of technology-related acquisitions and spin-offs, upon inventiveness and growth. The basic idea of this work is that an economic system consisting of large and small firms which interact through ownership changes is highly conducive to overall innovativeness and long-term growth. Important implications of the study will be formulated in this section, primarily for managers of large as well as small technology-based firms, but also (to some extent) for different policy-makers. This research area is quite unexplored, and the study has been a first attempt to investigate *both* technology-related acquisition and spin-off mechanisms. Thus the implications drawn here will primarily be stimulative, and more specific conclusions will have to await additional studies.

Implications for Policy-Makers

By definition, both technology-related spin-offs and acquisitions are fundamental and necessary ingredients in an extended systems approach. The spin-off firms are useful for spinning off subtechnologies which are currently not preferred within a certain organisation. In the independent small spin-off firm, small-scale advantages can be utilised in the early stages of the innovation process. Also, the spin-off process allows the less preferred subtechnologies to be further developed, a development that would not certainly have taken place within the incubator organisation. In this context, it can be argued that the spin-off process is likely to increase the overall innovativeness of the total (extended) economic system. Further, it has been demonstrated that after approximately a 10-year period as independent firms, the entrepreneurial spin-offs have a significantly higher growth than other independently established non-spin-off firms. Thus, it can also be argued that the spin-off process is likely to increase the long-term growth of the (extended) system. Additionally, the majority of technology-related acquisitions are made from the population of technology-related spin-offs (entrepreneurial spin-offs and divestments). Hence, without a properly-functioning spin-off mechanism, the population of firms available for acquisition will be decreased. The acquisition mechanism may also suffer because of a limited number of acquisition candidates (with higher acquisition prices as a consequence) and a lack of high-growing entrepreneurial spin-offs as potentially successful candidates.

It has been concluded that the technology-related acquisitions contribute to the growth of the small technology-based firm and, possibly, to the growth of the acquiring firm. Moreover, the inventiveness does not suffer – as sometimes claimed in popular debate – because of technology-related acquisitions. It may then be argued that, on the one hand, technology-related acquisitions and spin-offs are important for the growth and innovativeness of the (extended) system. On the other hand, since often (and at least in Sweden) the majority of the acquired firms are earlier spin-offs, a sufficient population of spin-offs is critical to the (extended) system. Possibly the most important implication for policy-makers concerns the necessary circumstances for establishing a sufficient population of spin-off firms.

In the LTBF case studies (see Lindholm, 1994), it was indicated that the large firms in the extended system were not aware of the potential of the spin-off process, and the spin-offs were seldom sponsored by the large firms. If large firms fail to spin off new firms (with less preferred subtechnologies), this will further underline the importance of having some sort of spin-off promotion policy. Policy-makers should establish a climate which encourages spin-offs, resulting in a sufficient population of – primarily – entrepreneurial spin-offs from both corporate and academic organisations.

Such a promoting policy ought, at least, to provide information and help about the possibilities of research financing and (more practically) the establishment of a new firm. Also, a spin-off promotion policy should include different means by which unpreferred subtechnologies may be identified and externalised from the incubator organisations. In Sweden, there are recent examples of university spin-off-promoting activities, both government-initiated and university-initiated. In addition to these efforts, some spin-off promoting activities for corporate spin-offs ought also to be considered, such as a 'technology transfer advisory committee' acting independently in relation to, but including contacts with, established firms. In other words, policy-makers should encourage both the potential spin-off founders and potential incubator organisations to take part in the spin-off process.

Implications for Practitioners

Important implications for managers concern both technology-related spin-offs and acquisitions. First, it has been argued that the large technology-based firms may not take full advantage of the potential benefits of the spin-off process. By actively engaging in internal development ventures and friendly spin-offs, the small-scale advantages early in the innovation process could be better utilised. It seems that large firms use divestments, especially of earlier acquired units, in order to dispose of unwanted business or unsuccessful units, but that they are relatively unsuccessful in divesting new internal technology ventures. The main difference results from whether or not the divesting firm is able to find an acquirer. Quite naturally, a subsequent acquirer prefers to acquire (and may also pay a higher price for) ventures with more ready-developed technology, than units (or licences) that require additional technology development resources, which the acquirer may not have. This may be especially so when the current technology of the potential acquirer is not related to the technology of the venture, and there are no perceived potential technology synergies.

When a spin-off parent wants to dispose of such a venture, without any interested external acquirers, the only alternatives may be either to disclose the development or to engage in an entrepreneurial spin-off. Often, the first of these is preferred, because the parent does not recognise the potential benefits of the spin-off process. Rather, the potential spin-off parent seems to avoid entrepreneurial spin-offs because of the risk of losing competent personnel and proprietary knowledge, and the risk that later the personnel may also turn into competitors. Actually, as argued in this study (as well as by Roberts, 1991b), entrepreneurial spin-offs are more often formed from general technological skills than from proprietary knowledge. Also, it was found that almost half of all spin-off founders left their prior employer when their ideas were not utilised. Thus, when a spin-off parent (an incubator) discloses a certain technology, and tries to hinder an entrepreneurial spin-off, there is a risk that this will result in a hostile spin-off.

Naturally, in a hostile spin-off the benefits to the incubator organisation will be relatively low, especially when compared to the potential benefits of friendly and sponsored spin-offs. In friendly spin-offs, there are potential benefits of post-spin-off co-operation which can help both firms. In a sponsored spin-off, this potential can be quite well developed and, if properly managed, can result in several externalisation disadvantages being avoided. The sponsored spin-off, including the spin-off parent holding a minority share in the entrepreneurial spin-off, may be an efficient procedure for combining large- and small-scale innovation advantages. It is also possible that, after some time of development within the spin-off, there will be opportunities for a subsequent reintegration into the large firm, or there might be a subsequent acquisition made by an external firm. In both cases, the spin-off parent is likely to benefit either from the reintegration, or from the price paid in the external acquisition (a 'time-delayed divestment' in the view of the incubator organisation.)

Some managerial implications concerning the technology-related acquisitions can also be discussed. It has been argued that acquisition includes potential advantages (with lowered transaction costs) because of the internalisation. Additionally, technology-related acquisitions may increase the possibilities of both technology and product diversification and also, to some extent, market diversification. The sourcing of technology from outside the organisation is becoming increasingly important for large technology-based firms. In areas of rapid and expensive technology development, it can be costly to develop all subtechnologies internally, and to source technology externally may save both time and costs. However, for the long-run competitiveness of the organisation, it is often important for the competitiveness of the firm to have at least some of the current and future core technologies developed internally. Among the external sourcing strategies, it may be argued that the technology-related acquisitions have some advantages because of the integration and internalisation possibilities. Nevertheless, external technology sourcing must be complemented by an internal technology development, and it is also important that technology-related acquisitions are complemented by the acquirer's internal technology. Without an internal technology development, the acquiring organisation may have difficulties in realising technology synergies and in the continued development of the acquired technology. It is an important managerial task to find a balance between internal technology development and external technology acquisition, and for this to result in well-formulated and managed acquisition strategies.

Finally, it is important for managers to consider both the acquisition and spin-off processes of the (extended) system. A technology-related acquisition is usually the result of technology development undertaken in another parent organisation (and is therefore part of a spin-off process). Similarly, a spin-off from this organisation may very well, either directly or later on, be acquired by another large technology-based firm. The organisational arrangements of the extended systems approach are dynamically changing and are never frozen in a given structure. The benefits of the system include both various acquisition and spin-off advantages, as well as the size-related innovation advantages of combining large and small firms.

Bibliography

Aaker, D. and Day, G. (1986), 'The Perils of High Growth Markets' *Strategic Management Journal*, Vol. 7, pp. 409–21.

Abbanat, R.F. (1967), 'Strategies for Size', PhD dissertation, Harvard University.

Achilladis, B., Robertson, A. and Jervis, P. (1971), *Project SAPPHO: A Study of Success and Failure in Innovation*, two volumes, (University of Sussex: Science Policy Research Unit).

Acs, Z.J. and Audretsch, D.B. (1988), 'Innovation and firm size in manufacturing', *Technovation*, Vol. 7, pp. 197–210.

Acs, Z.J. and Audretsch, D.B. (1990), *Innovation and Small Firms* (Cambridge, Mass.: MIT Press).

Adizes, I. (1987), *Organisationers livscykler* (Malmö: Liber).

Aharoni, Y. (1966), *The Foreign Investment Decision Process* (Cambridge, Mass.: Division of Research, Graduate School of Business Administration, Harvard University).

Ahola, E. (1990), *Examples of companies spun off from the Technical Research Center of Finland* (Finland: Espoo).

Aldrich, H. (1979), *Organizations and Environment* (Englewoood Cliffs, NJ: Prentice-Hall).

Aldrich, H.E. (1985), *A Population Perspective of Organisational Change*, Working Paper (Chapel Hill: University of North Carolina).

Aldrich, H.E. and Auster, E.R. (1986), 'Even Dwarfs Started Small: Liabilities of Age and Size and their Strategic Implication', in Aldrich, H.E. (ed.), *Population Perspectives on Organizations* (Uppsala: Acta Universitatis, Studia Oeconomiae, Negotiorum), pp. 29–59.

Aldrich, H.E. and Whetten, D. (1981), 'Organisation-Sets, Action-Sets, and Networks: Making the Most of Simplicity' in Nystrom, P. and Starbuck, W. (eds), *Handbook of Organizational Design*, Volume One (New York: Oxford University Press), pp. 385–408.

Aldrich, H.E. and Zimmer, C. (1986), 'Entrepreneurship through Social Networks', in Sexton, D.L. and Smilor, R.M. (eds), *The Art and Science of Entrepreneurship* (Cambridge, Mass.: Ballinger) pp. 3–23.

Aldrich, J.H. and Nelson, F.D. (1984), *Linear Probability, Logit and Probit Models* (London: Sage).

Allen, P. (1990), 'Why Future is not what it was – New Models of Evolution', *Futures*, July–August, pp. 555–70.

Allen, T. (1977), *Managing the Flow of Technology: Technology Transfer and the Dissemination of Technological Information within the R&D Organization* (Cambridge, Mass.: MIT Press).

Allen, T., Hyman, D. and Pinckney, D. (1983), 'Transferring Technology to the Small Manufacturing Firm: A Study of Technology Transfer in Three Countries', *Research Policy*, Vol. 12, No. 2, pp. 199–211.

Amendola, M. and Bruno, S. (1990), 'The Behavior of the Innovating Firm: Relations to the Environment', *Research Policy*, Vol. 19, pp. 419–33

Andersen, E.S. and Lundvall, B. (1988), 'Small National Systems of Innovation Facing Technological Revolutions: An Analytical Framework', in Freeman, C. and Lundvall, B. (eds), *Small Countries Facing the Technological Revolution* (London: Pinter), pp. 9–36.

Anderson, C.R., and Zeithmal, C.P. (1984), 'Stage of the Product Life Cycle, Business Strategy, and Business Performance', *Academy of Management Journal*, Vol. 27, pp. 5–24.

Ansoff, I. (1965), *Corporate Strategy* (Harmondsworth: Penguin).

Ansoff, I., Brandenburg, G., Portner, F. and Radosevich, R. (1971), *Acquisition Behavior of U.S. Manufacturing Firms, 1946–1965* (Vanderbilt University Press).

Arrow, K.J. (1962), 'Economic Welfare and the Allocation of Resources for Invention', in Nelson, R.R. (ed.), *The Rate and Direction of Inventive Activity* (Princeton University Press), pp. 609–25.

Audretsch, D.B. (1995), *Innovation and Industry Evolution* (Cambridge, Mass.: MIT Press).

Auster, E. (1990), 'The Interorganizational Environment: Network Theory, Tools, and Applications', in Williams, F. and Gibson, D. (eds), *Technology Transfer: A Communication Perspective* (London: Sage), pp. 63–89.

Autio, E. (1993a), *Spin-Off Companies as Agents of Technology Transfer: An Empirical Study of the Spin-off Companies of the Technical Research Centre of Finland* (Espoo: VTT).

Autio, E. (1993b), *Technology Transfer Effects of New, Technology-based Companies: An Empirical Study* (Espoo: Helsinki University of Technology, Institute of Industrial Management, Research reports 1993/1).

Autio, E. (1994), 'New, Technology Based Firms as Agents of R&D and Innovation: An Empirical Study', *Technovation*, Vol. 14, pp. 259–73.

Autio, E. (1995), *Technological and Manufacturing Embeddedness among Traditional and High Technology Small Firms*, 3rd International Conference on High Technology Small Firms, Manchester Business School, 18–19 September.

Autio, E. (1997), '"Atomistic" and "Systemic" Approaches to Research on New, Technology-based Firms: A Literature Study', *Small Business Economics*, forthcoming.

Autio, E. and Hameri, A.-P. (1995), 'The Structure and Dynamics of Technological Systems: A Conceptual Model', *Technology in Society*, Vol.17, pp. 365–84.

Autio, E. and Kauranen, I. (1992), 'Science Parks As Tools of Technology Policy: Some Empirical Evidence', paper presented at the Conference on User-Producer Relations and the Innovation Process, Six Countries Programme, Espoo, November.

Autio, E, Kaila, M., Kanerva, R. and Kauranen, I. (1989), *Uudet teknologiayritykset (New Technology-Based Firms)* (Helsinki: Finnish National Fund for Research and Development), SITRA, B 101.

Ayal I. and Raban J. (1990), 'Developing Hi-Tech Industrial Products for World Markets', *IEEE Transactions on Engineering Management*, Vol. 37, No. 3, pp. 177–83.

Aydalot, P. and Keeble, D. (eds) (1988), *Technology Industry and Innovative Environments: The European Experience* (London: Routledge.)

Badaracco, J. (1991), *The Knowledge Link: How Firms Compete through Strategic Alliances* (Cambridge, Mass.: Harvard Business School Press).

Bailetti, A.J. and Guild, P.D. (1991), 'A Method for Projects Seeking to Merge Technical Advancements with Potential Markets', *R&D Management*, Vol. 21, No. 4, pp. 291–300.

Baker, N., Green, S. and Bean, A. (1985), 'How Management Can Influence the Generation of Ideas', *Research Management*, Vol. 28, No. 6, pp. 35–42.

Balazs, K. and Plonski, G.A. (1994), 'Academic-Industry Relationships in Middle-Income Countries: East Europe and Ibero-America', *Science and Public Policy*, Vol. 21, No. 2, pp. 109–16.

Balconi, M. (1993), 'The Notion of Industry and Knowledge Bases: The Evidence of Steel and Mini-Mills', *Industrial and Corporate Change,* Vol. 2, No. 3, pp. 471–507.

Barber, J., Metcalfe, J.S. and Porteous, M. (1990), *Barriers to Growth in Small Firms* (London: Routledge).

Baumann, D.M. (1981), 'Second Generation Innovation-Center Entrepreneurs', in Vesper, K.H. (ed.), *Frontiers of Entrepreneurship Research* (Wellesley, Mass.: Babson college) pp. 428–42.

Baumback, M.C. and Mancuso, R.J. (1987), *Entrepreneurship and Venture Management*, 2nd edn (Englewood Cliffs, NJ: Prentice-Hall.)

Begley, T.M. and Boyd, D.P. (1986), 'Psychological Characteristics Associated with Entrepreneurial Performance', in Ronstadt, R., Hornaday, J.A., Peterson, R. and Vesper, K.H. (eds), *Frontiers of Entrepreneurship Research* (Wellesley, Mass.: Badson College) pp. 146–65.

Bell, M. and Pavitt, K. (1993), 'Technological Accumulation and Industrial Growth: Contrasts Between Developed and Developing Countries', *Industrial and Corporate Change*, Vol. 2, pp. 157–210.

Bessant, J. (1995), 'Networking as a Mechanism for Enabling Organisational Innovations: The Case of Continuous Improvement', in *Europe's Next Step*, pp. 253–70.

Bhave, M.P. (1994), 'A Process Model of Entrepreneurial Venture Creation', *Journal of Business Venturing,* Vol. 9, pp. 223–42.

Biggadike, R. (1976), *Corporate Diversification: Entry, Strategy and Performance* (Cambridge, Mass.: Division of Research, Graduate School of Business Administration, Harvard University).

Biggadike, R. (1979), 'The Risky Business of Diversification', *Harvard Business Review*, Vol. 57 (May–June), pp. 103–11.

Bilkey, W.J. and Tesar, G. (1977), 'The Export Behavior of Smaller-Sized Wisconsin Manufacturing Firms', *Journal of International Business Studies*, Spring/Summer, pp. 93–8.

Birch, D.L. (1979), *The Job Generation Process. MIT Program on Neighbourhood and Regional Change* (Cambridge, Mass.: MIT Press).

Birley, S. (1985), 'The Role of Networks in the Entrepreneurial Process', in Hornaday, J.A., Shils, E.B., Timmons, J. and Vesper, K.H. (eds), *Frontiers of Entrepreneurship Research* (Wellesley, Mass.: Babson College), pp. 325–37.

Birley, S. and Norburn, D. (1985), 'Small vs. Large Companies: The Entrepreneurial Conundrum', *Journal of Business Strategy,* Vol. 6, No. 1, pp. 81–7.

Birley, S., Cromie, S. and Myers, A. (1991), 'Entrepreneurial Networks: Their Emergence in Ireland and Overseas', *International Small Business Journal*, Vol. 9, No. 4, pp. 56–74.

Boeker, W. (1989), 'Strategic Change: The Effects of Founding and History', *Academy of Management Journal,* Vol. 32, pp. 489–515.

Boissevain, J. (1974), *Friends of Friends: Networks, Manipulators and Coalitions* (Oxford: Basil Blackwell).

Bollinger, L. Hope K. and Utterback, J.M. (1983) 'A Review of Literature and Hypothesis on New Technology Based Firms', *Research Policy*, Vol. 12, pp. 1–14.

Bollinger, L., Hope, K. and Utterback, J.M. (1981), *Technology and Industrial Innovation in Sweden. A Review of Literature and Hypothesis on New Technology-Based Firms* (Stockholm: National Swedish Board For Technical Development).

Bollinger, L., Hope, K. and Utterback, J.M. (1983), 'A Review of Literature and Hypotheses on New Technology-Based Firms', *Research Policy*, Vol. 12, pp. 1–14.

Bolton, J.E. (1971), *Small Firms: Report of the Commission of Inquiry on Small Firms*, Cmnd 4811 (London: HMSO).

Boswell, J. (1972) *The Rise and Decline of Small Firms* (London: Allen & Unwin).

Braden, P.L. (1977), *Technological Entrepreneurship – The Allocation of Time and Money in Technology Based Firms*, Michigan Business Reports, No. 62 (University of Michigan).

Brockhaus, R.H. (1980), 'Risk-Taking Propensity of Entrepreneurs', *Academy of Management Journal*, Vol. 23, No. 3, pp. 509–20.

Brockhaus, R.H. (1982), 'The Psychology of the Entrepreneur', in Kent, C.A., Sexton, D.L., and Vesper, K.A. (eds), *Encyclopaedia of Entrepreneurship*. (Englewood Cliffs, NJ: Prentice Hall), pp. 35–57.

Brockhoff, K. (1985), 'Die Produktinnovationsrate als Instrument der strategischen Unternehmensplanung', *Zeitschrift für Betriebswirtschaft*, Vol. 55, No. 5, pp. 451–76.

Brockhoff, K. and Chakrabarti, A.K. (1988), 'R&D/Marketing Linkage and Innovation Strategy: Some West German Experience', *IEEE Transactions on Engineering Management*, Vol. EM-35, No. 3, pp. 167–74.

Brunner, H. (1991), 'Small Scale Industry and Technology in India: The Case of Computer Industry', *Small Business Economics*, Vol. 3, pp. 121–9.

Bruno, A.V. and Cooper, A.C. (1982), 'Patterns of Development and Acquisitions for Silicon Valley Start-Ups', *Technovation*, Vol. 7, pp. 275–90.

Bruno, A.V. and Tyebjee, T.T. (1984), 'The Entrepreneurs' Search for Capital', in Hornaday, J.A., Tarpley, F., Timmons, J. and Vesper, K.H. (eds), *Frontiers Of Entrepreneurship Research* (Wellesley, Mass.: Babson College), pp. 18–31.

Bruno, A.V., McQuarrie, E.F. and Torgrimson, C.G. (1992), 'The Evolution of New Technology Ventures over 20 Years: Patterns of Failure, Merger and Survival', *Journal of Business Venturing*, Vol. 7, pp. 291–302.

Bryman, A. (1989), *Research Methods and Organisational Studies* (London: Unwin Hyman).

Brynjolfsson, E., Malone, T.W., Gurbaxani, V. and Kambil, A. (1993), 'An Empirical Analysis of the Relationship between Information Technology and Firm Size', mimeo (Cambridge, Mass.: Sloan School of Management, Massachusetts Institute of Technology).

Bullock, M. (1983), *Academic Enterprise, Industrial Innovation, and the Development of High Technology Financing in the United States* (London: Brand Brothers).

Burgelman, R.A. (1983), 'A Process Model of Internal Corporate Venturing In the Diversified Major Firm', *Administrative Science Quarterly*, Vol. 28, pp. 223–44.

Burgelman, R.A. (1985), 'Managing the New Venture Division: Research Findings and Implications for Strategic Management', *Strategic Management Journal*, Vol. 6. No. 1, pp. 39–54.

Burns, T. (1969), 'Models, Images and Myths', in Gruber, W. and Marquis, D., *Factors in the Transfer of Technology* (Cambridge, Mass.: MIT Press), pp. 11–23.

Burt, D.N., Norquist, W.E. and Anklesaria, J. (1990), *Zero Base Pricing™: Achieving World Class Competitiveness through Reduced All-in Costs. A Proactive Handbook for General Managers, Program Managers and Procurement Professionals* (Chicago: Probus).

Burt, R., Minor, M. and Associates (1983), *Applied Network Analysis: A Methodological Introduction* (Beverly Hills, Calif: Sage).

Buzzell, R.D. and Gale, B.T. (1987), *The PIMS Principles* (New York: The Free Press).

Buzzell, R.D. and Wiersema, F.D. (1981), 'Successful Share-Building Strategies', *Harvard Business Review*, Vol. 53, No. 1, pp. 135–44.

Bygrave, W.D. (1988), 'The entrepreneurship Paradigm (I): A Philosophical Look at its Research Methodologies', paper presented at the Entrepreneurship Doctoral Consortium, Babson Research Conference, University of Calgary.

Calvet, A.L. (1981), 'A Synthesis of Foreign Direct Investment Theories and Theories of the Multinational Firm', *Journal of International Business Studies*, Spring/Summer, pp. 43–59.

Cambridge Small Business Research Centre (1992), *The State of British Enterprise* (University of Cambridge: Department of Applied Economics).

Carland, J.W. (1982), 'Entrepreneurship in a Small Business Setting: An Exploratory Study', doctoral dissertation, University of Georgia.

Carlson, S. (1975), *How Foreign is Foreign Trade? A Problem in International Business Research* (Uppsala: Borgströms).

Carlson, S. (1979), *Swedish Industry Goes Abroad – An Essay on Industrialization and Internationalization* (Lund: Studentlitteratur).

Carlsson, B. and Jacobsson, S. (1994), 'Technological Systems and Economic Policy: The Diffusion of Factory Automation in Sweden', *Research Policy*, Vol. 23, pp. 235–48.

Carlsson, B. and Stankiewicz, R. (1991), 'On the Nature, Function, and Composition of Technological Systems', *Journal of Evolutionary Economics*, Vol. 1, pp. 93–118.

Carroll, G.R. and Delacroix, J. (1982), 'Organisational Mortality in the Newspaper Industries of Argentina and Ireland: An Ecological Approach', *Administrative Science Quarterly*, Vol. 27, pp. 169–98.

Carter, C. and Williams, B. (1957), *Industry and Technical Progress: Factors Affecting the Speed and Application of Science* (London: Oxford University Press).

Cavanagh, R.E. and Clifford, D.K. (1983), 'Lessons from America's mid-sized growth companies', *The McKinsey Quarterly*, Autumn, pp. 2–23.

Chakrabarti, A.K. (1990), 'Organizational factors in post-acquisition performance', *IEEE Transactions on Engineering Management*, Vol. 37, No. 4, pp. 259–68.

Chakrabarti, A.K. and Souder, W.E. (1987), 'Technology, Innovation and Performance in Corporate Mergers: A Managerial Evaluation', *Technovation*, No. 6, pp. 103–14.

Chakrabarti, A.K., Hauschildt, J. and Süverkrüp, C. (1994), 'Docs it Pay to Acquire Technological Firms?', *R&D Management*, Vol. 24, No. 1, pp. 47–56.

Chancellor of the Duchy of Lancaster (1993), *Realising Our Potential: A Strategy for Science, Engineering and Technology*, Government White Paper, Report No. CM2250 (London: HMSO).

Chandler, G.N. and Jansen, E. (1988), 'Founding Team Experience and New Firm Performance', in Kirchoff, B.A., Long, W.A., McMullan, W.E., Vesper K.H. and Wetzel, W.E. (eds), *Frontiers of Entrepreneurship Research* (Wellesley, Mass.: Babson College) pp. 106–18.

Channon, D. (1973), *The Strategy and Structure of British Enterprise* (London: Macmillan).

Charles, D.R. (1987), 'Technical Change and the Decentralised Corporation in the Electronics Industry: Regional Policy Implications', in K. Chapman and G. Humphrys (eds), *Technical Change and Industrial Policy* (Oxford: Basil Blackwell) pp.176–98.

Chell, E., Haworth, J.H. and Brearley, S. (1991), *The Entrepreneurial Personality: Concepts, Cases and Categories* (London: Routledge).

Chidamber, A., Shyam, R. and Henry, B. (1994), 'Research Retrospective of Innovation Inception and Success: The Technology-Push, Demand-Pull Question', *International Journal of Technology Management*, Vol. 9, pp. 94–112.

Child, J. and Kieser, A. (1981), 'Development of Organisations over Time', *Handbook of Organisational Design*, ch. 2, pp. 28–58.

Churchill, N.C. and Lewis, V.L. (1983), 'The Five Stages of Small Business Growth', *Harvard Business Review*, Vol. 61, pp. 30–50.

Churchill, N.C. and Lewis, V.L. (1986), 'Entrepreneurship Research : Directions and methods', In Sexton, D.L. and Smilor, R.M. (eds), *The Art and Science of Entrepreneurship* (Cambridge, Mass.: Ballinger), pp. 333–65.

Clark, N. and Juma, C. (1987), *Long-Run Economics: An Evolutionary Approach to Economic Growth*, (London: Pinter).

Cohen, W. and Levinthal, D. (1989), 'Innovation and Learning: The Two Faces of R&D', *The Economic Journal*, Vol. 99, pp. 569–96.

Cohn, T. and Lindberg, R. (1972), *How Management is Different in Small Companies* (New York: Harper & Row).

Collins, O.F., Moore, D.G. and Unwalla, D.B. (1964), *The Enterprising Man* (East Lansing, Michigan: Bureau of Business and Economic Research, Michigan State University).

Committee on Information in the Behavioural Sciences (1967), *Communication Systems and Resources in the Behavioural Sciences* (Washington, DC: National Academy of Sciences).

Contractor, F.J. (1984), 'Choosing between Direct Investment and Licensing: Theoretical Considerations and Empirical Tests', *Journal of International Business Studies*, Winter, pp. 167–88.

Conway, S. (1993), 'The Role of Users in the Innovation Process', Doctoral Working Paper Series, No. 10 (NS), Aston Business School, Aston University, Birmingham.

Conway, S. (1994), 'Informal Boundary-Spanning Links and Networks in Successful Technological Innovation', PhD Thesis, Aston Business School.

Conway, S. (1995), 'Informal Boundary-Spanning Networks in Successful Technological Innovation', *Technology Analysis and Strategic Management,* Vol. 7, No. 3, pp. 327–42.

Coombs, R. and Fontes, M. (1993), *Research and Technology Management in Enterprises: Issues for Community Policy – Case Study on Portugal* (Luxembourg: Commission of the European Communities).

Cooper, A.C. (1970a), *Incubator Organisations, Spin-Offs and Technical Entrepreneurship*, Proceedings of the Indiana Academy of the Social Sciences, 3rd Series, 4.

Cooper, A.C. (1970b), 'The Palo Alto Experience', *Industrial Research*, May, pp. 58–60.

Cooper, A.C. (1971a), 'Spin-Offs and Technical Entrepreneurship', *IEEE Transactions on Engineering Management*, EM-18 No. 1, pp. 2–6.

Cooper, A.C. (1971b), *The Founding of Technologically-Based Firms* (Milwaukee: Center for Venture Management).

Cooper, A.C. (1973), 'Technical Entrepreneurship: What Do We Know?', *R&D Management*, Vol. 3, pp. 59–64.

Cooper, A.C. (1981), 'Strategic Management: New Ventures and Small Business', *Long Range Planning*, Vol. 14, No. 5, pp. 39–45.

Cooper, A.C. (1984), 'Contrasts in the Role of Incubator Organizations in the Founding of Growth-Oriented Firms', in Hornaday, J.A. Tarpley, F., Timmons, J. and Vesper, K.H. (eds), *Frontiers of Entrepreneurship Research* (Wellesley, Mass.: Babson College), pp. 159–74.

Cooper, A.C. and Bruno, A.V. (1977), 'Success among High Technology Firms', *Business Horizons,* Vol. 20, No. 2, pp. 16–22.

Cooper, A.C. and Schendel, D. (1976), 'Stragtegic Responses to Technological Threats', *Business Horizons*, Vol. 19, No.1, pp. 61–9.

Cooper, A.C. and Dunkelberg, W.C. (1981) 'A new look of business entry: experiences of 1805 entrepreneurs', in Vesper, K.H. (ed.), *Frontiers of Entrepreneurship Research* (Wellesley, Mass.: Babson (Centre for Entrepreneurial Studies), pp. 1–20.

Cooper, R.G. (1984), 'New Product Strategies: What Distinguishes the Top Performers?', *Journal of Product Innovation Management*, Vol. 2, No. 2, pp. 151–64.

Cooper, R.G. (1985), 'Overall Corporate Strategies for New Product Programs', *Industrial Marketing Management*, Vol. 14, No. 3, pp. 179–93.

Courtney, N. and Leeming, A. (1994), *Meeting the Needs of Small IT firms*, International Conference on High Technology Small Firms, Manchester Business School, Manchester, September.

Covin, J. and Prescott, J. (1991), 'Strategies, Styles, and Structures of Small Product Innovative Firms in High and Low Technology Industries', *Journal of High Technology Management Research*, Vol. 1, pp. 39–56.

Crane, D. (1972), *Invisible Colleges: Diffusion of Knowledge in Scientific Communities* (University of Chicago Press).

Crevoisier, O. and Maillat, D. (1991), 'Milieu, Industrial Organization, and Territorial Production System: Towards a New Theory of Spatial Development', in Camagni, R. (ed.), *Innovation Networks: Spatial Perspectives* (London and New York: Belhaven Press), pp. 13–34.

Crone, J.L. and Crone, F.D. (1971), 'Some Considerations in Organizational Growth', *Pacific-Sociological Review*, Vol. 3 pp. 30–50.

Cunningham, M. and Homse, E. (1984), *The Role of Personal Contacts in Supplier-Customer Relationships*, Occasional Paper No. 8410 (Manchester: UMIST).

Cusumano, M.A. and Takeishi, A. (1991), 'Supplier Relations and Management: A Survey of Japanese, Japanese-Transplant, and U.S Auto Plants', *Strategic Management Journal*, Vol. 12, No. 8, pp. 563–88.

Cyert, R. and March, J.G.A. (1963), *Behavioral Theory of the Firm* (Englewood Cliffs, NJ: Prentice-Hall).

Dahlman C. and Westphal, L. (1982), 'Technological Effort in Industrial Development – An Interpretative Survey of Recent Research' in Stewart, F. and James, J. (eds), *The Economics of New Technology in Developing Countries* (London: Pinter) pp. 105–137.

Dahmén, E. (1950), *Svensk Industriell Företagsverksamhet – Kausalanalys av den svenska industriella utvecklingen 1919–1939* (Stockholm: Industrins Utvecklingsinstitut).

Dahmén, E. (1953), *Företagsbildning Förr Och Nu*, (Stockholmn).

Davidson, W.H. (1980), 'The Location of Foreign Direct Investment Activity: Country Characteristics and Experience Effects', *Journal of International Business Studies*, Fall, pp.9–22.

Davidson, W.H. and McFetridge, D.G. (1985), 'Key Characteristics in the Choice of International Technology Transfer Mode', *Journal of International Business Studies*, Vol. 16, Summer, pp. 5–21.

Davidsson, P. (1988) 'Type of Man and Type of Company Revisited: A Confirmatory Cluster Analysis Approach', in Kirchoff, B.A., Long, W.A., McMullan, W.E., Vesper, K.H. and Wetzel, W.E. (eds), *Frontiers of Entrepreneurship Research* (Wellesley, Mass.: Babson College), pp. 88–105.

Davidsson, P. (1989), 'Continued Entrepreneurship and Small Firm Growth', Dissertation, Stockholm.

Debackere, K., Clarysse, B., Wijnberg, M. and Rappa, M.A. (1994), 'Science and Industry: A Theory of Networks and Paradigms', *Technology Analysis and Strategic Management*, Vol. 6, No. 1, pp. 21–37.

DeBresson, C. and Amesse, F. (1991) 'Networks of Innovations: A Review and Introduction to the Issue', *Research Policy*, Vol. 20, No. 5, pp. 363–79.

Deeks, J. (1976), *The Small Firm Owner-Manager: Entrepreneurial Behavior and Management Practice*, (New York: Praeger).

Department for Trade and Industry (1991b) *The SMART scheme evalution report* Assessment Paper No. 13.

Dertouzos, M., Lester, R. and Solow, R. (1990), *Made in America: Regaining the Productive Edge* (Cambridge, Mass. : MIT Press).

Dietrich, G.B. and Gibson, D.V. (1990), 'New Business Ventures: the Spin-Out Process', in Williams, F. and Gibson, D.V. (eds), *Technology Transfer – A Communication Perspective* (London: Sage).

Dodgson, M. (1992), 'The Future for Technological Collaboration', *Futures*, Vol. 24, pp. 459–70.

Dodgson, M. and Rothwell, R. (1991), 'Technology Strategies in Small Firms', *Journal of General Management*, Vol. 17, No.1, pp. 45–55.

Dorfman, N.S. (1983), 'Route 128: The Development of a Regional High Technology economy', *Research Policy*, Vol. 12, pp. 299–316.

Dosi, G. (1982), 'Technological Paradigms and Technological Trajectories: A Suggested Interpretation of the Determinants and Directions of Technical Change', *Research Policy*, Vol. 11, pp. 147–62.

Dosi, G. (1988), 'The Nature of the Innovative Process', in Dosi, G., Freeman, C., Nelson, R., Silverberg, G. and Soete, L. (eds), *Technical Change and Economic Theory*, (London: Pinter), pp. 221–38.

Doutriaux, J. and Peterman, B. (1982), *Technology Transfer and Academic Entrepreneurship at Canadian Universities*, (Ottawa: Technological Innovations Studies Program).

Doutriaux, J. and Simyar, F. (1987), 'Duration of the Comparative Advantage Accruing from some Start-Up Factors in High-Tech Entrepreneurial Firms', in Churchill, N.C., Hornaday, J.A., Kirchhoff, B.A., Kranser, C.J. and Vesper, K.H. (eds), *Frontiers of Entrepreneurship Research*. (Wellesley, Mass.: Babson College), pp. 436–51.

Draheim, K.P. (1972), 'Factors Influencing the Rate of Formation of Technical Companies', in Cooper, A.C. and Komives, J.L. (eds), *Technical Entrepreneurship: A Symposium*, (Milwaukee: Center for Venture Management).

Dubini, P. (1988), 'The Influence of Motivations and Environment on Business Start-Ups: Some Hints for Public Policies', *Journal of Business Venturing*, Vol. 4, pp. 11–26.

Duffy, P.D. and Stevenson, H.H. (1984), 'Entrepreneurship and Self-Employment: Understanding the Distinctions', in Hornaday, J.A., Tarpley, F., Timmons, J. and Vesper, K.H. (eds), *Frontiers of Entrepreneurship Research* (Wellesley, Mass.: Babson College) pp. 461–77.

Duhaime, I.M. and Grant, J.H. (1984), 'Factors Influencing Divestment Decision-making: Evidence From A Field Study', *Strategic Management Journal*, Vol. 5, pp. 301–18.

Dunkelberg, W.C. and Cooper, A.C. (1982), 'Entrepreneurial Typologies', in Kent, C.A., Sexton, D.L., and Vesper, K.H. (eds), *Frontiers of Entrepreneurship Research* (Wellesley, Mass.: Babson College), pp. 1–15.

Dunkelberg, W.C. and Cooper, A.C, (1983), 'Financing the Start in a Small Enterprise', in Hornaday, J.A., Timmons, J.A. and Vesper, K.H. (eds), *Frontiers of Entrepreneurship Research* (Wellesley, Mass.: Babson College), pp. 369–81.

Easingwood, C. (1986), 'New Product Development for Service Companies', *Journal of Product Innovation Management*, Vol. 3, No. 4, pp. 264–75.

Eishenhardt, K. and Schoonhoven, C. (1990), 'Organisational Growth: Linking Founding Team, Strategy, Environment, and Growth among US Semiconductor Ventures, 1978–1988', *Administrative Science Quarterly*, Vol. 35, pp. 504–29.

ENSR (1994) *The European Observatory for SMEs – Second Annual Report*, (Zoetermeer, The Netherlands: EIM Business Research and Consultancy).

Ettinger, J. C. (1983), 'Some Belgian evidence on entrepreneurial personality', *European Small Business Journal*, Vol. 1, No. 2, pp. 48–56.

Evan, W. (1965), 'Toward a Theory of Interorganizational Relations', *Management Science*, Vol. 11, No. 10, pp. 217–30.

Fairtlough, G. (1992), 'Three Misconceptions About Innovation', *Technology Analysis and Strategic Management*, Vol. 4, pp. 77–82.

Fast, N.D. (1979), 'Key Managerial Factors in New Venture Departments', *Industrial Marketing Management*, Vol. 8, No. 3, pp. 221–35

Faulkner, W. and Senker, J. (1994), 'Making Sense of Diversity: Public-Private Sector Research Linkage in Three Technologies', *Research Policy*, Vol. 23, pp. 673–95.

Feeser, H. and Dugan, K. (1989), 'Entrepreneurial Motivation: A Comparison of High and Low Growth High Tech Founders', in Brockhaus, R.H., Churchill, N.C., Katz, J.A., Kirchoff, B.A., Vesper, K.H. and Wetzel, W.E. (eds), *Frontiers of Entrepreneurship Research* (Wellesley, Mass.: Babson College), pp. 13–27.

Feeser, H. and Willard, G.E. (1990), 'Founding Strategy and Performance: A Comparison of High and Low Growth High Tech Firms', *Strategic Management Journal*, Vol. 11, No. 2, pp. 87–98.

Feldman, M.P. (1994), 'Knowledge Complementarity and Innovation', *Small Business Economics*, Vol. 6, pp. 363–72.

Firnstahl, T.W. (1986), 'Letting Go', *Harvard Business Review* Vol. 64, No. 5, pp. 14–16.

Flamholtz, E.C. (1986) *How to make the transition from an enterpreneurship to a professionally managed firm* (San Francisco: Jossey Bass Publishers).

Flamholtz, E.G. (1990), *Growing Pains: How to Manage the Transition From An Entrepreneurship to a Professionally Managed Firm* (Oxford: Jossey-Bass).

Fombrun, C. (1982), 'Strategies for Network Research in Organisations', *Academy of Management Review*, Vol. 7, No. 2, pp. 280–91.

Fontes, M. (1995a), *Acquiring the Inputs for NTBF Creation: Technology, Funds and Market Demand. A Case Study on Portugal,* 3rd Annual High Technology Small Firms Conference, Manchester Business School, 18–19 September.

Fontes, M. (1995b), 'New Technology Based Firms and National Technological Capability: The Case of Portugal', PhD Thesis, University of Manchester Institute of Science and Technology, Manchester.

Fontes, M. and Coombs, R. (1995), 'New Technology Based Firms and Technology Acquisition in Portugal: Firms' Adaptive Responses to a Less Favourable Environment', *Technovation*, Vol. 15, pp. 497–510.

Forrest, J.E. and Martin, M.J.C. (1992), 'Strategic Alliances Between Large and Small Research Intensive Organizations: Experiences in the Biotechnology Industry', *R&D Management*, Vol. 22, pp. 41–67.

Forsström, B., Eskelinen, H. and Lindmark, L. (1994), 'Exportföretagen och hemmamarknadsföretagen', in L. Lindmark *et al.* (eds), *Småföretagens internationalisering – en nordisk jämförande studie* (NordREFO).

Freeman, C. (1971), *The Role of the Small Firm in Innovation in the United Kingdom since 1945*, Committee of Inquiry on Small Firms Report No. 6 (London: HMSO).

Freeman, C. (1974) *The Economics of Industrial Innovation* (Harmondsworth: Penguin).

Freeman, C. (1988), 'Technological Gaps, International Trade and the Problems of Smaller and Less Developed Economies', in Freeman, C. and Lundvall, B. (eds), *Small Countries Facing the Technological Revolution* (London: Pinter) pp. 67–84.

Freeman, C. (1991), 'Networks of Innovators: A Synthesis of Research Issues', *Research Policy,* Vol. 20, No. 5, pp. 499–514.

Freeman, J., Carrol, G.L. and Hannan, M.T. (1983), 'The Liability of Newness: Age Dependence in Organisational Death Rates', *American Sociological Review,* Vol. 48, pp. 692–710.

Galbraith, J.K. (1967), *The New Industrial State* (London: Hamish Hamilton).
Galbraith, J. (1982), 'The Stages of Growth', *The Journal of Business Strategy,* Vol. 3, No. 1.
Gallagher, C.C. and Miller, P. (1989), 'The acquisition of high technology firms – An Application of Strategic Groups', paper presented at the SMS Conference on 'The Wave of Mergers, Acquisitions and Alliances', Paris.
Gallagher, C.C. and Miller, P. (1991), 'New Fast Growth Companies Create Jobs', *Long Range Planning,* Vol. 24, No. 1, pp. 96–101.
Garnsey, E. and Roberts, J. (1992), 'Acquisition and Integration of New Ventures; Technology and Culture', in Marceau, J. (ed.), *Organisations, Technologies and Cultures in Comparative Perspective,* Studies in Organisation, No. 42 (De Gruter).
Garnsey, E.W., Galloway, S.C., and Mathisen, S.H. (1994), 'Flexibility and Specialization in Question; Birth, Growth and Death Rates of Cambridge New Technology-Based Firms 1988–92', *Entrepreneurship and Regional Development,* Vol. 6, pp. 81–107.
Gartner, W. (1984), 'Problems in Business Startup: The Relationships Among Entrepreneurial Skills and Problem Identification for Different Types of New Ventures', in Hornaday, J., Tarpley, F., Timmons, J. and Vesper, K.H. (eds), *Frontiers Of Entrepreneurship Research* (Wellesley, Mass.: Babson College), pp. 496–512.
Gartner, W. (1985), 'A Conceptual Framework for Describing the Phenomenon of New Venture Creation', *Academy of Management Review,* Vol. 10, No. 5, pp. 696–706.
Garud, R. and Kumaraswamy, A. (1993), 'Changing Competitive Dynamics in Network Industries: An Exploration of Sun Microsystems' Open Systems Strategy', *Strategic Management Journal,* Vol. 14, pp. 351–69.
Garud, R. and Kumaraswamy, A.(1995), 'Technological and organizational designs for realizing economies of substitution', *Strategic Management Journal,* Vol. 16, No. 1, pp. 93–109.
Gemünden, H.G. and Heydebreck, P. (1994a), 'Geschäftsbeziehungen in Netzwerken' Instrumente der Stabilitätssicherung und Innovation', in Kleinaltenkamp, M. and Schubert, K. (eds), *Netzwerkansätze im Business-to-Business Marketing. Absatz, Beschaffung und Implementierung Neuer Technologien* (Wiesbaden: Gabler, pp. 251–84).
Gemünden, H.G and Heyderbreck, P. (1994b), 'Matching Business Strategy and Technological Network Activities – the Impact on Success', in Biemans, W.G. and Ghauri, P.N. (eds), *Meeting the Challenges of New Frontiers,* Conference Proceedings of the X. IMP Conference, Groningen, Netherlands, 29–30 September, pp. 534–53.
Gemünden, H.G. and Heydebreck, P. (1994c), 'Technological Interweavement – A Key Success Factor for New Technology-Based Firms', in Sydow, J. and Windeler, A. (eds), *Management interorganisationaler Beziehungen. Vertrauen, Kontrolle und Informationstechnik* (Opladen: Westdeutscher Verlag), pp. 194–211.
Gemünden, H.G. and Heydebreck, P. (1995a), *Innovationskooperationen und Innovationserfolg – Eine empirische Analyse kleiner und mittlerer Unternehmen in Spitzentechnologiebranchen,* Final Report for the German Federal Ministry of Education, Science, Research and Technology (Karlsruhe University: IBU).

Gemünden, H.G. and Heydebreck, P. (1995b), 'The External Links and Networks of Small Firms – their Role and Nature', in O'Doherty, D.P (ed.), *Globalisation, Networking and Small Firm Innovation* (London: Graham & Trotman), pp. 87–100.

Gemünden, H.G. and Heydebreck, P. (1995c), 'The Influence of Business Strategies on Technological Network Activities', *Research Policy*, Vol. 24, pp. 831–49.

Gemünden, H.G., Heydebreck, P. and Herden, R. (1992), 'Technological Interweavement: A Means to Achieve Innovation Success', *R&D Management*, Vol. 22, No. 4, pp. 359–376.

Geust, N. and Autio, E. (1994), *External Technology Interfaces of New, Technology-Based Companies* (Helsinki University of Technology: Institute of Industrial Management, Espoo, Research Publications).

Gibb, A.A. and Ritchie, J. (1981) *The Shell Entrepreneurs Part 1: Entrepreneurialism as a Social Process towards a Framework for Analysis and Understanding* (Durham University: Business School Working paper).

Gibb, A.A. and Scott, M. (1986), 'Understanding Small Firms Growth', in Scott, M., Gibb, A.A., Lewis, J. and Faulkner, T. (eds), *Small Business Growth and Development* (Aldershot: Gower), pp. 81–104.

Gibbons, M. and Johnston, R. (1974), 'The Roles of Science in Technological Innovation', *Research Policy*, Vol. 3, pp. 220–42.

Gibson, D. (1991), *'Technology Companies and Global Markets: Programs, Policies and Strategies to Accelerate Innovation and Entrepreneurship'* (Rowman & Littlefield).

Giddens, A. (1979), *Central Problems in Social Theory. Action, Structure and Contradiction in Social Analysis* (University of California Press).

Glaser, B. (1978), *Theoretical Sensitivity: Advances in the Methodology of Grounded Theory* (Mill Valley, Calif.: Sociology Press).

Gnyawali, D.R. and Fogel, D.S. (1994), 'Environments for Entrepreneurship Development: Key Dimensions and Research Implications', *Entrepreneurship Theory and Practice*, Vol. 18, No. 4, pp. 43–62.

Goffee, R. and Scase, R. (1987), 'Patterns of Business Proprietorship among Women in Britain', in Goffee, R. and Scase, R. (eds), *Entrepreneurship in Europe – Social Analysis* (Worcester: Billing & Sons).

Goldstein, J.(1984), 'Undercapitalization as a Winning Entrepreneurial Strategy', in Hornaday, J.A., Tarpley, F. Timmons, J. and Vesper, K.H. (eds), *Frontiers of Entrepreneurship Research* (Wellesley, Mass.: Babson College), 53–71.

Gould, A. and Keeble, D. (1984), 'New Firms and Rural Industrialization in East Anglia', *Regional Studies*, Vol. 18, pp. 189–201.

Grandori, A. and Soda, G. (1995), 'Inter-Firm Networks: Antecedents, Mechanisms, and forms', *Organization Studies*, Vol. 16, No. 2, pp. 183–214

Granstrand, O. (1982), *Technology, Management and Markets* (London: Pinter).

Granstrand, O. (1992), *Hi-Tech Entrepreneurship in Silicon Valley*, CIM-Working Paper (Gothenburg: Dept of Industrial Management and Economics, Chalmers University of Technology).

Granstrand, O. and Alänge, S. (1995), 'The Evolution of Corporate Entrepreneurship in Swedish Industry – Was Schumpeter Wrong?', *Journal of Evolutionary Economics*, Vol. 5, pp. 1–24.

Granstrand, O. and Sjölander, S. (1990a) 'Managing Innovation in Multi-Technology Corporations', *Research Policy*, Vol. 19, No. 1, pp. 35–60.

Granstrand, O. and Sjölander, S. (1990b), 'The Acquisition of Technology and Small Firms by Large Firms', *Journal of Economic Behavior and Organization*, Vol. 13, pp. 367–86.

Greiner, L.E. (1972), 'Evolution and Revolution As Organisations Grow', *Harvard Business Review*, Vol. 50, No. 4, pp. 37–46.

Gupta, A.K., Raj, S.P. and Wilemon, D. (1986), 'R&D and Marketing Managers in High-tech Companies: Are They Different?', *IEEE Transactions on Engineering Management*, Vol. EM-33 No. 1, pp. 25–32.

Haataja, M., Kauranen, I., Autio, E. and Kaila, M. (1992), *The Three First Years: A Study of a New Science Park and its Tenants* (Espoo: Otaniemi Science Park).

Habermeier, K. (1990), 'Product Use and Product Improvement', *Research Policy*, Vol. 19, No. 3, pp. 271–83.

Hagedoorn, J. (1989), *The Dynamic Analysis of Innovation and Diffusion: A Study in Process Control* (London: Pinter).

Hagedoorn, J. and Schakenraad, J. (1990a), 'Organizational Modes of Inter-Firm Co-Operation and Technology Transfer', *Technovation*, Vol. 10, No. 1, pp. 17–30.

Hagedoorn, J. and Schakenraad, J. (1990b), 'Strategic Partnering and Technological Cooperation', in Dankbaar, B., Groenewegen, J. and Schenk, H. (eds), *Perspectives in Industrial Economics* (Dordrecht: Kluwer), pp. 171–91.

Hagedoorn, J. and Schakenraad, J. (1992), 'Leading Companies and Networks of Strategic Alliances in Information Technologies', *Research Policy*, Vol. 21, No. 2, pp. 163–90.

Hagen, E.E. (1962), *On the Theory of Social Change: How Economic Growth Begins*, (Homewood, Ill.: Dorsey)

Hahn R., Gaiser, A. Héraud, J.-A. and Muller, E. (1995), 'Innovationstätigkeit und Unternehmensnetzwerke. Eine vergleichende Untersuchung von Unternehmen im Elsaß und im Bodenseeraum', *Zeitschrift für Betriebswirtschaft*, Vol. 65, No. 3, pp. 247–66.

Håkansson, H. (1987) *Industrial Technological Development: A Network Approch* London: Croom Helm).

Håkansson, H. (1989) *Corporate Technological Behavior: Co-Operation and Networks* (London: Routledge), pp. 37–38.

Håkansson, H. and Johanson, J. (1990), 'Formal and Informal Co-operation Strategies in International Industrial Networks', in Ford, D. (ed.), *Understanding Business Markets* (London: Academic Press), pp. 459–67.

Hambrick, D.C., MacMillan, I.C., and Day, D.L (1982), 'Strategic Attributes and Performance in the BCG Matrix – a PIMS-Based Analysis of Industrial-Product Business', *Academy of Management Journal*, Vol. 25, pp. 510–31.

Hameri, A.P. (1993), *Technical Change, Innovations, and Technological Causality – An Empirical and Philosophical Inquiry* (Helsinki: Acta Polytechnica Scandinavica).

Hammermesh, R.G., Anderson, M.J. and Harris, J.E. (1978), 'Strategies for Low Market Share Businesses', *Harvard Business Review*, Vol. 56, No. 3, pp. 95–102.

Hannan, M. (1976), 'Venturing Corporations – Think Small to Stay Strong', *Harvard Business Review*, May–June, pp. 139–48.

Hannan, M.T. and Freeman, J. (1989), *Organizational Ecology* (Cambridge, Mass.: Harvard University Press).

Hayes, R.H., and Abernathy, W.J. (1980), 'Managing Our Way to Economic Decline', *Harvard Business Review*, July–August.

Helper, S. (1990), *An Exit/Voice Approach to Supplier Relations*, Working Paper presented at the Networks! Workshop at the Wissenschaftszentrum Berlin, 11–13 June.

Helper, S. (1991), 'How Much Has Really Changed between U. S. Auto-makers and their Suppliers?', *Sloan Management Review*, Vol. 32, No. 4, pp. 15–28.

Henderson, B.D. (1973), 'The Experience Curve Reviewed, IV: the Growth Share Matrix of the Product Portfolio', *Perspectives*, No. 135, Boston Consulting Group, Boston, Mass.

Herden, R. (1992), *Technologieorientierte Auß enbeziehungen im betrieblichen Innovations management. Ergebnisse einer empirischen Untersuchung* (Heidelberg: Physika-Verlag).

Herstatt, C. and Hippel, E. von (1991), *An Implementation of the Lead User Market Research Method in a 'Low Tech' Product Area: Pipe Hangers*, Working Paper No. 3249-91-BPS (Cambridge, Mass.: Sloan School of Management, Massachusetts Institute of Technology).

Heydebreck, P. (1996), 'Technologische Verflechtung: Ein Instrument zum Erreichen von Produkt- und Prozeß innovationserfolg', in Gaul, W. and Gemünden, H.G. (eds), *Entscheidungsunterstützung für ökonomische Probleme* (Frankfurt: Peter Lang Verlag), Dissertation.

Hippel, E. von (1976), 'The dominant role of users in the scientific instrumentation process', *Research Policy*, Vol. 5, No. 3, pp. 212–39.

Hippel, E. von (1977), 'The Dominant Role of the User in Semiconductor and Electronic Subassembly Process Innovation', *IEEE Transactions on Engineering Management*, Vol. EM-24, No. 2, pp. 60–71.

Hippel, E. von (1986a), *Cooperation Between Competing Firms. Informal Know-How trading* (Cambridge, Mass.: Sloan School of Management Working Paper, Massachusetts Institute of Technology).

Hippel, E. von (1986b), 'Lead Users: A Source of Novel Product Concepts', *Management Science*, Vol. 32, No. 7, pp. 791–805.

Hippel, E. von (1987), 'Cooperation Between Rivals: Informal Know-How Trading', *Research Policy*, Vol. 16, pp. 291–302.

Hippel, E. von (1988), *The Sources of Innovation* (Oxford University Press).

Hobday, M. (1995), 'Complex System vs Mass Production Industries: A New Innovation Research Agenda', mimeo, University of Sussex, Science Policy Research Unit.

Hofer, C.W. (1975), 'Toward a contingency theory of business strategy', *Academy of Management Journal*, Vol. 18, pp. 784–810.

Hofer, C.W. and Schendel, D. (1978) *Strategy formulation: analytial concepts* (St Paul, Minn.: West Publishing Company).

Hörnell, E., Vahlne, J.-E. and Wiedersheim-Paul, F. (1973), *Export och utlandsetableringar* (Uppsala: Almqvist & Wiksell).

Horowitz, M. (1968), 'Organizational Processes Underlying Differences between Listening and Reading as a Function of Complexity of Material', *The Journal of Communication*, Vol. 18, pp. 37–46.

Howells, J. (1987), 'Developments in the Location, Technology and Industrial Organisation of Computer Services: Some Trends and Research Issues', *Regional Studies*, Vol. 21, pp. 493–503.

Howells, J. and Green, A.E. (1986), 'Location, Technology and Industrial Organisation in UK Services', *Progress in Planning*, Vol. 27, pp. 83–184.

Hull, C. and Hjern, B. (1989), Helping Small Firms Grow: An Implementation Approach (London: Routledge).

Hull, D.L., Bosley, J.J. and Udell, G.G. (1980), 'Renewing the Hunt for the Heffalump: Identifying Potential Entrepreneurs by Personality Characteristics', *Journal of Small Business Management*, Vol. 18, No. 1, pp. 11–18.

Hult, M. and Odéen, G. (1986), 'Etableringsprocessen', Dissertation, Uppsala.

Hyvärinen, A. and Ahola, E. (1989), *Survey of the Spin-Off Companies of the Technical Research Center of Finland* (Espoo: Technical Research Center).

Illinois Institute of Technology (1968), *'Technology in Retrospect and Critical Events in Science'*, Report to the National Science Foundation, NSF-C235.

Jacobsson, S. (1984), *Acquisition and Management of Innovative Companies* (Gothenburg: Department of Industrial Management and Economics, Chalmers University of Technology).

Jarillo, J.C. (1989) 'Entrepreneurship and Growth: The Strategic Use of External Resources', *Journal of Business Venturing*, Vol. 4, pp. 133–47.

Jevons, F.R. and Saupin, M. (1991), 'Capturing Regional Benefits from Science and Technology: The Question of Regional Appropriability', *Prometheus*, Vol. 9, pp. 265–73.

Jewkes, J., Sawers, D. and Stillerman, R. (1969), *The Sources of Invention*, 2nd edn (London: Macmillan).

Johannisson, B. (1978), *Företag och Närsamhälle, En Studie i Organisation* (Högskolan i Växjö).

Johannisson, B. and Peterson, R. (1984), 'The Personal Networks of Entrepreneurs', paper presented at the Third Canadian Conference, International Council for Small Business, Toronto, 23–25 May.

Johanson, J. and Vahlne, J.-E. (1977), 'The Internationalization Process of the Firm – A Model of Knowledge Development and Increasing Foreign Market Commitments', *Journal of International Business Studies*, Vol. 8 (Spring/Summer), pp. 23–32.

Johanson, J. and Vahlne, J.-E. (1990), 'The Mechanism of Internationalization', *International Marketing Review*, Vol. 7, No. 4, pp. 11–24.

Johanson, J. and Wiedersheim-Paul, F. (1974), 'Internationaliseringsprocessen i några svenska företag', in Vahlne, J.E. (ed.), *Företagsekonomisk forskning inom internationellt företagande* (Stockholm: Norstedts), pp. 31–49.

Jones-Evans, D. (1992), 'Technical Entrepreneurship in the UK – An Examination of the Relationship between the Previous Occupational Background of the Technical Entrepreneur and the Management of the Small Technology-Based Venture', unpublished PhD dissertation, Aston University, Birmingham.

Jones-Evans, D. (1995), 'A Typology of Technology-Based Entrepreneurs: A Model Based on Previous Occupational Background', *International Journal of Entrepreneurial Behaviour and Research*, Vol. 1, No. 1, pp. 26–47.

Jones-Evans, D. (1996a), 'Experience and Entrepreneurship – Technology-Based Owner-Managers in the UK', *New Technology Work and Employment*, Vol. 11, No. 1, pp. 39–54.

Jones-Evans, D. (1996b) 'Technical Entrepreneurship, Strategy and Experience', *International Small Business Journal*, Vol. 14, No. 3, pp. 15–40.

Jones-Evans, D. and Kirby, D.A. (1995), 'Small Technical Consultancies and their Client Customers: An Analysis in North East England', *Entrepreneurship and Regional Development*, Vol. 7, pp. 21–40.

Jones-Evans, D. and Steward, F. (1991), 'How Does Previous Experience Contribute to Entrepreneurial Success – An Examination of Technical Entrepreneurs as a Case Study', in Oliga, J.C. and Kim, T.B. (eds), *Proceedings of the World Conference on Entrepreneurship and Innovative Change* (Singapore: Nanyang Technological University).

Jones-Evans, D. and Westhead, P. (1996), 'High Technology Small Firm Sector in the UK', *International Journal of Entrepreneurial Behaviour and Research,* Vol. 2, No. 1, pp. 15–35.

Kadushin, C. (1966), 'The Friends and Supporters of Psychotherapy: On Social Circles in Urban Life', *American Sociological Review,* Vol. 31, No. 6, pp. 786–802.

Kalleberg, A. and Leicht, K. (1991), 'Gender and Organisational Performance: Determinants of Small Business Survival and Success', *Academy of Management Journal,* Vol. 34, No. 1, pp. 136–61.

Katz, D. and Kahn, R.L. (1978), *The Social Psychology of Organizations* (New York: Wiley).

Katz, J.A. (1981), 'One Person Organizations as a Resource for Researchers and Practioners', *American Journal of Small Business,* Vol. 8, No. 3, pp. 24–30.

Katz, J.A. and Gartner, W.B. (1988), 'Properties of Emerging Organizations', Academy of Management Review, Vol. 13, No. 3, pp. 429–41.

Katz, R.L. (1970), *Cases and Concepts in Corporate Strategy* (Englewood Cliffs, N.J: Prentice-Hall).

Kauranen, I., Takala, M., Autio, E. and Kaila, M. (1990), *Three First Years: A Study on the First Phases of a New Science Park and of its Tenants* (Finland: Otaniemi Science Park).

Kazanjian, R.K. (1983), 'The Organizational Evolution of High Technology New Ventures: The Impact of Stage of Growth on the Nature and Structure of the Planning Process', doctoral dissertation, Wharton Business School, Pennsylvania.

Kazanjian, R.K. (1988), 'Relation of Dominant Problems to Stages of Growth in Technology-Based New Ventures', *Academy of Management Journal,* Vol. 31, No. 2, pp. 257–79.

Keeble, D. (1994), 'Regional Influences and Policy in New Technology-Based Firm Creation and Growth', in R. Oakey (ed.), *New Technology-Based Firms in the 1990s* (London: Paul Chapman), pp. 204–18.

Keeble, D. and Kelly, T. (1986), 'New Firms and High-technology Industry in the United Kingdom: The Case of Computer Electronics', in Keeble, D. and Wever, E. (eds), *New Firms and Regional Development in Europe* (London: Croom Helm), pp. 75–104.

Kelley, M. and Brooks, H. (1991), 'External Learning Opportunities and the Diffusion of Process Innovations to Small Firms: The Case of Programmable Automation', *Technological Forecasting and Social Change,* Vol. 39, pp. 103–125.

Kellock, M. (1992), *On Barriers to Growth* (Cranfield School of Management).

Kenney, M. (1986), 'Schumpeterian Innovation and Entrepreneurs in Capitalism: A Case Study of the US Biotechnology Industry', *Research Policy,* Vol. 15, pp. 21–31.

Kets de Vries, M.F.R. (1970), 'The Entrepreneur as Catalyst of Economic and Cultural Change', Dissertation, Harvard Graduate School of Business Administration.

Kets De Vries, M.F.R. (1977) 'The Entrepreneurial Personality; A Person at the Crossroads', *Journal of Management Studies* Febuarary, pp. 34–57.

380   *Bibliography*

Kim, L. (1988), 'Entrepreneurship and Innovation in a Rapidly Developing Country', *Journal of Development Planning*, Vol. 18, pp. 183–94.

Kim, L. and Dahlman, C. J. (1992), 'Technology Policy for Industrialisation: An Integrative Framework and Korea's Experience', *Research Policy*, Vol. 21, pp. 437–52.

Kimberly, J.R. (1979), 'Issues in the Creation of Organizations: Initiation, Innovation and Institutionalization', *Academy of Management Journal*, Vol. 22, pp. 437–47.

Kimberly, J.R. (1980) 'Initiation, Innovation, and Institutionalization in the Creation Process', in J.R. Kimberly and R.H. Miles (eds), *The Organizational Life Cycle* San Francisco: Jossey-Bass) pp. 18–43.

Kimberly, J.R. and Miles, R.H. (1980), *The Organizational Life Cycle* (San Francisco: Jossey-Bass).

Kinsella, R., Clarke, W., Coyne, D., Mulvenna, D. and Storey, D.J. (1993), *Fast Growth Firms and Selectivity* (Dublin: Irish Management Institute).

Kirby, D.A. and Jones-Evans, D. (1997), 'Small Technology-based Professional Consultancy Services in the United Kingdom', *Service Industries Journal.* Vol.17., No.1 pp.155–72.

Kitching, J. (1973), *Acquisitions in Europe – Causes of Corporate Successes and Failures* (Geneva: Business International).

Kitching, J. (1976), 'Why do Mergers Miscarry?', *Harvard Business Review*, (November/December), pp. 84–7.

Klandt, H. (1987), 'Trends in Small Business Start-up in West Germany', in Goffee, R. and Scase, R. (eds), *Entrepreneurship in Europe – in Social Analysis*, (Worcester: Billing & son).

Klandt, H. (1990), 'Zur Person des Unternehmensgründers', in Dieterle, W.K.M, and Winckler, E.M. (eds), *Unternehmensgründung. Handbuch des Gründungsmanagements* (Munich:) pp. 29–43.

Kline, S.J. and Rosenberg, N. (1986), 'An overview on innovation', in *The Positive Sum Strategy: Harnessing Technology for Economic Growth*, (Washington, DC: National Academy Press), pp. 275–305.

Klofsten, M. (1987), *On Understanding Business Development in Small Technology Based Companies*. Working paper 87-4 (Linköping University: Economics Institute).

Klofsten M. (1992), Tidiga utvecklingsprocesser i teknikbaserade företag. ('Early Development Processes in Technology-Based firms'), PhD Dissertation. Linköping University, Department of Management and Economics.

Klofsten, M. (1996) *Ideas that Really Mean Business* (Linköping University: Centre for Innovation and Entrepreneurship).

Klofsten, M., Jones-Evans, D. and Lindell, P. (1997) 'Growth Factors in Technology-Based Spin-Offs: A Swedish Study', *Piccola Impressa,* forthcoming.

Klofsten, M., Lindell, P., Olofsson, C. and Wahlbin, C. (1988), 'Internal and External Resources in Technology-Based Spin-Offs', in Kirchoff, B.A., Long, W.A., McMullan, W.E., Vesper K.H. and Wetzel, W.E. (eds), *Frontiers of Entrepreneurship Research* (Wellesley, Mass.: Babson College), pp. 430–43.

Knight, R.M. (1986), 'Product Innovation by Smaller High Technology Firms in Canada', *Journal of Product Innovation Management*, Vol. 3, pp. 195–203.

Knight, R.M. (1988), 'Spin-Off Entrepreneurs: How Corporations Really Create Entrepreneurs', in Kirchoff, B.A., Long, W.A., McMullan, W.E., Vesper K.H.

and Wetzel, W.E. (eds), *Frontiers of Entrepreneurship Research* (Wellesley, Mass.: Babson College), pp. 134–49.

Komives, J.L. (1972), 'A Preliminary Study of the Personal Values of High Technology Entrepreneurs', in Cooper, A.C. and Komives, J.L. (eds), *Technical Entrepreneurship: A Symposium* (Milwaukee: Center for Venture Management).

Kreiner, K. and Schultz, M. (1993), 'Informal Collaboration in R&D: The Formation of Networks Across Organizations', *Organization Studies*, Vol. 14, No. 2, pp. 189–209.

Kudla, R.J., and McInish, T.H. (1988) 'Divergence of Opinion and Corporate Spin-Offs', *Quarterly Review of Economics and Business*, Vol. 28, No. 2, pp. 20–9.

Kuhn, R.L. (1982), *Mid-Sized Businesses: Success Strategies and Methodology* (New York: Praeger).

Kumar, M.S. (1984), *Growth, Acquisition, and Investment – An Analysis of the Growth of Industrial Firms and their Overseas Activities* (Cambridge University Press).

Landström, H. (1990), *Riskkapitalföretagens Resurstillförsel till Små Företag* (University of Lund: Institute for Management of Innovation and Technology).

Langlois, R.N. and Robertson, P.L. (1992) 'Networks and Innovation in a Modular System: Lessons from the Microcomputer and Stereo Component Industries', *Research Policy*, Vol. 21, pp. 297–313.

Langrish, J., Gibbons, M., Evans, W. and Jevons, F. (1972), '*Wealth From Knowledge: A Study of Innovation in Industry*' (London: Macmillan).

Larsen, J.K. and Rogers, E.M. (1984), *Silicon Valley Fever* (New York: Basic).

Larson A. and Starr, J. A. (1993), 'A Network Model of Organisation Formation', *Entrepreneurship Theory and Practice*, Vol. 17, No. 2, pp. 5–15.

Laumann, E., Marsden, P. and Prensky, D. (1983), 'The Boundary Specification Problem in Network Analysis', in Burt, R. and Minor, M. (eds), *Applied Network Analysis: A Methodological Introduction*' (Beverly Hills, Calif.: Sage), pp. 18–34.

Lawton-Smith, H., Dickson, K. and Lloyd Smith, S. (1991) '"There Are Two Sides to Every Story": Innovation and Collaboration Within Networks of Large and Small Firms', *Research Policy*, Vol. 20, pp. 457–68.

Lemola T. and Lovio, R. (1988), 'Possibilities for a Small Country in High-Technology Production: The Electronics Industry in Finland', in Freeman, C. and Lundvall, B. (eds) *Small Countries Facing the Technological Revolution* (London: Pinter), pp.139–55.

Leonard-Barton, D. (1983), 'Interpersonal Communication Patterns among Swedish and Boston Area Entrepreneurs', in Hornaday, J.A., Timmons, J.A. and Vesper, K.H. (eds), *Frontiers of Entrepreneurship Research* (Wellesley, Mass.: Babson College), pp. 538–63.

Leonard-Barton, D. (1984), 'Interpersonal Communication Patterns among Swedish and Boston-Area Entrepreneurs', *Research Policy*, Vol. 13, No. 2, pp. 101–14.

Leone, A., Keeley, R.H. and Miller, W.F. (1992), 'A survey of technology-based companies founded by members of the Stanford University community', Stanford University, Office of Technology Licensing.

Levine, J. (1972), 'The Sphere of Influence', *American Sociological Review*, Vol. 37, No. 1, pp. 14–27.

Liles, P.R. (1974), *New Business Ventures and the Entrepreneur* Inc. (Homewood, Ill.: Richard D. Irwin).

Lindgren, U. (1982), *Foreign Acquisitions – Management of the Integration Process, Institute of International Business*, Stockholm School of Economics, Stockholm, Sweden.

Lindholm, Å. (1990), *Acquisition of Technology-Based Firms. A Study of Acquisition and Growth Patterns among Swedish Firms* (Gothenburg: Department of Industrial Management and Economics, Chalmers University of Technology).

Lindholm, Å. (1994), 'The Economics of Technology-Related Ownership Changes – A Study of Innovativeness and Growth through Aquisitions and Spin-Offs', PhD dissertation, Department of Industrial Management and Economics, Chalmers University of Technology, Gothenburg.

Lindqvist, M. (1991), *Infant Multinationals – The Internationalization of Young, Technology-Based Swedish Firms* (Stockholm: IIB).

Lipparini, A. and Sobrero, M. (1994), 'The Glue and the Pieces: Entrepreneurship and Innovation in Small Firm Networks', *Journal of Business Venturing*, Vol. 9, pp. 125–40.

Lippman, S. and Rumelt, R. (1982), 'Uncertain Imitability: An Analysis of Interfirm Differences in Efficiency under Competition', *The Bell Journal of Economics*, Vol. 13, pp. 418–38.

Lipsey, R.E. and O'Connor, L. (1982) *Swedish Firms Acquired by Foreigners: A Comparison of Before and After Takeover,* Working Paper Series (Cambridge: National Bureau of Economic Research).

Little, Arthur D. (1977), *New Technology-Based Firms in the United Kingdom and the Federal Republic of Germany: A Report Prepared for the Anglo-German Foundation for the Study of Industrial Society*, (London: A.D. Little).

Littler, D. and Sweeting, R.C. (1990), 'The Management of New Technology Based Businesses: The Existentialist Firm', *Omega*, Vol. 18, No. 3, pp. 231–40.

Litvak, I.A. and Maule, C.J. (1972), 'Managing the Entrepreneurial Enterprise', *Business Quarterly*, Vol. 37, No. 2, p. 43.

Litvak, I.A. and Maule, C.J. (1982), 'Successful Canadian entrepreneurship and innovation', in Kent, C.A., Sexton, D.L. and Vesper, K.H. (eds), *Frontiers of Entrepreneurship Research* (Wellesley, Mass.: Babson College), pp. 189–203.

Lorrain, J. and Dussault, L. (1988), 'Relation between Psychological Characteristics, Administrative Behaviors and Success of Founder Entrepreneurs at the Start-Up stage', in Kirchoff, B.A., Long, W.A., McMullan, W.E., Vesper K.H. and Wetzel, W.E. (eds), *Frontiers of Entrepreneurship Research* (Wellesley, Mass.: Babson College) pp. 150–64.

Lumme, A. (1994a), *Potential for Growth: Societal Contributions of the Most Promising Technology-Based Entrepreneurial Companies in Finland – Empirical Evidence*, International Conference on High Technology Small Firms, Manchester Business School, Manchester, September.

Lumme, A. (1994b), *Uusteollistamisen avaimet – Tutkimus suomalaisten pienten ja keskisuurten teknologiayritysten näkemyksistä kasvupotentiaalistaan (Keys of reindustrialisation – A Study of the Growth Potential of Small and Medium Sized Technology Intensive Firms)* (Helsinki: National Fund for Research and Development SITRA).

Lumme, A., Kauranen, I. and Autio, E. (1994) 'The Growth and Funding Mechanisms of New, Technology-Based Companies', *The Finnish Journal of Business Economics*, Vol. 1, pp. 20–35.

Lumme, A., Kauranen, I., Autio, E. and Kaila, M. (1992) *New, Technology-Based Companies in the United Kingdom and in Finland: A Comparative Study* (Helsinki: National Fund for Research and Development SITRA).

Lundvall, B. (1988), 'Innovation as an Interactive Process: From User-Producer Interaction to National Systems of Innovation', in Dosi, G. *et al* (eds), *Technical Change and Economic Theory* (London: Pinter), pp. 349–69.

Macmillan, I.C., Hambrick D.C. and Day, D.L. (1982), 'The Product Portfolio and Profitability – A PIMS-Based Analysis of Industrial Product Businesses', *Academy of Management Journal*, Vol. 25, pp. 733–55.

Macrae, D. (1991), *Characteristics of High and Low Growth Small and Medium Sized Businesses*, 21st European Small Business Seminar, Barcelona, Spain.

Magee, S.P. (1977), 'Information and the Multinational Corporation: An Appropriability Theory of Foreign Direct Investment', in Bhagwati, J.N. (ed.), *The New International Economic Order: The North-South Debate* (Cambridge, Mass.: MIT Press) pp. 317–40

Maidique, M.A. (1980), 'Entrepreneurs, Champions and Technological Innovation', *Sloan Management Review*, Vol. 21, No. 2, pp. 59–74.

Maillat, D. and Vasserot, J.-Y. (1988), 'Economic and Territorial Conditions for Indigenous Revival in Europe's Industrial Regions', in Keeble, D. and Aydalot, P. (eds), *High Technology Industry and Innovative Environments – The European Experience* (London: Routledge), pp. 163–83.

Marques, J.M.A. and Laranja, M. (1994), *As Tecnologias de Informação e Electrónica em Portugal: Importância, Realidade e Perspectivas* (Lisbon: Direcção Geral Indústria).

Marquis, D.G. (1969), 'The Anatomy of Successful Innovations', *Innovation Magazine*, November.

Marshall, A. (1890), *The Principles of Economics* (New York: Macmillan).

Massey, D., Quintas, P. and Wield, D. (1992), *High Tech Fantasies: Science Parks in Society, Science and Space* (London: Routledge).

Mayer, M., Heinzel, W. and Muller, R. (1990), 'Performance of New Technology-Based Firms in the Federal Republic of Germany at the Stage of Market Entry', *Entrepreneurship and Regional Development*, Vol. 2, pp. 125–38.

McClelland, D.C. (1961), *The Achieving Society* (Princeton, Nj: Van Nostrand).

McClelland, D.C. (1965), 'Achievement Motivation can be Developed', *Harvard Business Review*, Vol. 43, No. 6, pp. 6–24.

McClelland, D.C. (1969), 'Toward the Theory of Motive Acquisition', *American Psychologist*, Vol. 20, pp. 321–33.

McGee, J.E. and Dowling, M.J. (1994), 'Using R&D Cooperative Arrangements to Leverage Managerial Experience: A Study of Technology-Intensive New Ventures', *Journal of Business Venturing*, Vol. 9, pp. 33–48.

McKenna, R. (1985), *The Regis Touch: Million Dollar Advice from American Top Marketing Consultant* (Reading, Mass.: Addison-Wesley).

McLaughlin, C., Rosenbloom, R. and Wolek, F. (1965), *Technology Transfer and the Flow of Technical Information in a Large Industrial Group* (Cambridge, Mass.: Harvard University Press).

McQueen, D.H. and Wallmark, J.T. (1982), 'Spin-off Companies from Chalmers University of Technology', *Technovation*, Vol. 1, pp. 305–15

Menzel, H. (1962), 'Planned and Unplanned Scientific Communication', in Barber, B. and Hirsch, W. (eds), *The Sociology of Science* (New York: Free Press) pp. 417–41.

Meyer, K.B. and Goldstein, S. (1961), *The First Two Years: Problems of Small Firm Growth and Survival* (Washington, DC: Small Business Administration).

Meyer, M. H. and Roberts, E. B. (1988), 'Focusing Product Technology for Corporate Growth', *Sloan Management Review*, Vol. 29 (Summer), pp. 7–16.

Miles, M.B. and Huberman, A.M. (1994), *Qualitative Data Analysis – An Expanded Sourcebook* (London: Sage).

Miles, R.H. and Snow, C.C. (1978), *Organizational Strategy, Structure, and Process* (New York and London: McGraw-Hill).

Miles, R.H. and Snow, C.C. (1986), 'Organizations: New Concepts for New Forms', *California Management Review*, Vol. 28, No. 3, pp. 62–73.

Miller, D. and Friesen, P.H. (1984), 'A Longitudinal Study of the Corporate Life Cycle', *Management Science*, Vol. 30, No. 10, pp. 1161–83.

Miller, J.G. and Roth, A.V. (1994), 'A Taxonomy of Manufacturing Strategies', *Management Science*, Vol. 40, No. 3, pp. 285–304.

Mintzberg, H. (1973), 'Strategy Making in Three Modes', *California Management Review*, Vol. 16, No. 2, pp. 44–53.

Mitchell, J. (1969), 'Introduction', and 'The Concept and Use of Social Networks', in Mitchell, J., *Social Networks in Urban Situations* (Manchester University Press), pp. 1–50.

Monck, C.S.P., Porter, R.P., Quintas, P., Storey, D.J. and Wynarczyk, P. (1988), *Science Parks* and the Growth of High Technology Firms (London: Croom Helm), pp. 127–52.

Morton-Williams, J. (1977), 'Unstructured Design Work', in Hoinville, G. and Jowell, R. (eds), *Survey Research Practice* (London: Heinemann), pp. 9–26.

Müller-Böling, D. and Klandt, H. (1993), 'Unternehmensgründungen', in Hauschildt, J. and Grün, O. (eds), *Ergebnisse empirischer betriebswirtschaftlicher Forschung. Zu einer Realtheorie der Unternehmensplanung, Festschrift für Eberhard Witte* (Stuttgart: Schäffer-Poeschel), pp. 135–78.

Murray, J.A. (1984), 'A Concept of Entrepreneurial Strategy', *Strategic Management Journal*, Vol. 5, pp. 1–13.

Murray, J.A. and O'Gorman. C. (1994), 'Growth Strategies for Smaller Business', *Journal of Strategic Change*, Vol. 3, pp. 175–83.

Mustar, P. (1994), 'Organisations, Technologies et Marches en Création: La Genèse des PME High-Tech', *Revue d'Economie Industrielle*, Vol. 67, pp. 156–74.

Myers, S. and Marquis, D. (1969), *Successful Commercial Innovations* (Washington, DC: National Science Foundation).

Nelson, R. (1987), 'The Public and Private Faces of Technology', in Nelson, R. (ed.), *Understanding Technical Change as an Evolutionary Process* (Amsterdam: Elsevier Science), pp. 73–91.

Nelson, R. (1994), 'The Co-Evolution of Technology, Industrial Structure, and Supporting Organization', *Industrial and Corporate Change*, Vol. 3, No. 1, pp. 47–63.

Nelson, R. and Winter, S. (1982), *An Evolutionary Theory of Economic Change* (Cambridge, Mass.: Harvard University Press).

Newbould, G.D., Buckley, P.J. and Thurwell, J. (1978), *Going International – The Experience of Smaller Companies Overseas* (London: Associate Business Press).
Nordström, K. (1991), 'The Internationalization Process of the Firm – Searching for New Patterns and Explanations', Doctoral dissertation, IIB, Stockholm.
Normann, R. (1975), *Skapande Företagsledning* (Stockholm: Bonniers).
Normann, R. (1977), *Management for Growth* (New York: Wiley).
O'Doherty, D. (1990), 'Strategic Alliances – a SME and Small Economy Perspective', *Science and Public Policy*, Vol. 17, pp. 303–10.
O'Doherty, D. (1993), 'Globalisation and Performance of Small Firm within the Smaller European Economies', in Humbert, M. (ed.), *The Impact of Globalisation on Europe's Firms and Industries* (London: Pinter), pp. 141–51.
Oakey, R.P. (1984), *High Technology Small Firms* (London: Pinter).
Oakey, R.P. (1991a), 'Government Policy towards High-Technology', in Curran, J. and Blackburn, R. (eds), *Paths of Enterprise – The Future for Small Business*, (London: Routledge), pp. 128–48.
Oakey, R.P. (1991b), 'High Technology Small Firms: Their Potential for Rapid Industrial Growth', *International Small Business Journal*, Vol. 9, No. 4, pp. 31–42.
Oakey, R.P. (1994), *New, Technology-Based Firms in the 1990's* (London: Paul Chapman).
Oakey, R.P. and White, T. (1993), 'Business Information and Regional Economic Development: Some Conceptual Observations', *Technovation*, Vol. 13, pp. 147–59.
Oakey, R.P., Rothwell, R. and Cooper, S. (1988) *The Management of Innovation in High Technology Small Firms – Innovation and Regional Development in Britain and the United States* (London: Pinter).
OECD (1993), *Reviews of National Science and Technology Policy – Portugal* (Paris: OECD).
OECD (1994), *Annual Employment Outlook* (Paris: OECD).
Olleros, F.J. (1986), 'Emerging Industries and the Burnout of Pioneers', *Journal of Product Innovation Management*, Vol. 3, No. 1, pp. 5–18.
Olofsson, C. (1969), *Produktutveckling – Miljöförankring* (SIAR-S 22), (Stockholm).
Olofsson, C. (1979), *Företagets exploatering av sina marknadsrelationer. En studie av produktutveckling* Forskningsrapport No. 91 (Linköping University: Department of Management and Economics).
Olofsson, C. and Wahlbin, C. (1984), 'Technology-Based New Ventures from Technical Universities: A Swedish Case', in Hornaday, J.A., Tarpley, F., Timmons, J. and Vesper, K.H. (eds), *Frontiers of Entrepreneurship Research* (Wellesley, Mass.: Babson College), pp. 192–211.
Olofsson, C. and Wahlbin, C. (1993), *Teknibaserade företag från högskolan* (Linköping: Institute for Management of Innovation and Technology).
Olofsson, C., Pettersson, G. and Wahlbin, C. (1986), 'Opportunities and Obstacles: A Study of Start-Ups and their Development', in Ronstadt, R.C., Hornaday, J.A., Peterson, R. and Vesper, K.H. (eds), *Frontiers Of Entrepreneurship Research* (Wellesley, Mass.: Babson College), pp. 482–501.
Olofsson, C., Wahlbin, C. and Tovman, P. (1987), 'Technology-Based New Ventures from Swedish Universities', in Churchill, N.C., Hornaday, J.A., Kirchoff, B.A., Kranser, C.J. and Vesper, K.H. (eds), *Frontiers of Entrepreneurship Research*, (Wellesley, Mass.: Babson College), pp. 605–16.

Oskarsson, C. (1990), 'Technology Diversification – The Phenomenon, its Causes and Effects', Licentiate dissertation, Department of Industrial Management and Economics, Chalmers University of Technology, Gothenburg, Sweden.

Patel, P. and Pavitt, K. (1994), *Technological Competencies in the World's Largest Firms: Characteristics, Constraints and Scope for Managerial Choice*, STEEP Discussion Paper No. 13, (University of Sussex: Science Policy Research Unit).

Paulin, W.L., Coffrey, R.E. and Spaulding, M.E. (1982) 'Entrepreneurship research: methods and directions', in Kent, C.A., Sexton, D.L. and Vesper, K.H. (eds) *Encyclopaedia of Entrepreneurship* (Englewood-Cliffs, N.J.: Prentice-Hall) pp. 352–73.

Pavia, T. (1990), 'Product Growth Strategies in Young High Technology Firms', *Journal of Product Innovation Management*, Vol. 7, No. 4, pp. 297–309.

Pavitt, K. (1984), 'Sectoral Patterns of Technical Change: Towards a Taxonomy and a Theory', *Research Policy*, Vol. 13, pp. 343–73.

Pavitt, K. (1990), 'What do we Know about the Strategic Management of Technology?', *California Management Review*, Spring, pp. 17–26.

Pavitt, K. (1991), 'Key Characteristics of the Large Innovating Firm', *British Journal of Management*, Vol. 2, pp. 41–50.

Pavitt, K., Robson, M. and Townsend, J. (1987), 'The Size Distribution of Innovating Firms in the UK: 1945–1983', *Journal of Industrial Economics*, Vol. 45, pp. 297–306.

Pavitt, K., Robson, M. and Townsend, J. (1989), 'Technological Accumulation, Diversification and Organization in UK companies, 1945–1983', *Management Science*, Vol. 35, pp. 81–99.

Peck, W.F. (1986), *The Leadership Transition from Scientist to Manager*, First International Conference on Engineering Management, Arlington, Virginia, 22–24 September.

Pennings, J.M. (1980), 'Environmental Influences on the Creation Process', in Kimberly, J.R. and Miles, R.H. (eds), *The Organizational Life Cycle* (San Francisco: Jossey-Bass), pp. 134–60.

Pennings, J.M., (1982), 'Elaborations on the Entrepreneur and his Environment', in Kent, C.A., Sexton, D.L. and Vesper, K.H. (eds), *Encyclopedia of Entrepreneurship* (Englewood Cliffs, NJ: Prentice-Hall).

Penrose, E.T. (1956), 'Foreign Investment and the Growth of the Firm', *Economic Journal*, Vol. 66, pp. 220–35.

Penrose, E.T. (1959), *The Theory of Growth of the Firm* (Oxford: Basil Blackwell).

Perez, C. and Soete, L. (1988), 'Catching Up in Technology: Entry Barriers and Windows of Opportunity', in Dosi, G., Freeman, C., Nelson, R., Silverberg, G. and Soete, L. (eds), *Technical Change and Economic Theory* (London: Pinter), pp. 458–79.

Perry, M. (1990), 'Business Service Specialisation and Regional Economic Change', *Regional Studies*, Vol. 24, No. 3, pp. 195–209.

Peters, T. and Waterman, R. (1982), *In Search of Excellence* (London: Harper & Row).

Philips, Å., Sundberg, L. and Uhlin, Å., (1991), I gränslandet mellan högskola och näringsliv: Drivkrafter för utveckling och tillväxt i små universitetsrelaterade företag (Stockholm: Sinova Managmentkonsulter).

Phillips, B.D. and Kirchhoff, B.A., (1989), 'Formation, Growth and Survival: Small Firm Dynamics in the US Economy', *Small Business Economics*, Vol.1, pp. 65–74.

Phillips, B.D., Kirchhoff, B.A., and Brown, H.S. (1991), 'Formation, Growth, and Mobility of Technology-Based Firms in the US Economy', *Entrepreneurship & Regional Development*, Vol. 3, pp.129–44.

Plosila, W.H. and Allen, D.N. (1987), 'State-Sponsored Seed Venture Capital Programs: The Pennsylvania Experience', *Policy Studies Review*, Vol. 6, pp. 529–37.

Porter, M.E. (1980), *Competitive Strategy: Creating and Sustaining Superior Performance*, (New York: The Free Press).

Porter, M.E. (1985) *Competitive Advantage. Techniques for Analyzing Industries and Competitors*, (New York: The Free Press).

Poza, E.J. (1989), *Smart Growth: Critical Choices for Business Continuity and Prosperity* (London: Jossey-Bass).

Prahalad, C. and Hamel, G. (1990), 'The Core Competence of the Corporation', *Harvard Business Review*, May–June, pp. 79–91.

Raffa, M., Zollo, G. and Caponi, R. (1995) *Organizational Transformations of Small Innovative Firms'*, paper presented at the Babson Entrepreneurship Research Conference, London, 9–11 April.

Ramos, R. (1989), 'High Tech Entrepreneurship in Madrid', In Birley, S. (ed.), *European Entrepreneurship: Emerging Growth Companies*, Proceedings of the First Annual EFER Forum, EFER, Cranfield School of Management, pp. 159–85.

Reitberger, G. (1987), 'Nya Företag med rötter i forskande miljöer', *Teknik och kunskapsspridning*, SIND, STU, SÖ, UHÄ, pp. 23–30.

Reuber, A.R. and Fischer, E.M. (1994), 'Entrepreneurs experience, expertise and the performance of small technology-based firms', *IEEE Transactions on Engineering Management*, Vol. 41, No. 4, pp. 365–74.

Reynolds, P. and Miller, B. (1989), 'New Firm Survival: Analysis of a Panel's Fourth Year', in Brockhaus, R.H., Churchill N.C., Katz, J.A., Kirchoff, B.A., Vesper, K.H. and Wetzel, W.E. (eds), *Frontiers of Entrepreneurship Research* (Wellesley, Mass.: Babson College, pp. 159–72.

Rhenman, E. (1973), *Organisation Theory for Long Range Planning*, (Chichester: John Wiley)

Richardson, G.B. (1972), 'The Organization of Industry', *Economic Journal*, Vol. 82 (September), pp. 883–96.

Riley, J. (1990), *Getting the Most from your data – A Handbook of Practical Ideas on How to Analyse Qualitative Data.* (Bristol: Technical and Educational Services).

Ritchie, J. (1991) 'Enterprise Cultures: A Frame Analysis, in Burrows, R. (ed.), *Deciphering the Enterprise Culture: Entrepreneurship, Petty Capitalism and the Restructuring of Britain*, (London: Routledge) pp. 17–35.

Rizzi, J.V. (1987), 'What Restructuring has to Offer', *Journal of Business Strategy*, Vol. 8, No. 2, pp. 38–42.

Rizzoni, A. (1991), 'Technological Innovation and Small Firms: A Taxonomy', *International Journal of Small Business*, Vol. 9, No. 4, pp. 31–42.

Roberts, E.B. (1968), 'Entrepreneurship and Technology: A Basic Study of Innovators', *Research Management*, Vol. 11, No. 4, pp. 249–66.

Roberts, E.B. (1969), 'Entrepreneurship and Technology', in Gruber, W. and Marquis, D. (eds), *Factors in the Transfer of Technology* (Cambridge, Mass.: MIT Press), pp. 219–237.

Roberts, E.B. (1980), 'Getting New Ventures off the Ground', *Management Review*, Vol. 69 (June) pp. 51–9.

Roberts, E.B. (1991a), *Entrepreneurs in High Technology: Lessons from MIT and Beyond*, (New York: Oxford University Press).

Roberts, E.B. (1991b), 'The Technological Base of the New Enterprise', *Research Policy*, Vol. 20, No. 4, pp. 283–98.

Roberts, E.B. and Berry, C. (1985), 'Entering New Businesses: Selecting Strategies for Success', *Sloan Management Review*, Vol. 26, No. 3, published in Roberts. (1987), *Generating Technological Innovation* (Oxford: OUP) pp. 3–17.

Roberts, E.B. and Hauptmann, O. (1986), 'The Process of Technology Transfer to the New Biomedical and Pharmaceutical Firm', *Research Policy*, Vol. 15, pp. 107–19.

Roberts, E.B. and Wainer, H.A. (1966), *Some characteristics of technological entrepreneurs*, Working Paper No. 195–6 (Cambridge, Mass.: Sloan School of Management, MIT).

Roberts, E.B. and Wainer, H.A. (1968). 'New Enterprises on Route 128', *Science Journal*, Vol. 4 (December), pp. 78–84.

Roberts, E.B. and Wainer, H.A. (1971), 'Some Characteristics of Technical Entrepreneurs', *IEEE Transactions of Engineering Management*, Vol. EM-18, No. 3, pp. 100–09

Robinson, R.B. Jr, McDougall, P. and Herron, L. (1988), 'Towards a New Venture Strategy Typology,' *Academy of Management Proceedings*, pp. 74–8.

Robson, M. and Townsend, J. (1984), 'Trends and Characteristics of Significant Innovations and their Innovators in the U.K. since 1945', mimeo, University of Brighton, Science Policy Research Unit.

Rodenberger C. and McCray J. (1981), 'Start ups from a large university in a small town, Texas A&M University, Texas', in Vesper, K.H. (ed.), Frontiers of Entrepreneurship Research (Wellesley, Mass.: Babson College), pp. 84–91.

Rogers, E. (1987), 'Progress, Problems and Prospects for Network Research:-Investigating Relationships in the Age of Electronic Communication', paper presented at the VII Sunbelt Social Networks Conference, Florida, 12–15 February.

Rogers, E. and Kincaid, D. (1981), *Communication Networks* (New York: Free Press).

Romanelli, E. (1989), 'Environments and Strategies of Organisation Start-Up: Effects on Early Survival', *Administrative Science Quarterly*, Vol. 34, pp. 369–87.

Romano, C.A. (1989), 'Research Strategies for Small Business – A Case Study Approach', *International Small Business Journal*, Vol. 7, No. 4, pp. 35–43.

Rosenbloom, R. and Wolek, F. (1970) 'Technology and Information Transfer: A survey of Practice in Industrial Organisations' (Boston: Haward Business School).

Rothwell, R. (1983), 'Innovation and Firm Size: A Case of Dynamic Complementarity; Or, Is Small Really So Beautiful?', *Journal of General Management*, Vol. 8, No. 3, pp. 5–25.

Rothwell, R. (1986), 'Innovation and Re-Innovation: A Role for the User', *Journal of Marketing Management*, Vol. 2, No. 2, pp. 109–23.

Rothwell, R. (1991), 'External Networking and Innovation in Small and Medium-Sized Manufacturing Firms in Europe', *Technovation*, Vol. 11, No. 2, pp. 93–112.

Rothwell, R. (1992), 'Successful Industrial Innovation: Critical Factors for the 1990s', *R&D Management*, Vol. 22, No. 3, pp. 221–39.

Rothwell, R. (1994a), 'Issues in User-Producer Relations in the Innovation Process: The Role of Government', *International Journal of Technology Management*, Vol. 9, pp. 629–49.

Rothwell, R. (1994b), 'The Changing Nature of the Innovation Process: Implications for SMEs', in Oakey, R. (ed.), *New Technology-Based Firms in the 1990s* (London: Paul Chapman), pp. 11–21.

Rothwell, R. and Dodgson, M. (1991), 'External Linkages and Innovation in Small and Medium Sized Enterprises', *R&D Management*, Vol. 21, pp. 125–37.

Rothwell, R. and Gardiner, P. (1985), 'Invention, Innovation, Re-Innovation and the Role of the User: A Case Study of British Hovercraft Development', *Technovation*, Vol. 3, pp. 167–86.

Rothwell, R. and Robertson, A. (1973), 'The Role of Communications in Technological Innovation', *Research Policy*, Vol. 2, No. 3, pp. 204–25.

Rothwell, R. and Zegveld, W. (1982), *Innovation and the Small and Medium Sized Firm – Their Role in Employment and in Economic Change* (London: Pinter).

Rothwell, R., Freeman, C., Horsley, A., Jervis, P., Robertson, A. and Townsend, J. (1974), 'SAPPHO Updated – Project SAPPHO Phase II', *Research Policy*, Vol. 3, No. 3, pp. 258–91.

Rotter, J.B. (1966), 'Generalised Expectations for Internal vs External Control of Reinforcement', *Psychological Monographs,* Whole No. 609, 801.

Roure, J.B. and Keeley, R.H. (1991) 'Predictors of Success in New, Technology-Based Ventures', *Engineering Management Review*, Fall, pp. 69–79.

Routamaa, V. and Vesalainen, J. (1987), 'Types of Entrepreneur and Strategic Level Goal Setting', *International Small Business Journal*, Vol. 5, No. 3, pp. 19–29.

Rubenson, G.C. and Gupta, A.K. (1990), 'The Founder's Disease: A Critical Re-Examination', in Churchill, N.C., Bygrave, W.D., Hornaday, J.A., Myzuka, D.F., Vesper, K.H. and Wetzel, W.E. (eds), *Frontiers of Entrepreneurship Research*, (Wellesley, Mass.: Babson College), pp. 167–83.

Ruhnka, J. and Young, J. (1987), 'A Venture Capital Model of Development Process for New Ventures', *Journal of Business Venturing*, Vol. 2, No. 2, pp. 167–84.

Rumelt, R.P. (1974), *Strategy, Structure, and Economic Performance* (Cambridge, Mass.: Harvard University Press).

Rumelt, R.P. (1979), 'Evaluation of Strategy Theory and Models', in Schendel, D.E. and Cooper, C.W. (eds), *Strategic Management: A New View of Business Policy and Planning* (Boston, Mass.: Little, Brown).

Sahal, D. (1985), 'Technology Guide-Posts and Innovation Avenues', *Research Policy*, Vol. 14, pp. 61–82.

Salter, M.S. and Weinhold, W.A. (1979), *Diversification through Acquisition* (New York: Free Press).

Samson, K.J. and Gurdon, M.A. (1990), 'Entrepreneurial Scientists: Organisational Performance in Scientist-Started High Technology Firms', in Churchill, N.C., Bygrave, W.D., Hornaday, J.A., Myzuka, D.F., Vesper, K.H.

and Wetzel, W.E. (eds), *Frontiers of Entrepreneurship Research* (Wellesley, Mass.: Babson College) pp. 437–51.

Samsom, K.J. and Gurdon, M.A. (1993), 'University Scientists as Entrepreneurs – a Special Case of Technology Transfer and High Tech Venturing', *Technovation*, Vol. 13, No. 2, pp. 63–71.

Sanchez, A.M. (1992), 'Regional Innovation and Small High Technology Firms in Peripheral Regions',*Small Business Economics*, Vol. 4, No. 2, pp. 153–68.

Sandberg, W. (1986), *New Venture Performance: The Role of Strategy and Industry Structure* (Toronto: Lexington Books).

Sandberg, W. and Hofer, C. (1987), 'Improving New Venture Performance: The Role of Strategy, Industry Structure, and the Entrepreneur', *Journal of Business Venturing*, Vol. 2, pp. 5–28.

Saxenian, A. (1991), 'The Origins and Dynamics of Production Networks in Silicon Valley' *Research Policy*, Vol. 20, pp. 423–37.

Scase, R. and Goffee, R. (1980), *The Real World of the Small Business Owner* (London: Croom Helm).

Schell, D.W. and Davig, W. (1981), 'The Community Infrastructure of Entrepreneurship: A Sociopolitical Analysis', in Vesper, Karl H. (ed.), *Frontiers of Entrepreneurship Research* (Wellesley, Mass.: Babson College), pp. 563–90.

Scherer, F.M. (1980), *Industrial Market Structure and Economic Performance* (Chicago: Rand McNally).

Scholz, L. (1989), *Comments on the State-of-the-Art Measuring of Innovation Output*, Working Paper, NESTI, Room Document 17 (Paris: OECD).

Schrage, H. (1965), 'The R&D Entrepreneur: Profile of Success', *Harvard Business Review*, Vol. 43, No. 6, pp. 8–21.

Schumpeter, J.A. (1934), *A Theory of Economic Development* (Cambridge, Mass.: Harvard University Press).

Schumpeter, J.A. (1976), *Capitalism, Socialism and Democracy* (New York: Harper Torchbooks).

Scott, J. (1991), *Social Network Analysis: A Handbook* (London: Sage).

Scott, M. and Bruce, R. (1987), Five Stages of Growth in Small Business', *Long Range Planning*, Vol. 20, No. 3, pp. 45–52.

Scott, W.R. (1987), *Organizations: Rational, Natural, and Open Systems*, 2nd edn (Englewood Cliffs, NJ: Prentice-Hall).

Segal Quince, (1985), *The Cambridge Phenomenon: The Growth of High Technology industry In and around a University Town* (Cambridge: Segal Quince Wicksteed).

Senker, J. (1985), 'Small High Technology Firms: Some Regional Implications', *Technovation*, Vol. 3, No. 4, pp. 243–62.

Senker, J. and Faulkner, W. (1993), '*Networks, Tacit Knowledge and Innovation*', Technological Collaboration: Networks, Institutions and States, ASEAT Second International Conference, Manchester, 21st–23 April.

Shapero, A. and Sokol, L. (1982), 'The Social Dimension of Entrepreneurship', in Kent, C.A., Sexton, D.L. and Vesper, K.H. (eds), *Encyclopedia of Entrepreneurship* (Englewood Cliffs, NJ: Prentice-Hall).

Shaw, B. (1985), 'The Role of Interaction Between the User and the Manufacturer in Medical Equipment Innovation', *R&D Management*, Vol. 15, No. 4, pp. 283–92.

Shaw, B. (1993), 'Formal and Informal Networks in the UK Medical Equipment Industry' *Technovation*, Vol. 13, No. 6, pp. 349–65.

Sherwin, E. and Isenson, R. (1967), 'Project Hindsight', *Science*, Vol. 156, No. 3782, pp. 1571–7.

Shirvastava, P. (1986), 'Postmerger Integration', *The Journal of Business Strategy*, Vol. 7, No.1, pp. 65–76.

Simon, H. (1947), *Administrative Behaviour*, 3rd edn (New York: Free Press).

SIND (1985), *Konkursutredning* (Stockholm: SIND).

Singh, J.V. and Lumsden, C.J. (1990), 'Theory and Research in Organisational Ecology', *Annual Review of Sociology*, Vol. 16, pp. 161–95.

Singh, J.V., Tucker D.J. and House, R.J. (1986), 'Organisational Legitimacy and the Liability of Newness', *Administrative Science Quarterly*, Vol. 31, pp. 171–93.

Sirilli, G. (1987), 'Patents and Inventors: an Empirical Study', *Research Policy*, Vol. 16, pp. 157–74.

Slatter, S. (1992), *Gambling on Growth: How to Manage the Small High-Tech Firm*, (Chichester John Wiley).

Smallbone, D., Leigh, R. and North, D. (1991), 'Growth Characteristics of Mature Small and Medium-sized Manufacturing Enterprises', in Robertson, M., Chell, E. and Mason, C., *Towards the Twenty-First Century: The Challenge for Small Business* (Macclesfield: Nadamal Books).

Smallbone, D., Leigh, R. and North, D. (1993a), 'The Growth and Survival of Mature Manufacturing SMEs in the 1980s: An Urban and Rural Comparison', in Curran, J. and Storey, D.J. (eds), *Small Firms in Urban and Rural Locations*, (London: Routledge).

Smallbone, D., Leigh, R. and North, D (1993b), 'The Use of External Assistance by Mature SMEs in the UK: Some Policy Implications', *Entrepreneurship & Regional Development*, Vol. 5, pp. 279–95.

Smallbone, D., Leigh, R. and North, D. (1995), 'The characteristics and Strategies of High Growth SMEs', *International Journal of Entrepreneurial Behaviour and Research*, Vol. 1, No. 3, pp. 44–62.

Smilor, R. W. (1987), 'Commercializing Technology through New Business Incubators' *Research Management*, Vol. 30, pp. 36–41.

Smilor, R.W. and Feeser, H.R. (1991), 'Chaos and the Entrepreneurial Process: Patterns and Policy Implications for Technological Entrepreneurship', *Journal of Business Venturing*, Vol. 6, pp. 165–172.

Smilor, R.W., Gibson, D.V. and Kozmetsky, G. (1988), 'Creating the Technopolis: High Technology Development in Austin, Texas', *Journal of Business Venturing*, Vol. 4, pp. 49–67.

Smith, N.R. (1967), *The Entrepreneur and His Firm: The Relationship between Type of Man and Type of Company* (East Lansing: Michigan State University).

Soete, L. and Arundel, A. (1993), *An Integrated Approach to European Innovation and Technology Diffusion Policy: A Maastricht Memorandum*, publication EUR 15090 (Brussels-Luxemburg: Commission of the European Communities).

Solem, O. and Steiner, M. (1989), 'Factors for Success in Small Manufacturing Firms – and with Special Emphasis on Growing Firms', paper presented at Conference on Small and Medium Sized Enterprises and the Challenges of 1992, Mikkeli, Finland.

Sowrey, T. (1989), 'Idea Generation: Identifying the Most Useful Techniques', *European Journal of Marketing*, Vol. 24, No. 5, pp. 20–9.

Spital, F. (1979), 'An Analysis of the Role of Users in the Total R & D Portfolios of Scientific Instrument Firms', *Research Policy*, Vol. 8, No. 3, pp. 284–96.

Stankiewicz, R. (1990), 'Basic Technologies and the Innovation Process', in Sigurdson, J. (ed.), *Measuring the Dynamics of Technological Change* (London: Pinter), pp. 13–38.

Stankiewicz, R. (1994), 'Spin-off Companies from Universities', *Science and Public Policy*, Vol. 21, No. 2, pp. 99–107.

Stanworth, J. and Curran, J. (1973), *Management Motivation in the Smaller Business* (Epping: Gower).

Stanworth, J. and Curran, J. (1976), 'Growth and the Small Firm: An Alternative View', *Journal of Management Studies*, Vol. 13, No. 2, pp. 95–110.

Stanworth, J. and Curran, J. (1986), 'Growth and the Small Firm', in Curran, J. and Stanworth, J.(eds), *The Survival of the Small Firm*, Vol. 2, pp. 81–99.

Starbuck, W.H. (1965), 'Organisational Growth and Development', in March, J.C. (ed.), *Handbook of Organisations*, (Chicago: Rand McNally) pp. 451–533.

Steen, R. (1991) *Tillvaxforetagen och Naringspolitken*, Ahrens & Partner, Tillväxtkonsulter, AB.

Stevenson, H. (1988), '*A Perspective on Entrepreneurship*', Harvard Business School, class discussion document.

Steward, F. and Conway, S. (1993), *Informal Networks in the Origination of Successful Innovations,* Technological Collaboration: Networks, Institutions and States, ASEAT Second International Conference, Manchester, 21–23 April.

Stinchcombe, A.L. (1965), 'Social Structure and Organizations', in March, J.G. (ed.), *Handbook of Organizations*, (Chicago: Rand McNally), pp. 142–93.

Stone-Romero, E.F., Alliger, G.M. and Aguinis, H. (1994), 'Type II Error Problems in the Use of Moderated Multiple Regression for the Detection of Moderating Effects of Dichotomous Variables', *Journal of Management*, Vol. 20, No. 1, pp. 167–78.

Stoner, C.R. (1987), 'Distinctive Competence and Competitive Advantage', *Journal of Small Business Management*, April, pp. 33–9.

Stoner, C.R. and Fry, F.L. (1982), 'The Entrepreneurial Decision – Dissatisfaction or Opportunity?', *Journal of Small Business Management*, Vol. 20, No. 2, pp. 39–45.

Storey, D.J. (1982), *Entrepreneurship and the New Firm* (London: Croom Helm).

Storey, D.J. (1994), *Understanding the Small Business Sector*, (London: Routledge).

Strauss, A. and Corbin, J. (1990), *Basics of Qualitative Research: Grounded Theory Procedures and Techniques.* (London: Sage).

Stuart, R.W. and Abetti, P.A. (1988), 'Field Studies of Technical Ventures – Part III: The Impact of Entrepreneurial and Management Experience on Early Performance', in Kirchoff, B.A., Long, W.A., McMullan, W.E., Vesper K.H. and Wetzel, W.E (eds), *Frontiers Of Entrepreneurship Research* (Wellesley, Mass.: Babson College), pp. 177–93.

Stuart, R.W. and Abetti, P.A. (1990), 'Impact of Entrepreneurial and Management Experience on early performance', *Journal of Business Venturing*, Vol. 5, pp.151–62.

Suárez, F. and Utterback, J.M. (1995), 'Dominant designs and the Survival of Firms', *Strategic Management Journal*, Vol. 16, pp. 415–30.

Susbauer, J.C. (1967). 'The Science Entrepreneur', *Industrial Research*, Vol. 8, No. 2, pp. 23–30.

Susbauer, J.C. (1972), 'The Technical Entrepreneurship Process in Austin, Texas', in Cooper, A.C. and Komives, J.L. (eds), *Technical Entrepreneurship: A Symposium* (Milwaukee: The Center for Venture Management).

Susbauer, J.C. and Baker, R.J. (1975), *The Venture Formation/Development Process: A Framework for the Evaluation of Venture Assistance Programs*, Project ISEED.

Task Force on Small Business (1994), *Report of the Task Force on Small Business* Dublin Stationery Office.

Teece, D.J. (1980), 'Economies of Scope and the Scope of the Enterprise', *Journal of Economic Behavior and Organization*, Vol. 3, pp. 39–63.

Teece, D.J. (1983), 'Technological and Organizational Factors in the Theory of the Multinational Enterprise', in Casson, M.C. (ed.), *The Growth of International Business* (London: Allen & Unwin), pp. 51–62.

Teece, D.J. (1986), 'Profiting from Technological Innovation: Implications for Integration, Collaboration Licensing and Public Policy', *Research Policy*, Vol. 15, pp. 285–305.

Telesio, P. (1984), 'Foreign Licensing in Multinational Enterprises', in Stobaugh, R. and Wells, L.T. (eds), *Technology Crossing Borders* (Cambridge, Mass.: Harvard Business School Press), pp. 177–201.

Tesfaye, B. (1991) 'The Formation of Small Technology-Based Companies – A Case Study of Factors Affecting a Company Formation Decision' Department of Business Administration, Stockholm University.

Thain, D.H. (1969), 'Stages of Corporate Development', *The Business Quarterly*, Vol. 34, pp. 33–45.

The SAPPHO-Project (1972), *Success and Failure in Industrial Innovation – Report on Project SAPPHO*, (University of Sussex: Science Policy Research Unit).

Thomas, R.E. (1986), 'Parent-to-Parent Divestment', in Coyne, J. and Wright, M. (eds), *Divestment and Strategic Change* (Oxford: Philip Allan).

Tichy, N., Tushman, M. and Fombrun, C. (1979), 'Social Network Analysis for Organisations", *Academy of Management Review*, Vol. 4, No. 4, pp. 507–19.

Tidd, J. (1995), 'Development of Novel Products through Intraorganizational and Interorganizational Networks: The Case of Home Automation', *Journal of Product Innovation Management*, Vol. 12, pp. 307–22.

Tiler, C. Metcalfe, S. and Connell, D. (1993), 'Business Expansion through Entrepreneurship: The Influence of Internal and External Barriers to Growth', *International Journal of Technology Management*, Special Publication on Small Firms and Innovation, pp. 119–32

Timmons, J.A. and Bygrave, W.D. (1986), 'Venture Capital's Role in Financing Innovation for Economic Growth', *Journal of Business Venturing*, Vol. 1, pp. 161–76.

Tucker, D.J., Singh, J.V. and Meinhard, A.G. (1990), 'Organizational Form, Population Dynamics, and Institutional Change: The Founding Pattern of Voluntary Organizations', *Academy of Management Journal*, Vol. 33, No. 1, pp. 151–78.

Tucker, D.J. *et al.* (1990), 'The Founding Pattern of Voluntary Organizations', *Academy of Management Journal*, Vol. 33, pp. 151–73.

Tyebjee, T. and Bruno, A.V. (1982), 'A Comparative Analysis of California Start-Ups from 1977 to 1980", in Vesper, K. (ed.), *Frontiers of Entrepreneurship Research* (Wellesley, Mass.: Babson College), pp. 163–76.

Udell, G. (1990), 'It's Still Caveat, Inventor', *Journal of Product Innovation Management*, Vol. 7, No. 3, pp. 230–43.

Utterback, J.M. (1971), 'The Process of Innovation: A Study of the Origination and Development of Ideas for Scientific Instruments', *IEEE Transactions on Engineering Management*, Vol. EM-18, No. 4, pp. 124–31.

Utterback, J.M. (1974), 'Innovation in Industry and the Diffusion of Technology', *Science*, 183, pp. 620–31.

Utterback, J.M. and Reitberger, G. (1982), *Technology and Industrial Innovation in Sweden – a Study of New Technology-Based Firms*, (Stockholm: National Swedish Board for Technical Development MIT).

Utterback, J.M., Meyer, M., Roberts, E. and Reitberger, G. (1988), 'Technology and Industrial Innovation in Sweden: a Study of Technology-Based Firms formed between 1965 and 1980', *Research Policy*, Vol. 17, No. 1, pp. 15–26.

Valls, J. (1993), 'Small Firms Facing Globalisation in R&D Activities. Lessons From Case Studies of Spanish Small Firms', in Humbert, M. (ed.), *The Impact of Globalisation on Europe's Firms and Industries* (London: Pinter), pp. 200–10.

Van de Ven, A.H. (1993), 'The Development of an Infrastructure for Entrepreneurship' *Journal of Business Venturing*, Vol. 8, pp. 211–30.

Van de Ven, A.H. and Garud, R. (1989), 'A Framework for Understanding the Emergence of New Industries', in Rosenbloom, R.S. and Burgelman, R.A. (eds), *Research on Technological Innovation, Management and Policy* (Greenwich, Conn: Jai Press), pp. 195–225.

Van Maanen, J. (1979), 'Reclaiming Qualitative Methods for Organizational Research: A Preface', *Administrative Quarterly*, Vol. 24, pp. 520–6.

Vanderwerf, P. (1990), 'Product Tying and Innovation in US Wire Preparation Equipment', *Research Policy*, Vol. 19, No. 1, pp. 83–96.

Vesper, K. (1990), *New Venture Strategies* (Englewood Cliffs, NJ: Prentice-Hall).

von Wright, G.H. (1987). *Tiede ja ihmisjärki* (Helsinki: Otava).

Wade, J. (1995), 'Dynamics of Organizational Communities and Technological Bandwagons: An Empirical Investigation of Community Evolution in the Microprocessor Market', *Strategic Management Journal*, Vol. 16, pp. 111–33.

Wainer, H.A. and Rubin, I.M. (1969) 'Motivation of Research and Development Entrepreneurs: Determinants of Company Success', *Journal of Applied Psychology*, Vol. 53, No. 3, pp. 178–84.

Wallmark, T., and McQueen, D.(1983), *100 viktiga innovationer i Sverige 1945–1980* STU-information No. 350-1983, Report submitted to National Swedish Board for Technical Development (STU), Stockholm.

Wallmark, T., and McQueen, D. (1986), *100 viktiga svenska innovationer* (Lund: Studentlitteratur).

Wallmark, J. T. and Sjösten, J. (1994), *Stability and Turbulence among Spin-Off Companies from Chalmers University*, 8th Nordic Congress on Small Business Research, Halmstad, June.

Walsh, V. (1987), 'Technology, Competitiveness and the Special Problems of Small Countries', *STI Review*, Vol. 2, No. 2, pp. 81–133.

Watkins, D.S. (1973), 'Technical entrepreneurship', *R&D Management*, Vol. 3, No. 2, pp. 65–9.

Watkins, D.S. (1975) *Regional Variations in the Industrial Ecology for New Growth Oriented Businesses in the UK* Project ISEED report.

Watkins, D.S. (1976), *Entry into Independent Entrepreneurship: Toward a Model of Business Initiation Process*, paper presented at EIASM Seminar on Entrepreneurship and Institution Building.

Weber, M., (1930) *The Protestant Ethic and the Spirit of Capitalism (London:* Allen & Unwin).

Webster, F. (1976), 'A Model of New Venture Initiation', *Academy of Management Review*, Vol. 1, No. 1, pp. 23–35.

Webster, F.A. (1977) 'Entrepreneurs and Ventures: an attempt of classification and clarification', *Academy of Management Review*, Vol. 2, No.1, pp. 54–61.

Weick, K.E. (1979), *The Social Psychology of Organizing*, 2nd edn (Reading, Mass.: Addison-Wesley).

Weiner, B. (1980), *Human motivation* (Los Angeles, Calif: Holt, Rinehart & Winston Press of W.B. Saunders).

Weisenfeld-Schenk, U. (1994), 'Technology Strategies and the Miles and Snow Typology: A Study of the Biotechnology Industries', *R&D Management*, Vol. 24, No. 1, pp. 57–64.

Westhead, P. (1994), *Survival and Employment Growth Contrasts between 'Types' of Owner-Managed High-Technology Firms*, International Workshop on Innovation and Entrepreneurship in SMEs, Jönköping Business School, September.

Westhead, P. and Birley, S. (1993), *Employment Growth in New Independent Owner-Managed Firms in Great Britain*, University of Warwick, Working Paper.

Westhead, P. and Cowling, M. (1994), *Employment Change in Independent Owner-Managed High-Technology Firms in Great Britain*, 2nd International Conference on High Technology Small Firms, Manchester, September.

Westhead, P. and Cowling, M. (1995), 'Employment Change in Independent Owner-Managed High-Technology Firms in Great Britain', *Small Business Economics*, Vol. 7, pp. 111–40.

Westhead, P., and Storey, D.J. (1994), *An Assessment of Firms Located on and off Science Parks in the United Kingdom* (London: HMSO).

Whalley, P. (1991), 'The Social Practice of Independent Inventing', *Science, Technology and Human Values*, Vol. 16, No. 2, pp. 208–32.

Wholey, D.R. and Brittain, J.W. (1986), 'Organisational Ecology: Findings and Implications', *Academy of Management Review*, Vol. 11, No. 3, pp. 513–33.

Willard, G.E., Kruger, D.A. and Feeser, H.R. (1992), 'In Order to Grow, Must the Founder Go: A Comparison between Founder and Non-Founder Managed High Growth Manufacturing Firms', *Journal of Business Venturing*, Vol. 7, No. 3, pp. 181–94.

Williamson, O.E. (1975), *Markets and Hierarchies: Analysis and Antitrust Implications* (New York: Free Press).

Wolek, F. (1970), 'The Complexity of Messages in Science and Engineering: An Influence on Patterns of Communication', In Nelson, C. and Pollock, D. (eds), *Communication among Scientists and Engineers*, (Lexington: Lexington Books) pp. 233–65.

Wolek, F. and Griffith, B. (1974), 'Policy and Informal Communication in Applied Science and Technology', *Science Studies*, Vol. 4, pp. 411–20.

Woo, C.Y., Dunkelberg, W.C. and Cooper, A.C. (1988), 'Entrepreneurial Typologies: Definition and Implications', in Kirchoff, B.A., Long, W.A.,

McMullan, W.E., Vesper K.H. and Wetzel, W.E. (eds), *Frontiers of Entrepreneurship Research* (Wellesley, Mass.: Babson College), pp. 165–76.

Woo, C.Y., Willard, G.E. and Daellenbach, U.S. (1992), 'Spin-Off Performance: A Case of Overstated Expectations?', *Strategic Management Journal,* Vol.13, pp. 433–47.

Woodward, H. (1976), 'Managerial Strategies for Small Companies', *Harvard Business Review*, January–Febuary, pp. 113–21.

Wynarczyk, P. (1996), *The Economic Success of UK Innovative Small Firms,* Proceedings of the 41st ICSB Conference, Stockholm, 17–19 June.

Wynarczyk, P. and Thwaites, A. (1994), *The Financial Performance of Innovative Small Firms in the UK*, Proceedings of the 2nd Annual High Technology Small Firms Conference, Manchester Business School, 19–20 September.

Wynarczyk, P., Watson, R., Storey, D.J., Short, H. and Keasey K. (1993), *The Managerial Labour Market in Small and Medium Sized Enterprises* (London: Routledge).

Yip, G. (1982), 'Gateways to Entry', *Harvard Business Review*, Vol. 60, No. 5, pp. 85–92.

Yuchtman, E. and Seashore, S.E. (1967), 'A System Resource Approach to Organizational Effectiveness', *American Sociological Review*, Vol. 32, pp. 891–903.

Index